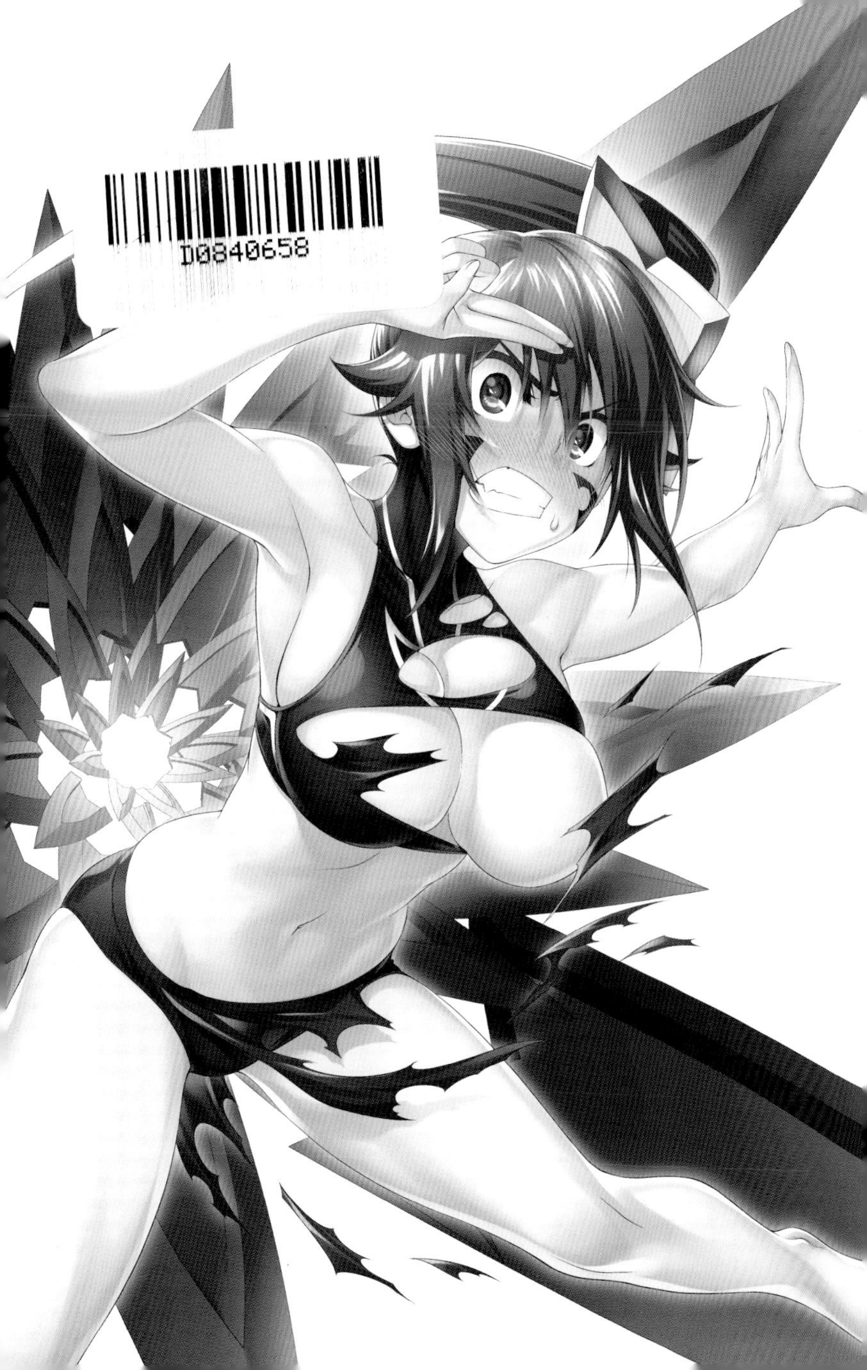

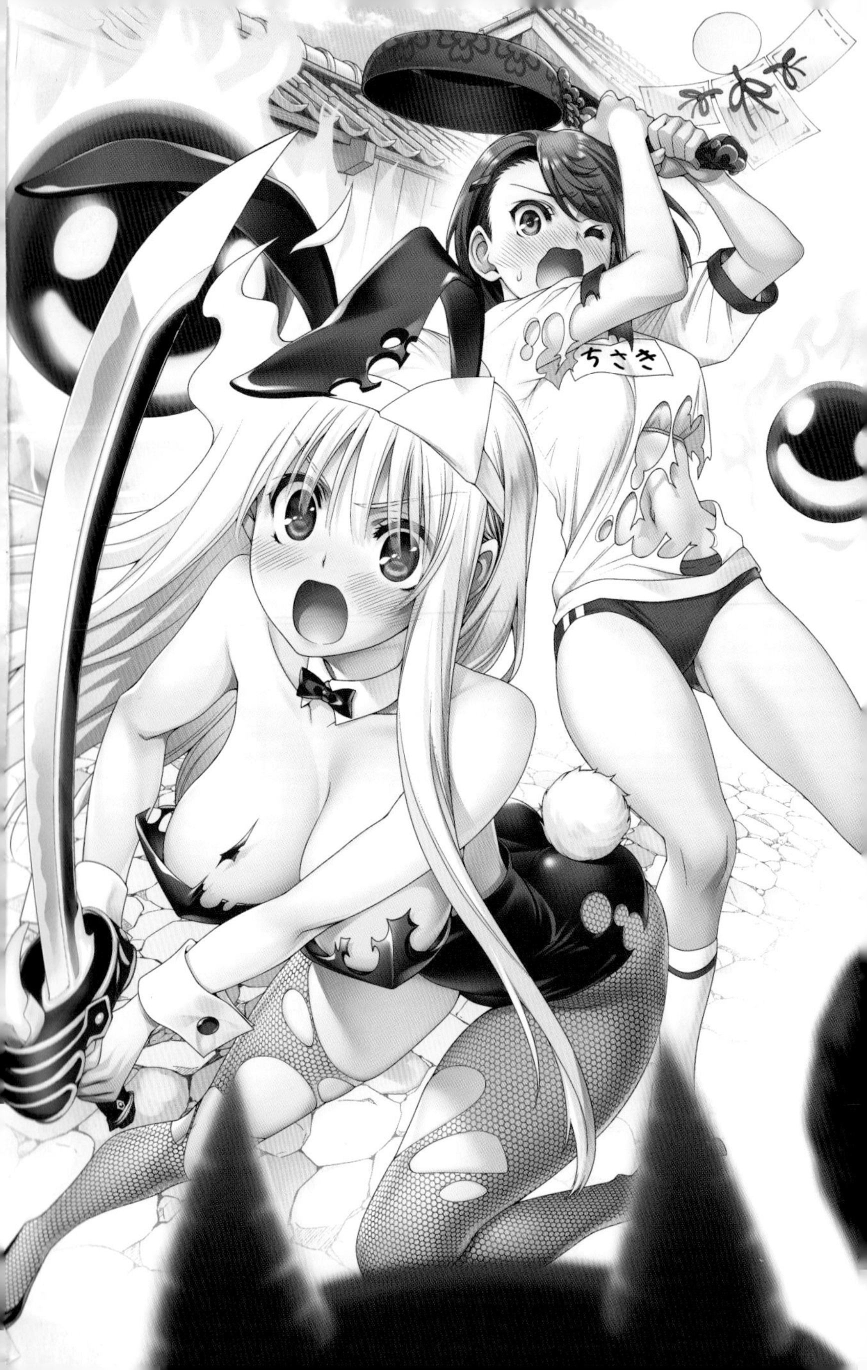
ちさき

Yuuna and the Haunted Hot Springs

16

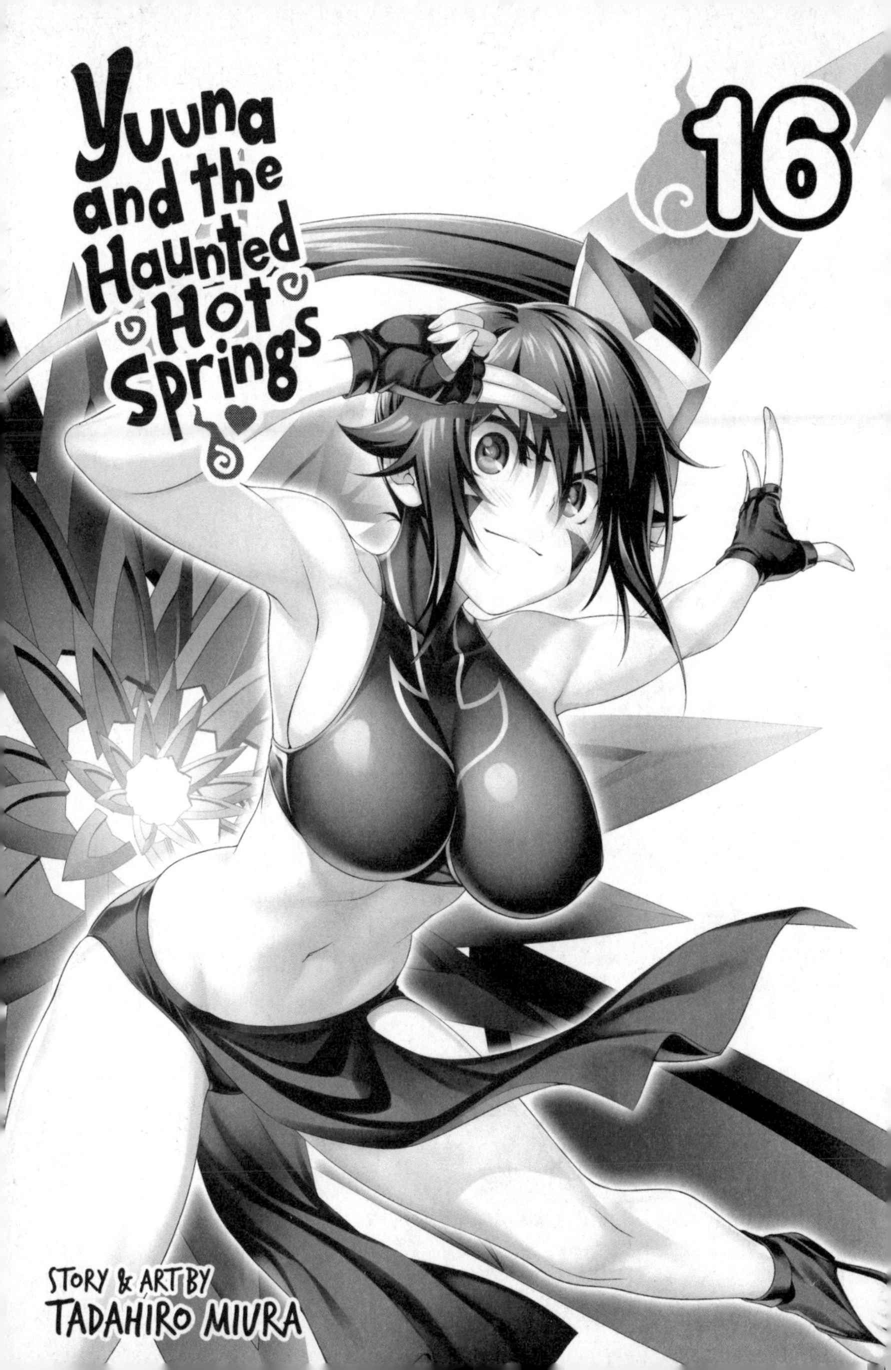

STORY & ART BY
TADAHIRO MIURA

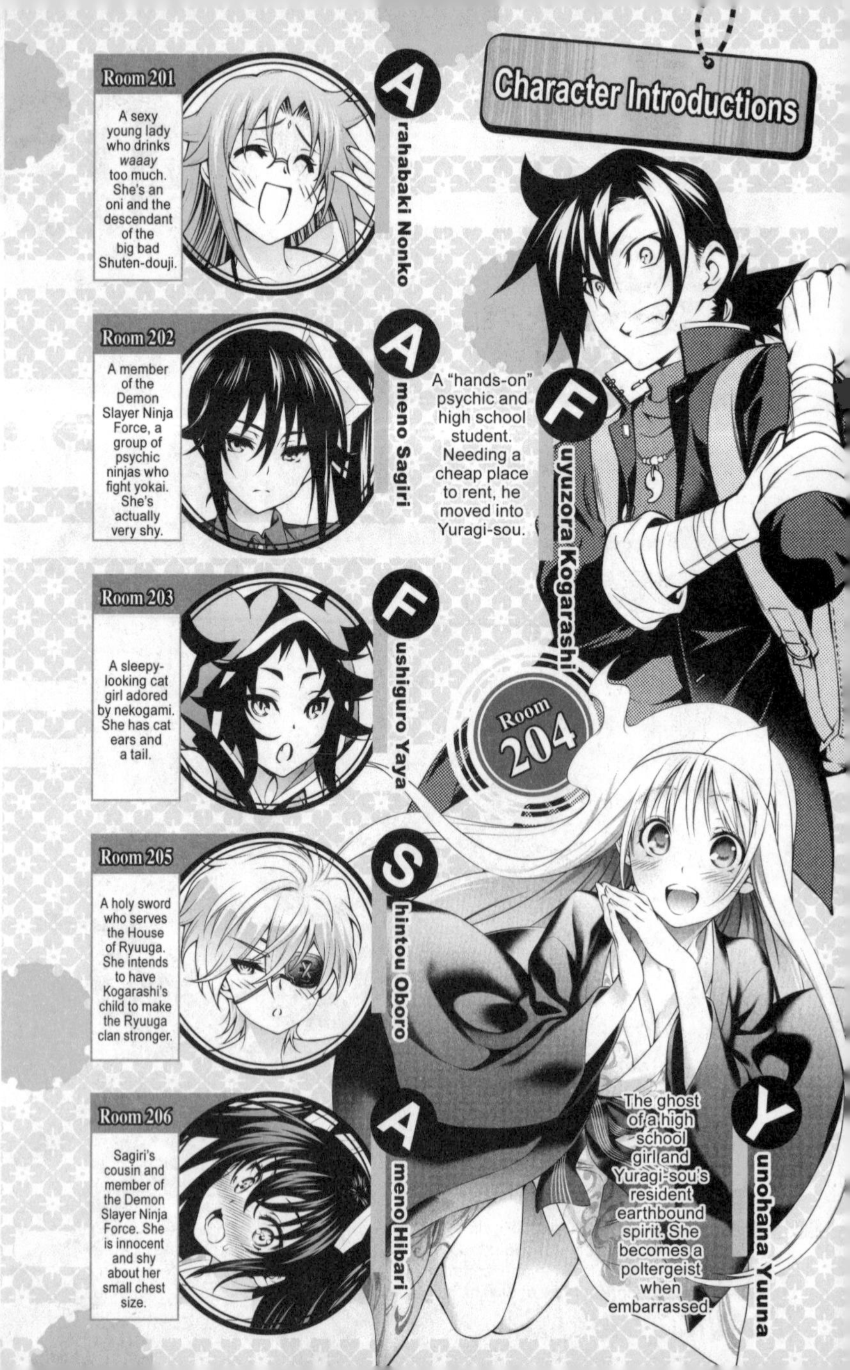

Character Introductions
Fuyuzora Kogarashi
A "hands-on" psychic and high school student. Needing a cheap place to rent, he moved into Yuragi-sou.
Room 204
Yunohana Yuuna
The ghost of a high school girl and Yuragi-sou's resident earthbound spirit. She becomes a poltergeist when embarrassed.
Room 201
Arahabaki Nonko
A sexy young lady who drinks *waaay* too much. She's an oni and the descendant of the big bad Shuten-douji.
Room 202
Ameno Sagiri
A member of the Demon Slayer Ninja Force, a group of psychic ninjas who fight yokai. She's actually very shy.
Room 203
Fushiguro Yaya
A sleepy-looking cat girl adored by nekogami. She has cat ears and a tail.
Room 205
Shintou Oboro
A holy sword who serves the House of Ryuuga. She intends to have Kogarashi's child to make the Ryuuga clan stronger.
Room 206
Ameno Hibari
Sagiri's cousin and member of the Demon Slayer Ninja Force. She is innocent and shy about her small chest size.

Hiougi Karura

Daughter of the Dai-tengu, who governs Kyoto. Praised as a genius, she studies various magics, reviving them in the modern era.

Nakai Chitose

Caretaker's Room

Despite her youthful appearance, she's a zashiki-warashi and Yuragi-sou's oldest resident. She can manipulate people's luck.

Mikogami Matora

An extremely powerful yokai known as a nue. Her hobby is fighting, and she is always seeking out stronger opponents.

Shigaraki Koyuzu

Caretaker's Room

A young bake-danuki girl. She looks up to Chisaki and envies her boobs.

Yumesaki Harumu

Kogarashi's new homeroom teacher. Being half succubus, her pupils are charged with charming magic.

Miyazaki Chisaki

The most beautiful and popular girl in Kogarashi's class. She has a naughty imagination.

Todoroki Shion

Seri's kouhai and former head delinquent in middle school. Her teddy bear panties are her favorite.

Katsuragi Miria

A youko girl. Part of the Katsuragi family; has long desired to be among the top of the Tenko clan, and to accomplish that she will get close to Yuuna.

Summary

While living in Yuragi-sou, a hot spring inn-turned-boarding house with an unusual history, "hands-on" psychic Fuyuzora Kogarashi promised Yuuna, the earthbound spirit of a high school girl, that he would make her happy and help her pass on. Realizing she is Tenko Genryusai, Yuuna wins in her showdown with Makyouin Ouga. Then, together with Kogarashi they defeat Tenko Byakuei, the one controlling Garandou. Later, Sagiri begins acting strange in front of Kogarashi, only to have her fiancé, Yoinozaka Shakuhito appear...

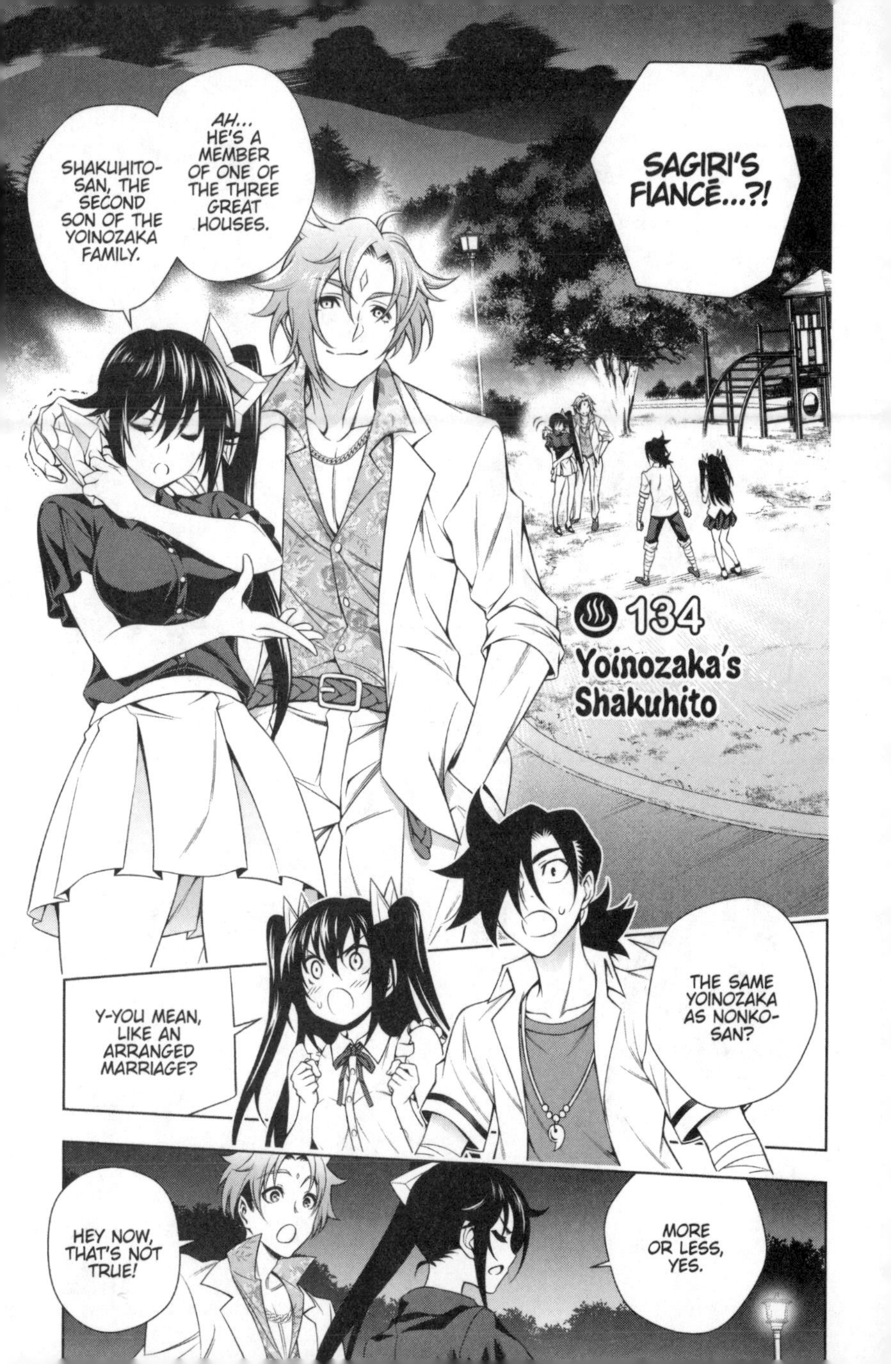
SAGIRI'S FIANCÉ...?!
AH... HE'S A MEMBER OF ONE OF THE THREE GREAT HOUSES.
SHAKUHITO-SAN, THE SECOND SON OF THE YOINOZAKA FAMILY.
134
Yoinozaka's Shakuhito
THE SAME YOINOZAKA AS NONKO-SAN?
Y-YOU MEAN, LIKE AN ARRANGED MARRIAGE?
MORE OR LESS, YES.
HEY NOW, THAT'S NOT TRUE!

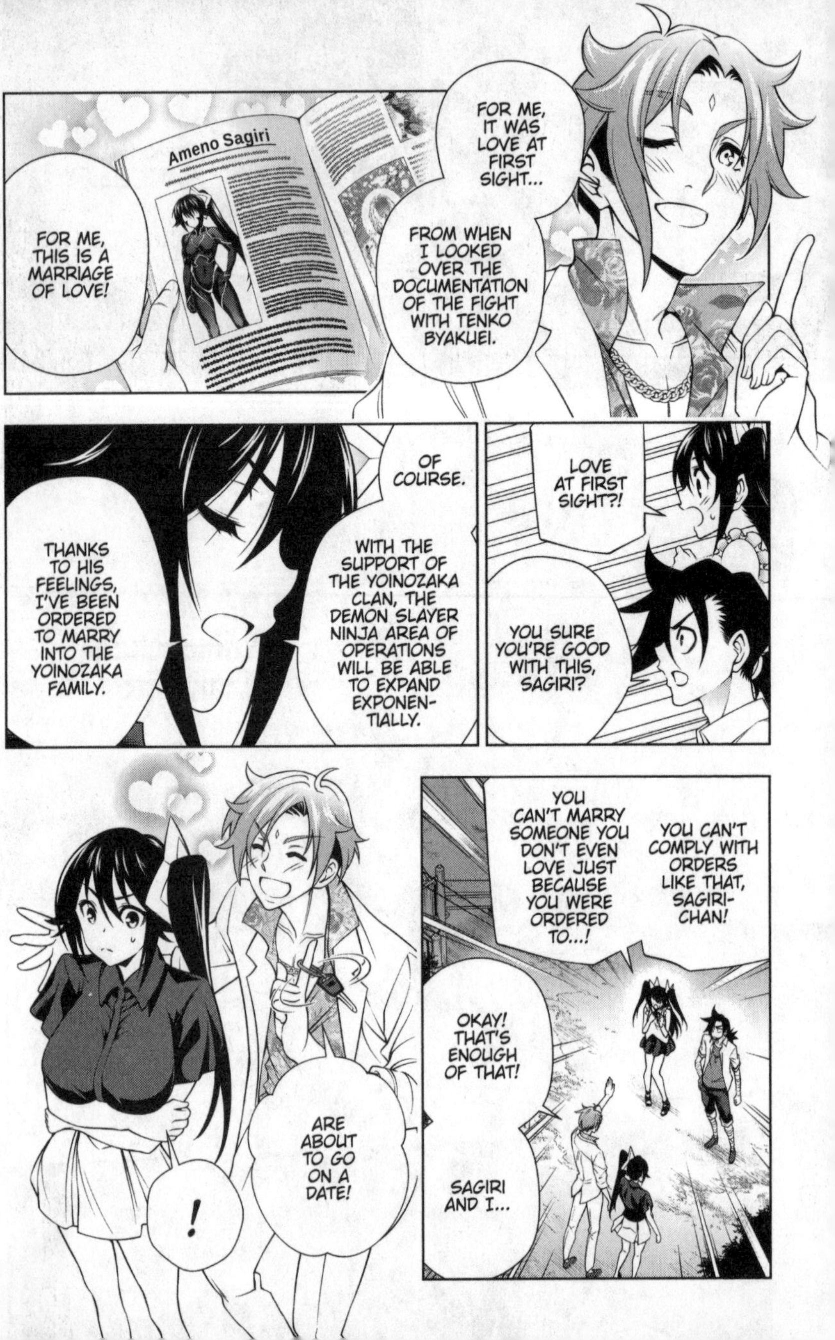
FOR ME, IT WAS LOVE AT FIRST SIGHT...
FROM WHEN I LOOKED OVER THE DOCUMENTATION OF THE FIGHT WITH TENKO BYAKUEI.
Ameno Sagiri
FOR ME, THIS IS A MARRIAGE OF LOVE!
LOVE AT FIRST SIGHT?!
YOU SURE YOU'RE GOOD WITH THIS, SAGIRI?
OF COURSE.
WITH THE SUPPORT OF THE YOINOZAKA CLAN, THE DEMON SLAYER NINJA AREA OF OPERATIONS WILL BE ABLE TO EXPAND EXPONEN-TIALLY.
THANKS TO HIS FEELINGS, I'VE BEEN ORDERED TO MARRY INTO THE YOINOZAKA FAMILY.
YOU CAN'T COMPLY WITH ORDERS LIKE THAT, SAGIRI-CHAN!
YOU CAN'T MARRY SOMEONE YOU DON'T EVEN LOVE JUST BECAUSE YOU WERE ORDERED TO...!
OKAY! THAT'S ENOUGH OF THAT!
SAGIRI AND I...
ARE ABOUT TO GO ON A DATE!
!

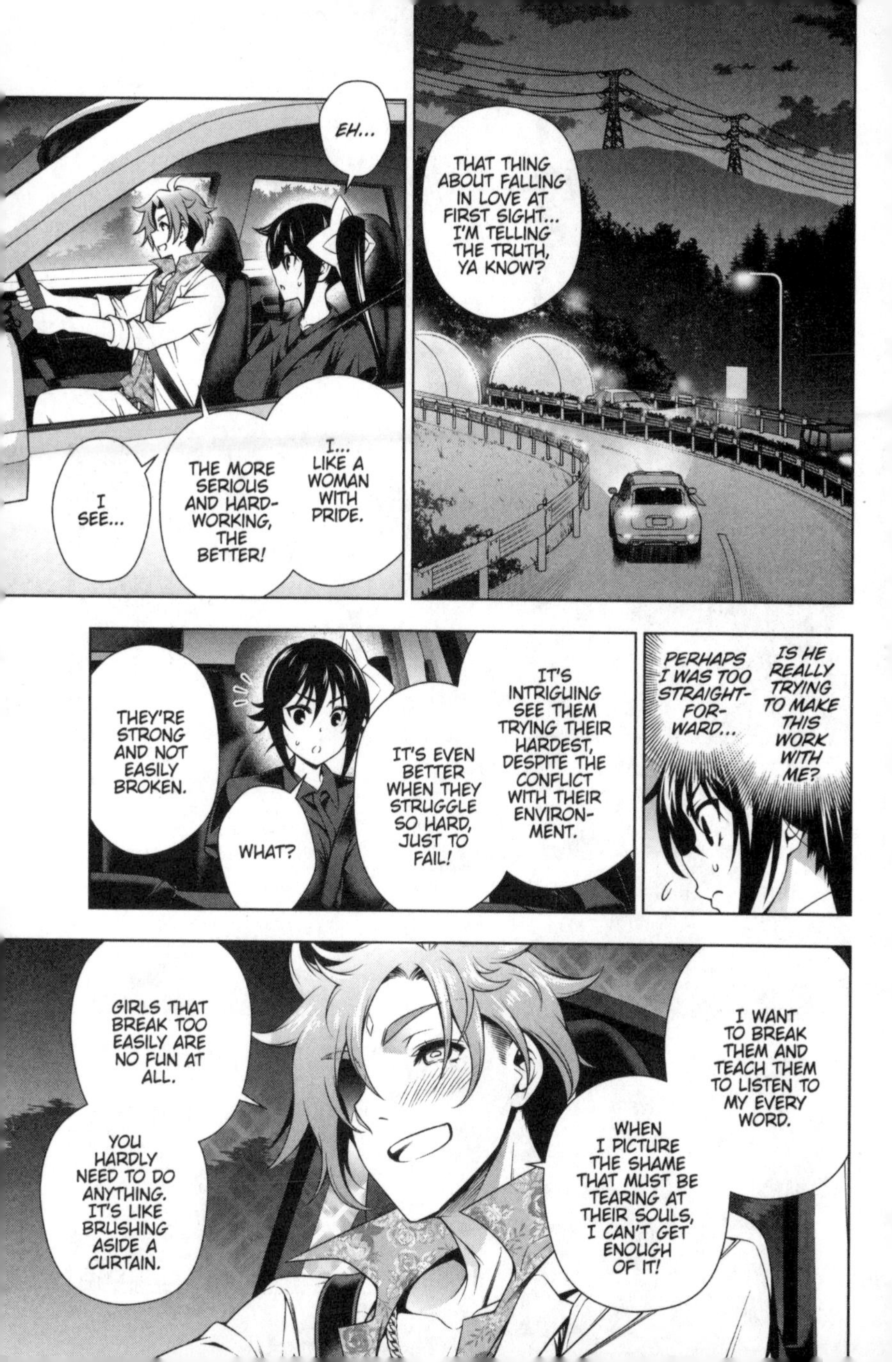
THAT THING ABOUT FALLING IN LOVE AT FIRST SIGHT... I'M TELLING THE TRUTH, YA KNOW?
EH...
I... LIKE A WOMAN WITH PRIDE.
THE MORE SERIOUS AND HARD-WORKING, THE BETTER!
I SEE...
IS HE REALLY TRYING TO MAKE THIS WORK WITH ME?
PERHAPS I WAS TOO STRAIGHT-FORWARD...
IT'S INTRIGUING SEE THEM TRYING THEIR HARDEST, DESPITE THE CONFLICT WITH THEIR ENVIRONMENT.
IT'S EVEN BETTER WHEN THEY STRUGGLE SO HARD, JUST TO FAIL!
WHAT?
THEY'RE STRONG AND NOT EASILY BROKEN.
I WANT TO BREAK THEM AND TEACH THEM TO LISTEN TO MY EVERY WORD.
WHEN I PICTURE THE SHAME THAT MUST BE TEARING AT THEIR SOULS, I CAN'T GET ENOUGH OF IT!
GIRLS THAT BREAK TOO EASILY ARE NO FUN AT ALL.
YOU HARDLY NEED TO DO ANYTHING. IT'S LIKE BRUSHING ASIDE A CURTAIN.

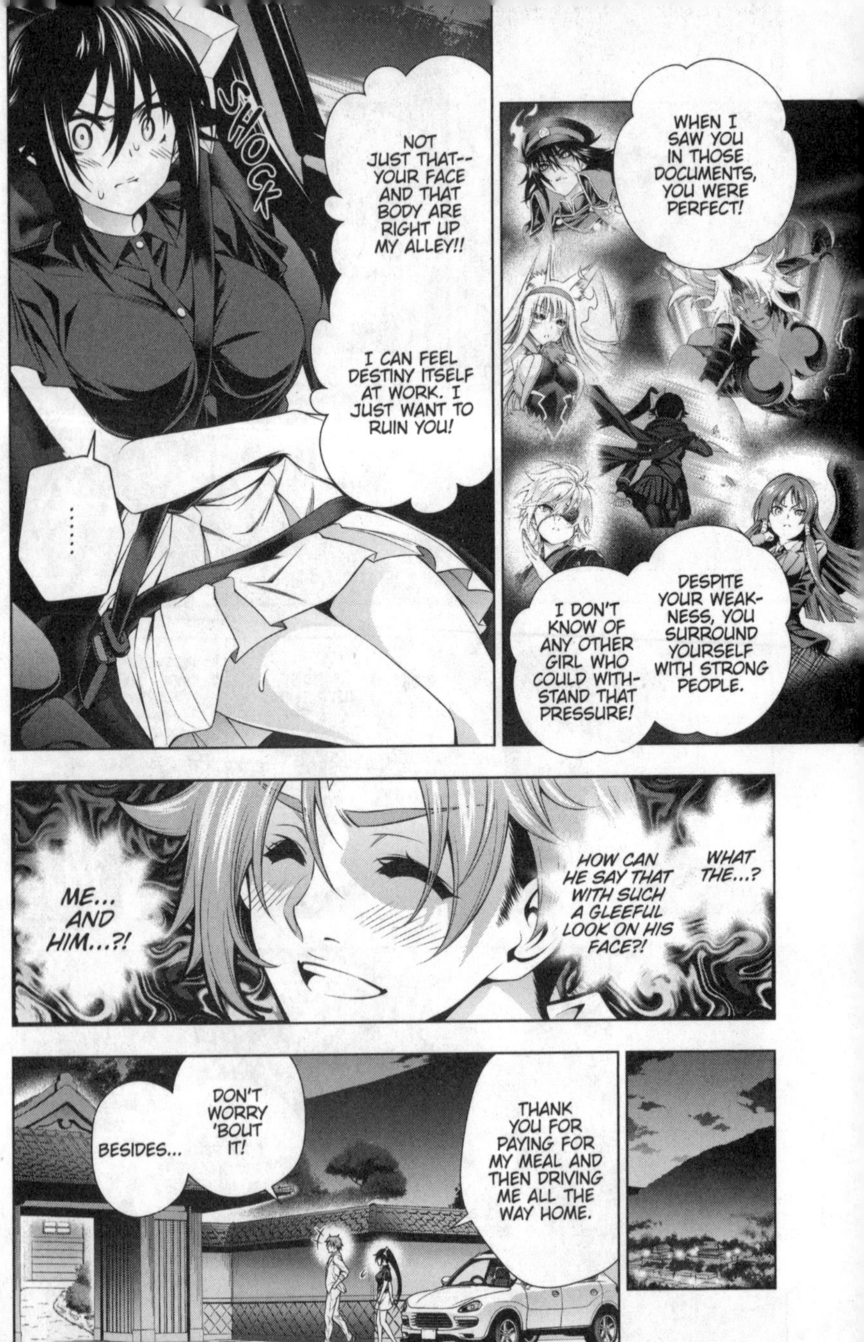
WHEN I SAW YOU IN THOSE DOCUMENTS, YOU WERE PERFECT!
DESPITE YOUR WEAKNESS, YOU SURROUND YOURSELF WITH STRONG PEOPLE.
I DON'T KNOW OF ANY OTHER GIRL WHO COULD WITHSTAND THAT PRESSURE!
SHOCK
NOT JUST THAT--YOUR FACE AND THAT BODY ARE RIGHT UP MY ALLEY!!
I CAN FEEL DESTINY ITSELF AT WORK. I JUST WANT TO RUIN YOU!
......
WHAT THE...?
HOW CAN HE SAY THAT WITH SUCH A GLEEFUL LOOK ON HIS FACE?!
ME... AND HIM...?!
THANK YOU FOR PAYING FOR MY MEAL AND THEN DRIVING ME ALL THE WAY HOME.
DON'T WORRY 'BOUT IT!
BESIDES...

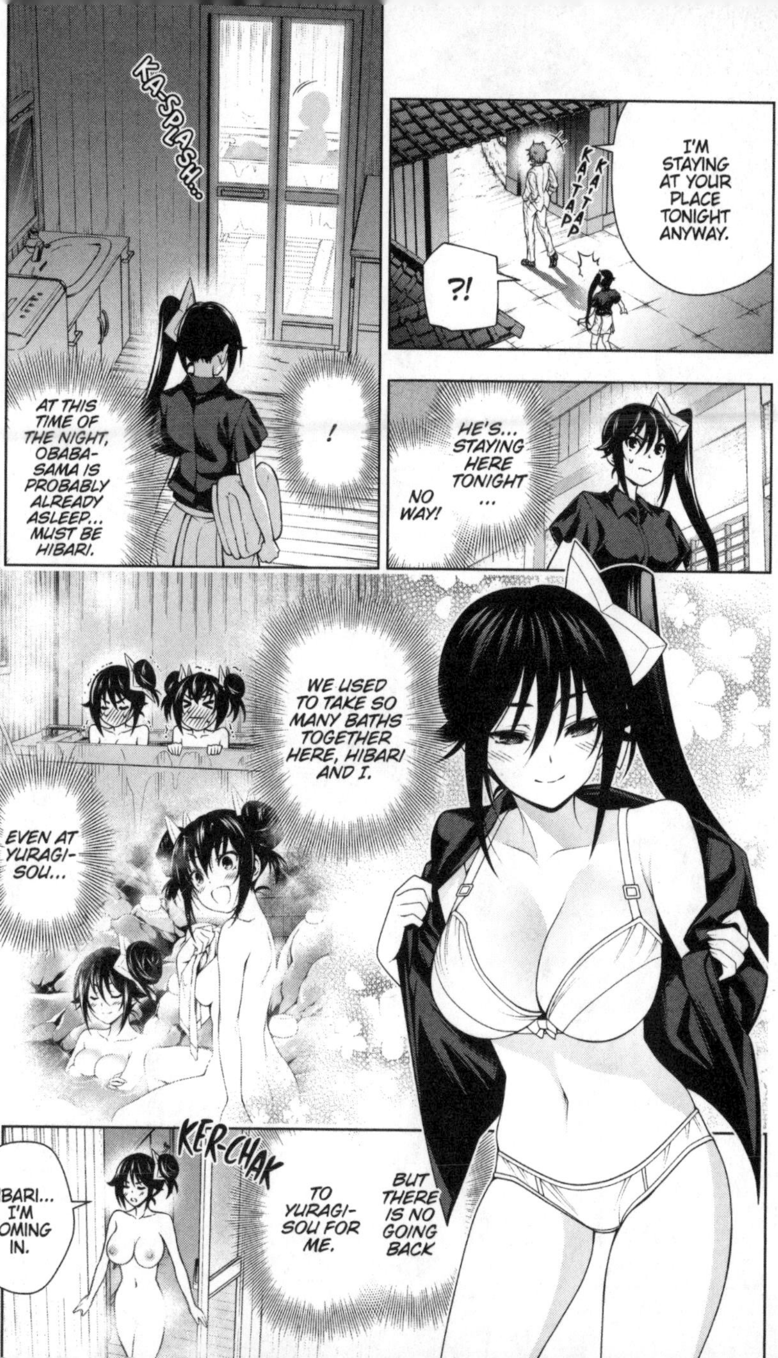
I'M STAYING AT YOUR PLACE TONIGHT ANYWAY.
KAITAP KAITAP
?!
HE'S... STAYING HERE TONIGHT...
NO WAY!
KA-SPLASH...
!
AT THIS TIME OF THE NIGHT, OBABA-SAMA IS PROBABLY ALREADY ASLEEP... MUST BE HIBARI.
WE USED TO TAKE SO MANY BATHS TOGETHER HERE, HIBARI AND I.
EVEN AT YURAGI-SOU...
BUT THERE IS NO GOING BACK
TO YURAGI-SOU FOR ME.
KER-CHAK
HIBARI... I'M COMING IN.

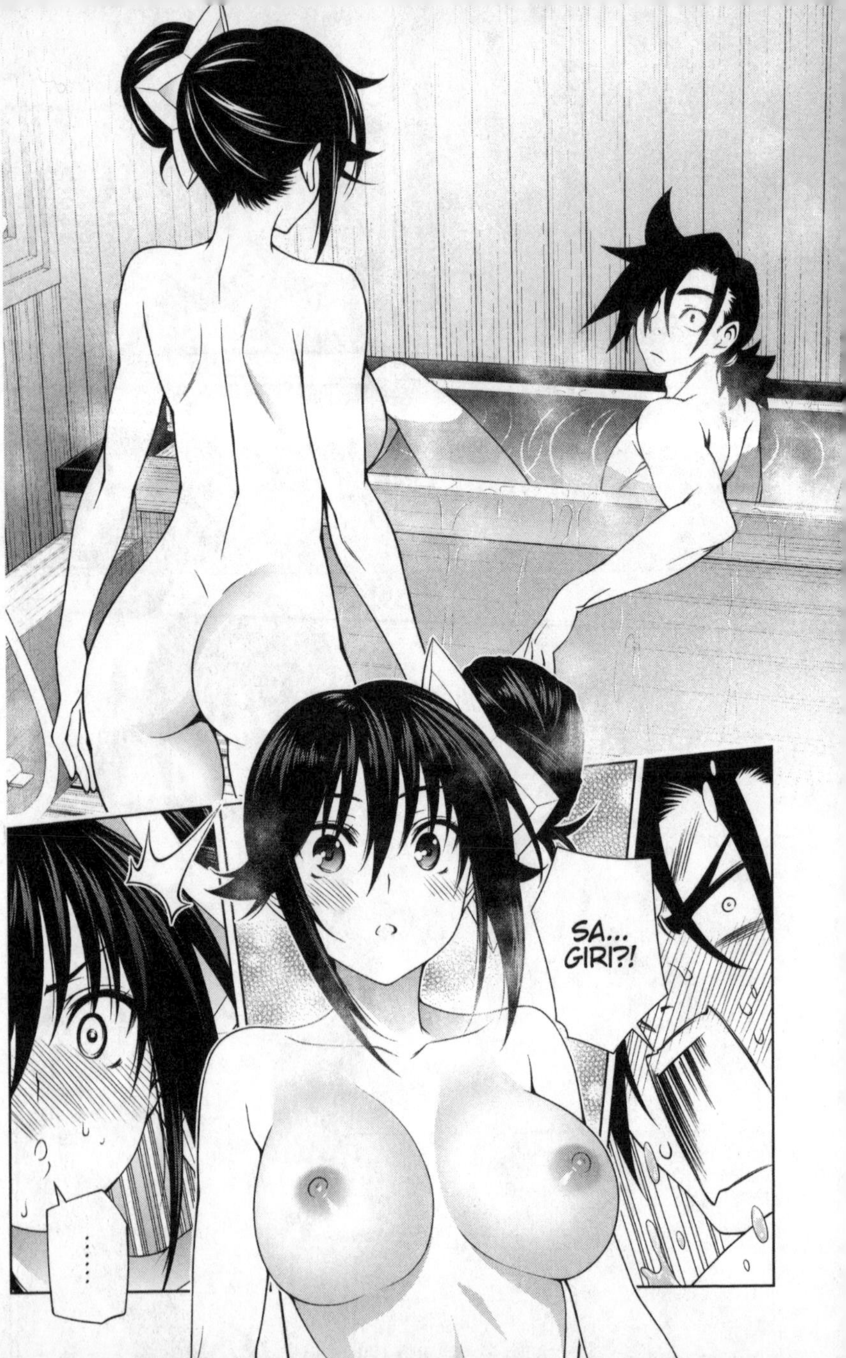
SA... GIRI?!
......

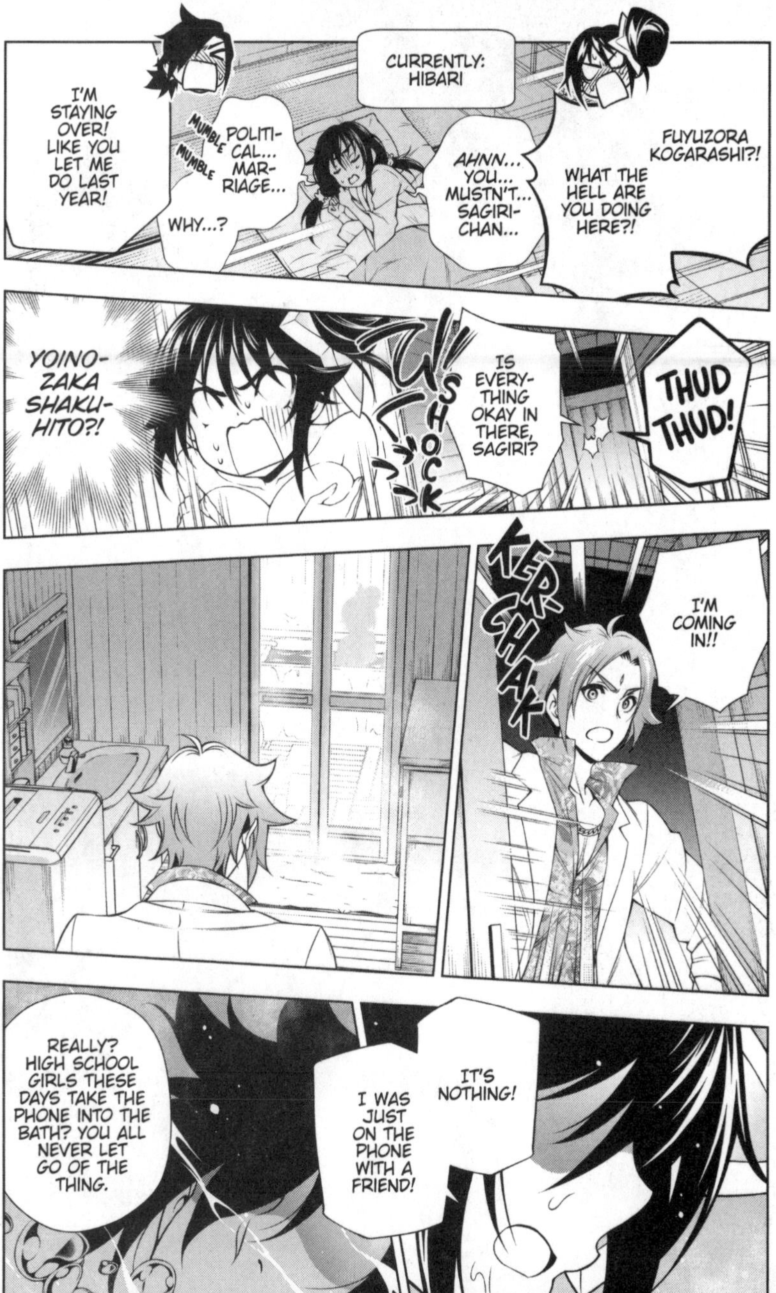
CURRENTLY: HIBARI
FUYUZORA KOGARASHI?!
WHAT THE HELL ARE YOU DOING HERE?!
AHNN... YOU... MUSTN'T... SAGIRI-CHAN...
MUMBLE MUMBLE
POLITICAL... MARRIAGE...
WHY...?
I'M STAYING OVER! LIKE YOU LET ME DO LAST YEAR!
THUD THUD!
IS EVERYTHING OKAY IN THERE, SAGIRI?
SHOCK
YOINOZAKA SHAKUHITO?!
KERCHAK
I'M COMING IN!!
IT'S NOTHING!
I WAS JUST ON THE PHONE WITH A FRIEND!
REALLY? HIGH SCHOOL GIRLS THESE DAYS TAKE THE PHONE INTO THE BATH? YOU ALL NEVER LET GO OF THE THING.

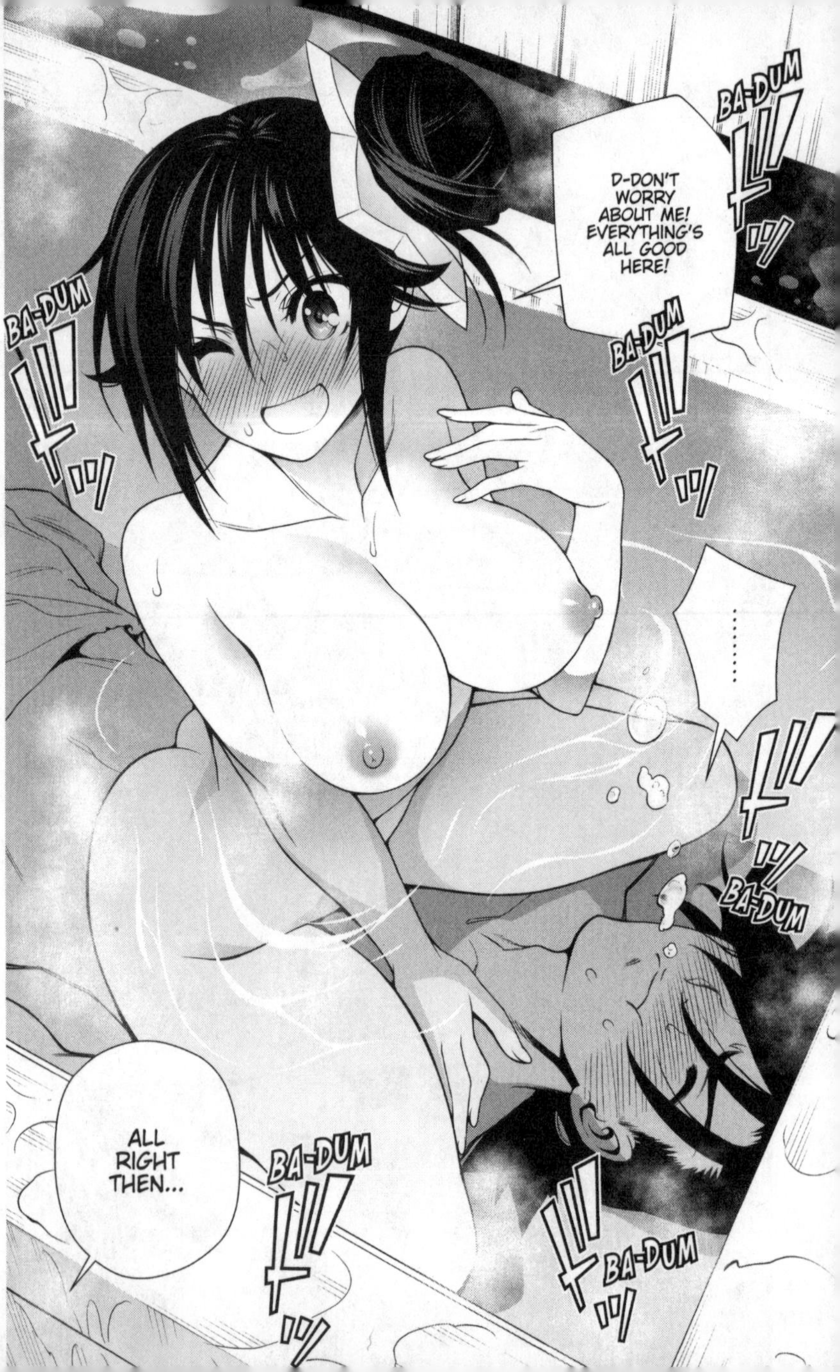
BA-DUM
D-DON'T WORRY ABOUT ME! EVERYTHING'S ALL GOOD HERE!
BA-DUM
BA-DUM
......
BA-DUM
BA-DUM
ALL RIGHT THEN...
BA-DUM

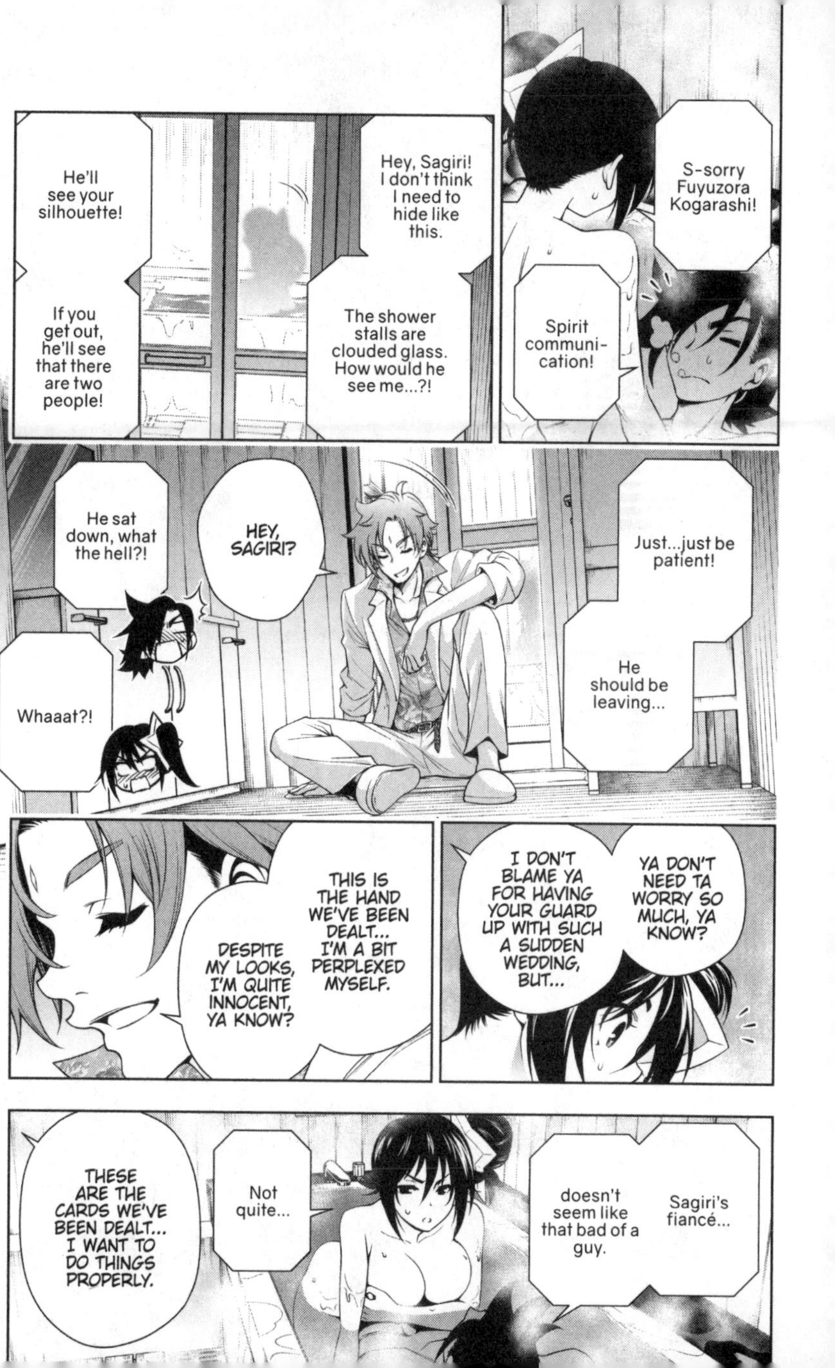
S-sorry Fuyuzora Kogarashi!
Spirit communi-cation!
Hey, Sagiri! I don't think I need to hide like this.
The shower stalls are clouded glass. How would he see me...?!
He'll see your silhouette!
If you get out, he'll see that there are two people!
Just...just be patient!
He should be leaving...
HEY, SAGIRI?
He sat down, what the hell?!
Whaaat?!
YA DON'T NEED TA WORRY SO MUCH, YA KNOW?
I DON'T BLAME YA FOR HAVING YOUR GUARD UP WITH SUCH A SUDDEN WEDDING, BUT...
THIS IS THE HAND WE'VE BEEN DEALT... I'M A BIT PERPLEXED MYSELF.
DESPITE MY LOOKS, I'M QUITE INNOCENT, YA KNOW?
Sagiri's fiancé...
doesn't seem like that bad of a guy.
Not quite...
THESE ARE THE CARDS WE'VE BEEN DEALT... I WANT TO DO THINGS PROPERLY.

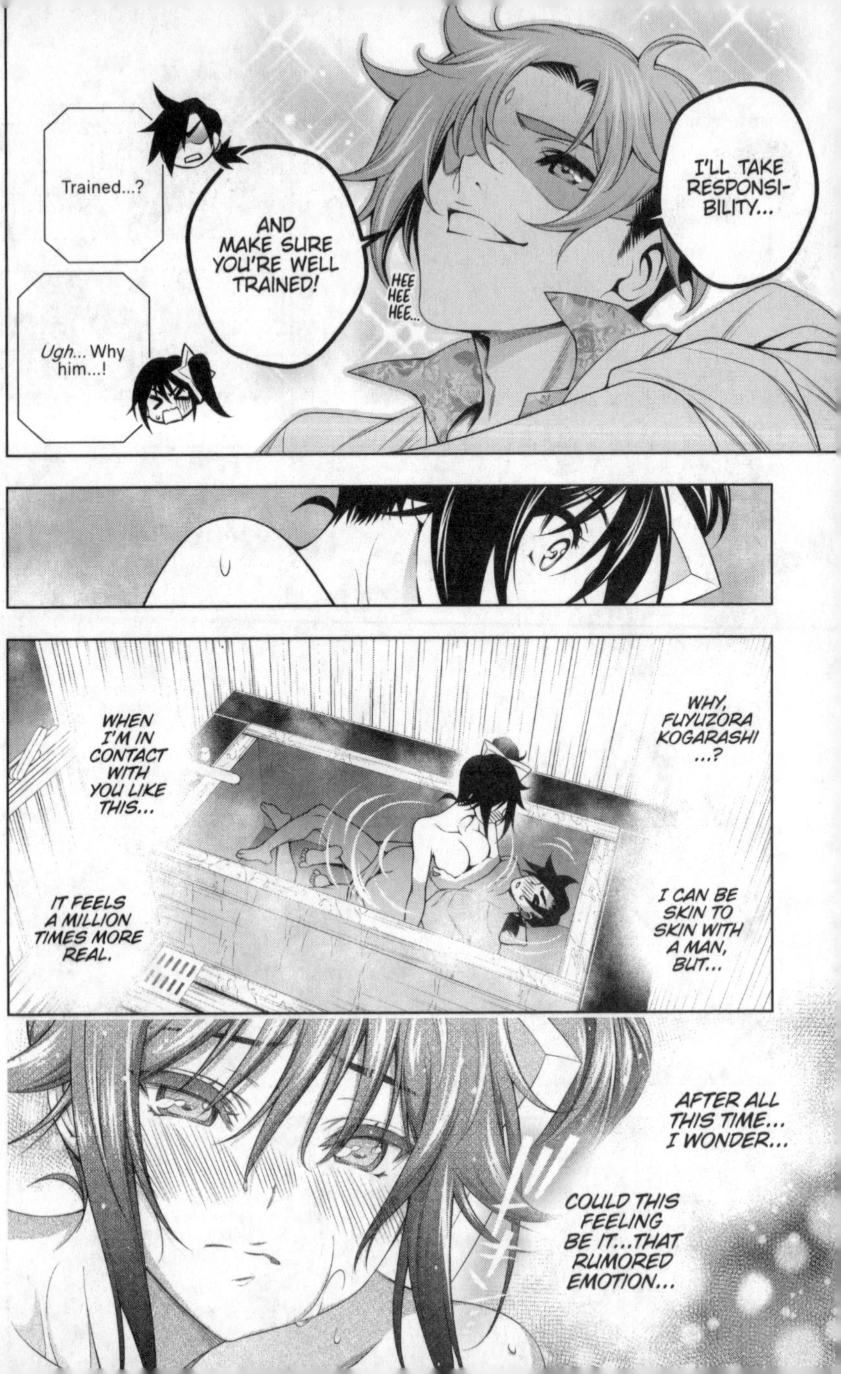

I'LL TAKE RESPONSI-BILITY...
AND MAKE SURE YOU'RE WELL TRAINED!
HEE HEE HEE...
Trained...?
Ugh... Why him...!
WHY, FUYUZORA KOGARASHI ...?
I CAN BE SKIN TO SKIN WITH A MAN, BUT...
WHEN I'M IN CONTACT WITH YOU LIKE THIS...
IT FEELS A MILLION TIMES MORE REAL.
AFTER ALL THIS TIME... I WONDER...
COULD THIS FEELING BE IT...THAT RUMORED EMOTION...

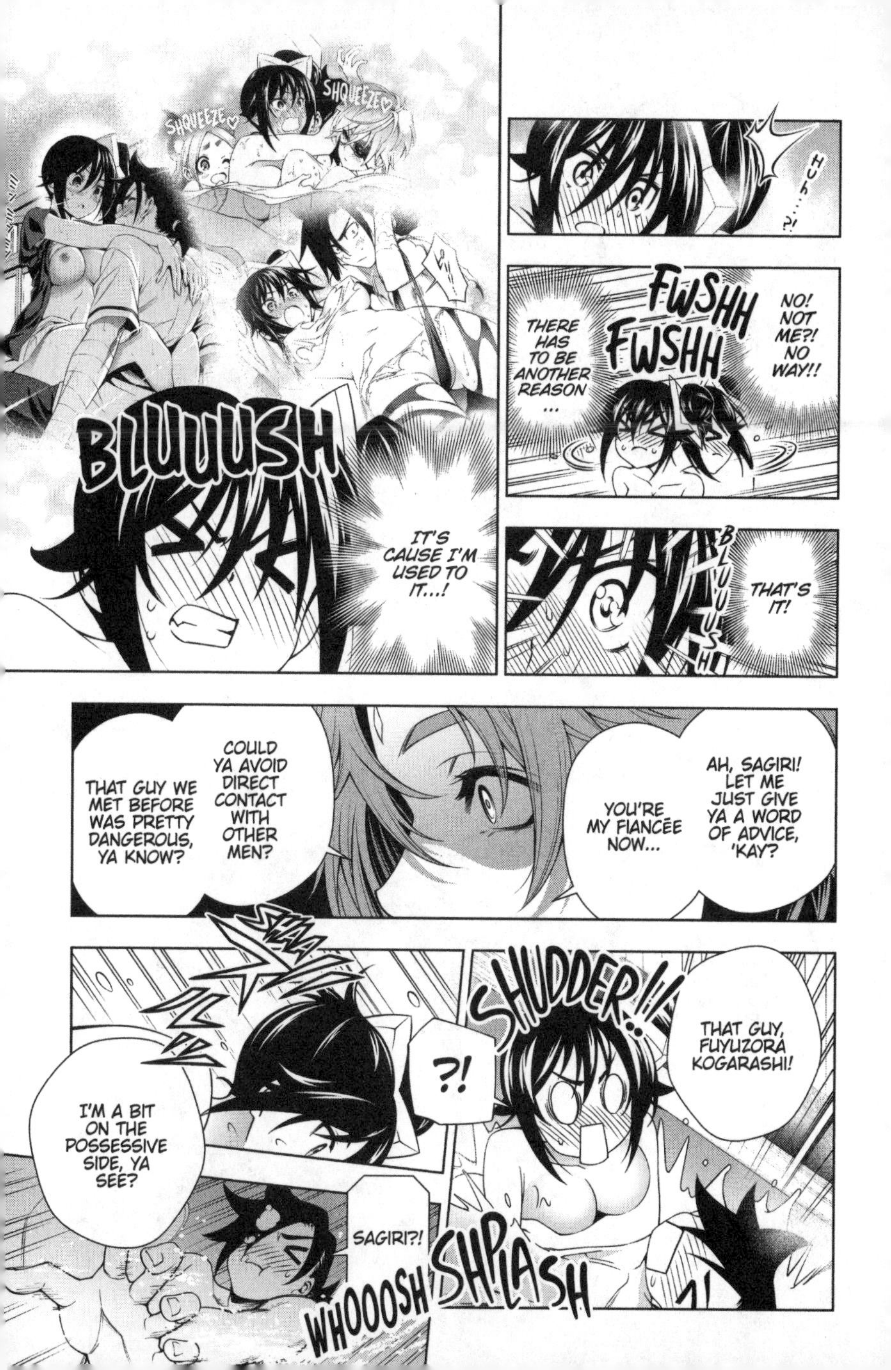
HUH...?!
NO! NOT ME?! NO WAY!!
FWSHH FWSHH
THERE HAS TO BE ANOTHER REASON ...
BLUUUUSH
THAT'S IT!
SHQUEEZE♡
SHQUEEZE♡
BLUUUSH
IT'S CAUSE I'M USED TO IT...!
AH, SAGIRI! LET ME JUST GIVE YA A WORD OF ADVICE, 'KAY?
YOU'RE MY FIANCÉE NOW...
COULD YA AVOID DIRECT CONTACT WITH OTHER MEN?
THAT GUY WE MET BEFORE WAS PRETTY DANGEROUS, YA KNOW?
THAT GUY, FUYUZORA KOGARASHI!
SHUDDER!!!
?!
I'M A BIT ON THE POSSESSIVE SIDE, YA SEE?
SAGIRI?!
SHPLASH
WHOOOSH

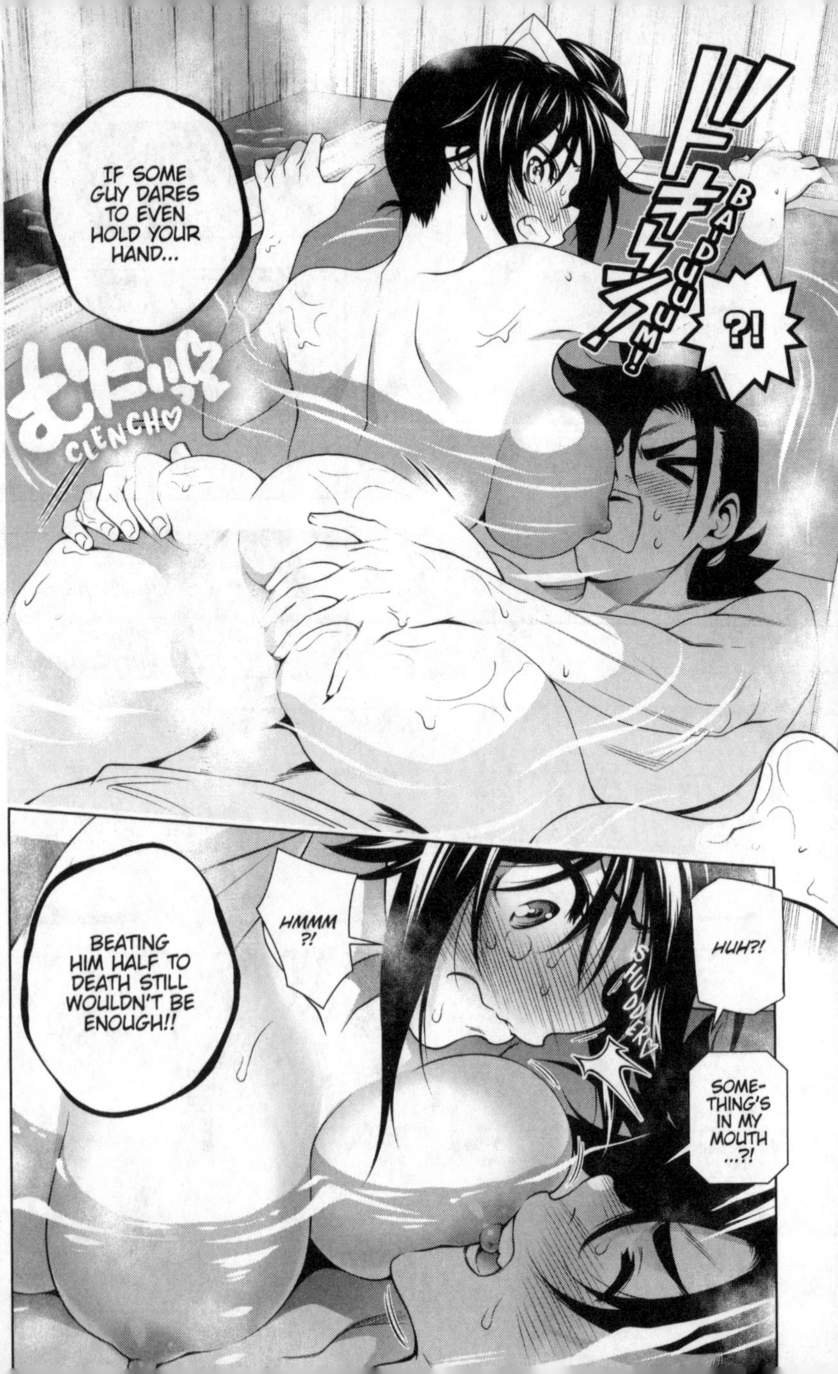
BA-DUUUM!
?!
IF SOME GUY DARES TO EVEN HOLD YOUR HAND...
CLENCH♥
HUH?!
SOME-THING'S IN MY MOUTH ...?!
SHUDDER♥
HMMM ?!
BEATING HIM HALF TO DEATH STILL WOULDN'T BE ENOUGH!!

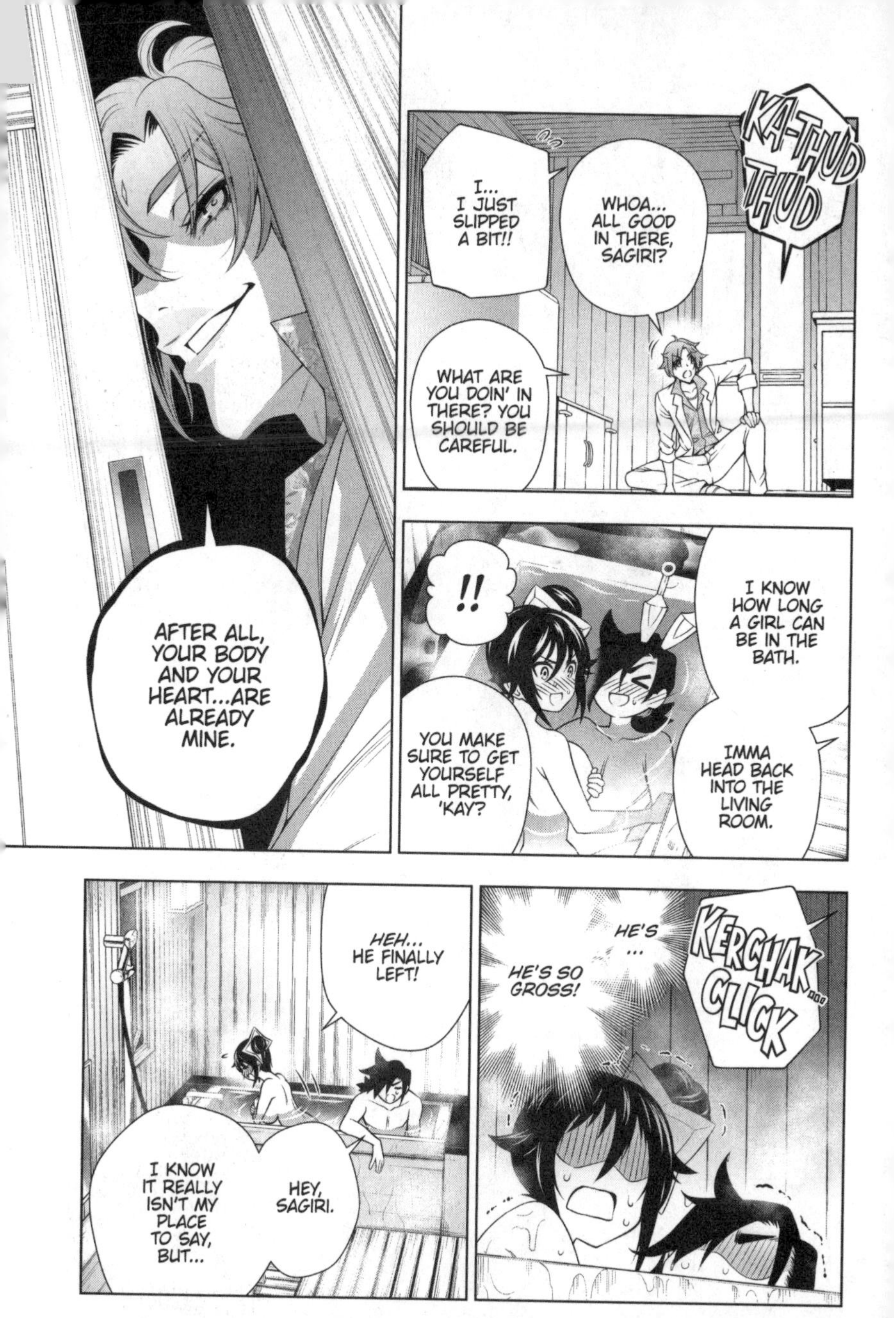
KA-THUD THUD
WHOA... ALL GOOD IN THERE, SAGIRI?
I... I JUST SLIPPED A BIT!!
WHAT ARE YOU DOIN' IN THERE? YOU SHOULD BE CAREFUL.
I KNOW HOW LONG A GIRL CAN BE IN THE BATH.
IMMA HEAD BACK INTO THE LIVING ROOM.
YOU MAKE SURE TO GET YOURSELF ALL PRETTY, 'KAY?
!!
AFTER ALL, YOUR BODY AND YOUR HEART...ARE ALREADY MINE.
KERCHAK... CLICK
HE'S ...
HE'S SO GROSS!
HEH... HE FINALLY LEFT!
HEY, SAGIRI.
I KNOW IT REALLY ISN'T MY PLACE TO SAY, BUT...

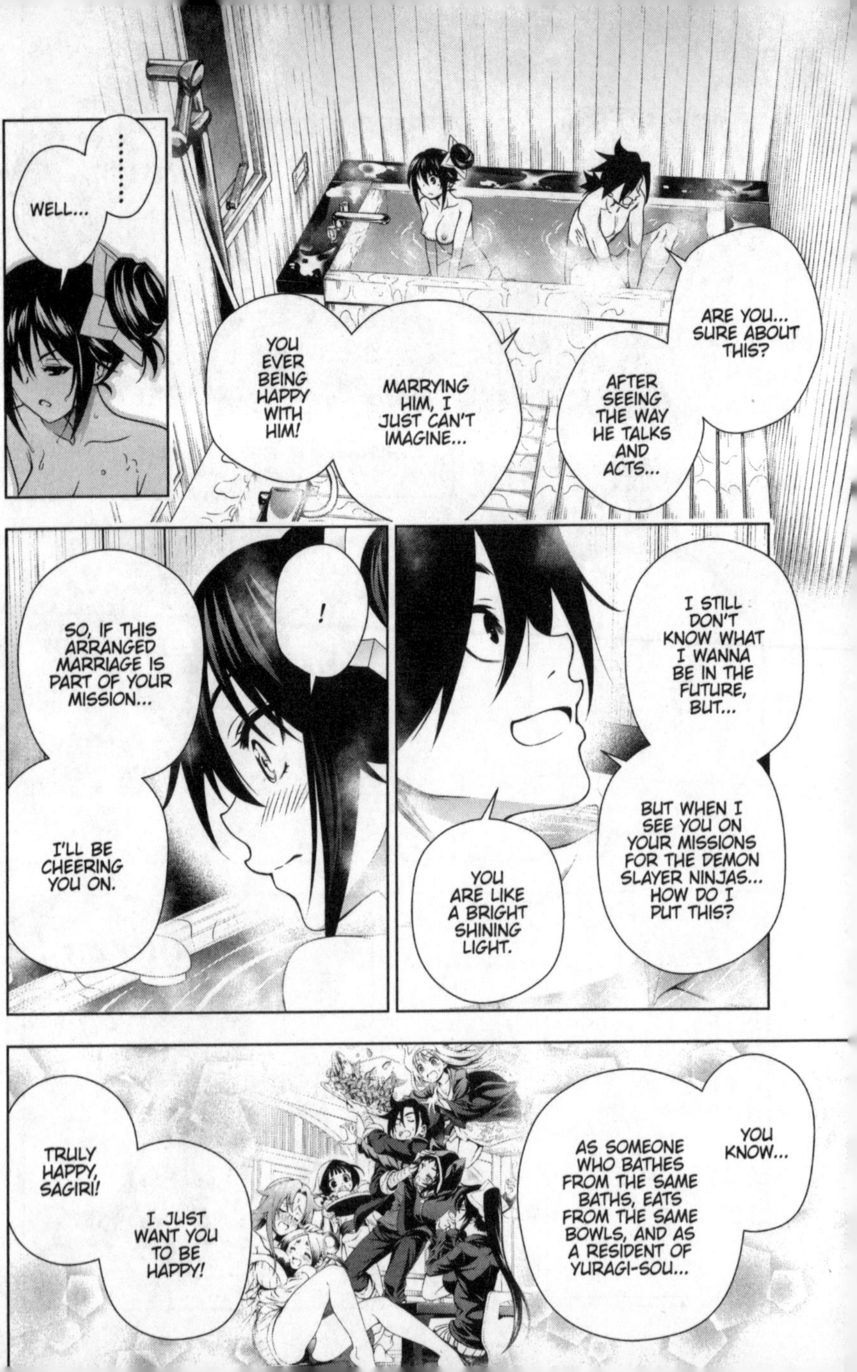
ARE YOU... SURE ABOUT THIS?
AFTER SEEING THE WAY HE TALKS AND ACTS...
MARRYING HIM, I JUST CAN'T IMAGINE...
YOU EVER BEING HAPPY WITH HIM!
......
WELL...
I STILL DON'T KNOW WHAT I WANNA BE IN THE FUTURE, BUT...
BUT WHEN I SEE YOU ON YOUR MISSIONS FOR THE DEMON SLAYER NINJAS... HOW DO I PUT THIS?
YOU ARE LIKE A BRIGHT SHINING LIGHT.
!
SO, IF THIS ARRANGED MARRIAGE IS PART OF YOUR MISSION...
I'LL BE CHEERING YOU ON.
YOU KNOW...
AS SOMEONE WHO BATHES FROM THE SAME BATHS, EATS FROM THE SAME BOWLS, AND AS A RESIDENT OF YURAGI-SOU...
I JUST WANT YOU TO BE HAPPY!
TRULY HAPPY, SAGIRI!

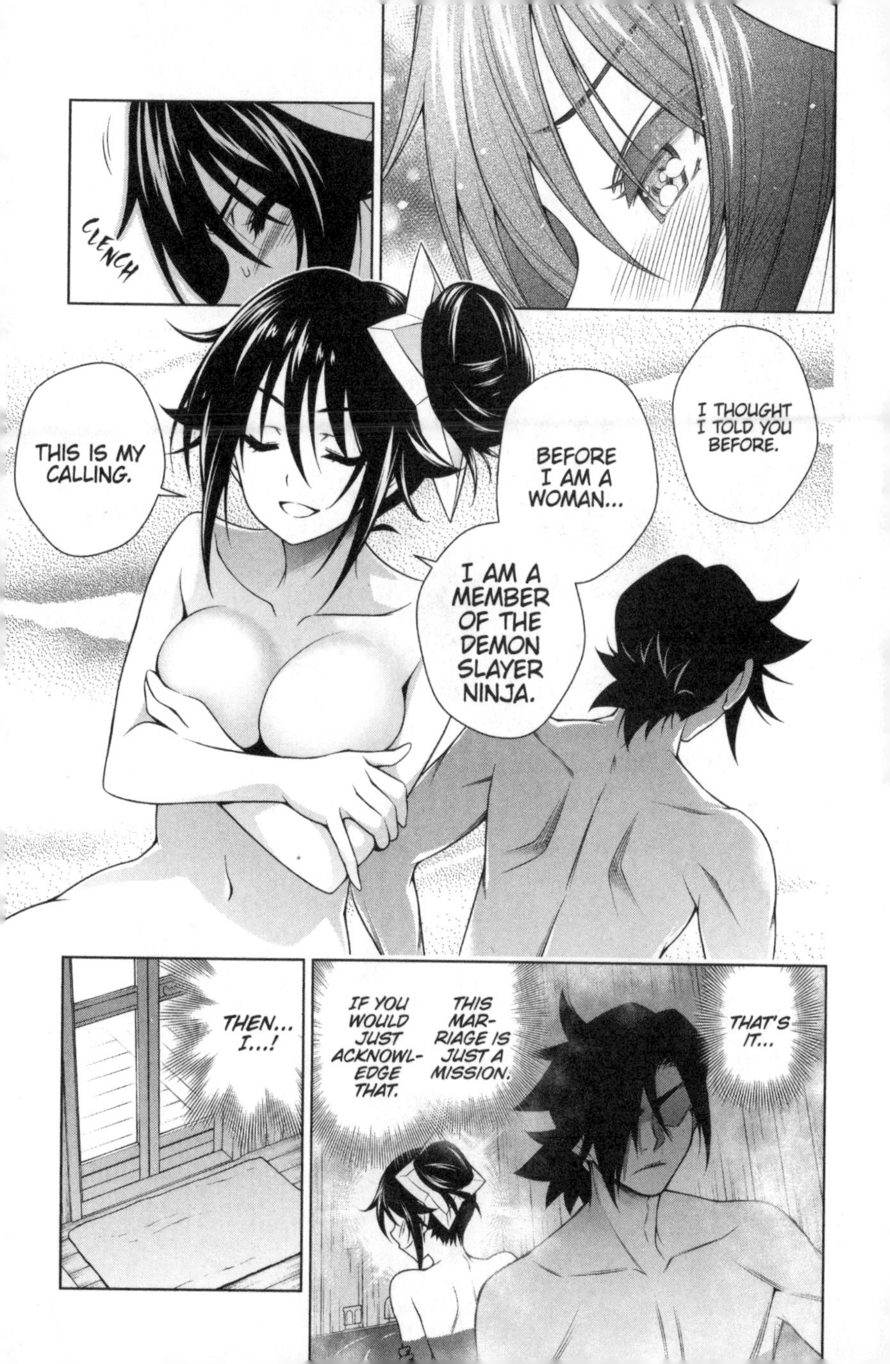
CLENCH
I THOUGHT I TOLD YOU BEFORE.
BEFORE I AM A WOMAN...
I AM A MEMBER OF THE DEMON SLAYER NINJA.
THIS IS MY CALLING.
THAT'S IT...
THIS MAR-RIAGE IS JUST A MISSION.
IF YOU WOULD JUST ACKNOWL-EDGE THAT.
THEN... I...!

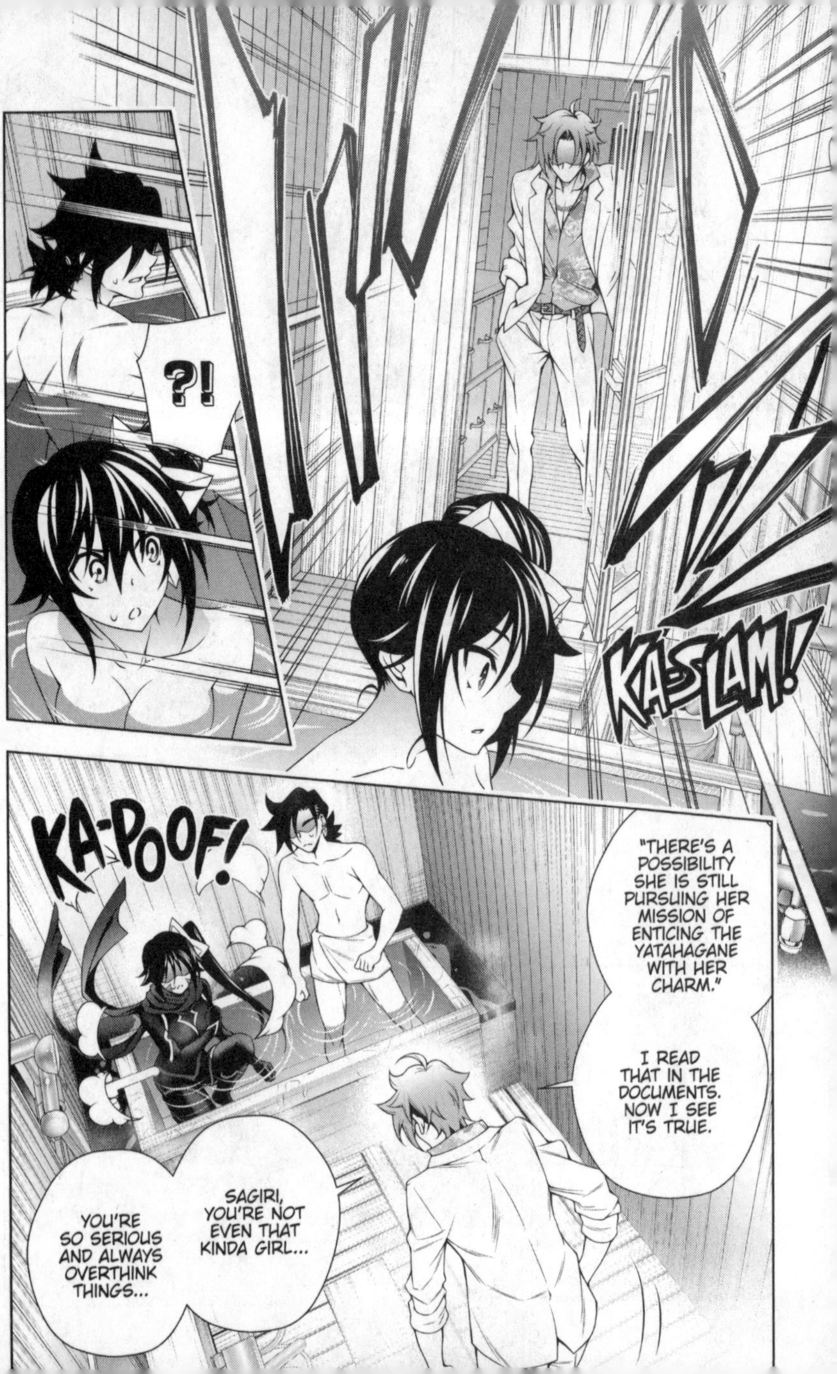
KA-SLAM!
?!
KA-POOF!
"THERE'S A POSSIBILITY SHE IS STILL PURSUING HER MISSION OF ENTICING THE YATAHAGANE WITH HER CHARM."
I READ THAT IN THE DOCUMENTS. NOW I SEE IT'S TRUE.
SAGIRI, YOU'RE NOT EVEN THAT KINDA GIRL...
YOU'RE SO SERIOUS AND ALWAYS OVERTHINK THINGS...

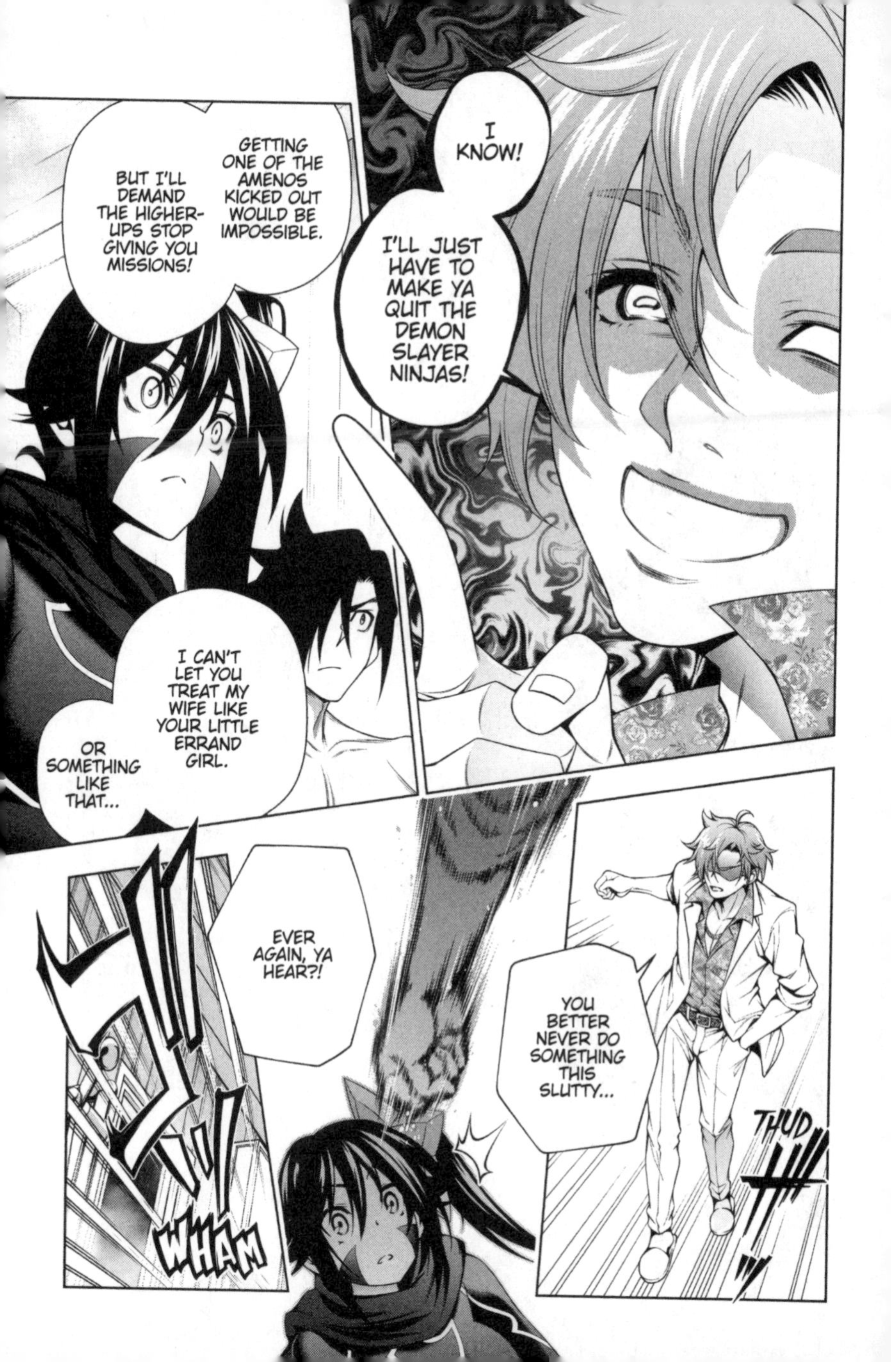
I KNOW!
I'LL JUST HAVE TO MAKE YA QUIT THE DEMON SLAYER NINJAS!
GETTING ONE OF THE AMENOS KICKED OUT WOULD BE IMPOSSIBLE.
BUT I'LL DEMAND THE HIGHER-UPS STOP GIVING YOU MISSIONS!
I CAN'T LET YOU TREAT MY WIFE LIKE YOUR LITTLE ERRAND GIRL.
OR SOMETHING LIKE THAT...
YOU BETTER NEVER DO SOMETHING THIS SLUTTY...
THUD
EVER AGAIN, YA HEAR?!
WHAM

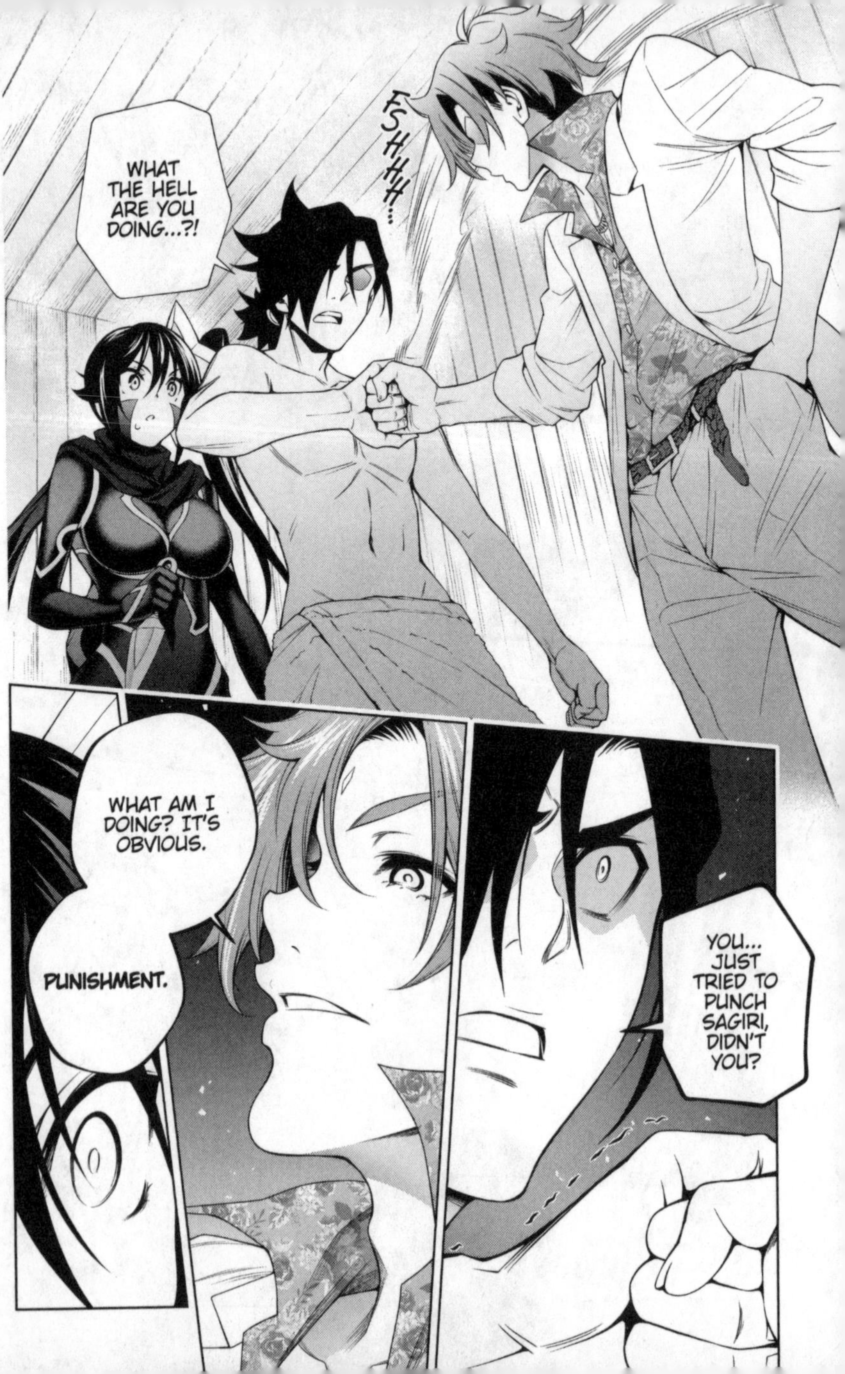
FSHHHH...
WHAT THE HELL ARE YOU DOING...?!
YOU... JUST TRIED TO PUNCH SAGIRI, DIDN'T YOU?
WHAT AM I DOING? IT'S OBVIOUS.
PUNISHMENT.

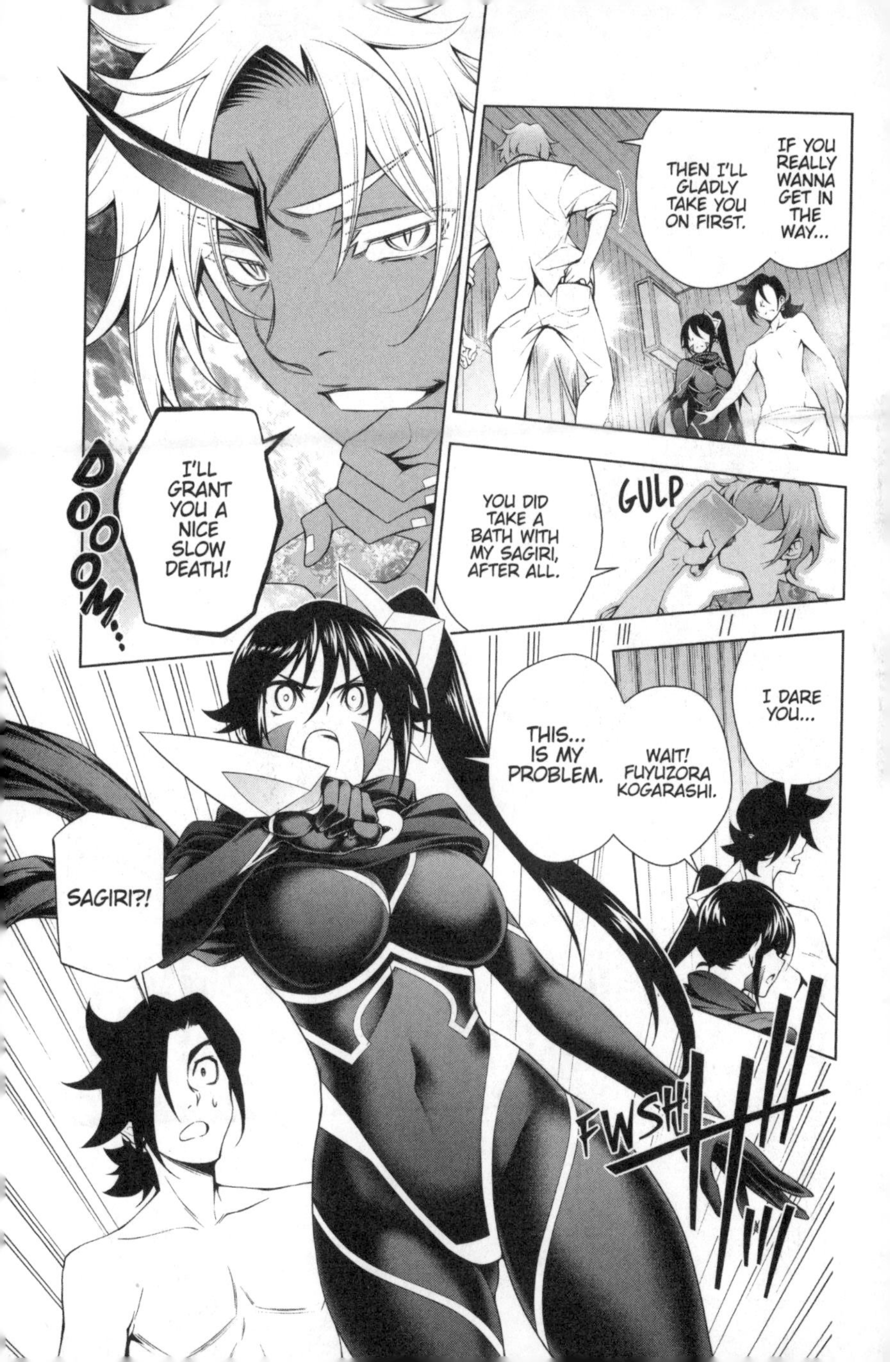
IF YOU REALLY WANNA GET IN THE WAY...
THEN I'LL GLADLY TAKE YOU ON FIRST.
GULP
YOU DID TAKE A BATH WITH MY SAGIRI, AFTER ALL.
I'LL GRANT YOU A NICE SLOW DEATH!
DOOOOM...
I DARE YOU...
WAIT! FUYUZORA KOGARASHI.
THIS... IS MY PROBLEM.
FWSH
SAGIRI?!

Yuuna
and the
Haunted
Hot
Springs

135 The Truth Behind Sagiri-san's Engagement

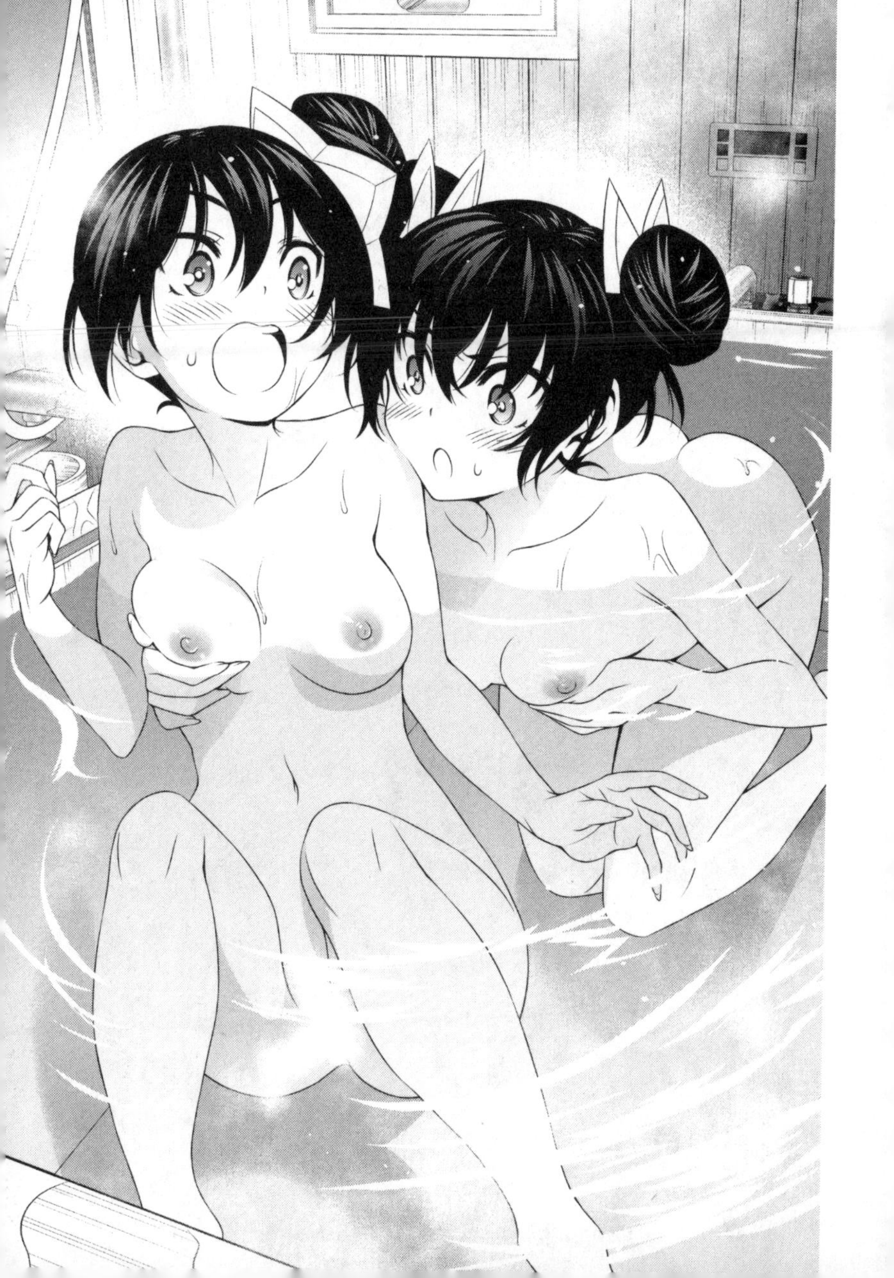

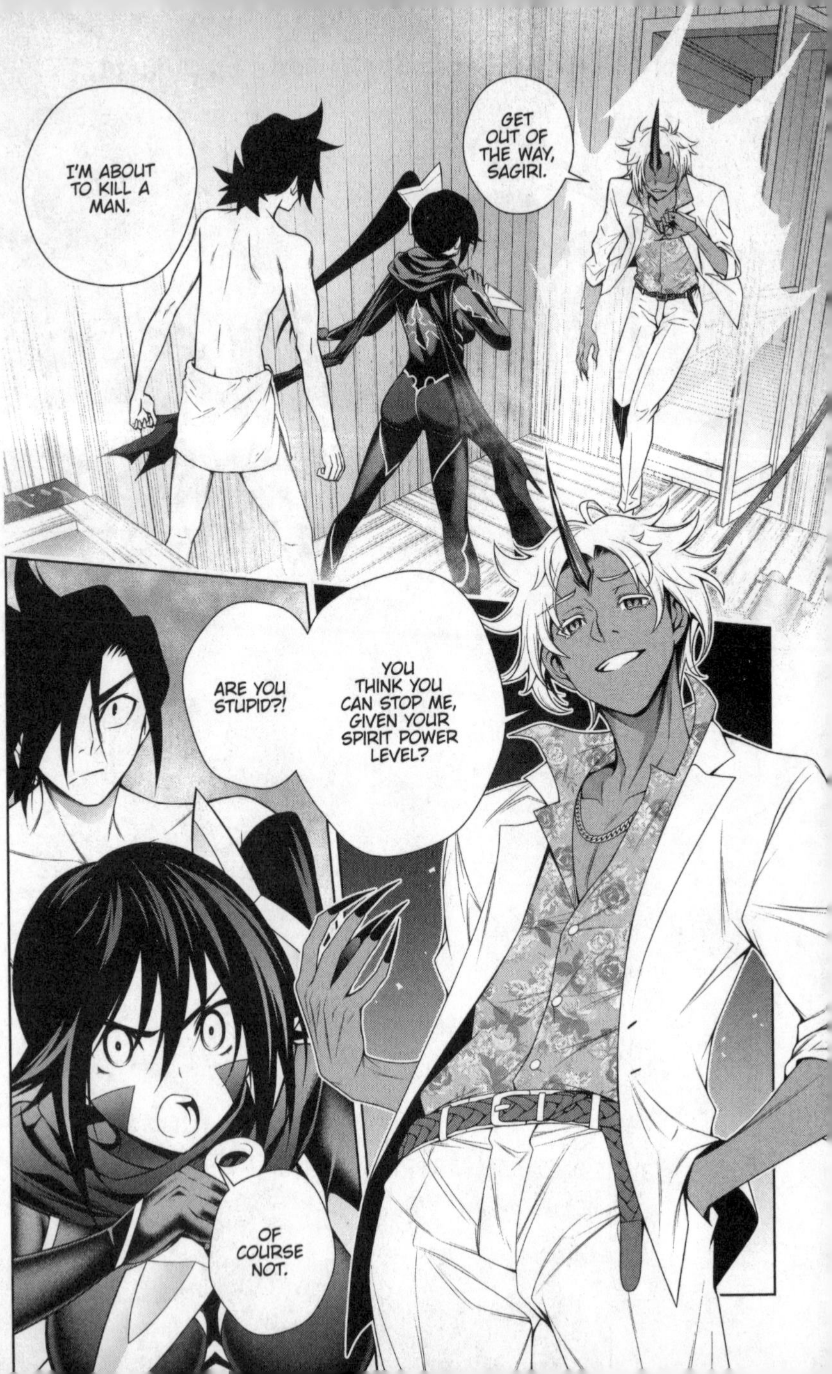
GET OUT OF THE WAY, SAGIRI.
I'M ABOUT TO KILL A MAN.
YOU THINK YOU CAN STOP ME, GIVEN YOUR SPIRIT POWER LEVEL?
ARE YOU STUPID?!
OF COURSE NOT.

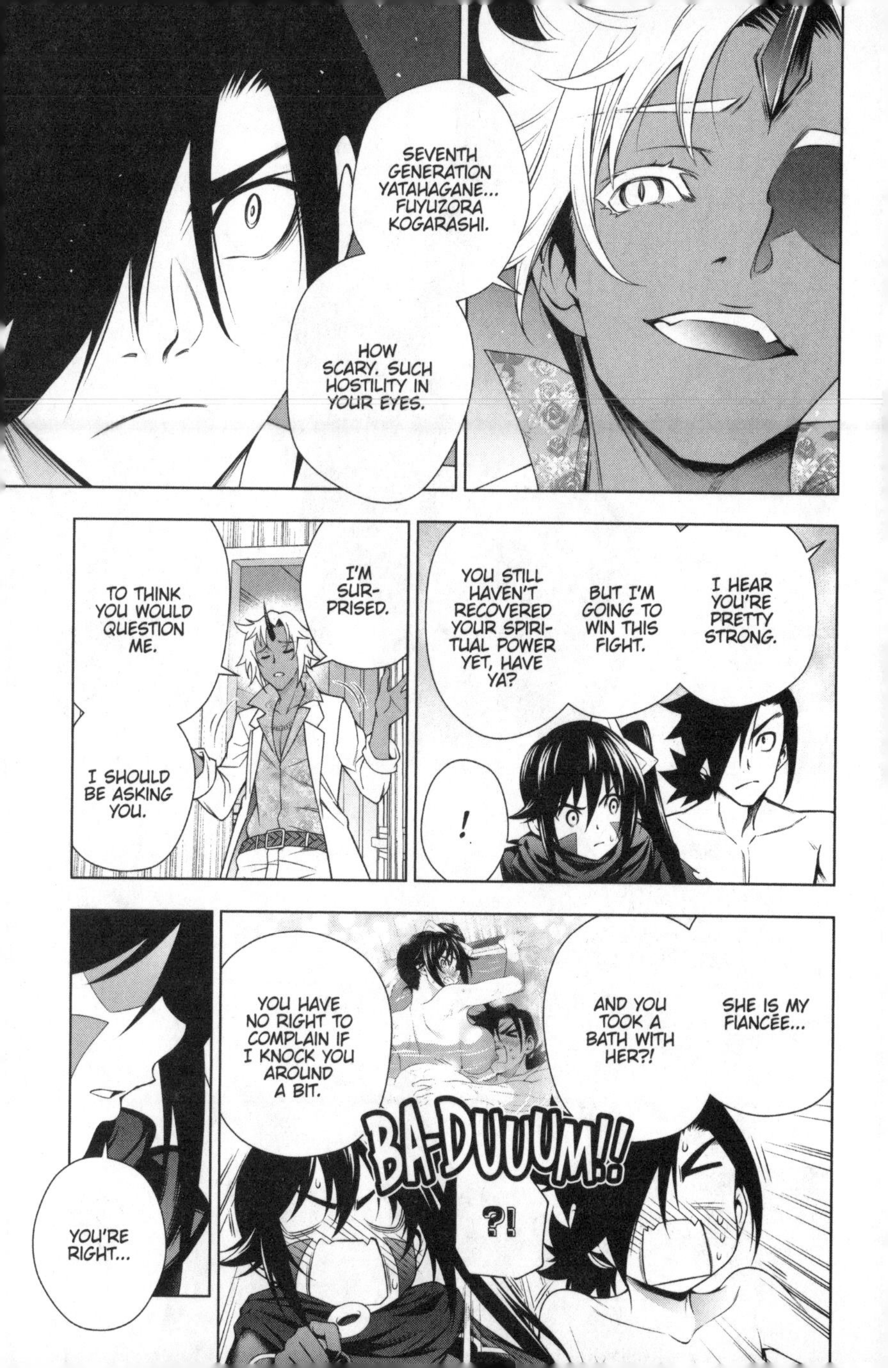
SEVENTH GENERATION YATAHAGANE... FUYUZORA KOGARASHI.
HOW SCARY. SUCH HOSTILITY IN YOUR EYES.
I HEAR YOU'RE PRETTY STRONG.
BUT I'M GOING TO WIN THIS FIGHT.
YOU STILL HAVEN'T RECOVERED YOUR SPIRITUAL POWER YET, HAVE YA?
!
I'M SURPRISED.
TO THINK YOU WOULD QUESTION ME.
I SHOULD BE ASKING YOU.
SHE IS MY FIANCÉE...
AND YOU TOOK A BATH WITH HER?!
YOU HAVE NO RIGHT TO COMPLAIN IF I KNOCK YOU AROUND A BIT.
BA-DUUUM!!
?!
YOU'RE RIGHT...

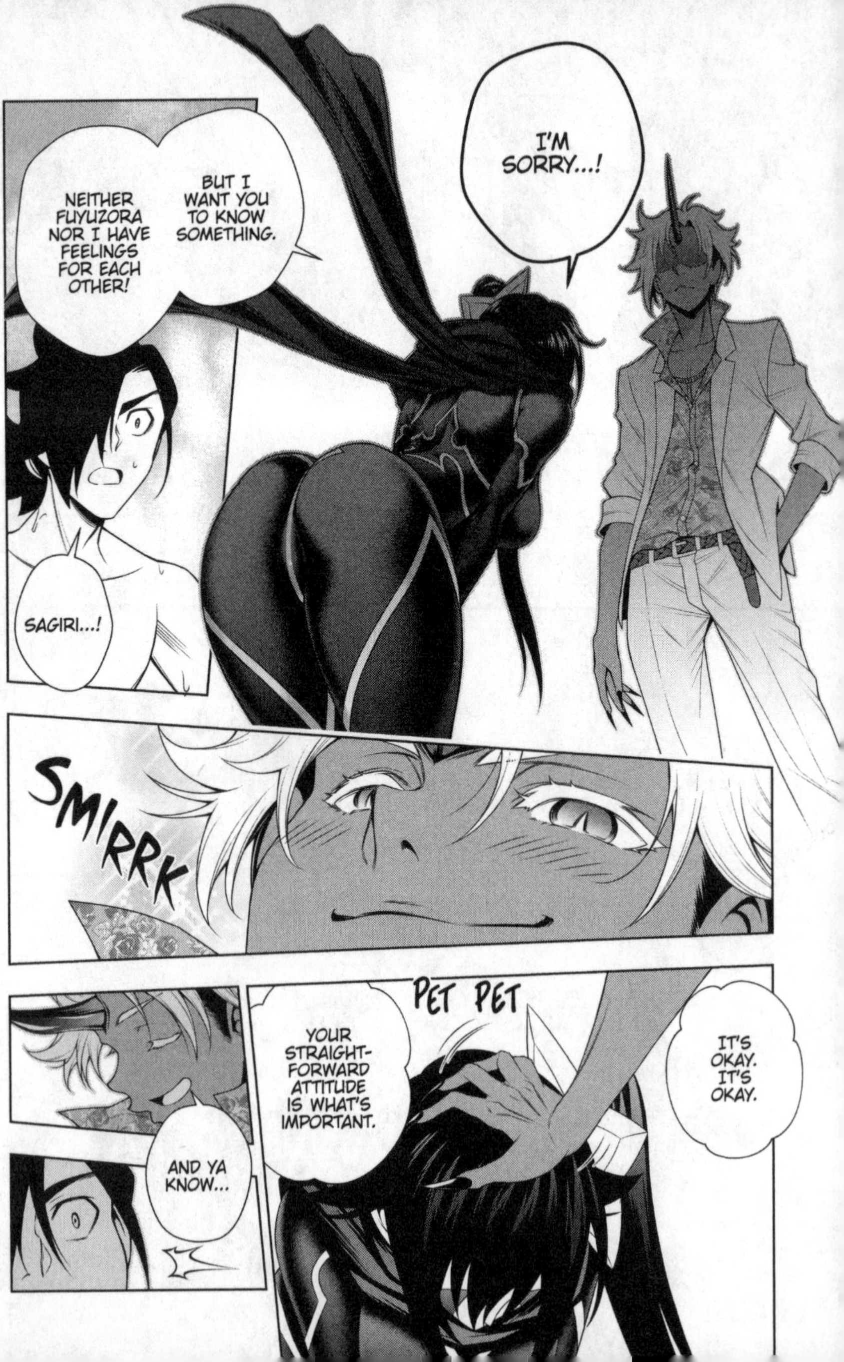
I'M SORRY...!
BUT I WANT YOU TO KNOW SOMETHING.
NEITHER FUYUZORA NOR I HAVE FEELINGS FOR EACH OTHER!
SAGIRI...!
SMIRRK
IT'S OKAY. IT'S OKAY.
PET PET
YOUR STRAIGHT-FORWARD ATTITUDE IS WHAT'S IMPORTANT.
AND YA KNOW...

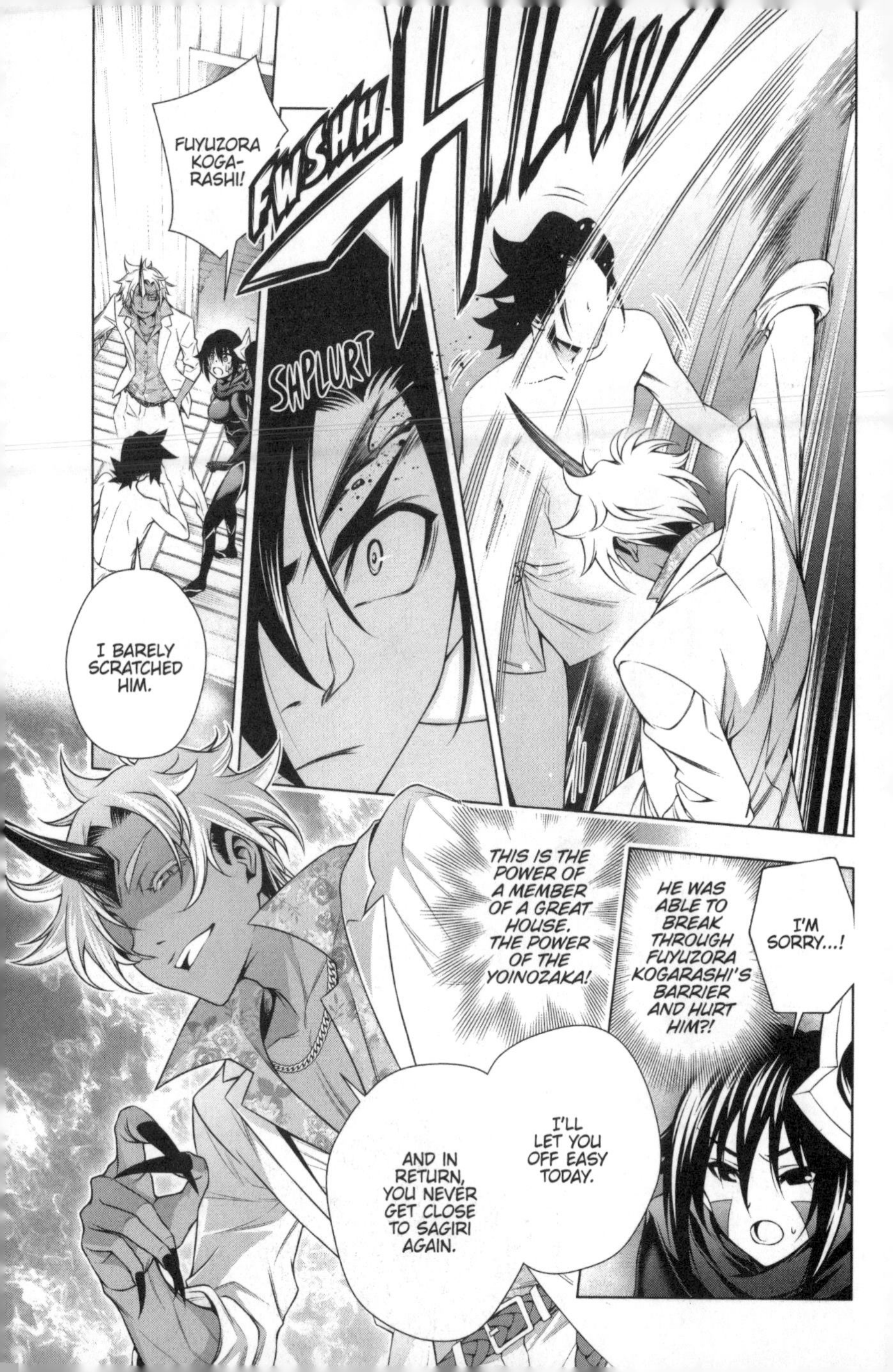

FWSHH
FUYUZORA KOGA-RASHI!
SHPLURT
I BARELY SCRATCHED HIM.
I'M SORRY...!
HE WAS ABLE TO BREAK THROUGH FUYUZORA KOGARASHI'S BARRIER AND HURT HIM?!
THIS IS THE POWER OF A MEMBER OF A GREAT HOUSE. THE POWER OF THE YOINOZAKA!
I'LL LET YOU OFF EASY TODAY.
AND IN RETURN, YOU NEVER GET CLOSE TO SAGIRI AGAIN.

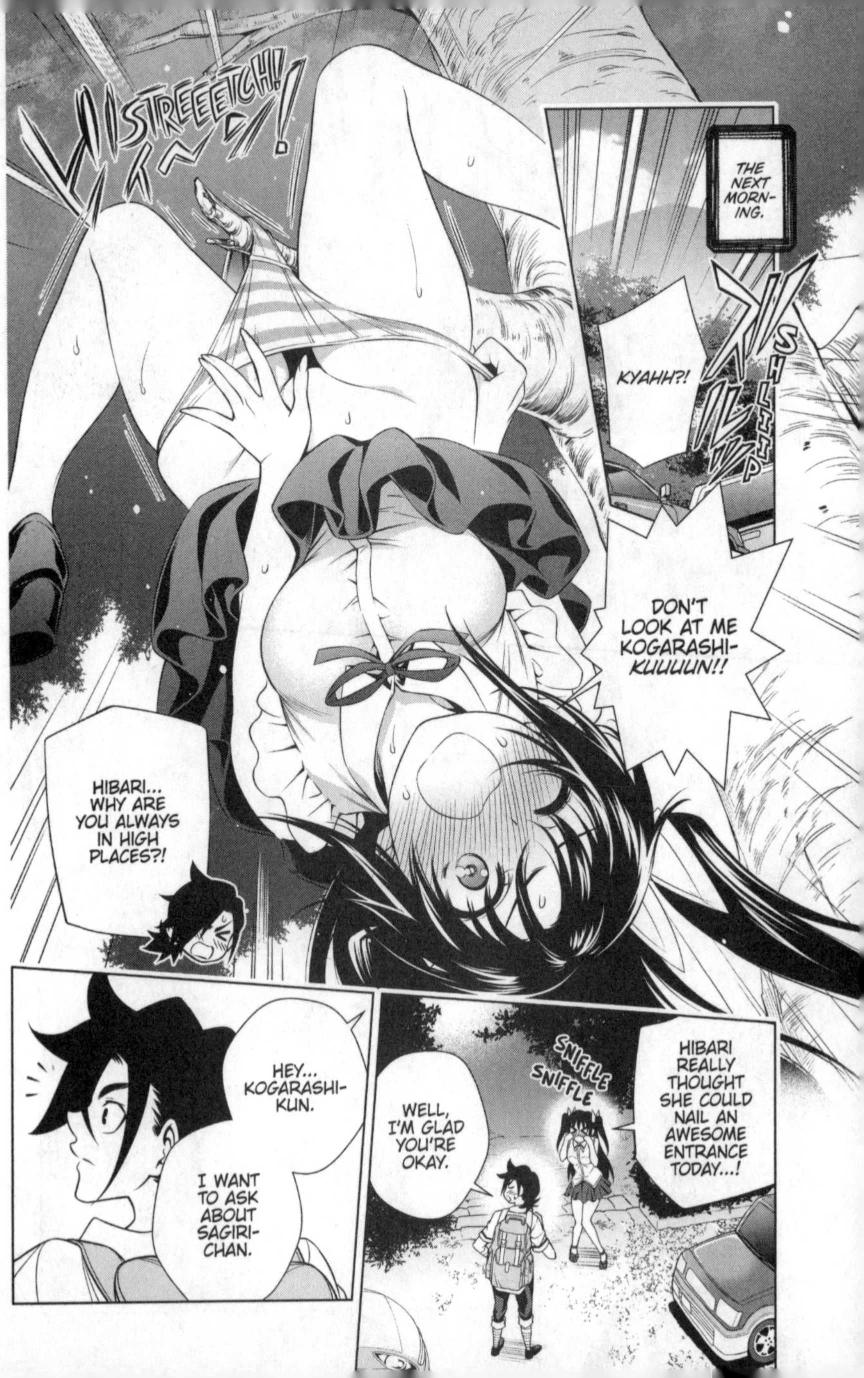
THE NEXT MORNING.
SHLIIIP
KYAHH?!
STREEEETCH!!
DON'T LOOK AT ME KOGARASHI-KUUUUN!!
HIBARI... WHY ARE YOU ALWAYS IN HIGH PLACES?!
SNIFFLE SNIFFLE
HIBARI REALLY THOUGHT SHE COULD NAIL AN AWESOME ENTRANCE TODAY...!
WELL, I'M GLAD YOU'RE OKAY.
HEY... KOGARASHI-KUN.
I WANT TO ASK ABOUT SAGIRI-CHAN.

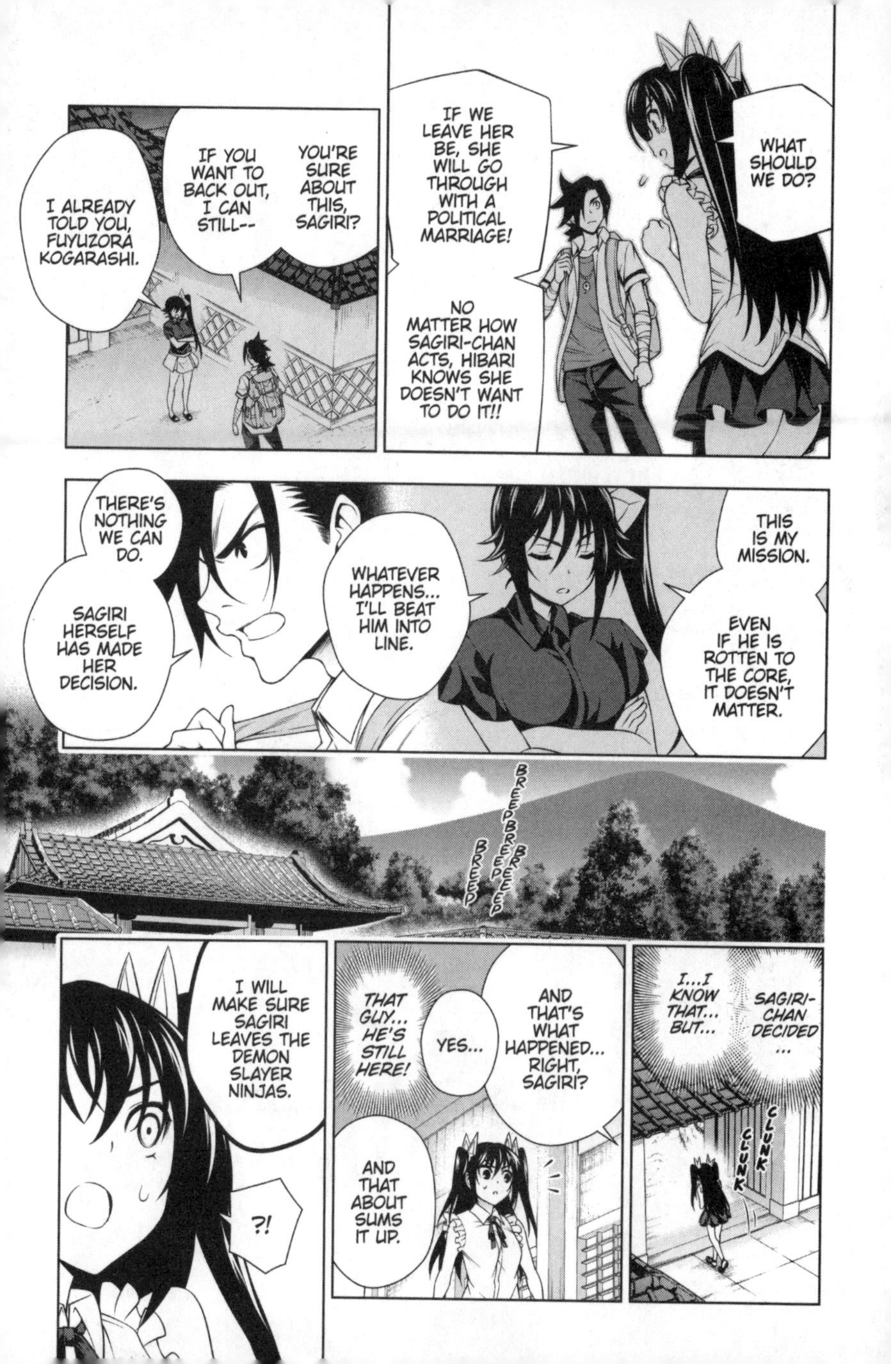
WHAT SHOULD WE DO?
IF WE LEAVE HER BE, SHE WILL GO THROUGH WITH A POLITICAL MARRIAGE!
NO MATTER HOW SAGIRI-CHAN ACTS, HIBARI KNOWS SHE DOESN'T WANT TO DO IT!!
YOU'RE SURE ABOUT THIS, SAGIRI?
IF YOU WANT TO BACK OUT, I CAN STILL--
I ALREADY TOLD YOU, FUYUZORA KOGARASHI.
THIS IS MY MISSION.
EVEN IF HE IS ROTTEN TO THE CORE, IT DOESN'T MATTER.
WHATEVER HAPPENS... I'LL BEAT HIM INTO LINE.
THERE'S NOTHING WE CAN DO.
SAGIRI HERSELF HAS MADE HER DECISION.
BREEP BREEP BREEP
BREEP BREEP
SAGIRI-CHAN DECIDED...
I...I KNOW THAT... BUT...
CLUNK CLUNK
AND THAT'S WHAT HAPPENED... RIGHT, SAGIRI?
YES...
THAT GUY... HE'S STILL HERE!
AND THAT ABOUT SUMS IT UP.
I WILL MAKE SURE SAGIRI LEAVES THE DEMON SLAYER NINJAS.
?!

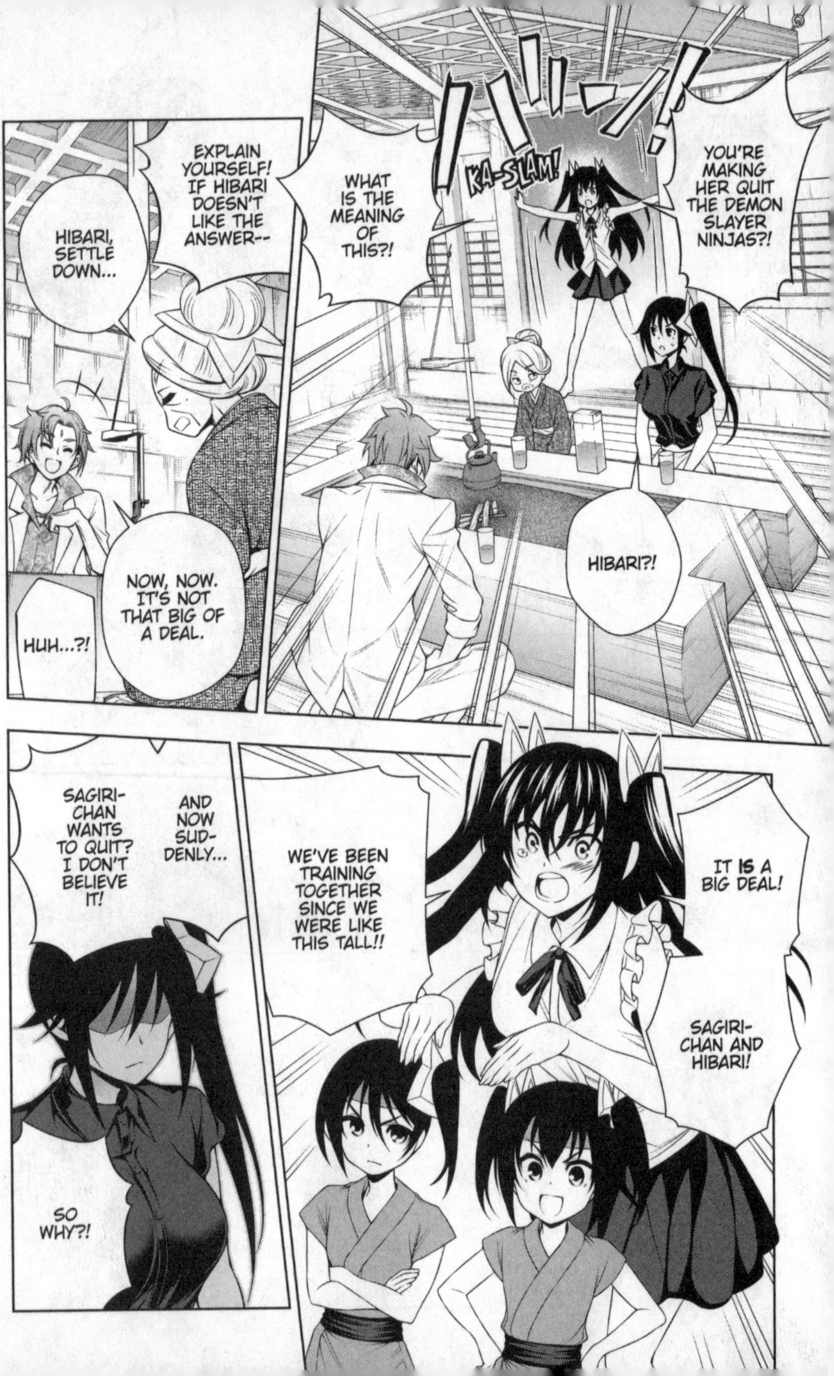
KA-SLAM!
YOU'RE MAKING HER QUIT THE DEMON SLAYER NINJAS?!
WHAT IS THE MEANING OF THIS?!
EXPLAIN YOURSELF! IF HIBARI DOESN'T LIKE THE ANSWER--
HIBARI, SETTLE DOWN...
HIBARI?!
NOW, NOW. IT'S NOT THAT BIG OF A DEAL.
HUH...?!
IT IS A BIG DEAL!
SAGIRI-CHAN AND HIBARI!
WE'VE BEEN TRAINING TOGETHER SINCE WE WERE LIKE THIS TALL!!
AND NOW SUD-DENLY...
SAGIRI-CHAN WANTS TO QUIT? I DON'T BELIEVE IT!
SO WHY?!

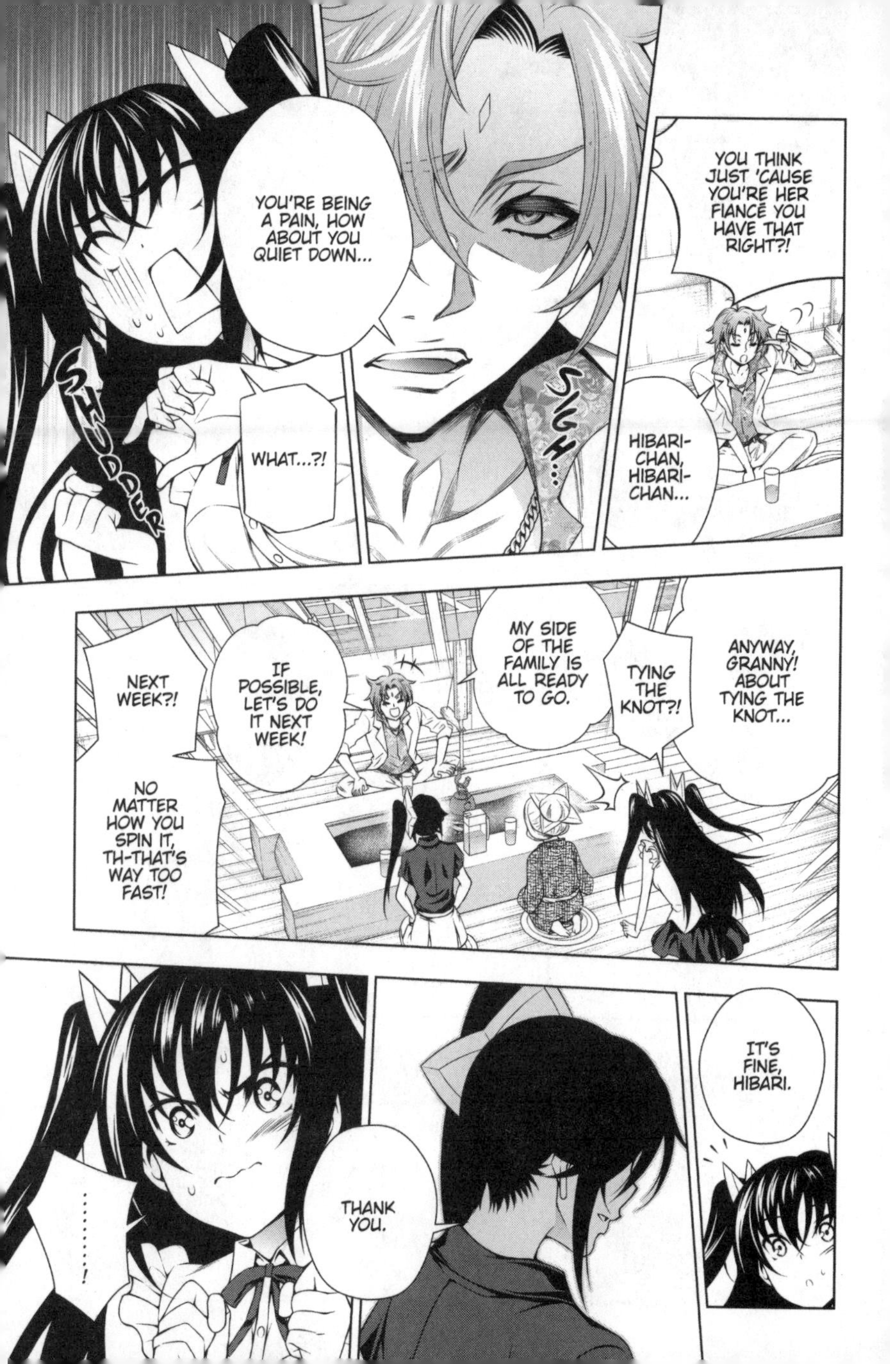
YOU THINK JUST 'CAUSE YOU'RE HER FIANCÉ YOU HAVE THAT RIGHT?!
HIBARI-CHAN, HIBARI-CHAN...
SIGH...
YOU'RE BEING A PAIN, HOW ABOUT YOU QUIET DOWN...
WHAT...?!
SHUDDER
ANYWAY, GRANNY! ABOUT TYING THE KNOT...
TYING THE KNOT?!
MY SIDE OF THE FAMILY IS ALL READY TO GO.
IF POSSIBLE, LET'S DO IT NEXT WEEK!
NEXT WEEK?!
NO MATTER HOW YOU SPIN IT, TH-THAT'S WAY TOO FAST!
IT'S FINE, HIBARI.
THANK YOU.
......!

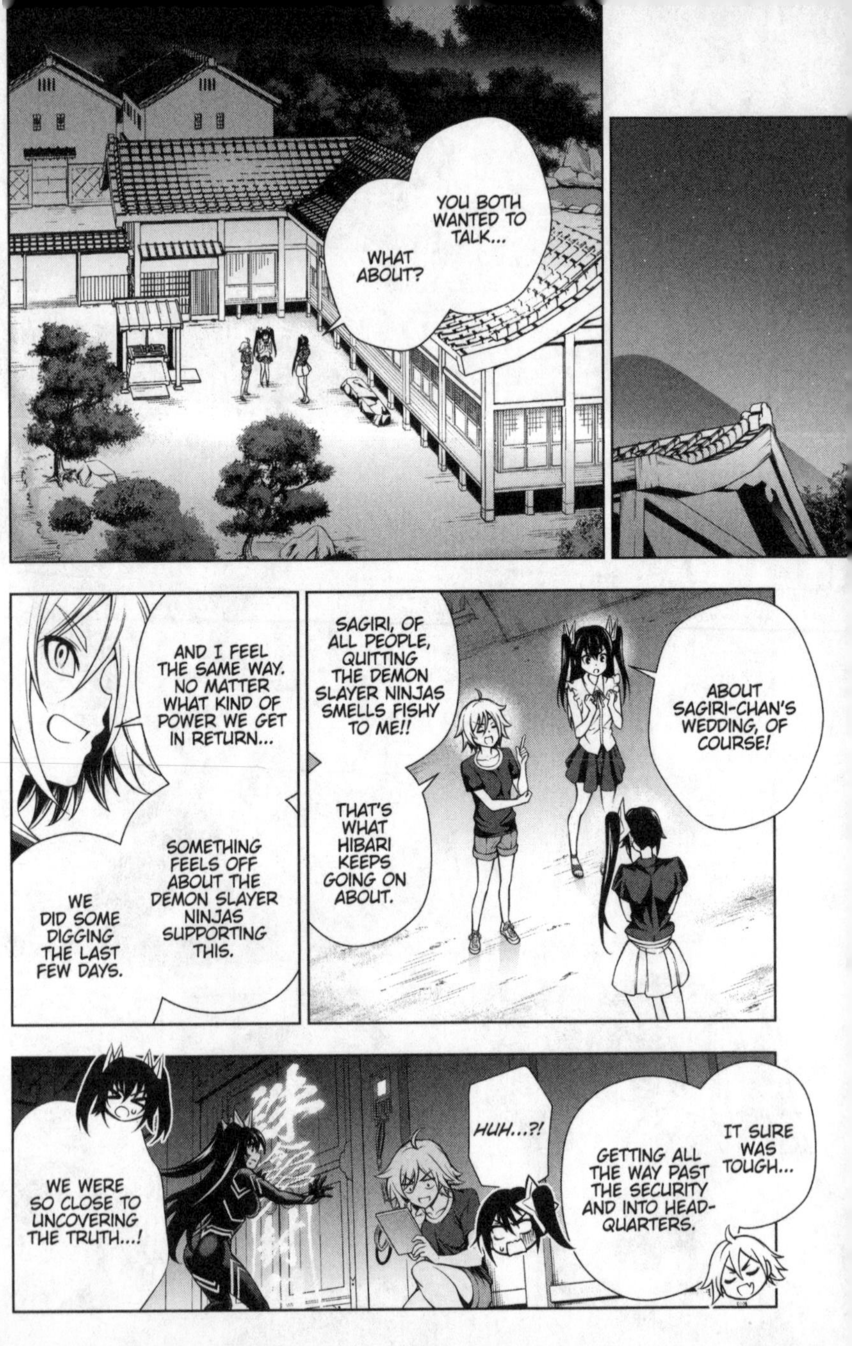
YOU BOTH WANTED TO TALK...
WHAT ABOUT?
ABOUT SAGIRI-CHAN'S WEDDING, OF COURSE!
SAGIRI, OF ALL PEOPLE, QUITTING THE DEMON SLAYER NINJAS SMELLS FISHY TO ME!!
THAT'S WHAT HIBARI KEEPS GOING ON ABOUT.
AND I FEEL THE SAME WAY. NO MATTER WHAT KIND OF POWER WE GET IN RETURN...
SOMETHING FEELS OFF ABOUT THE DEMON SLAYER NINJAS SUPPORTING THIS.
WE DID SOME DIGGING THE LAST FEW DAYS.
IT SURE WAS TOUGH...
GETTING ALL THE WAY PAST THE SECURITY AND INTO HEAD-QUARTERS.
HUH...?!
WE WERE SO CLOSE TO UNCOVERING THE TRUTH...!

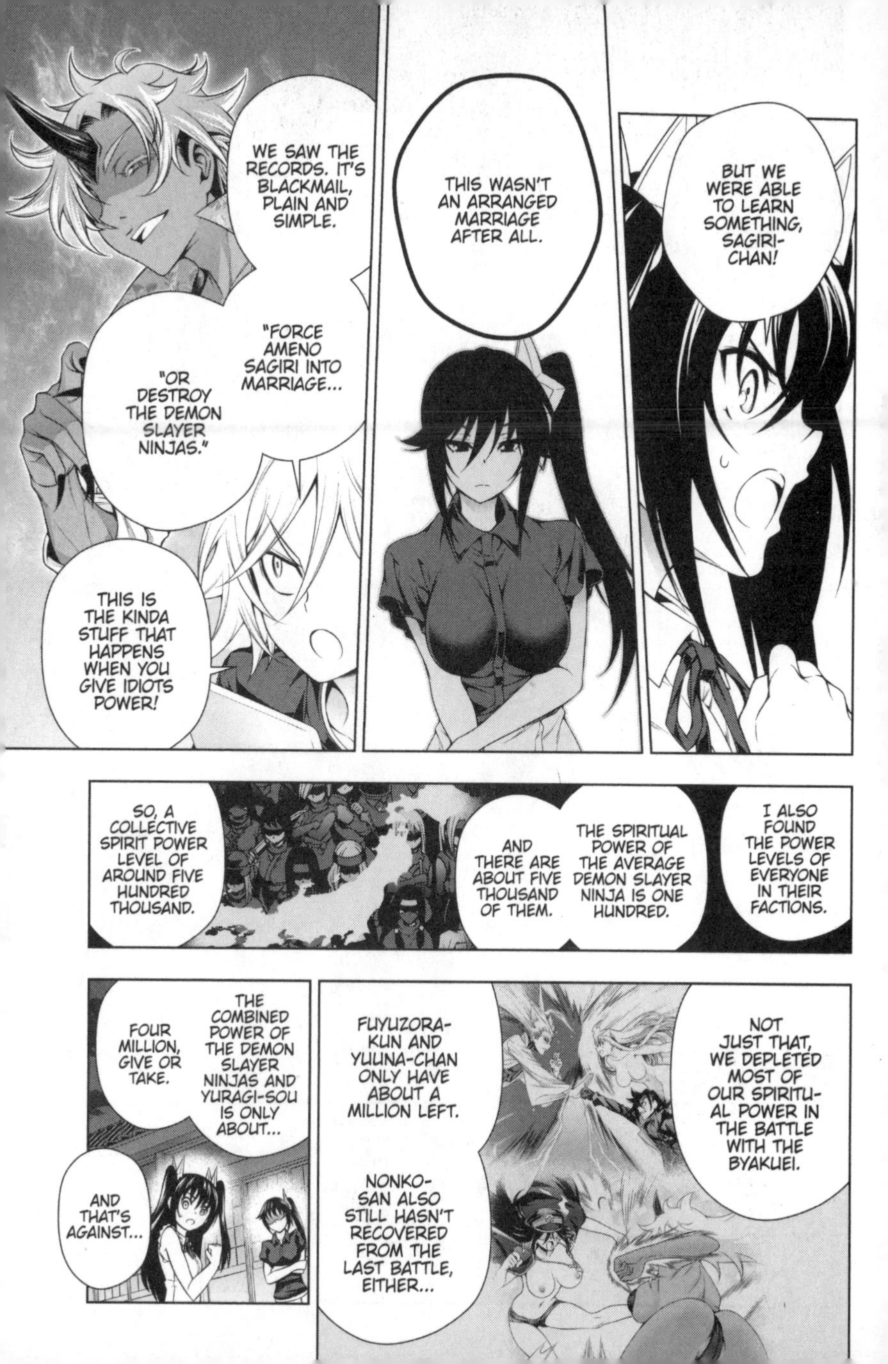
BUT WE WERE ABLE TO LEARN SOMETHING, SAGIRI-CHAN!
THIS WASN'T AN ARRANGED MARRIAGE AFTER ALL.
WE SAW THE RECORDS. IT'S BLACKMAIL, PLAIN AND SIMPLE.
"FORCE AMENO SAGIRI INTO MARRIAGE...
"OR DESTROY THE DEMON SLAYER NINJAS."
THIS IS THE KINDA STUFF THAT HAPPENS WHEN YOU GIVE IDIOTS POWER!
I ALSO FOUND THE POWER LEVELS OF EVERYONE IN THEIR FACTIONS.
THE SPIRITUAL POWER OF THE AVERAGE DEMON SLAYER NINJA IS ONE HUNDRED.
AND THERE ARE ABOUT FIVE THOUSAND OF THEM.
SO, A COLLECTIVE SPIRIT POWER LEVEL OF AROUND FIVE HUNDRED THOUSAND.
NOT JUST THAT, WE DEPLETED MOST OF OUR SPIRITU-AL POWER IN THE BATTLE WITH THE BYAKUEI.
FUYUZORA-KUN AND YUUNA-CHAN ONLY HAVE ABOUT A MILLION LEFT.
NONKO-SAN ALSO STILL HASN'T RECOVERED FROM THE LAST BATTLE, EITHER...
THE COMBINED POWER OF THE DEMON SLAYER NINJAS AND YURAGI-SOU IS ONLY ABOUT...
FOUR MILLION, GIVE OR TAKE.
AND THAT'S AGAINST...

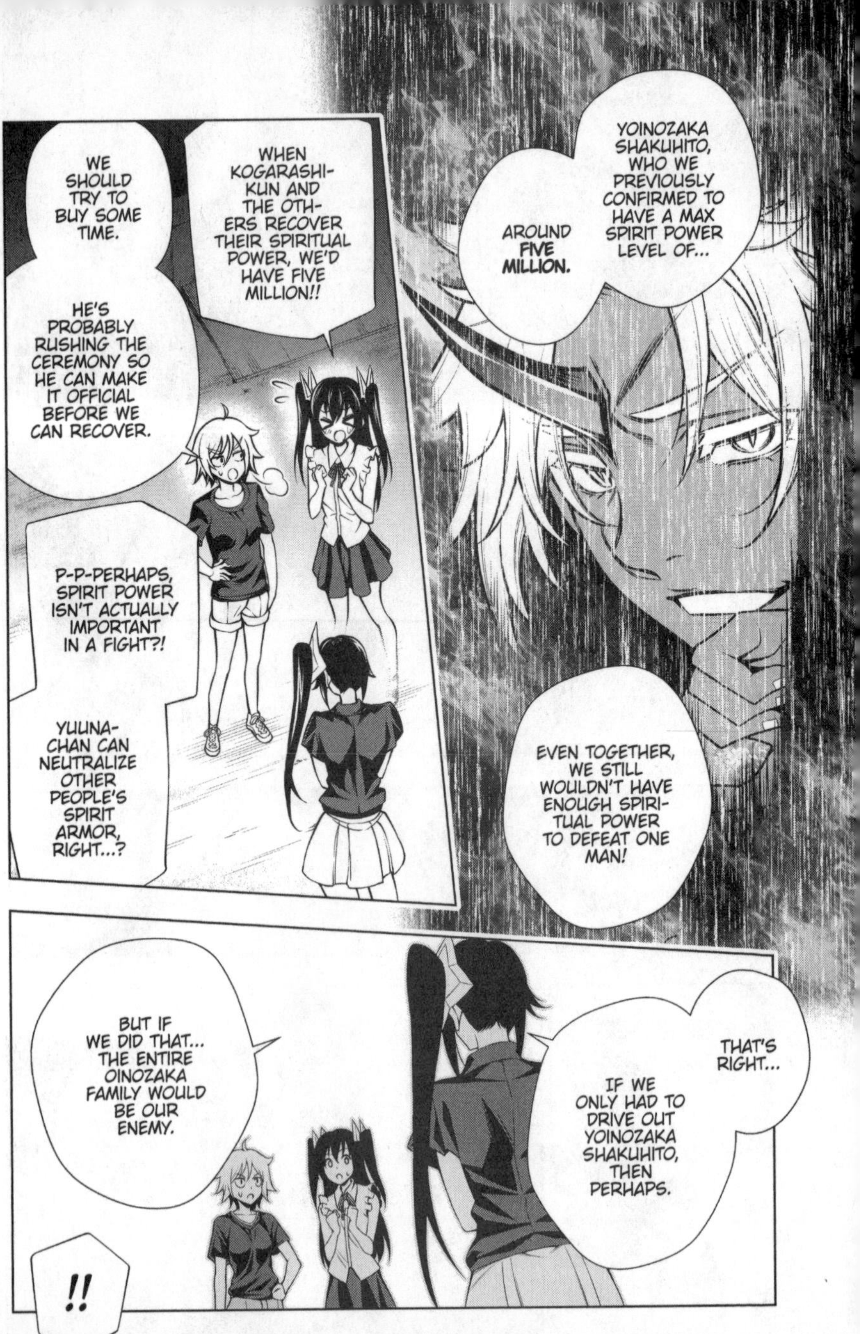
YOINOZAKA SHAKUHITO, WHO WE PREVIOUSLY CONFIRMED TO HAVE A MAX SPIRIT POWER LEVEL OF...
AROUND **FIVE MILLION.**
EVEN TOGETHER, WE STILL WOULDN'T HAVE ENOUGH SPIRITUAL POWER TO DEFEAT ONE MAN!
WHEN KOGARASHI-KUN AND THE OTHERS RECOVER THEIR SPIRITUAL POWER, WE'D HAVE FIVE MILLION!!
WE SHOULD TRY TO BUY SOME TIME.
HE'S PROBABLY RUSHING THE CEREMONY SO HE CAN MAKE IT OFFICIAL BEFORE WE CAN RECOVER.
P-P-PERHAPS, SPIRIT POWER ISN'T ACTUALLY IMPORTANT IN A FIGHT?!
YUUNA-CHAN CAN NEUTRALIZE OTHER PEOPLE'S SPIRIT ARMOR, RIGHT...?
THAT'S RIGHT...
IF WE ONLY HAD TO DRIVE OUT YOINOZAKA SHAKUHITO, THEN PERHAPS.
BUT IF WE DID THAT... THE ENTIRE OINOZAKA FAMILY WOULD BE OUR ENEMY.
!!

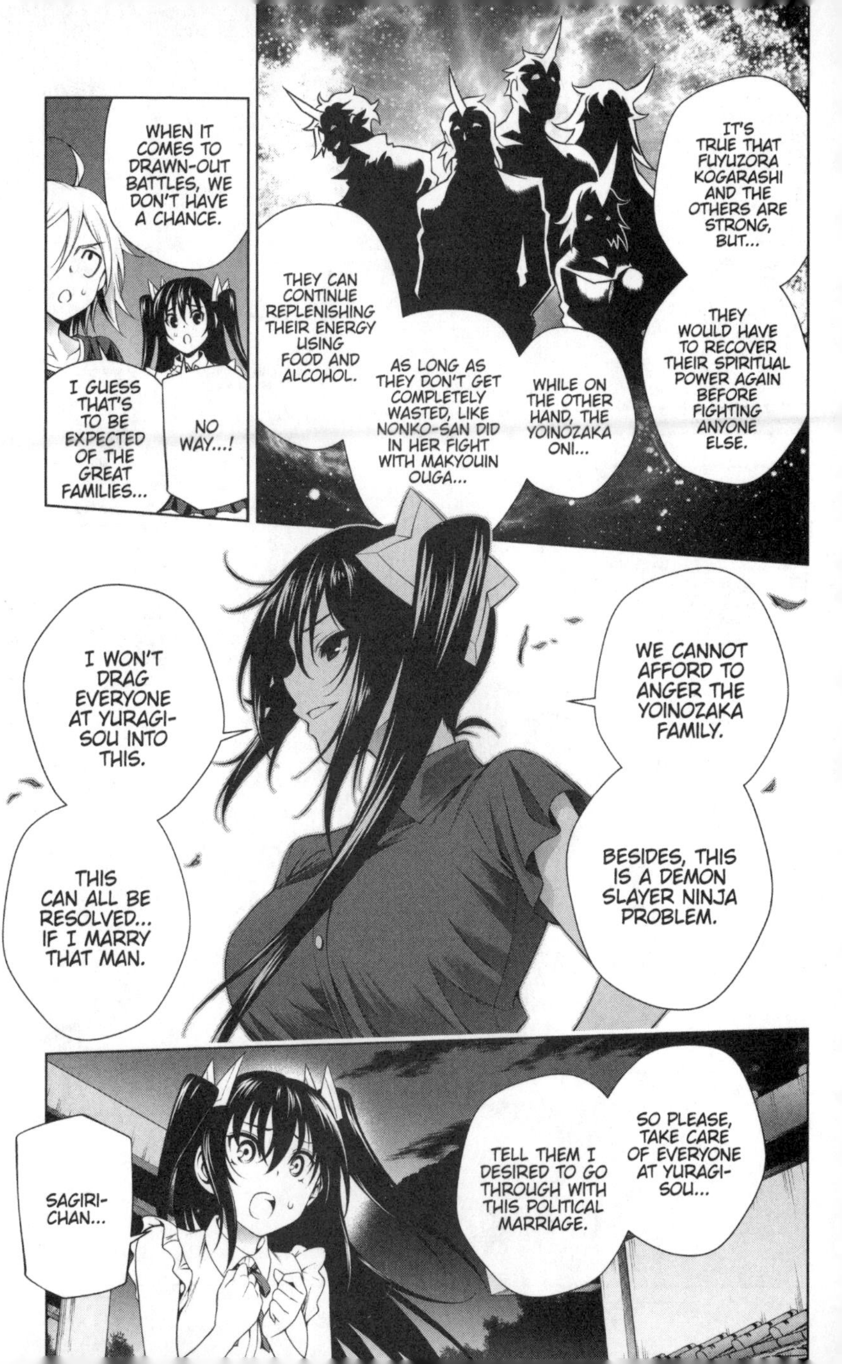

IT'S TRUE THAT FUYUZORA KOGARASHI AND THE OTHERS ARE STRONG, BUT...
THEY WOULD HAVE TO RECOVER THEIR SPIRITUAL POWER AGAIN BEFORE FIGHTING ANYONE ELSE.
WHILE ON THE OTHER HAND, THE YOINOZAKA ONI...
AS LONG AS THEY DON'T GET COMPLETELY WASTED, LIKE NONKO-SAN DID IN HER FIGHT WITH MAKYOUIN OUGA...
THEY CAN CONTINUE REPLENISHING THEIR ENERGY USING FOOD AND ALCOHOL.
WHEN IT COMES TO DRAWN-OUT BATTLES, WE DON'T HAVE A CHANCE.
NO WAY...!
I GUESS THAT'S TO BE EXPECTED OF THE GREAT FAMILIES...
WE CANNOT AFFORD TO ANGER THE YOINOZAKA FAMILY.
BESIDES, THIS IS A DEMON SLAYER NINJA PROBLEM.
I WON'T DRAG EVERYONE AT YURAGI-SOU INTO THIS.
THIS CAN ALL BE RESOLVED... IF I MARRY THAT MAN.
SO PLEASE, TAKE CARE OF EVERYONE AT YURAGI-SOU...
TELL THEM I DESIRED TO GO THROUGH WITH THIS POLITICAL MARRIAGE.
SAGIRI-CHAN...

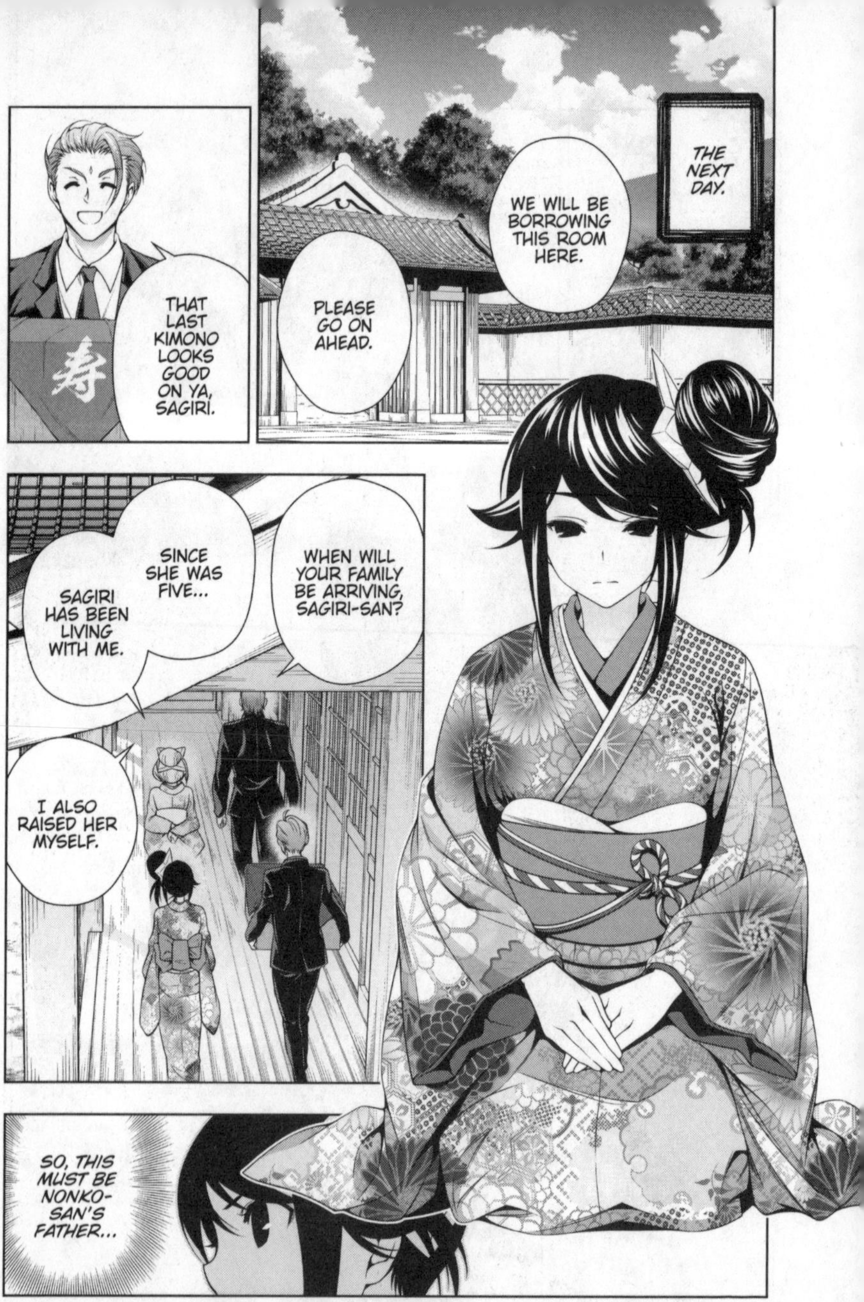
THE NEXT DAY.
WE WILL BE BORROWING THIS ROOM HERE.
PLEASE GO ON AHEAD.
THAT LAST KIMONO LOOKS GOOD ON YA, SAGIRI.
寿
WHEN WILL YOUR FAMILY BE ARRIVING, SAGIRI-SAN?
SINCE SHE WAS FIVE...
SAGIRI HAS BEEN LIVING WITH ME.
I ALSO RAISED HER MYSELF.
SO, THIS MUST BE NONKO-SAN'S FATHER...

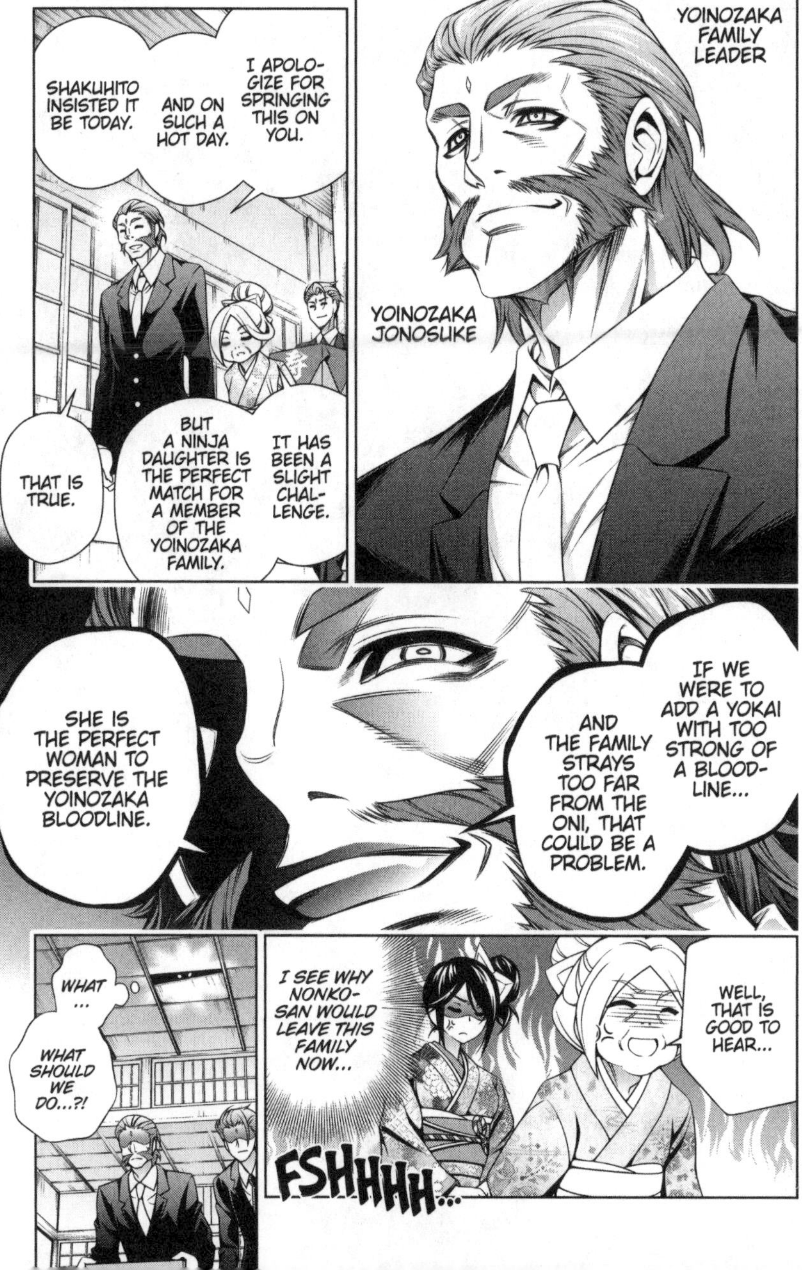
YOINOZAKA FAMILY LEADER
YOINOZAKA JONOSUKE
I APOLO-GIZE FOR SPRINGING THIS ON YOU.
AND ON SUCH A HOT DAY.
SHAKUHITO INSISTED IT BE TODAY.
IT HAS BEEN A SLIGHT CHAL-LENGE.
BUT A NINJA DAUGHTER IS THE PERFECT MATCH FOR A MEMBER OF THE YOINOZAKA FAMILY.
THAT IS TRUE.
IF WE WERE TO ADD A YOKAI WITH TOO STRONG OF A BLOOD-LINE...
AND THE FAMILY STRAYS TOO FAR FROM THE ONI, THAT COULD BE A PROBLEM.
SHE IS THE PERFECT WOMAN TO PRESERVE THE YOINOZAKA BLOODLINE.
WELL, THAT IS GOOD TO HEAR...
I SEE WHY NONKO-SAN WOULD LEAVE THIS FAMILY NOW...
FSHHHHH...
WHAT ...
WHAT SHOULD WE DO...?!

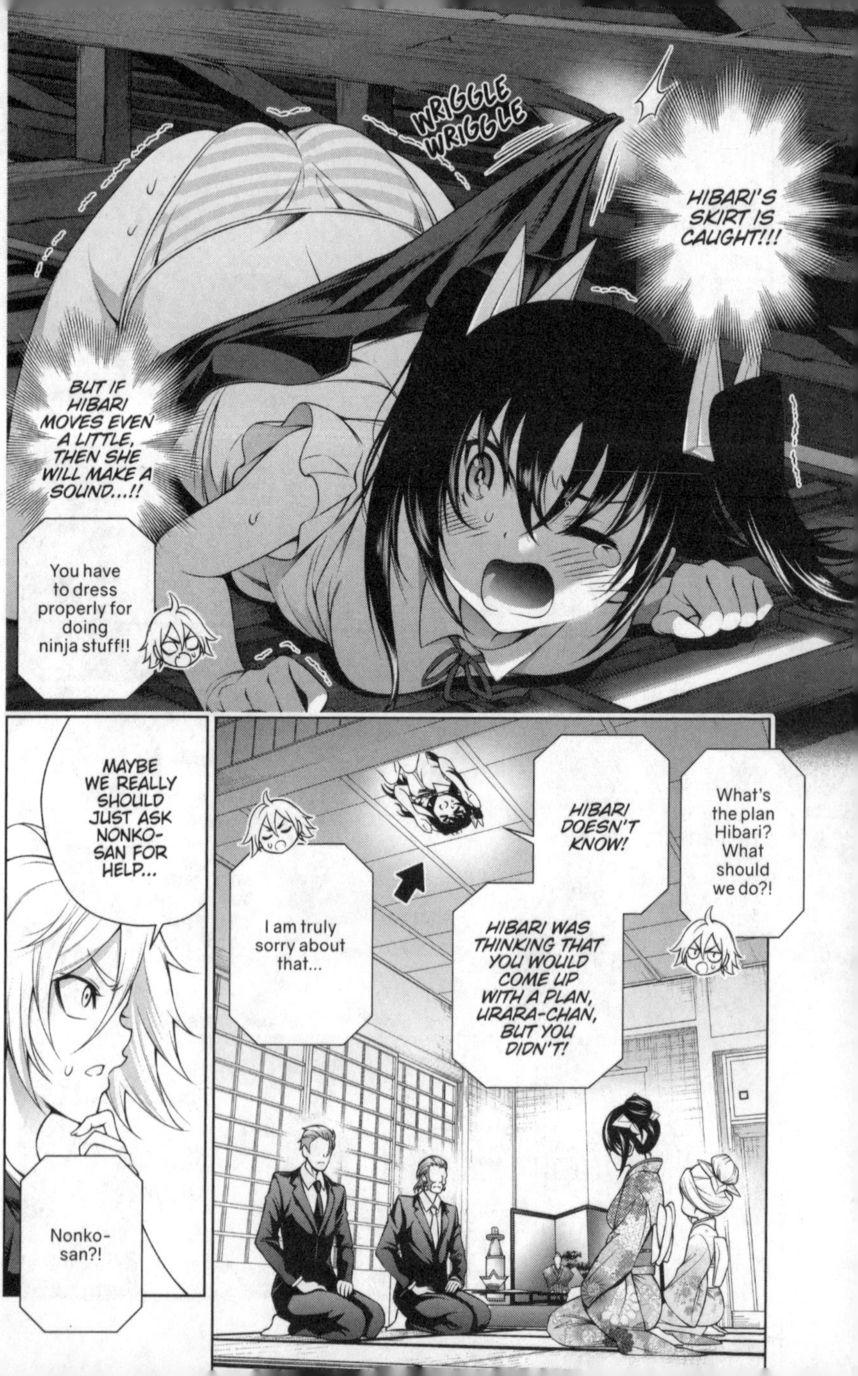
WRIGGLE WRIGGLE
HIBARI'S SKIRT IS CAUGHT!!!
BUT IF HIBARI MOVES EVEN A LITTLE, THEN SHE WILL MAKE A SOUND...!!
You have to dress properly for doing ninja stuff!!
What's the plan Hibari? What should we do?!
HIBARI DOESN'T KNOW!
HIBARI WAS THINKING THAT YOU WOULD COME UP WITH A PLAN, URARA-CHAN, BUT YOU DIDN'T!
I am truly sorry about that...
MAYBE WE REALLY SHOULD JUST ASK NONKO-SAN FOR HELP...
Nonko-san?!

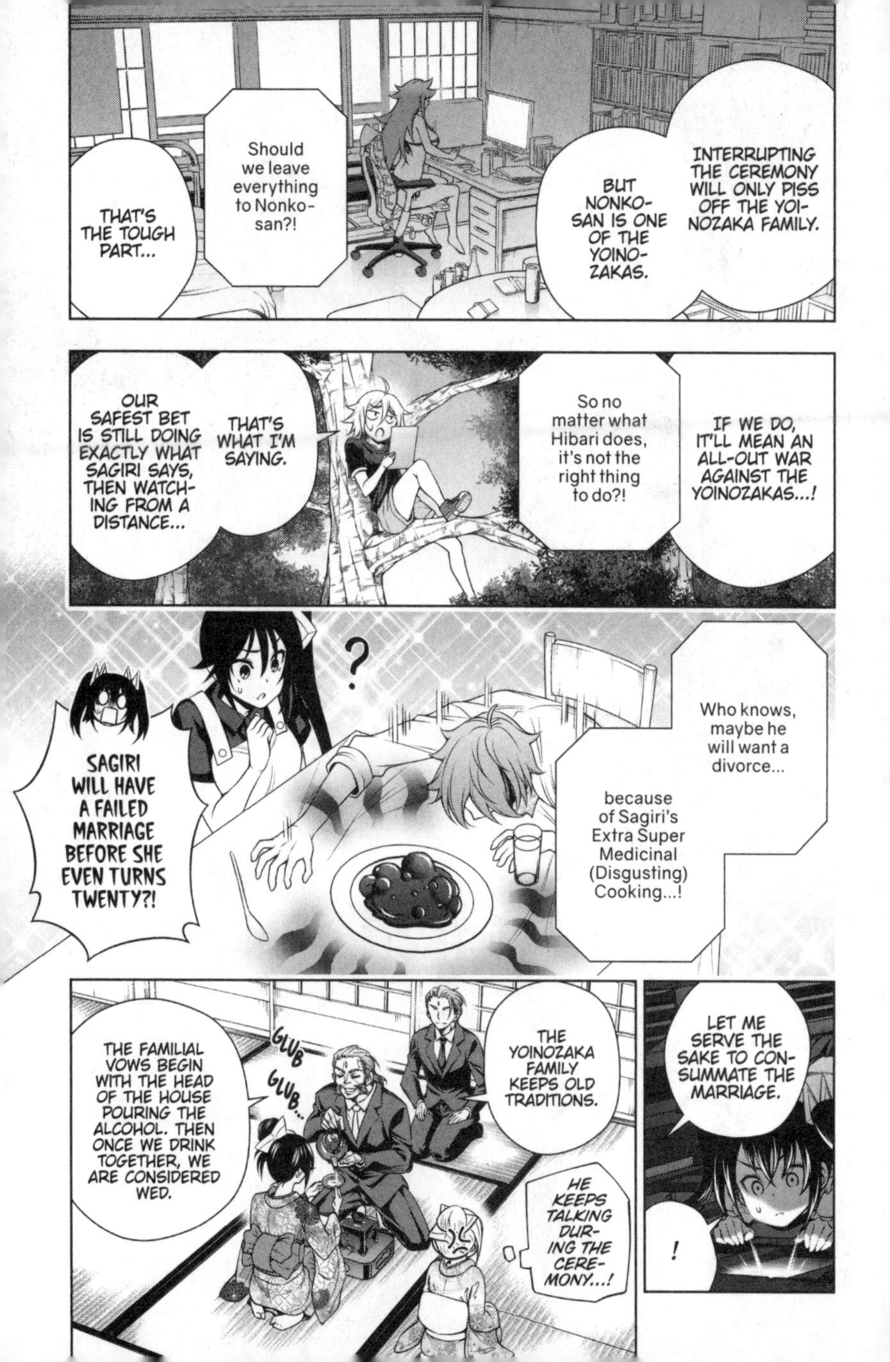
INTERRUPTING THE CEREMONY WILL ONLY PISS OFF THE YOINOZAKA FAMILY.
BUT NONKO-SAN IS ONE OF THE YOINO-ZAKAS.
Should we leave everything to Nonko-san?!
THAT'S THE TOUGH PART...
IF WE DO, IT'LL MEAN AN ALL-OUT WAR AGAINST THE YOINOZAKAS...!
So no matter what Hibari does, it's not the right thing to do?!
THAT'S WHAT I'M SAYING.
OUR SAFEST BET IS STILL DOING EXACTLY WHAT SAGIRI SAYS, THEN WATCHING FROM A DISTANCE...
Who knows, maybe he will want a divorce...
because of Sagiri's Extra Super Medicinal (Disgusting) Cooking...!
?
SAGIRI WILL HAVE A FAILED MARRIAGE BEFORE SHE EVEN TURNS TWENTY?!
LET ME SERVE THE SAKE TO CONSUMMATE THE MARRIAGE.
!
THE YOINOZAKA FAMILY KEEPS OLD TRADITIONS.
GLUB
GLUB...
THE FAMILIAL VOWS BEGIN WITH THE HEAD OF THE HOUSE POURING THE ALCOHOL. THEN ONCE WE DRINK TOGETHER, WE ARE CONSIDERED WED.
HE KEEPS TALKING DURING THE CEREMONY...!

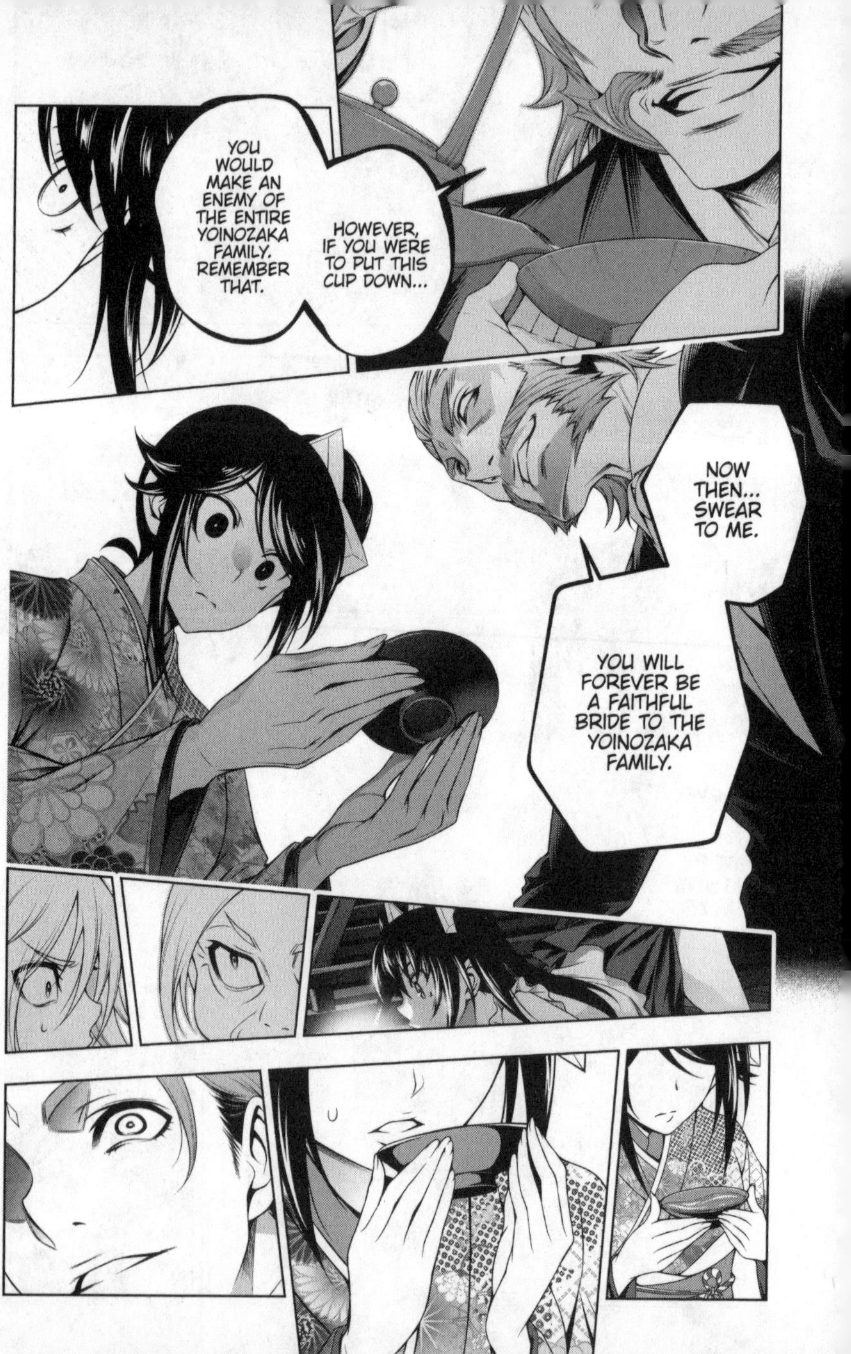
HOWEVER, IF YOU WERE TO PUT THIS CUP DOWN...
YOU WOULD MAKE AN ENEMY OF THE ENTIRE YOINOZAKA FAMILY. REMEMBER THAT.
NOW THEN... SWEAR TO ME.
YOU WILL FOREVER BE A FAITHFUL BRIDE TO THE YOINOZAKA FAMILY.

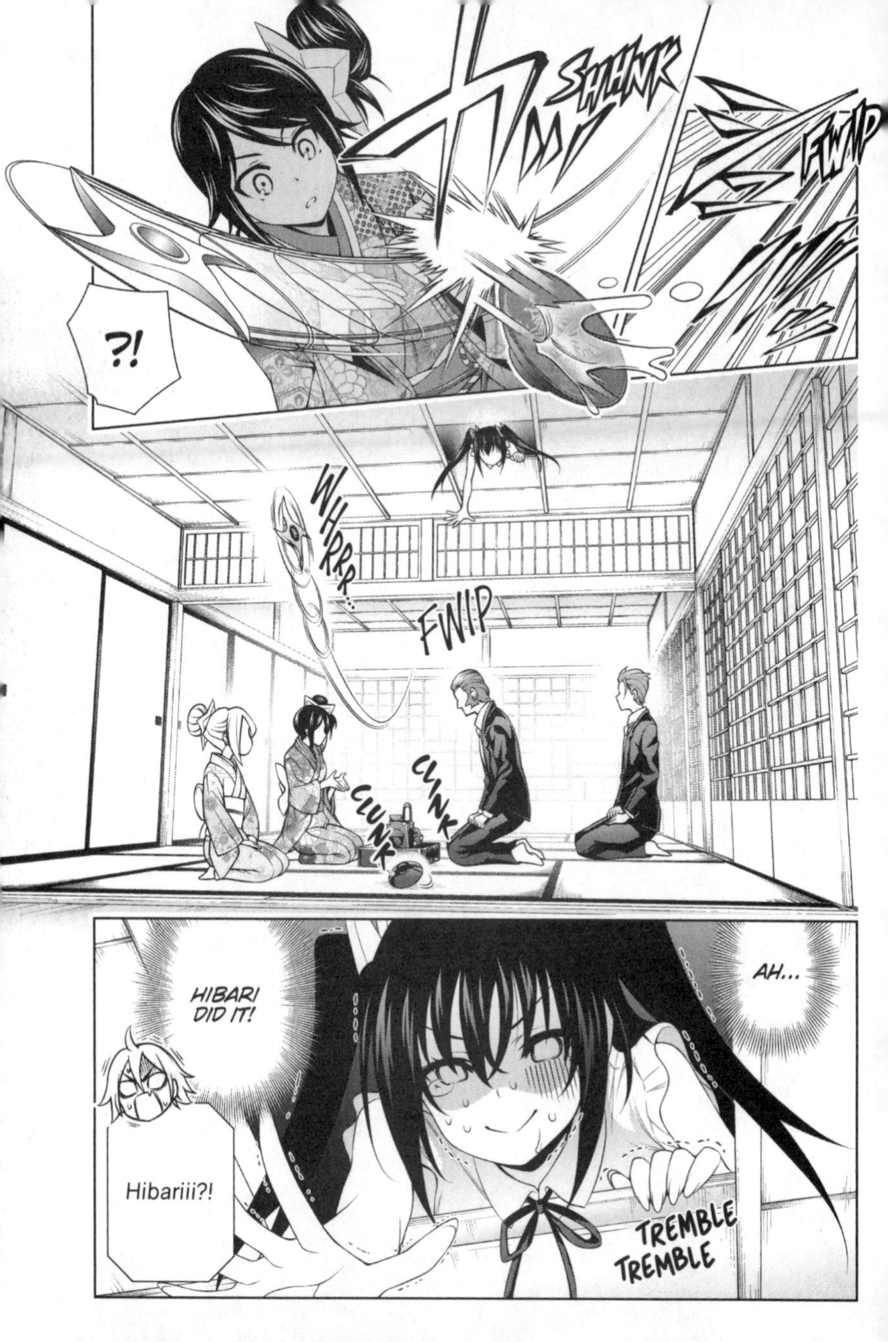
SHHNR
FWIP
?!
WHRRRR...
FWIP
CLINK
CLUNK
CLUNK
AH...
HIBARI DID IT!
Hibariii?!
TREMBLE TREMBLE

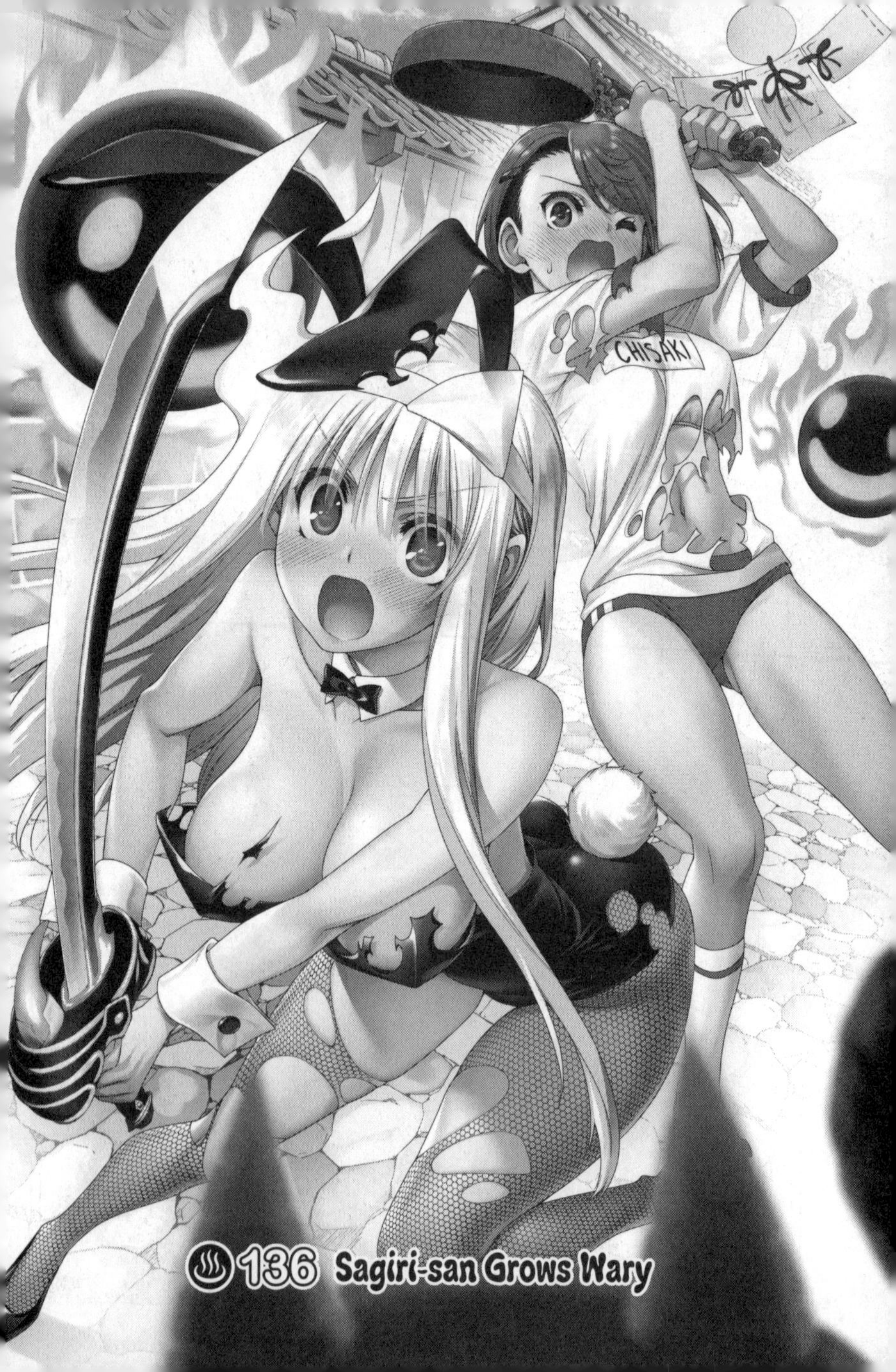
CHISAKI
♨136 Sagiri-san Grows Wary

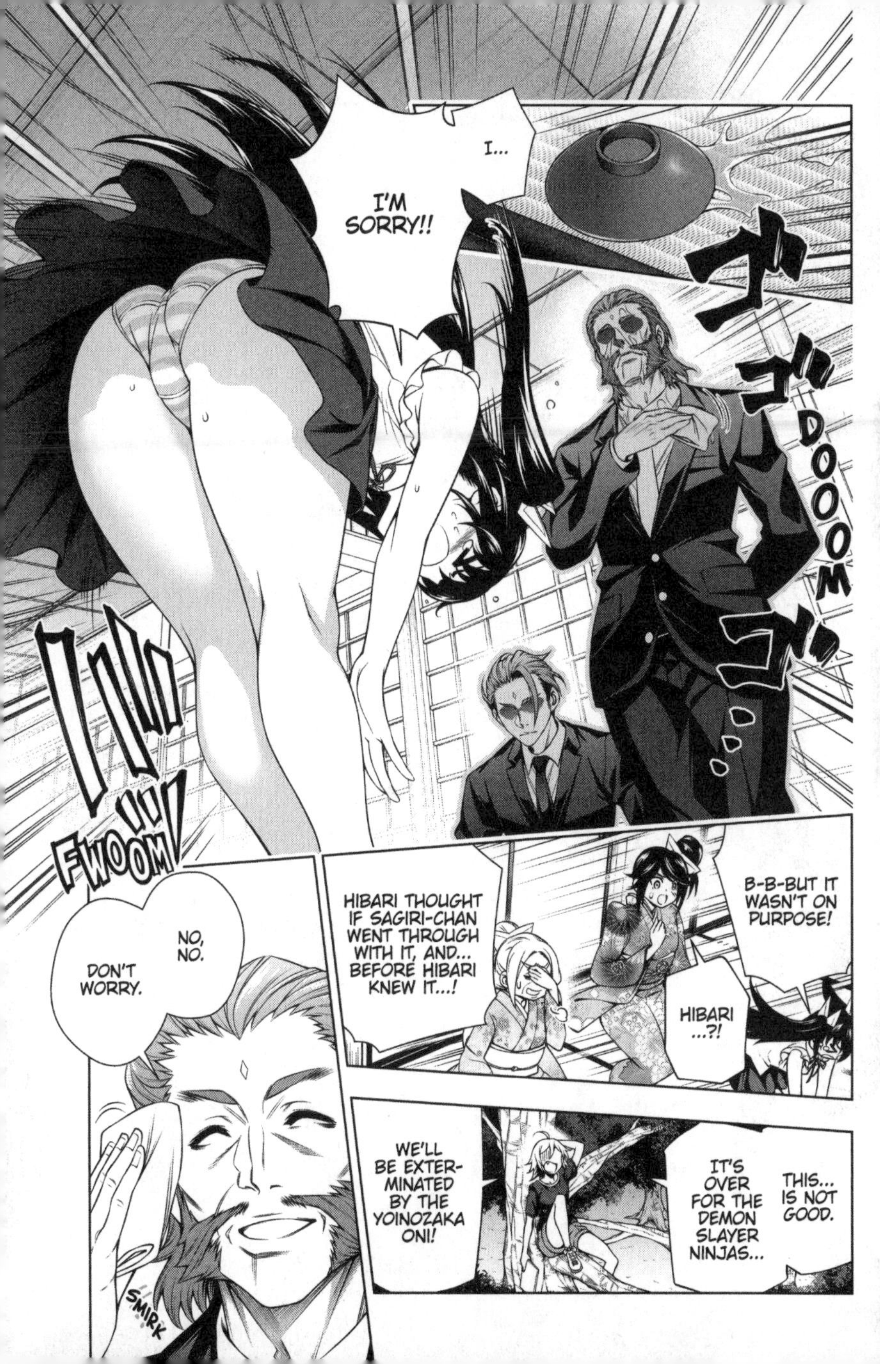
I...
I'M SORRY!!
DOOOOM
FWOOM!
B-B-BUT IT WASN'T ON PURPOSE!
HIBARI ...?!
HIBARI THOUGHT IF SAGIRI-CHAN WENT THROUGH WITH IT, AND... BEFORE HIBARI KNEW IT...!
THIS... IS NOT GOOD.
IT'S OVER FOR THE DEMON SLAYER NINJAS...
WE'LL BE EXTER-MINATED BY THE YOINOZAKA ONI!
NO, NO.
DON'T WORRY.
SMIRK

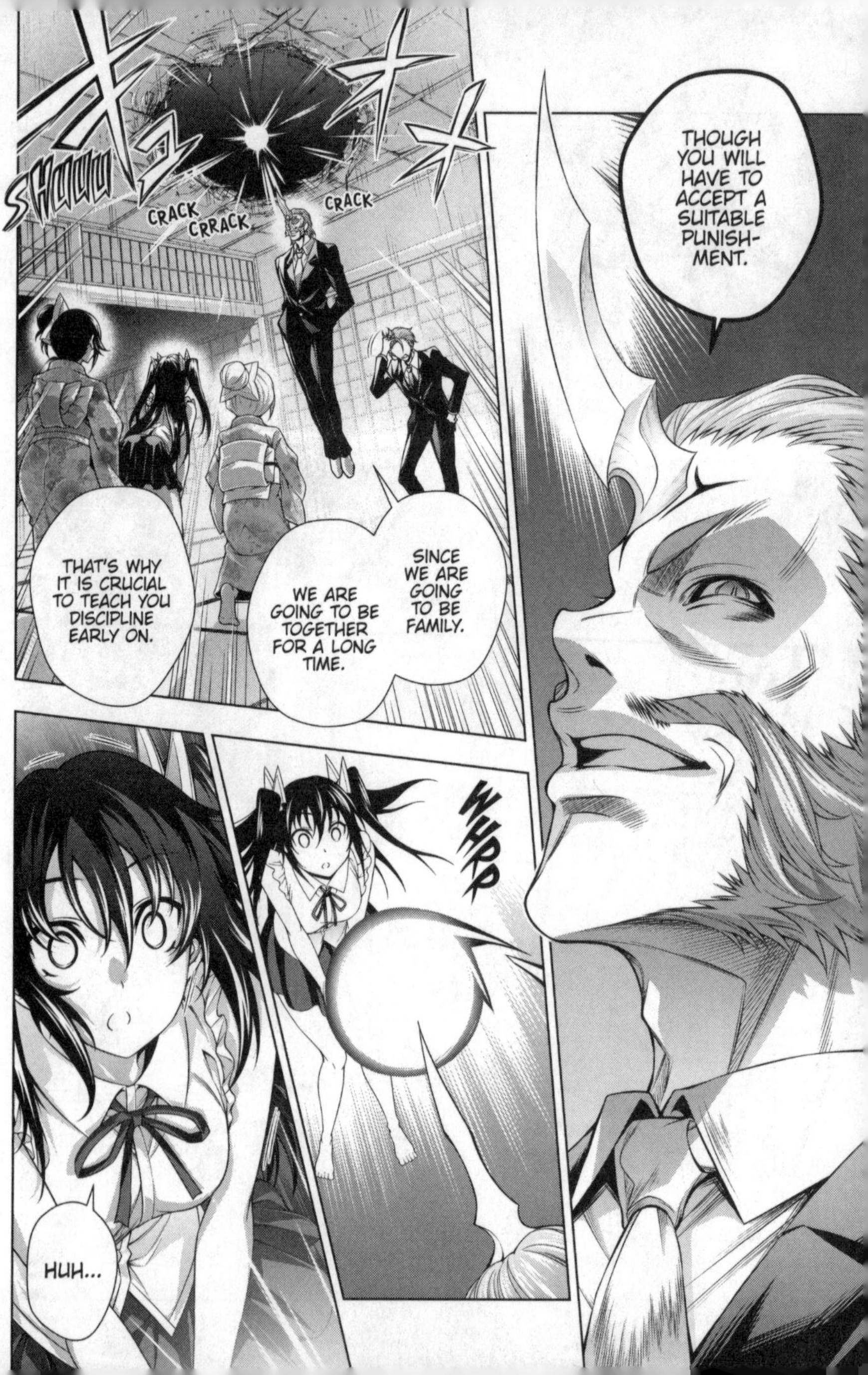
SHUUU
CRACK
CRRACK
CRACK
THOUGH YOU WILL HAVE TO ACCEPT A SUITABLE PUNISH-MENT.
SINCE WE ARE GOING TO BE FAMILY.
WE ARE GOING TO BE TOGETHER FOR A LONG TIME.
THAT'S WHY IT IS CRUCIAL TO TEACH YOU DISCIPLINE EARLY ON.
WHRR
HUH...

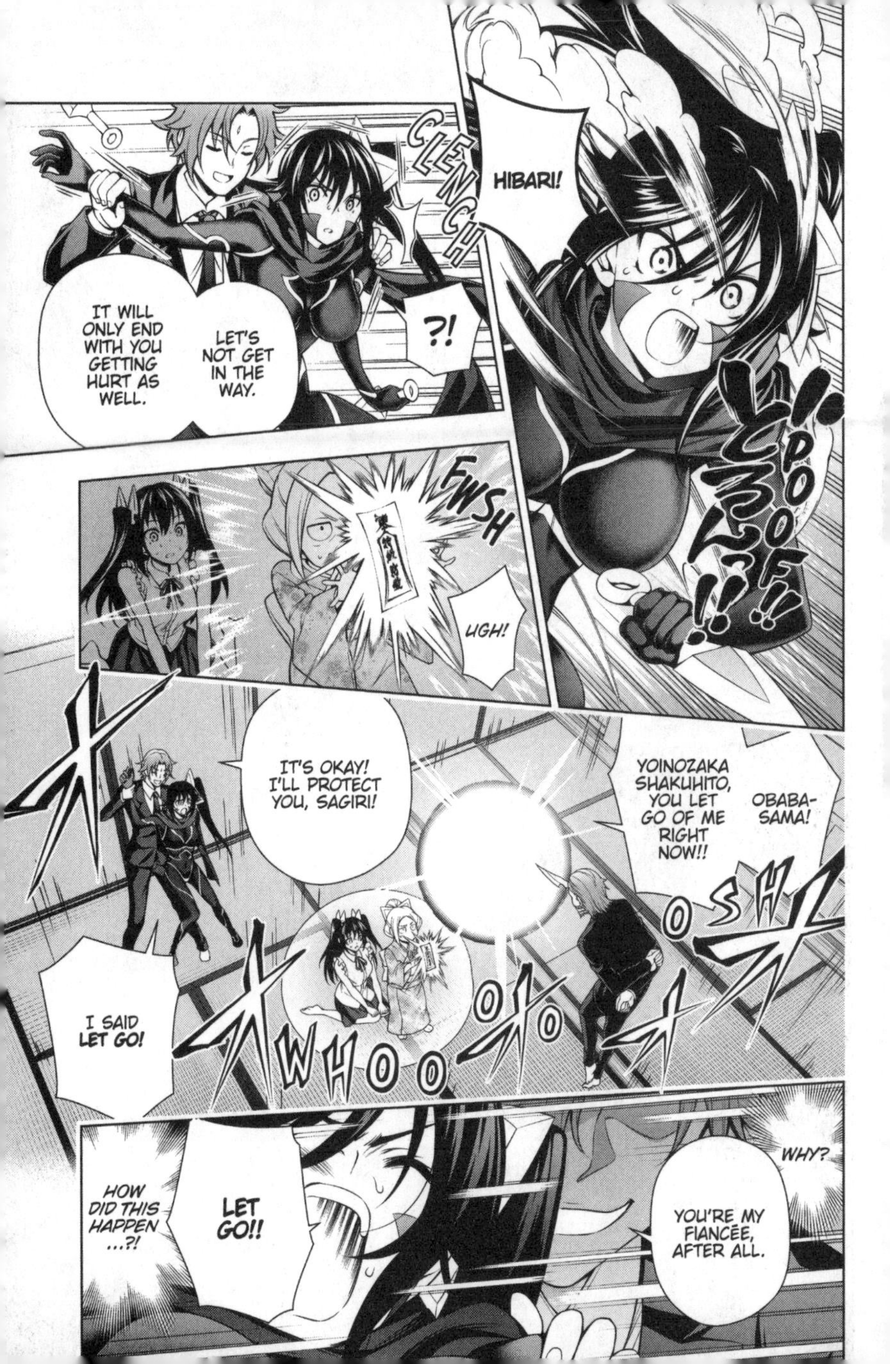
HIBARI!
CLENCH
?!
LET'S NOT GET IN THE WAY.
IT WILL ONLY END WITH YOU GETTING HURT AS WELL.
POOF!!
FWSH
UGH!
OBABA-SAMA!
YOINOZAKA SHAKUHITO, YOU LET GO OF ME RIGHT NOW!!
IT'S OKAY! I'LL PROTECT YOU, SAGIRI!
I SAID LET GO!
WHOOOOOSH
WHY?
YOU'RE MY FIANCÉE, AFTER ALL.
LET GO!!
HOW DID THIS HAPPEN ...?!

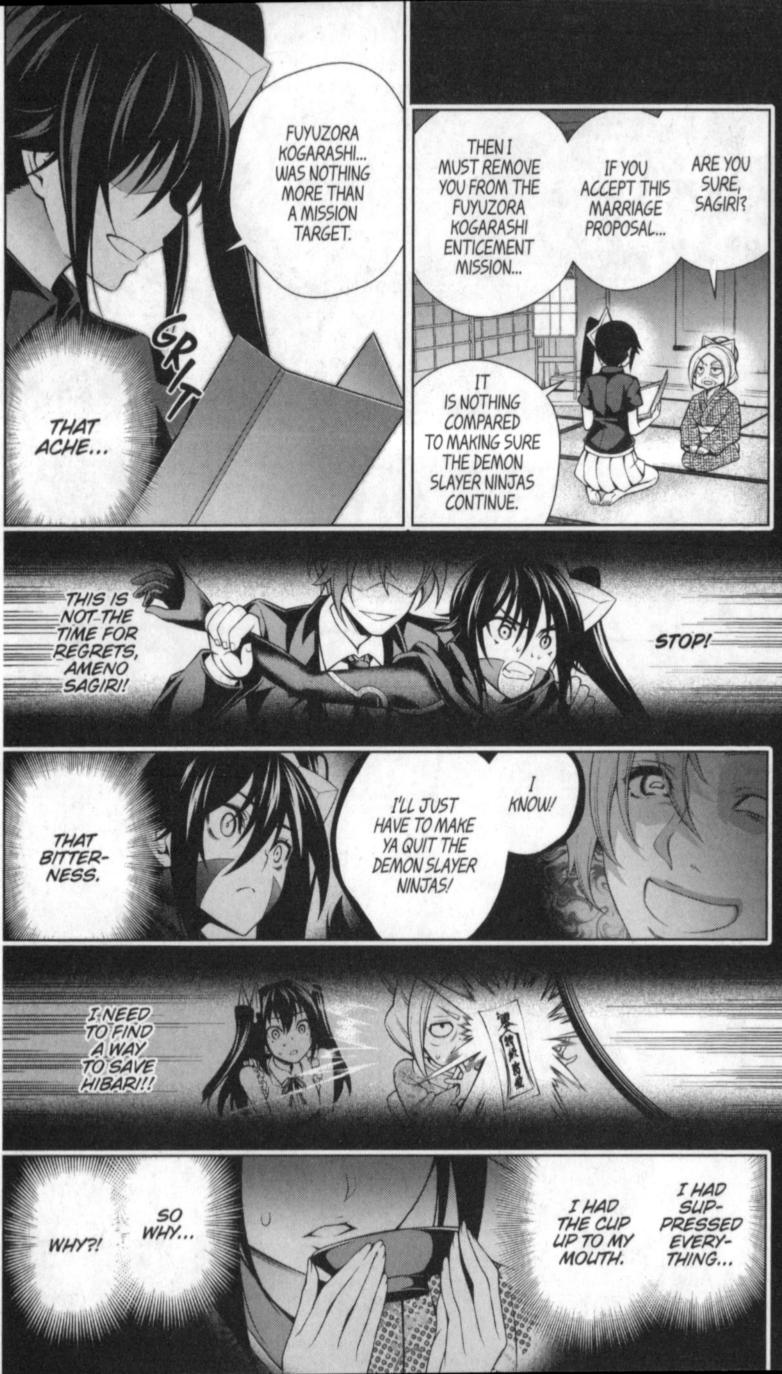
ARE YOU SURE, SAGIRI?
IF YOU ACCEPT THIS MARRIAGE PROPOSAL...
THEN I MUST REMOVE YOU FROM THE FUYUZORA KOGARASHI ENTICEMENT MISSION...
IT IS NOTHING COMPARED TO MAKING SURE THE DEMON SLAYER NINJAS CONTINUE.
FUYUZORA KOGARASHI... WAS NOTHING MORE THAN A MISSION TARGET.
GRIT
THAT ACHE...
STOP!
THIS IS NOT THE TIME FOR REGRETS, AMENO SAGIRI!
I KNOW!
I'LL JUST HAVE TO MAKE YA QUIT THE DEMON SLAYER NINJAS!
THAT BITTERNESS.
I NEED TO FIND A WAY TO SAVE HIBARI!!
I HAD SUP-PRESSED EVERY-THING...
I HAD THE CUP UP TO MY MOUTH.
SO WHY...
WHY?!

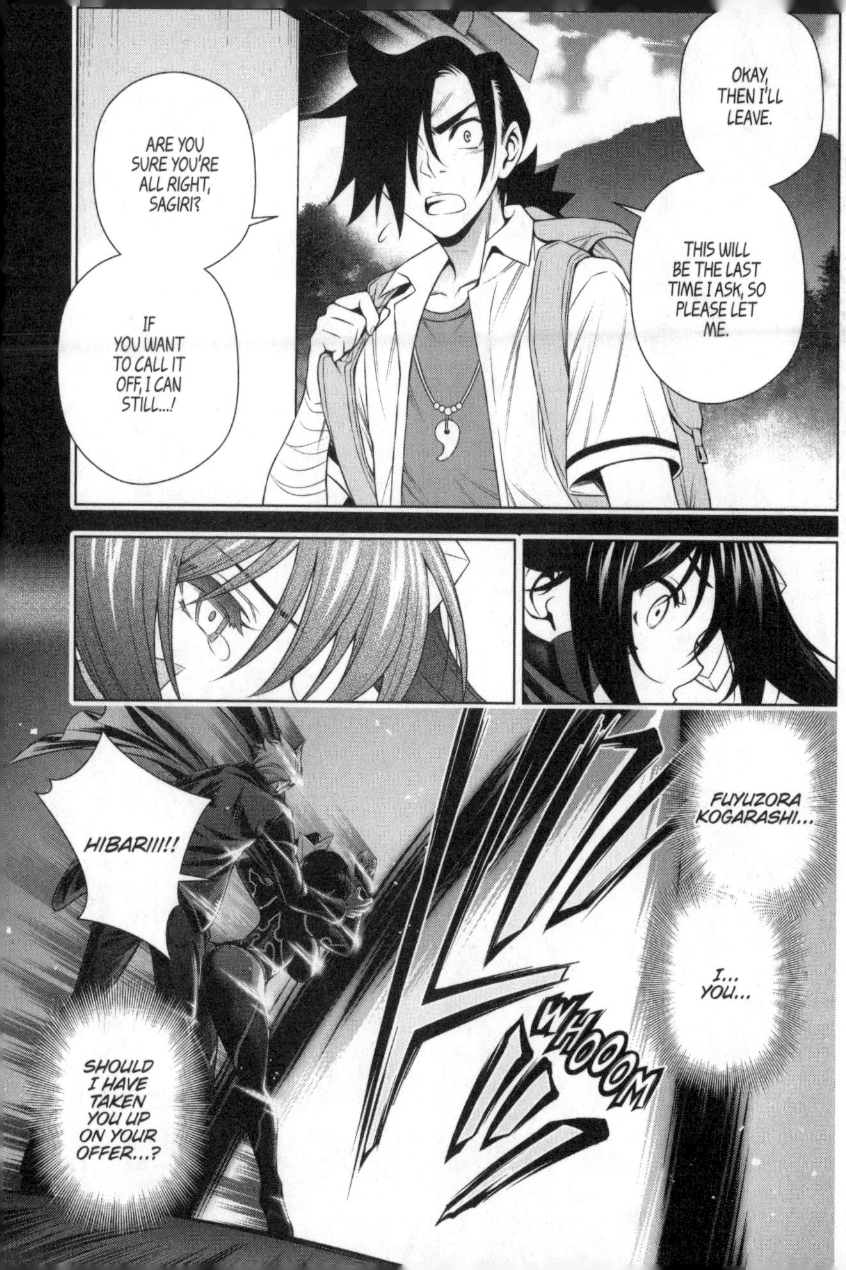
OKAY, THEN I'LL LEAVE.
THIS WILL BE THE LAST TIME I ASK, SO PLEASE LET ME.
ARE YOU SURE YOU'RE ALL RIGHT, SAGIRI?
IF YOU WANT TO CALL IT OFF, I CAN STILL...!
FUYUZORA KOGARASHI...
I... YOU...
WHOOOM
HIBARIII!!
SHOULD I HAVE TAKEN YOU UP ON YOUR OFFER...?

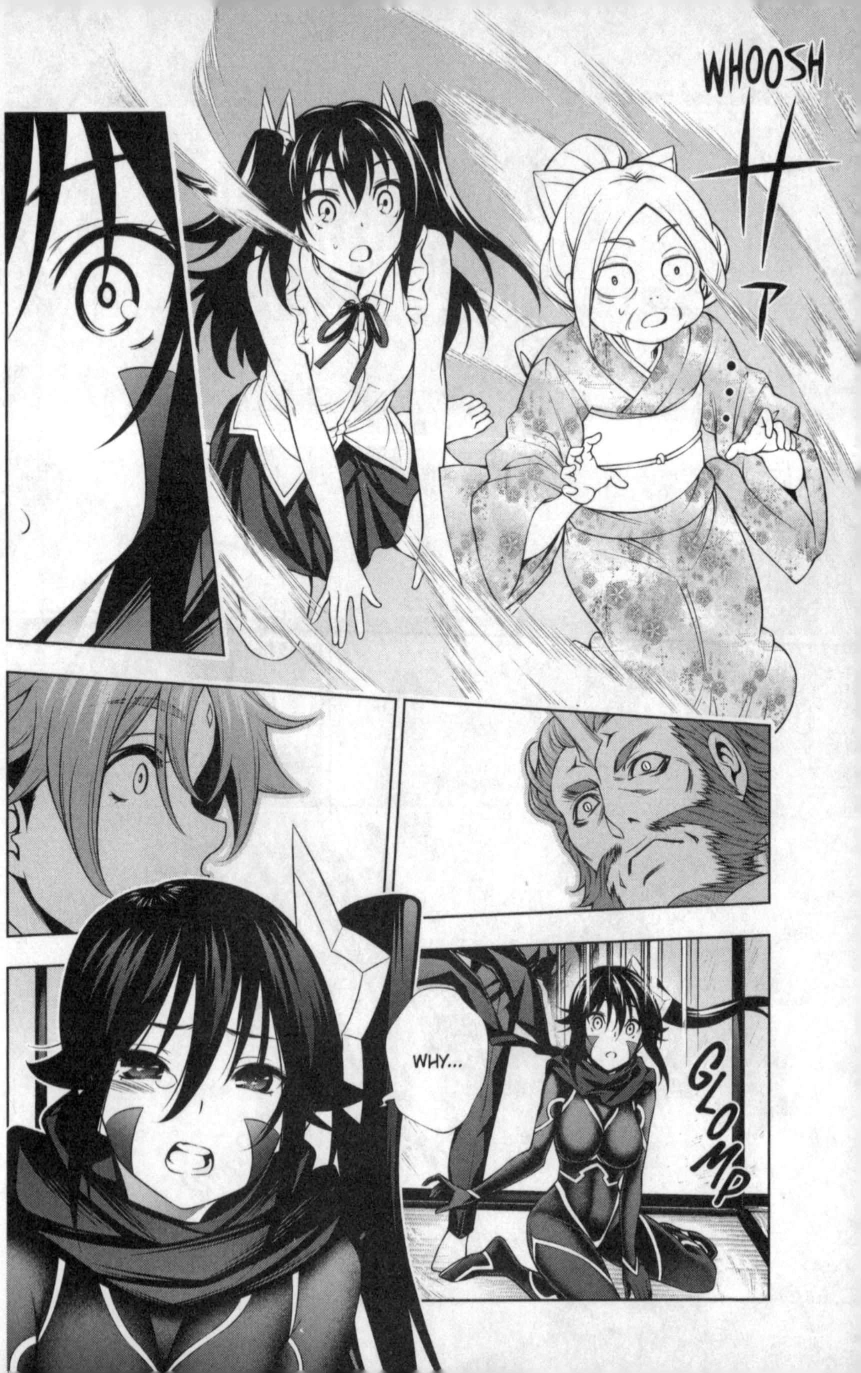
WHOOSH
サァ
GLOMP
WHY...

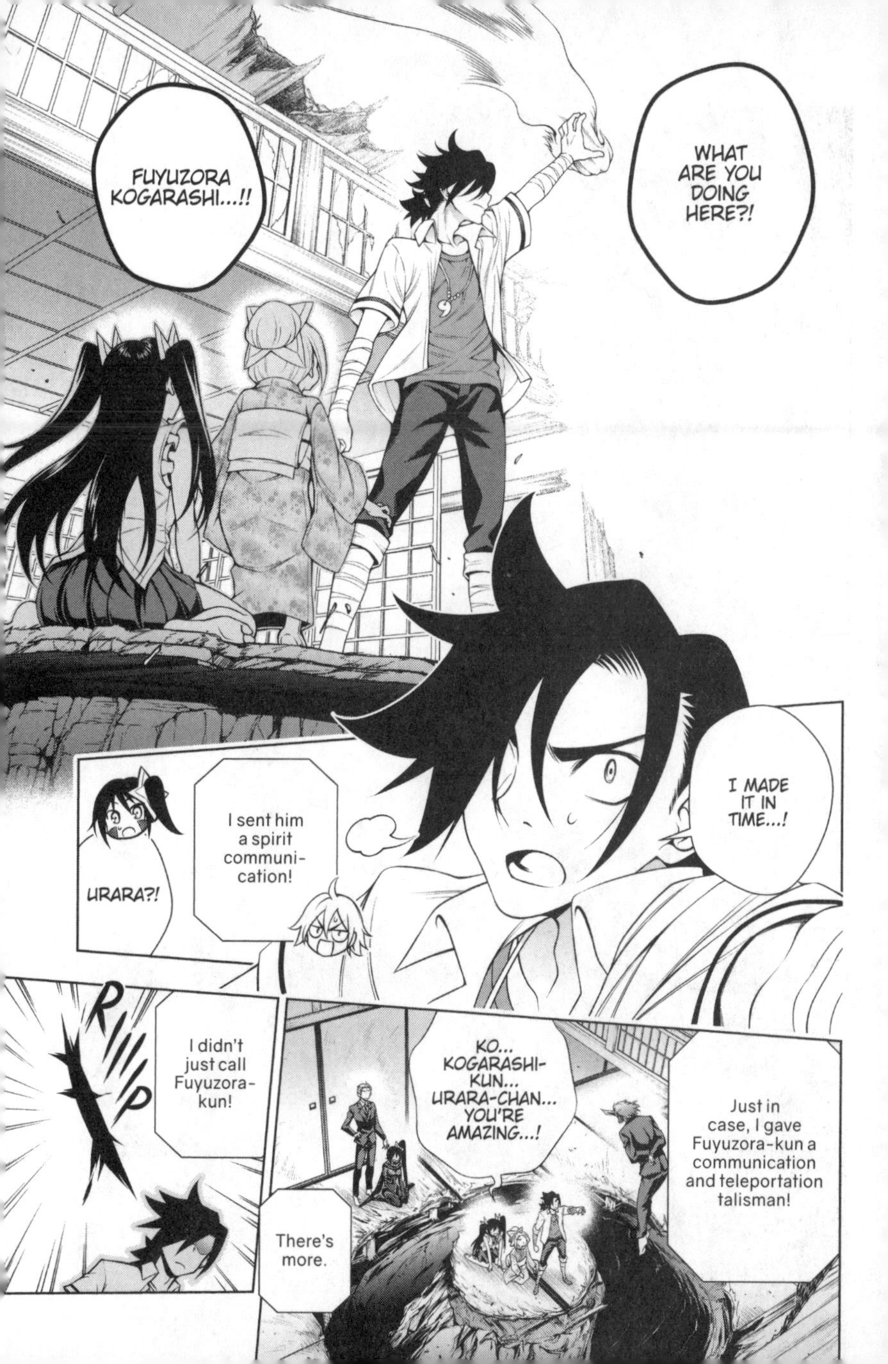
WHAT ARE YOU DOING HERE?!
FUYUZORA KOGARASHI...!!
I MADE IT IN TIME...!
URARA?!
I sent him a spirit communi-cation!
Just in case, I gave Fuyuzora-kun a communication and teleportation talisman!
KO... KOGARASHI-KUN... URARA-CHAN... YOU'RE AMAZING...!
I didn't just call Fuyuzora-kun!
There's more.
RIIIIP

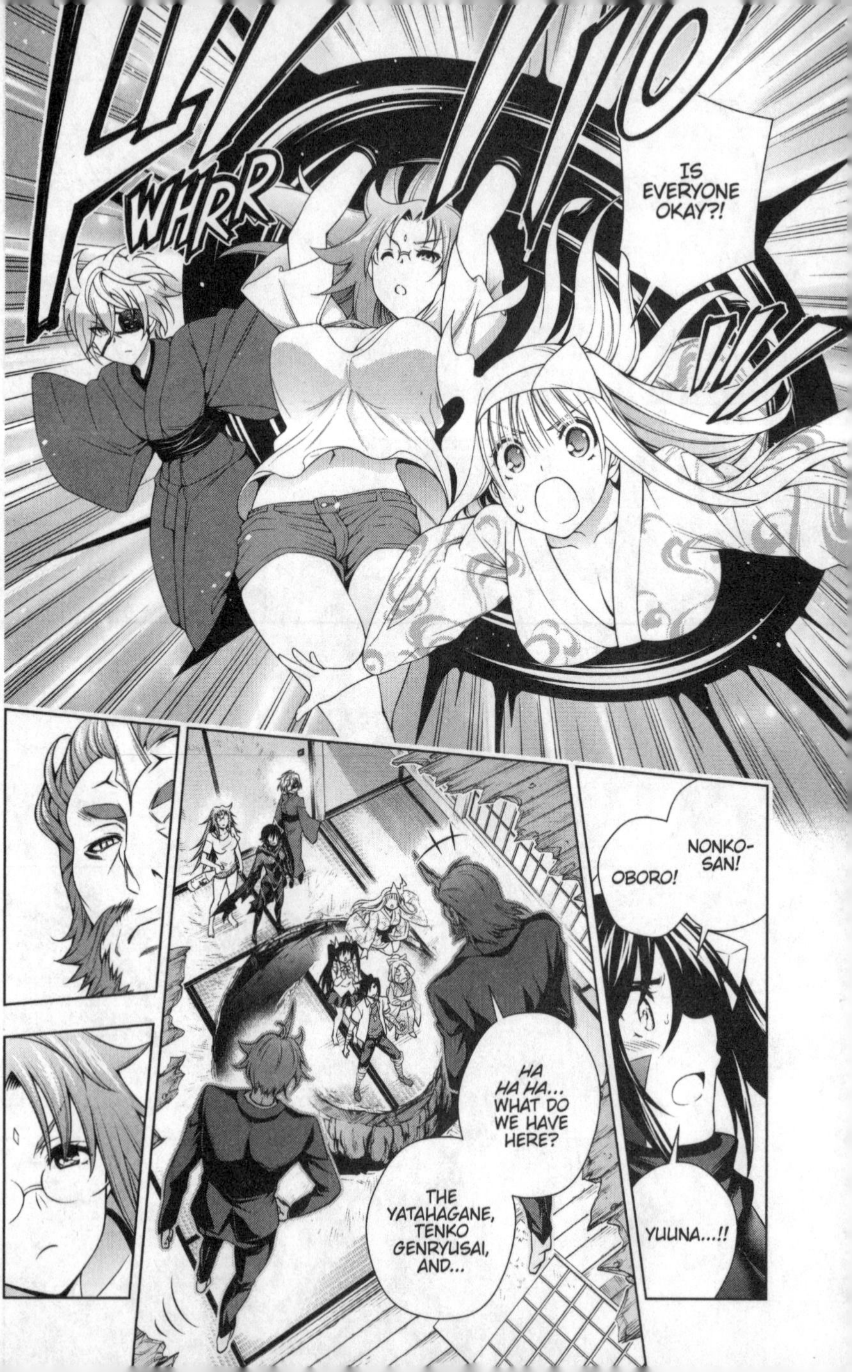
WHRR
IS EVERYONE OKAY?!
NONKO-SAN!
OBORO!
HA HA HA... WHAT DO WE HAVE HERE?
THE YATAHAGANE, TENKO GENRYUSAI, AND...
YUUNA...!!

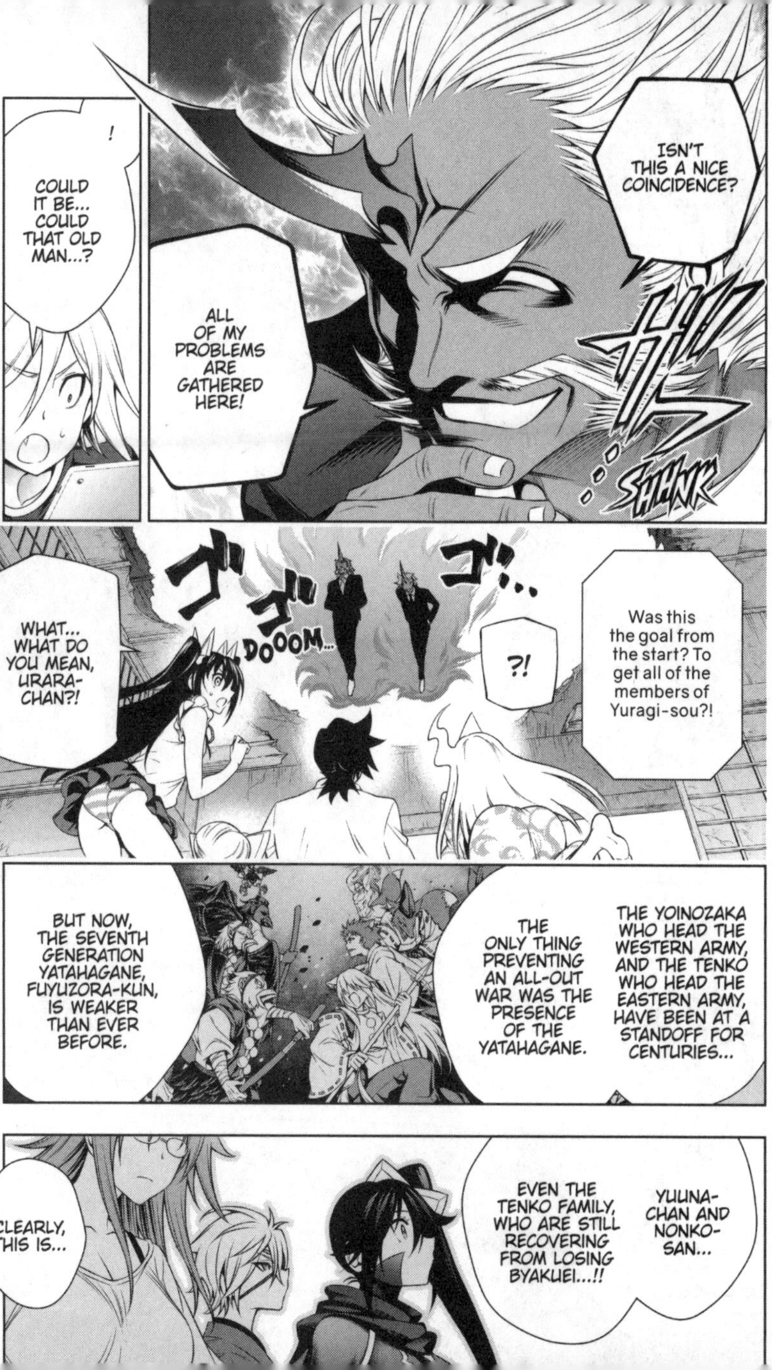
ISN'T THIS A NICE COINCIDENCE?
ALL OF MY PROBLEMS ARE GATHERED HERE!
SHHNK
!
COULD IT BE... COULD THAT OLD MAN...?
Was this the goal from the start? To get all of the members of Yuragi-sou?!
?!
DOOOM...
WHAT... WHAT DO YOU MEAN, URARA-CHAN?!
THE YOINOZAKA WHO HEAD THE WESTERN ARMY, AND THE TENKO WHO HEAD THE EASTERN ARMY, HAVE BEEN AT A STANDOFF FOR CENTURIES...
THE ONLY THING PREVENTING AN ALL-OUT WAR WAS THE PRESENCE OF THE YATAHAGANE.
BUT NOW, THE SEVENTH GENERATION YATAHAGANE, FUYUZORA-KUN, IS WEAKER THAN EVER BEFORE.
YUUNA-CHAN AND NONKO-SAN...
EVEN THE TENKO FAMILY, WHO ARE STILL RECOVERING FROM LOSING BYAKUEI...!!
CLEARLY, THIS IS...

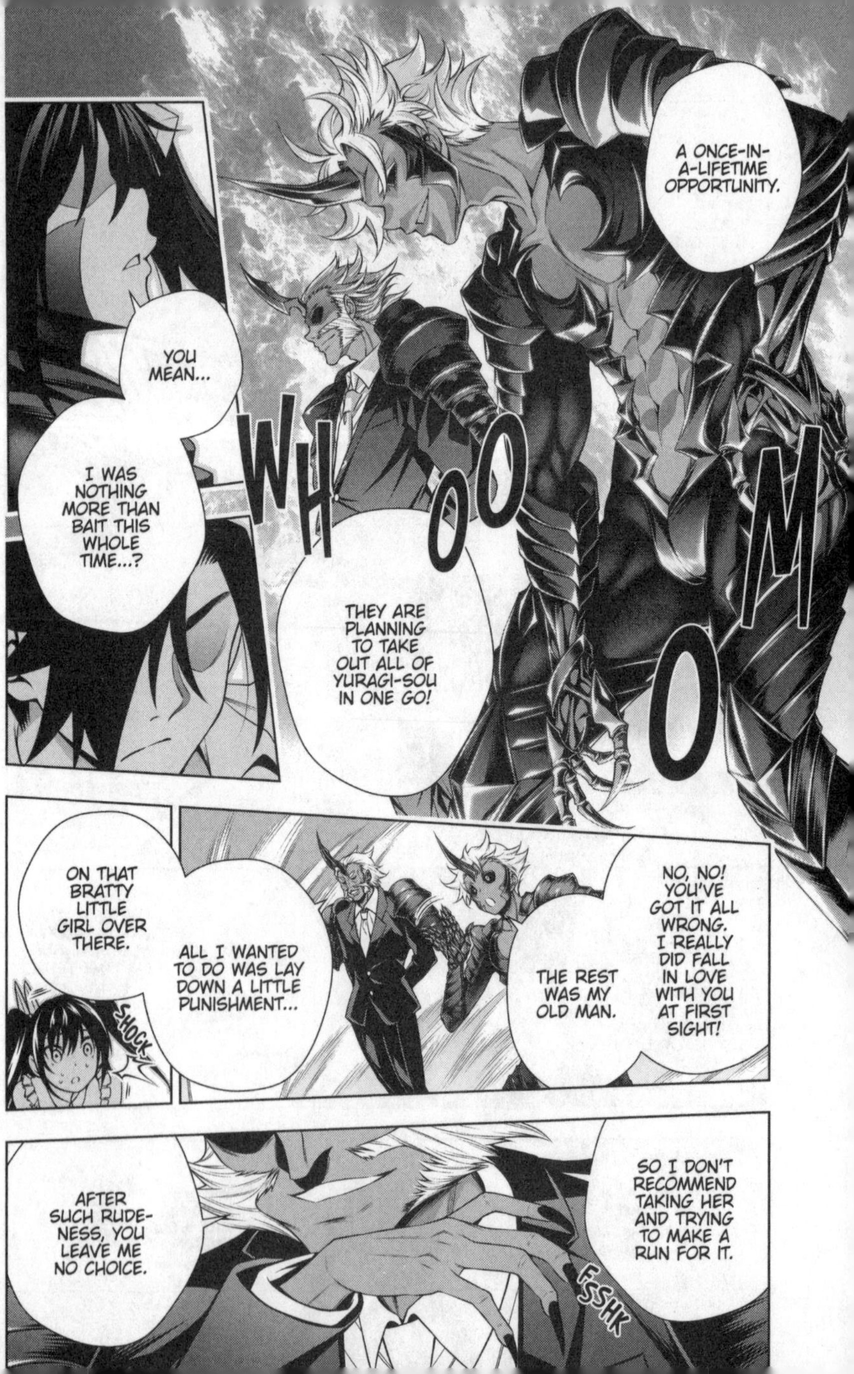
A ONCE-IN-A-LIFETIME OPPORTUNITY.
WHOOOOM
THEY ARE PLANNING TO TAKE OUT ALL OF YURAGI-SOU IN ONE GO!
YOU MEAN...
I WAS NOTHING MORE THAN BAIT THIS WHOLE TIME...?
NO, NO! YOU'VE GOT IT ALL WRONG. I REALLY DID FALL IN LOVE WITH YOU AT FIRST SIGHT!
THE REST WAS MY OLD MAN.
ALL I WANTED TO DO WAS LAY DOWN A LITTLE PUNISHMENT...
ON THAT BRATTY LITTLE GIRL OVER THERE.
SHOCK
SO I DON'T RECOMMEND TAKING HER AND TRYING TO MAKE A RUN FOR IT.
FSSHK
AFTER SUCH RUDENESS, YOU LEAVE ME NO CHOICE.

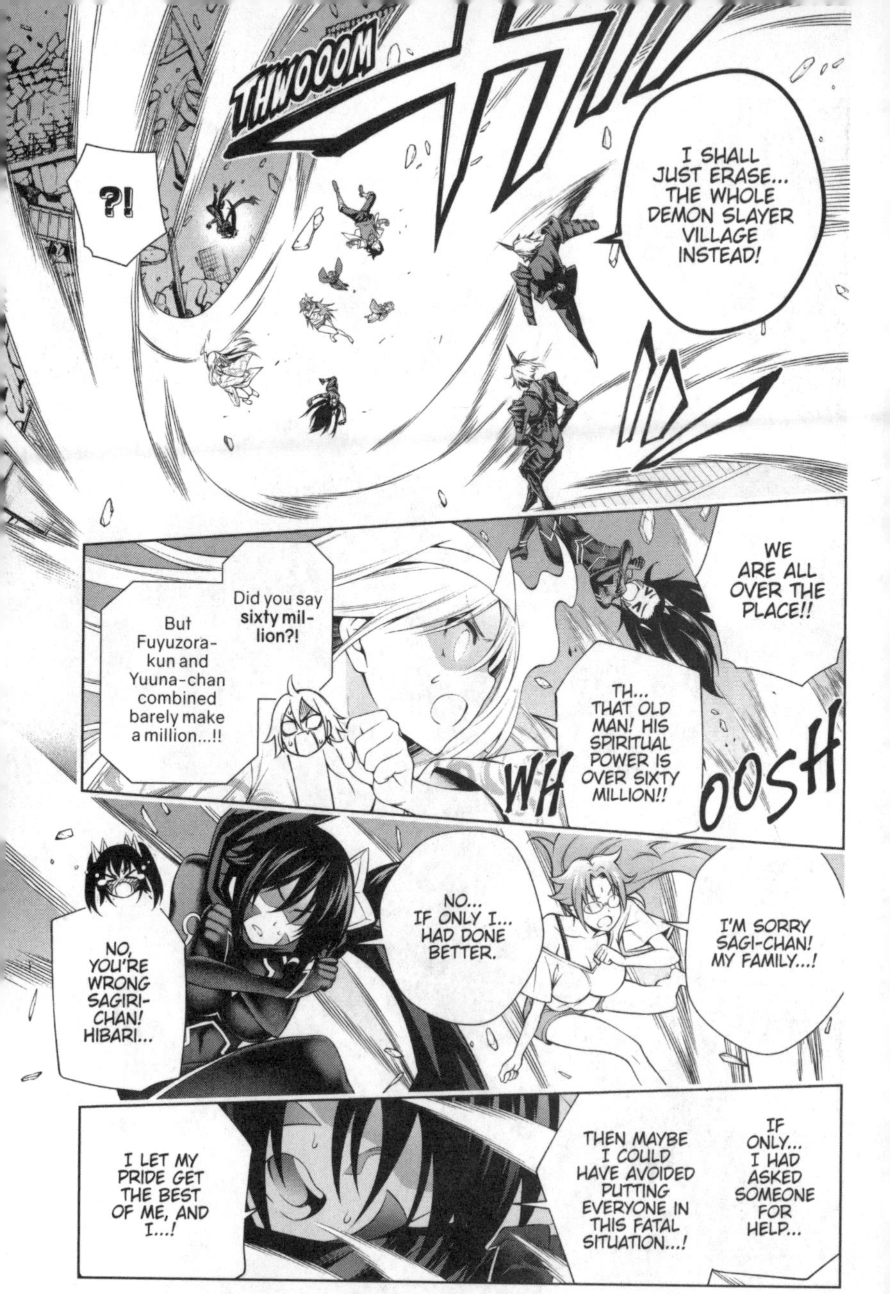
THWOOOM
I SHALL JUST ERASE... THE WHOLE DEMON SLAYER VILLAGE INSTEAD!
?!
WE ARE ALL OVER THE PLACE!!
TH... THAT OLD MAN! HIS SPIRITUAL POWER IS OVER SIXTY MILLION!!
WHOOSH
Did you say sixty million?!
But Fuyuzora-kun and Yuuna-chan combined barely make a million...!!
I'M SORRY SAGI-CHAN! MY FAMILY...!
NO... IF ONLY I... HAD DONE BETTER.
NO, YOU'RE WRONG SAGIRI-CHAN! HIBARI...
IF ONLY... I HAD ASKED SOMEONE FOR HELP...
THEN MAYBE I COULD HAVE AVOIDED PUTTING EVERYONE IN THIS FATAL SITUATION...!
I LET MY PRIDE GET THE BEST OF ME, AND I...!

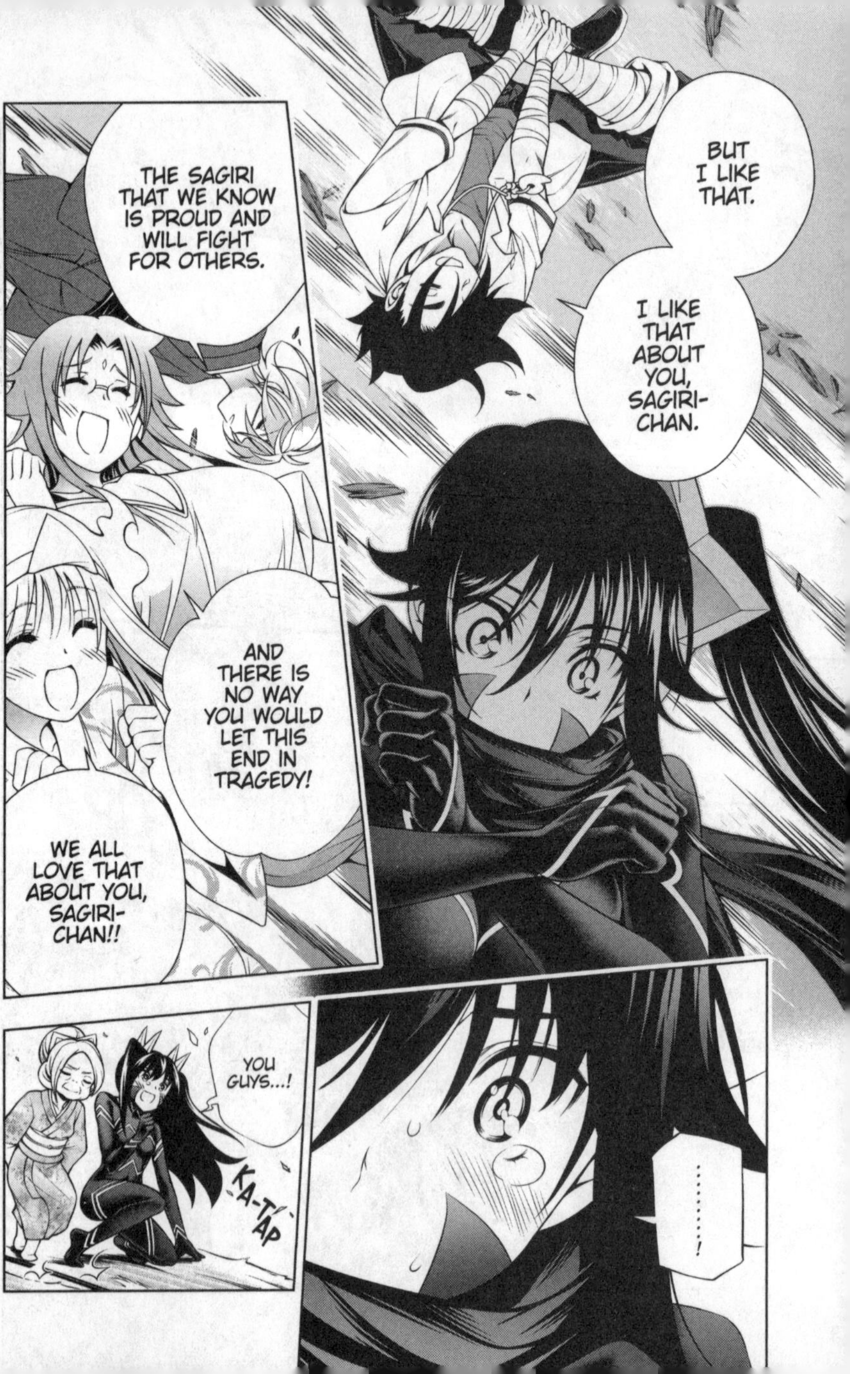
BUT I LIKE THAT.
I LIKE THAT ABOUT YOU, SAGIRI-CHAN.
THE SAGIRI THAT WE KNOW IS PROUD AND WILL FIGHT FOR OTHERS.
AND THERE IS NO WAY YOU WOULD LET THIS END IN TRAGEDY!
WE ALL LOVE THAT ABOUT YOU, SAGIRI-CHAN!!
......!
YOU GUYS...!
KA-TAP

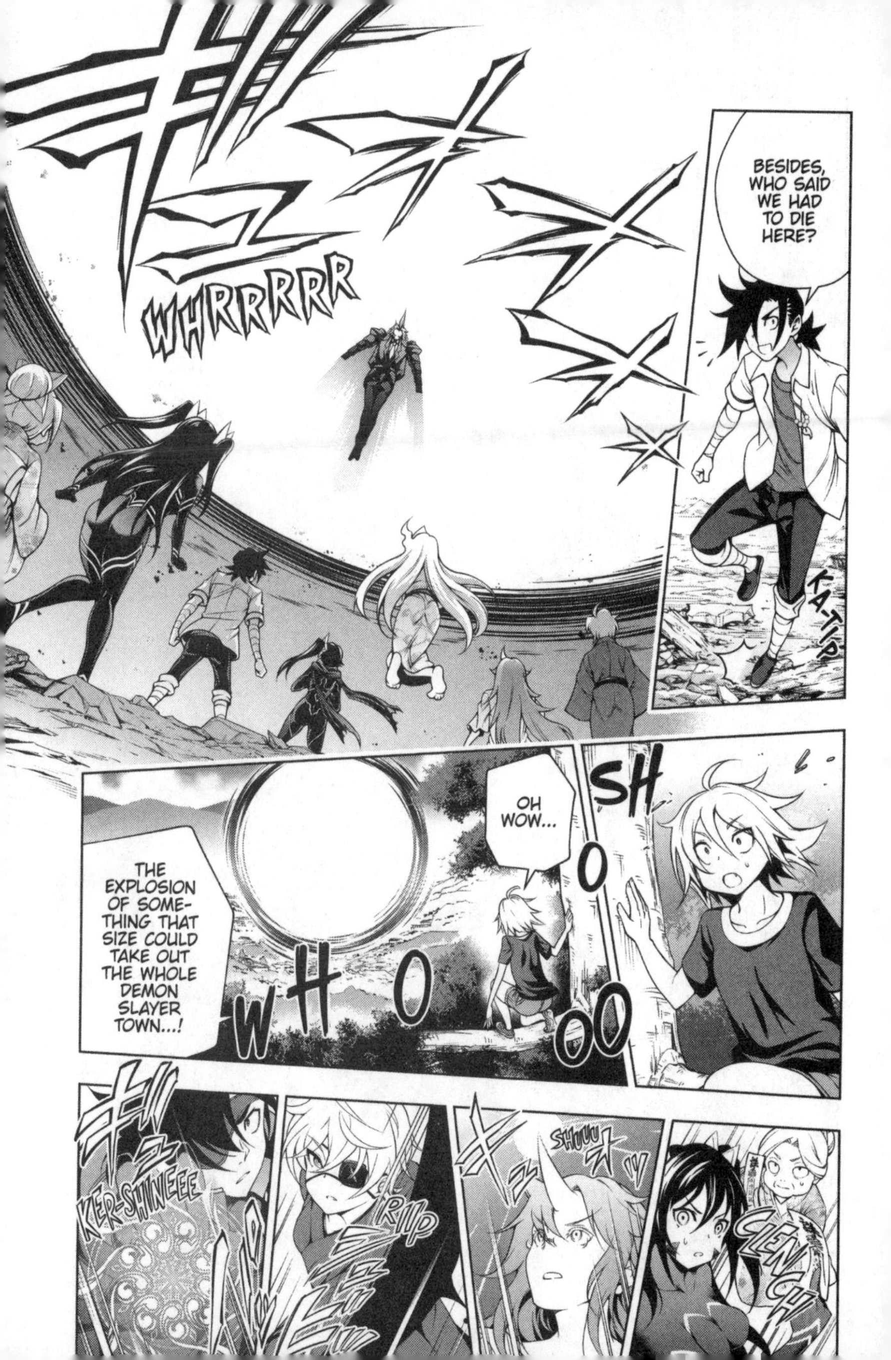
BESIDES, WHO SAID WE HAD TO DIE HERE?
KA-TIP
WHRRRRR
OH WOW...
THE EXPLOSION OF SOME-THING THAT SIZE COULD TAKE OUT THE WHOLE DEMON SLAYER TOWN...!
WHOOOOSH
CLENCH
SHUUU
RIIP
KER-SHINEEE

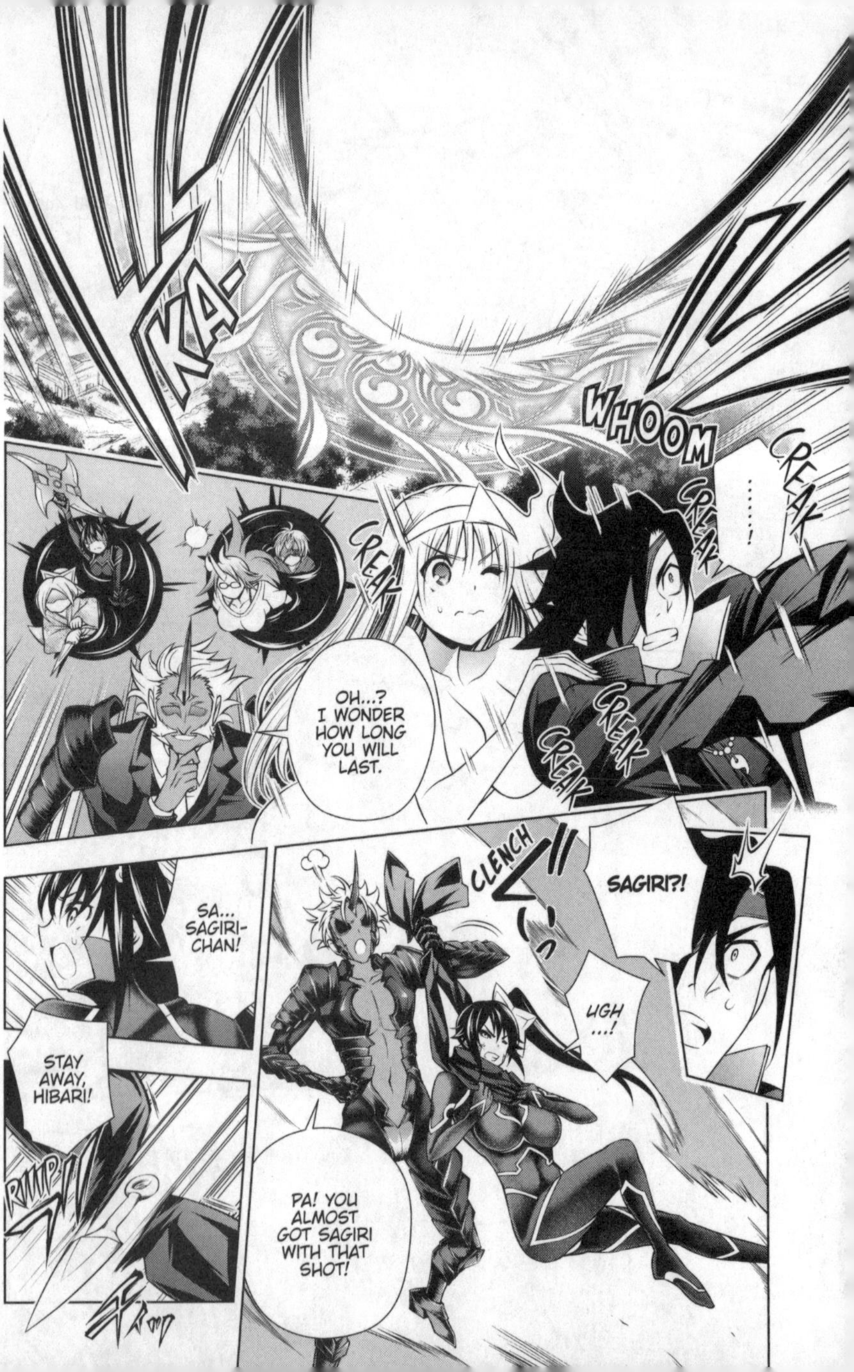

KA-
WHOOM
CREAK
CREAK
......!
CREAK
OH...? I WONDER HOW LONG YOU WILL LAST.
CREAK
CREAK
SAGIRI?!
CLENCH
UGH ...!
SA... SAGIRI-CHAN!
STAY AWAY, HIBARI!
PA! YOU ALMOST GOT SAGIRI WITH THAT SHOT!

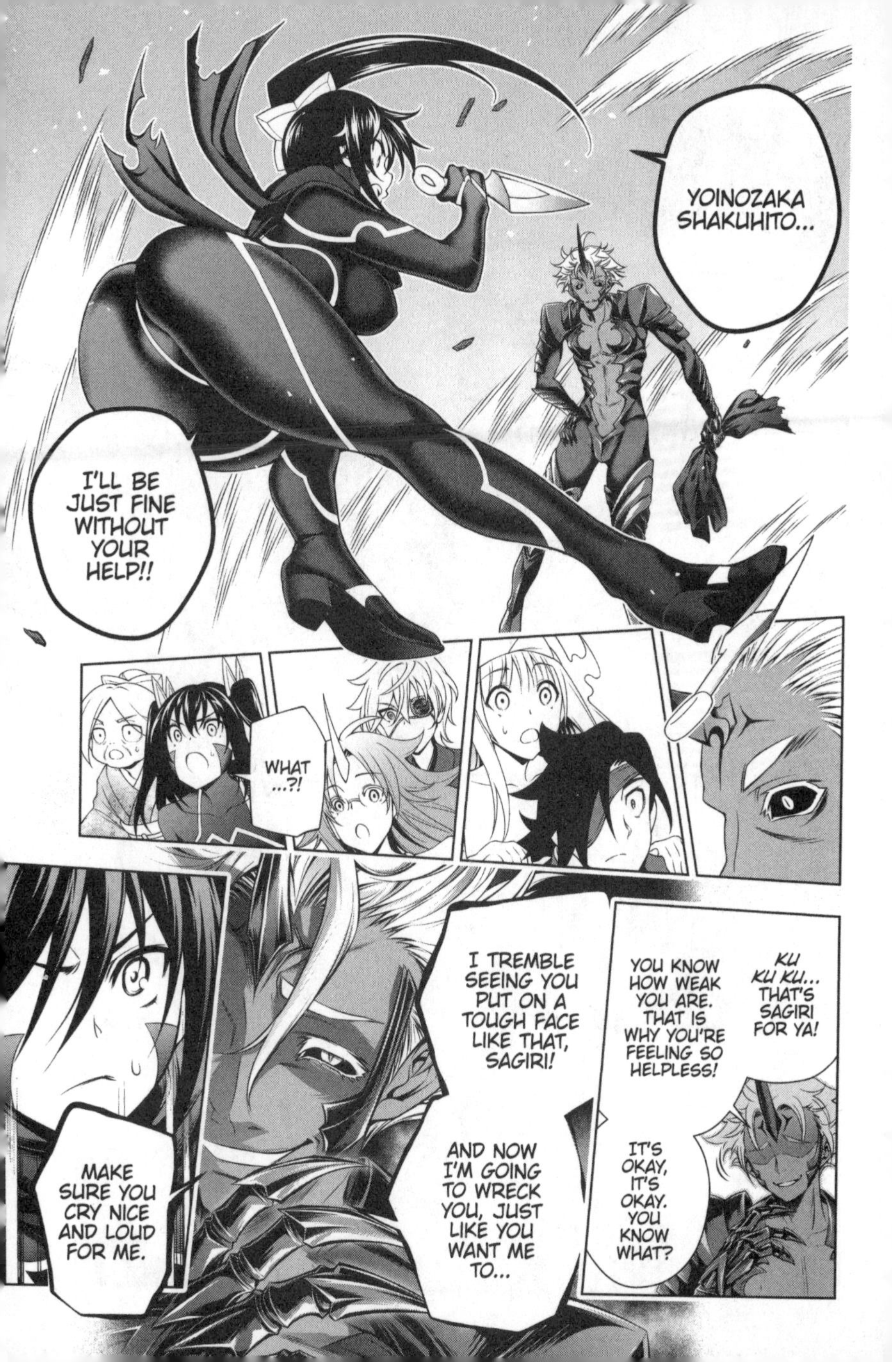
YOINOZAKA SHAKUHITO...
I'LL BE JUST FINE WITHOUT YOUR HELP!!
WHAT ...?!
KU KU KU... THAT'S SAGIRI FOR YA!
YOU KNOW HOW WEAK YOU ARE. THAT IS WHY YOU'RE FEELING SO HELPLESS!
I TREMBLE SEEING YOU PUT ON A TOUGH FACE LIKE THAT, SAGIRI!
IT'S OKAY, IT'S OKAY. YOU KNOW WHAT?
AND NOW I'M GOING TO WRECK YOU, JUST LIKE YOU WANT ME TO...
MAKE SURE YOU CRY NICE AND LOUD FOR ME.

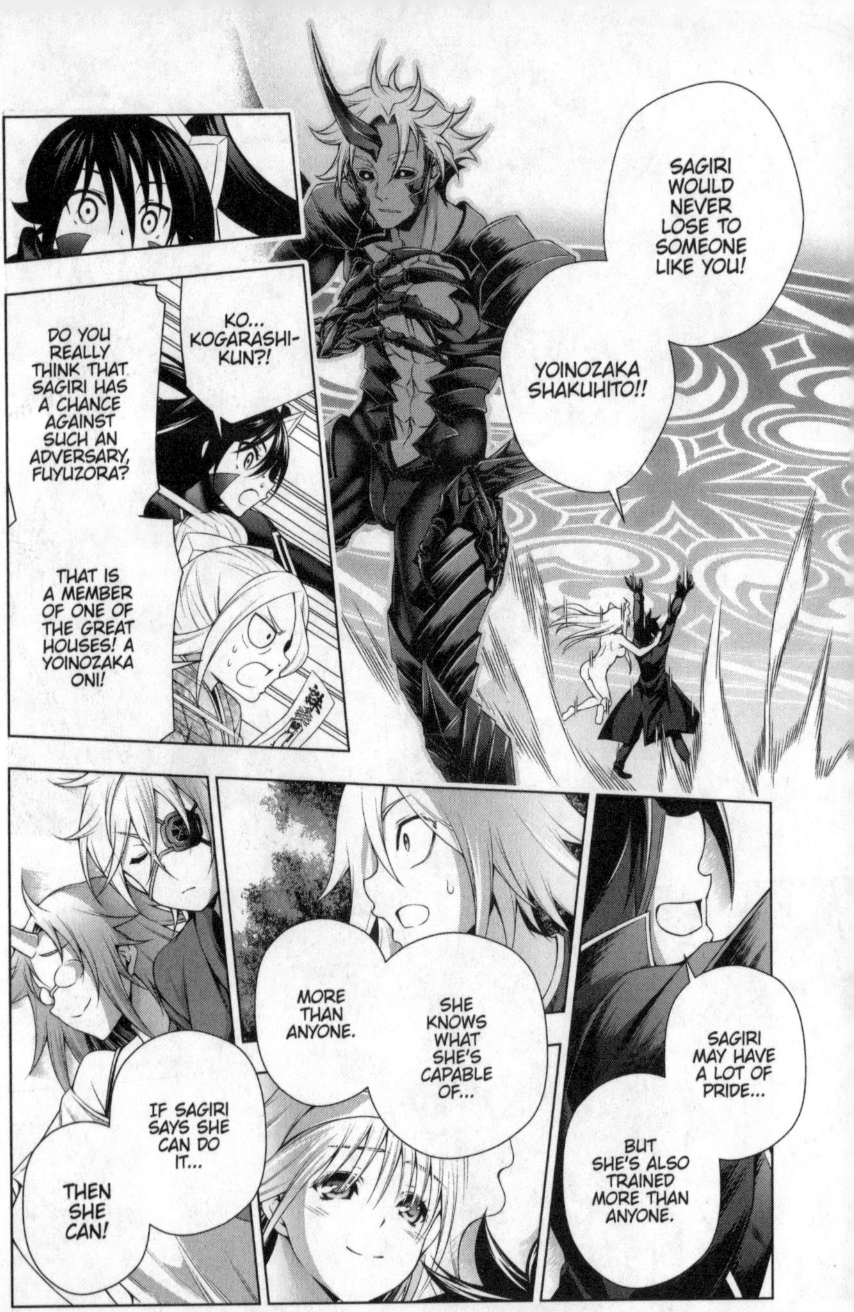
SAGIRI WOULD NEVER LOSE TO SOMEONE LIKE YOU!
YOINOZAKA SHAKUHITO!!
KO... KOGARASHI-KUN?!
DO YOU REALLY THINK THAT SAGIRI HAS A CHANCE AGAINST SUCH AN ADVERSARY, FUYUZORA?
THAT IS A MEMBER OF ONE OF THE GREAT HOUSES! A YOINOZAKA ONI!
SAGIRI MAY HAVE A LOT OF PRIDE...
BUT SHE'S ALSO TRAINED MORE THAN ANYONE.
SHE KNOWS WHAT SHE'S CAPABLE OF...
MORE THAN ANYONE.
IF SAGIRI SAYS SHE CAN DO IT...
THEN SHE CAN!

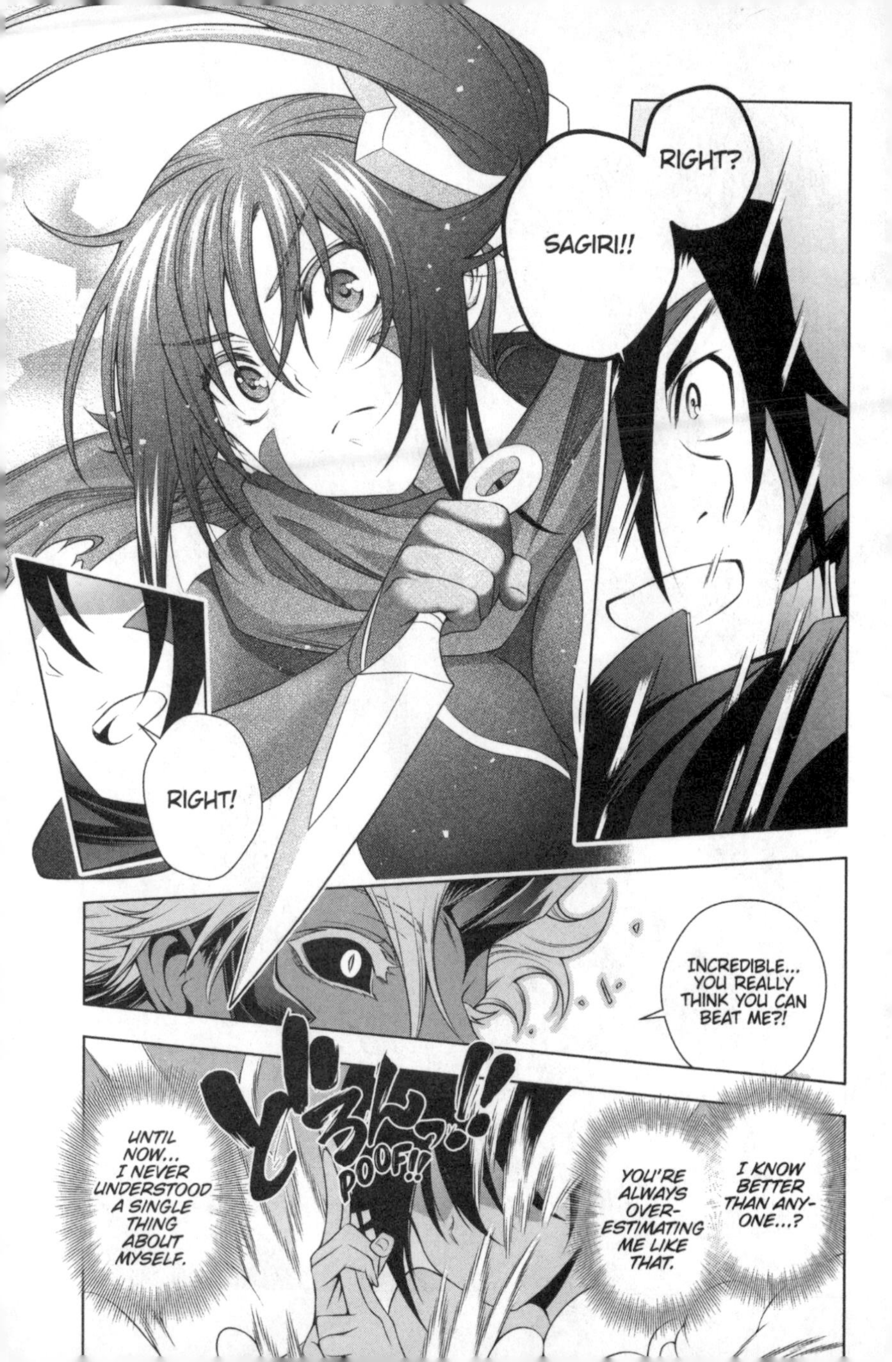
RIGHT?
SAGIRI!!
RIGHT!
INCREDIBLE... YOU REALLY THINK YOU CAN BEAT ME?!
I KNOW BETTER THAN ANY-ONE...?
YOU'RE ALWAYS OVER-ESTIMATING ME LIKE THAT.
どろんっ!!
POOF!!
UNTIL NOW... I NEVER UNDERSTOOD A SINGLE THING ABOUT MYSELF.

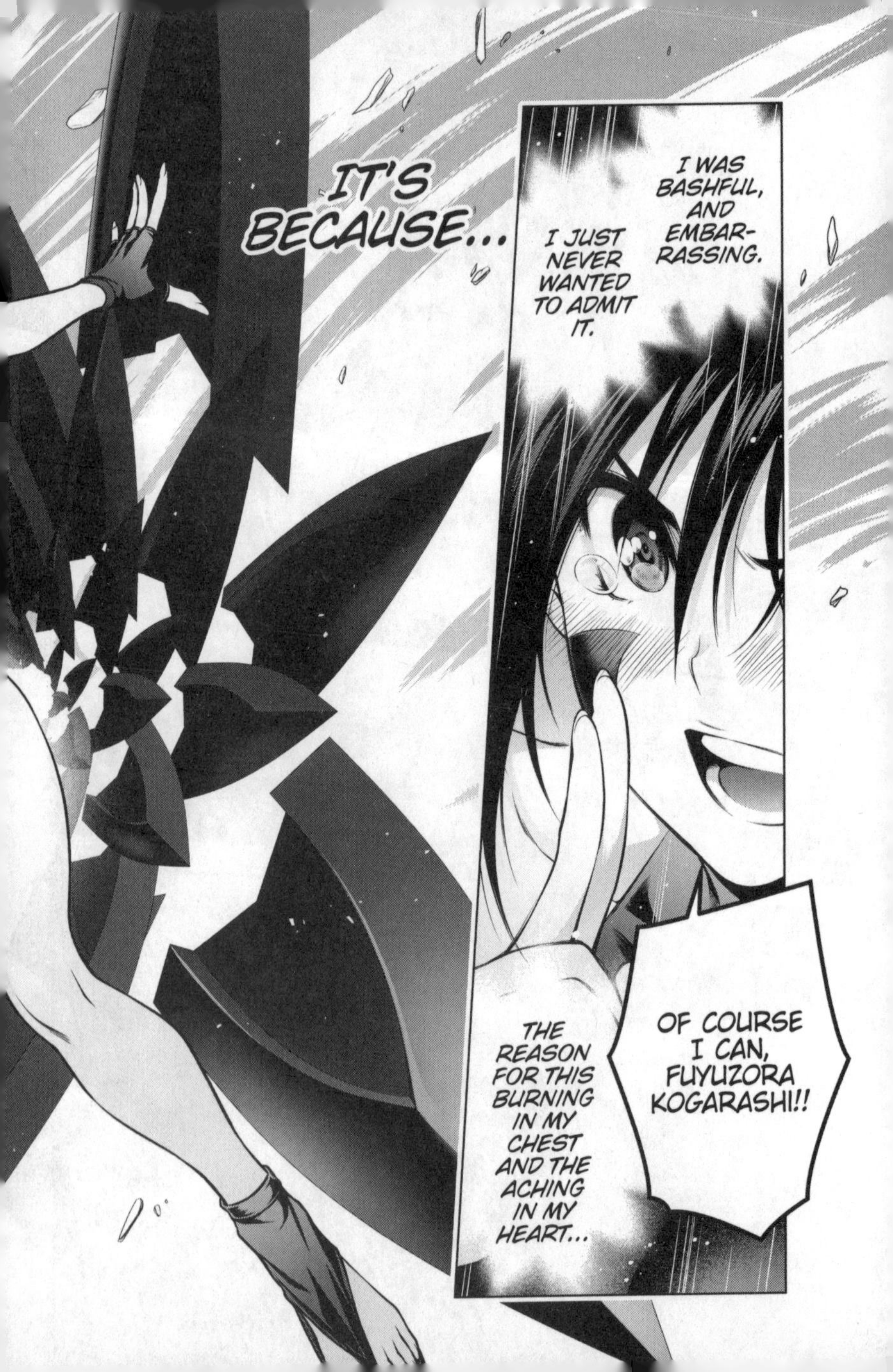
I WAS BASHFUL, AND EMBARRASSING.
I JUST NEVER WANTED TO ADMIT IT.
IT'S BECAUSE...
OF COURSE I CAN, FUYUZORA KOGARASHI!!
THE REASON FOR THIS BURNING IN MY CHEST AND THE ACHING IN MY HEART...

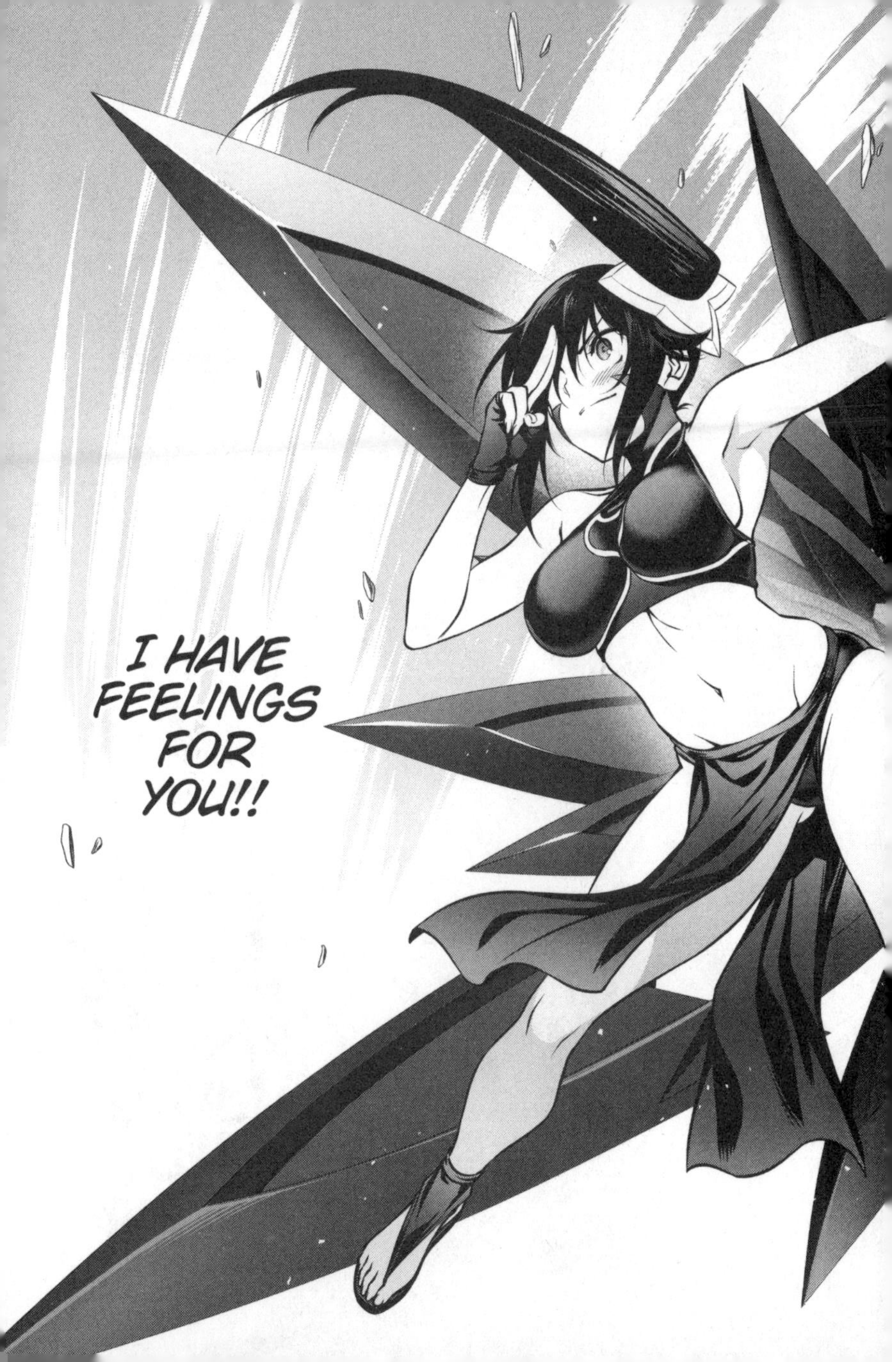
I HAVE FEELINGS FOR YOU!!

Yuuna
and the
Haunted
Hot
Springs

137 How Sagiri-san Fights

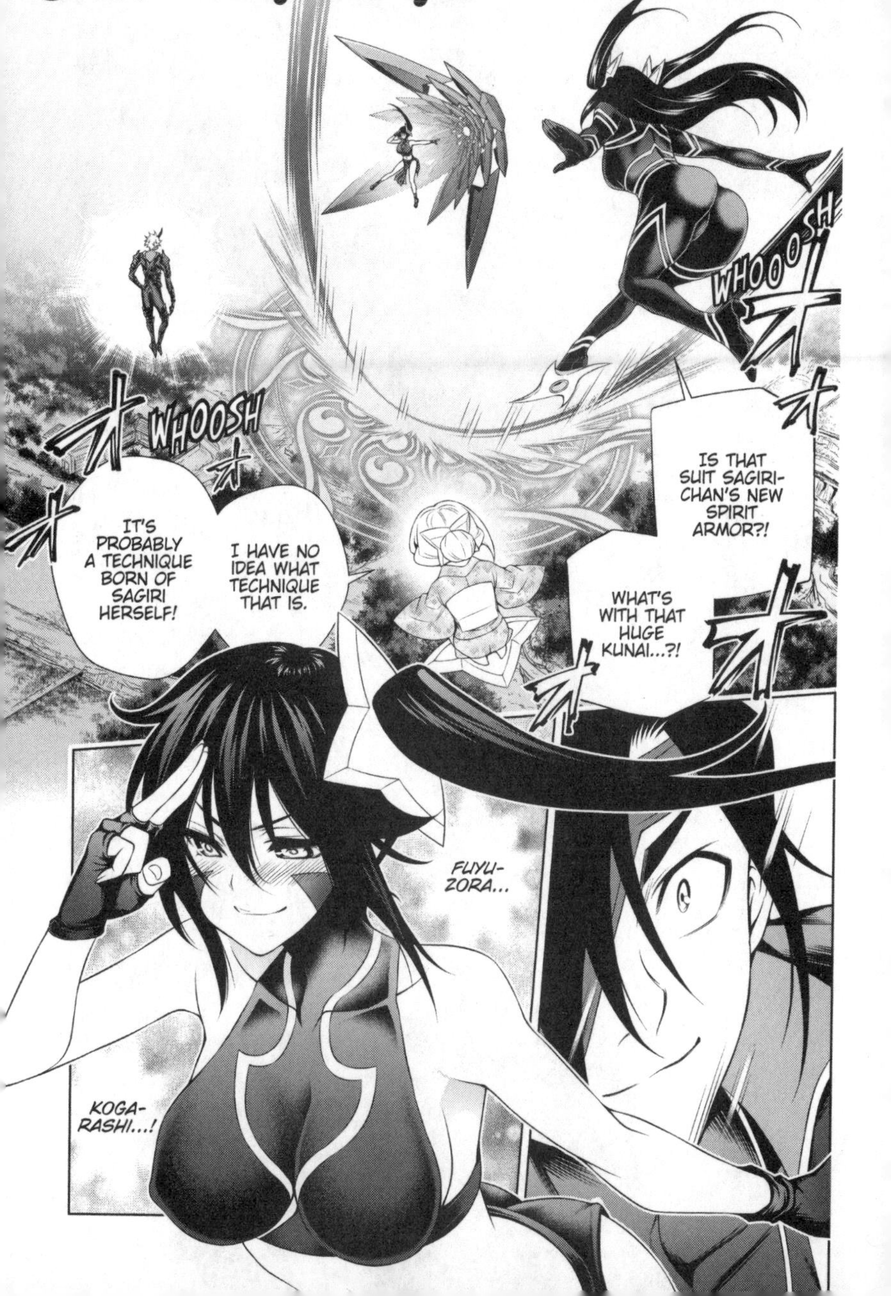
WHOOOSH
IS THAT SUIT SAGIRI-CHAN'S NEW SPIRIT ARMOR?!
WHAT'S WITH THAT HUGE KUNAI...?!
WHOOSH
I HAVE NO IDEA WHAT TECHNIQUE THAT IS.
IT'S PROBABLY A TECHNIQUE BORN OF SAGIRI HERSELF!
FUYU-ZORA...
KOGA-RASHI...!

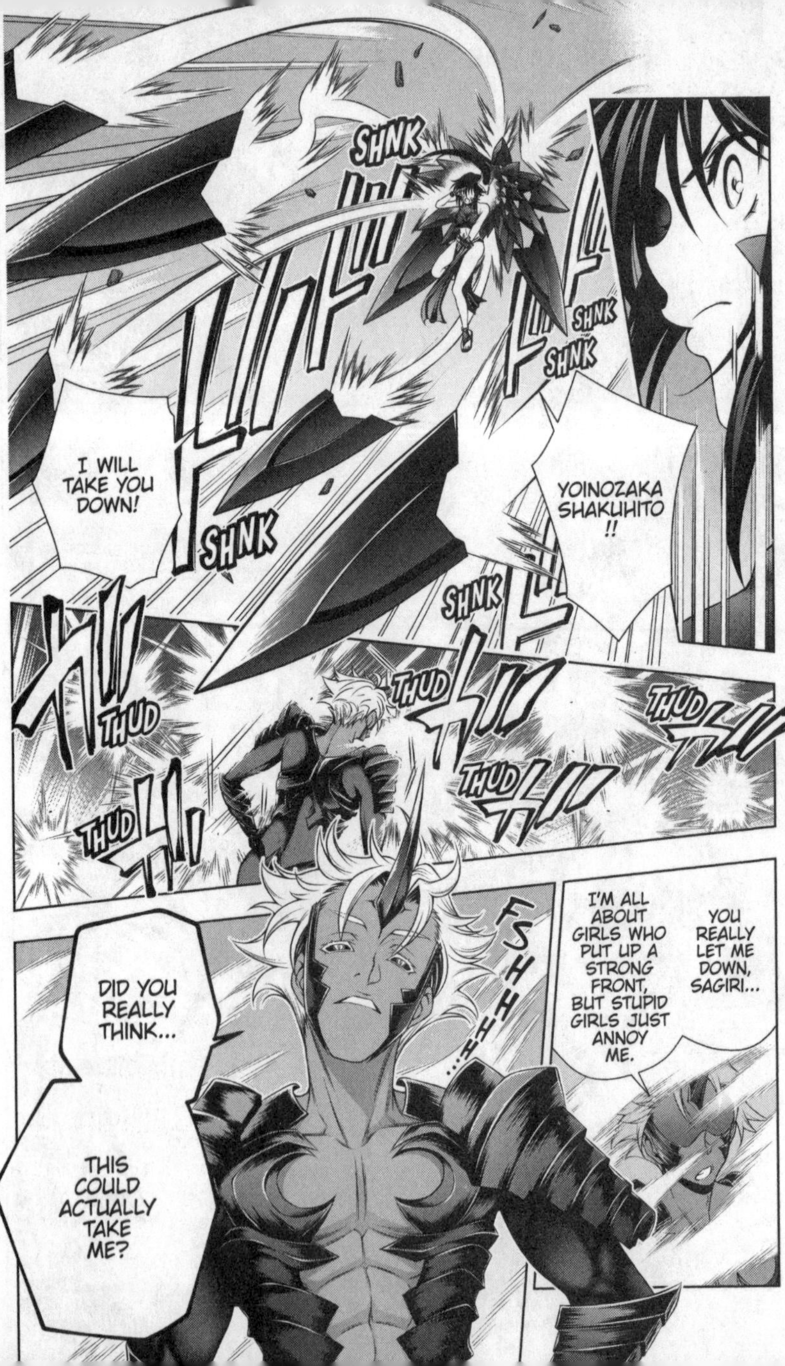
SHNK
YOINOZAKA SHAKUHITO !!
I WILL TAKE YOU DOWN!
SHNK
SHNK
SHNK
SHNK
THUD
THUD
THUD
THUD
THUD
YOU REALLY LET ME DOWN, SAGIRI...
I'M ALL ABOUT GIRLS WHO PUT UP A STRONG FRONT, BUT STUPID GIRLS JUST ANNOY ME.
FSHHHH...
DID YOU REALLY THINK...
THIS COULD ACTUALLY TAKE ME?

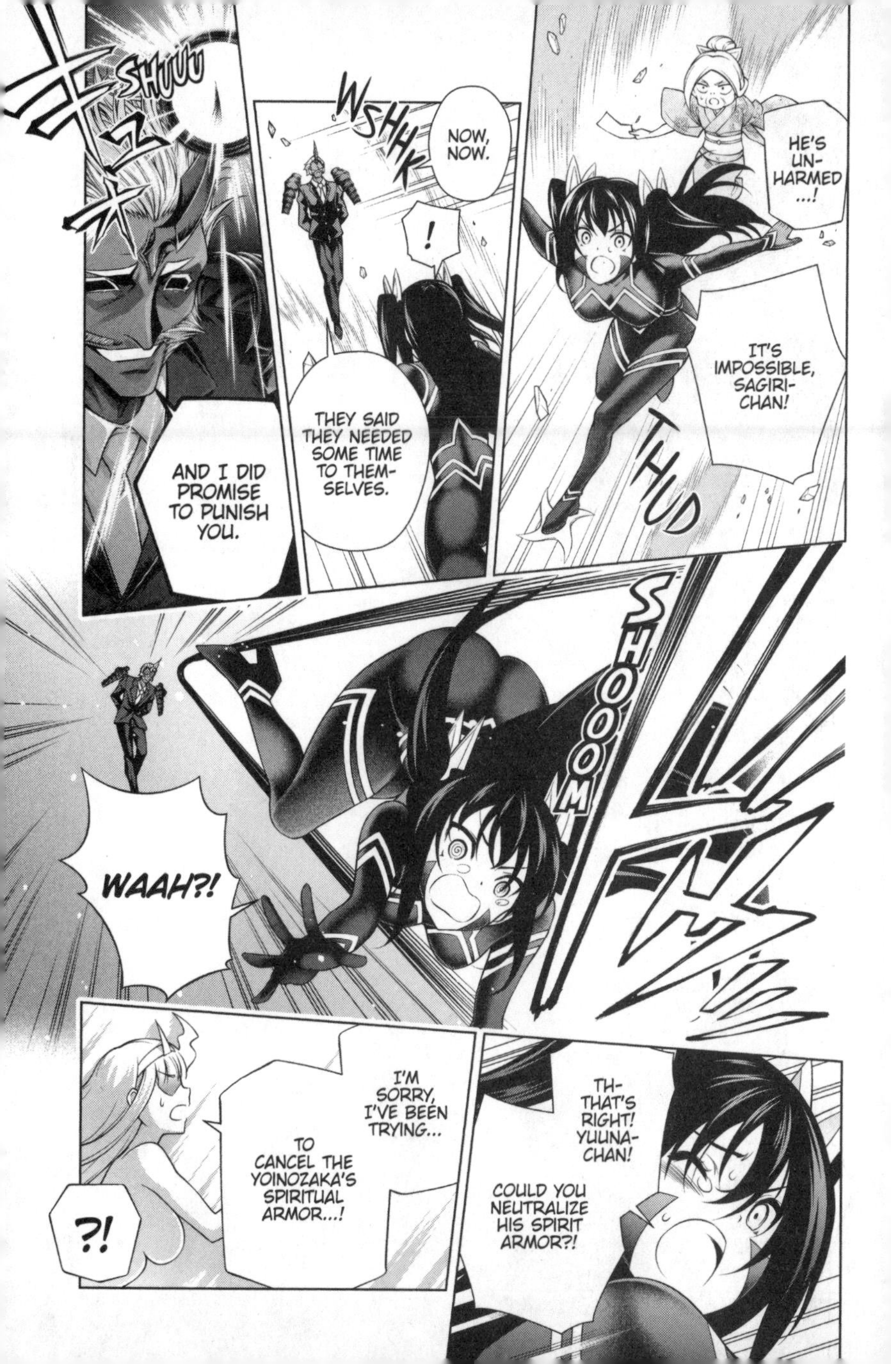
HE'S UN-HARMED ...!
IT'S IMPOSSIBLE, SAGIRI-CHAN!
THUD
WSHHK
NOW, NOW.
!
THEY SAID THEY NEEDED SOME TIME TO THEM-SELVES.
SHUUU
AND I DID PROMISE TO PUNISH YOU.
SHOOOM
WAAH?!
TH-THAT'S RIGHT! YUUNA-CHAN!
COULD YOU NEUTRALIZE HIS SPIRIT ARMOR?!
I'M SORRY, I'VE BEEN TRYING...
TO CANCEL THE YOINOZAKA'S SPIRITUAL ARMOR...!
?!

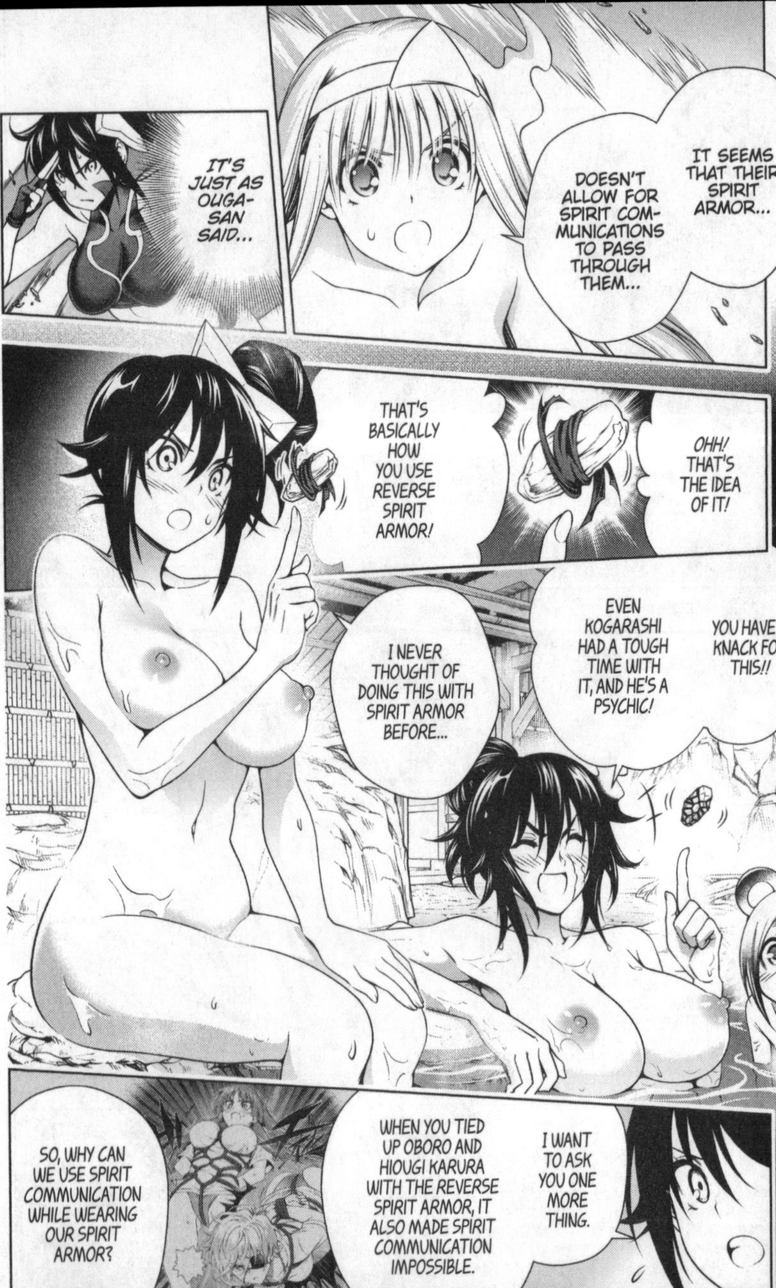
IT SEEMS THAT THEIR SPIRIT ARMOR...
DOESN'T ALLOW FOR SPIRIT COMMUNICATIONS TO PASS THROUGH THEM...
IT'S JUST AS OUGA-SAN SAID...
OHH! THAT'S THE IDEA OF IT!
THAT'S BASICALLY HOW YOU USE REVERSE SPIRIT ARMOR!
YOU HAVE A KNACK FOR THIS!!
EVEN KOGARASHI HAD A TOUGH TIME WITH IT, AND HE'S A PSYCHIC!
I NEVER THOUGHT OF DOING THIS WITH SPIRIT ARMOR BEFORE...
I WANT TO ASK YOU ONE MORE THING.
WHEN YOU TIED UP OBORO AND HIOUGI KARURA WITH THE REVERSE SPIRIT ARMOR, IT ALSO MADE SPIRIT COMMUNICATION IMPOSSIBLE.
SO, WHY CAN WE USE SPIRIT COMMUNICATION WHILE WEARING OUR SPIRIT ARMOR?

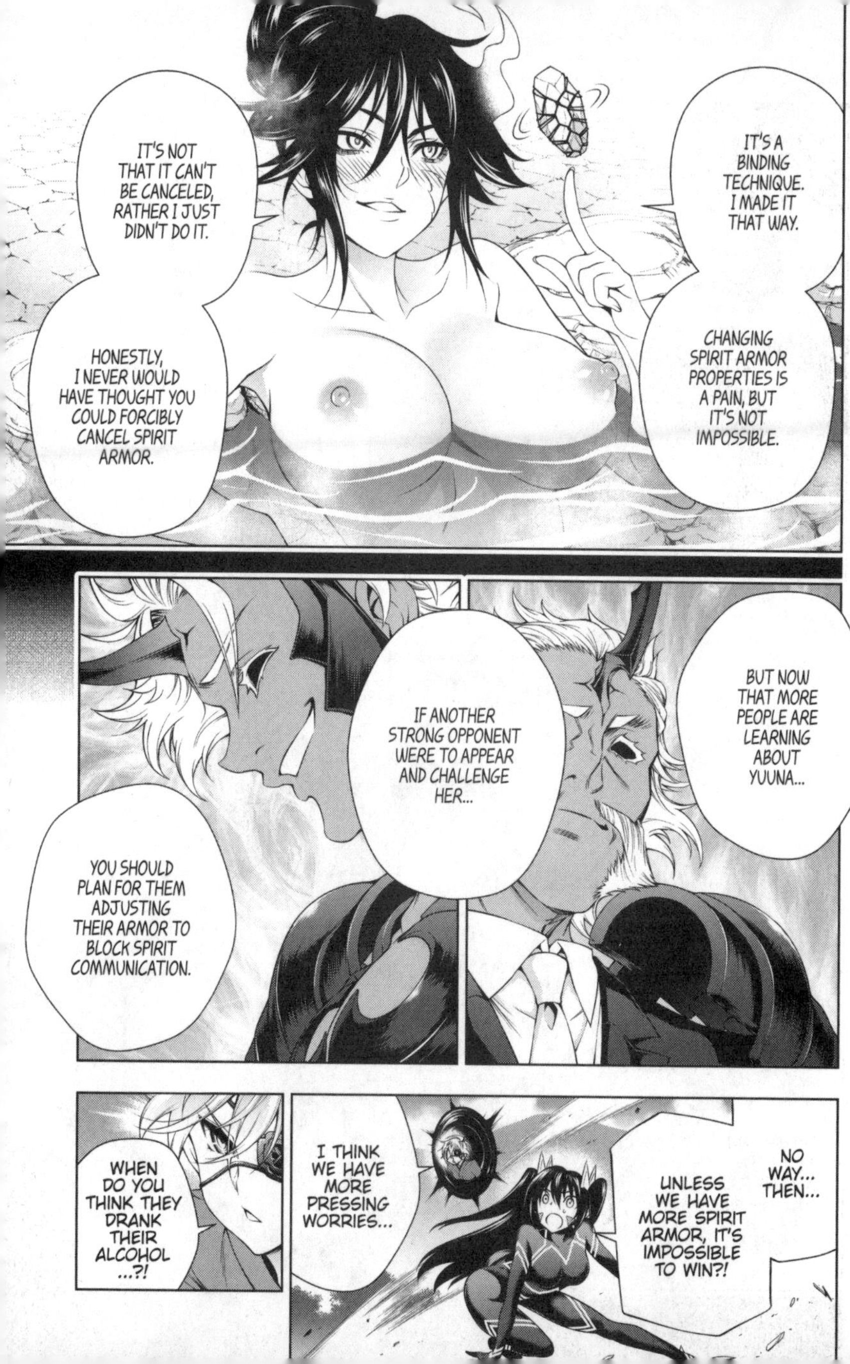
IT'S A BINDING TECHNIQUE. I MADE IT THAT WAY.
IT'S NOT THAT IT CAN'T BE CANCELED, RATHER I JUST DIDN'T DO IT.
CHANGING SPIRIT ARMOR PROPERTIES IS A PAIN, BUT IT'S NOT IMPOSSIBLE.
HONESTLY, I NEVER WOULD HAVE THOUGHT YOU COULD FORCIBLY CANCEL SPIRIT ARMOR.
BUT NOW THAT MORE PEOPLE ARE LEARNING ABOUT YUUNA...
IF ANOTHER STRONG OPPONENT WERE TO APPEAR AND CHALLENGE HER...
YOU SHOULD PLAN FOR THEM ADJUSTING THEIR ARMOR TO BLOCK SPIRIT COMMUNICATION.
NO WAY... THEN...
UNLESS WE HAVE MORE SPIRIT ARMOR, IT'S IMPOSSIBLE TO WIN?!
I THINK WE HAVE MORE PRESSING WORRIES...
WHEN DO YOU THINK THEY DRANK THEIR ALCOHOL ...?!

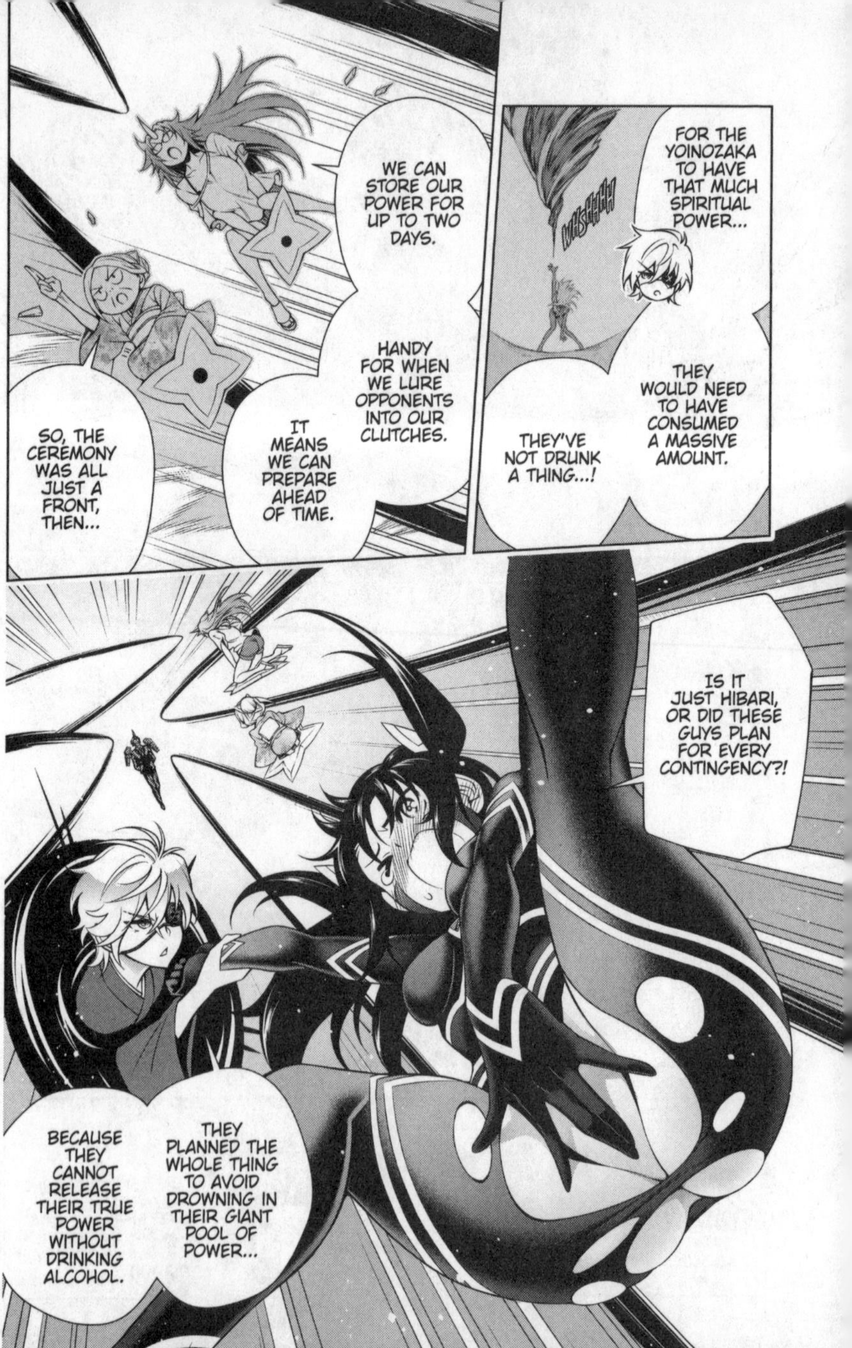
FOR THE YOINOZAKA TO HAVE THAT MUCH SPIRITUAL POWER...
WHSHHHH
THEY WOULD NEED TO HAVE CONSUMED A MASSIVE AMOUNT.
THEY'VE NOT DRUNK A THING...!
WE CAN STORE OUR POWER FOR UP TO TWO DAYS.
HANDY FOR WHEN WE LURE OPPONENTS INTO OUR CLUTCHES.
IT MEANS WE CAN PREPARE AHEAD OF TIME.
SO, THE CEREMONY WAS ALL JUST A FRONT, THEN...
IS IT JUST HIBARI, OR DID THESE GUYS PLAN FOR EVERY CONTINGENCY?!
THEY PLANNED THE WHOLE THING TO AVOID DROWNING IN THEIR GIANT POOL OF POWER...
BECAUSE THEY CANNOT RELEASE THEIR TRUE POWER WITHOUT DRINKING ALCOHOL.

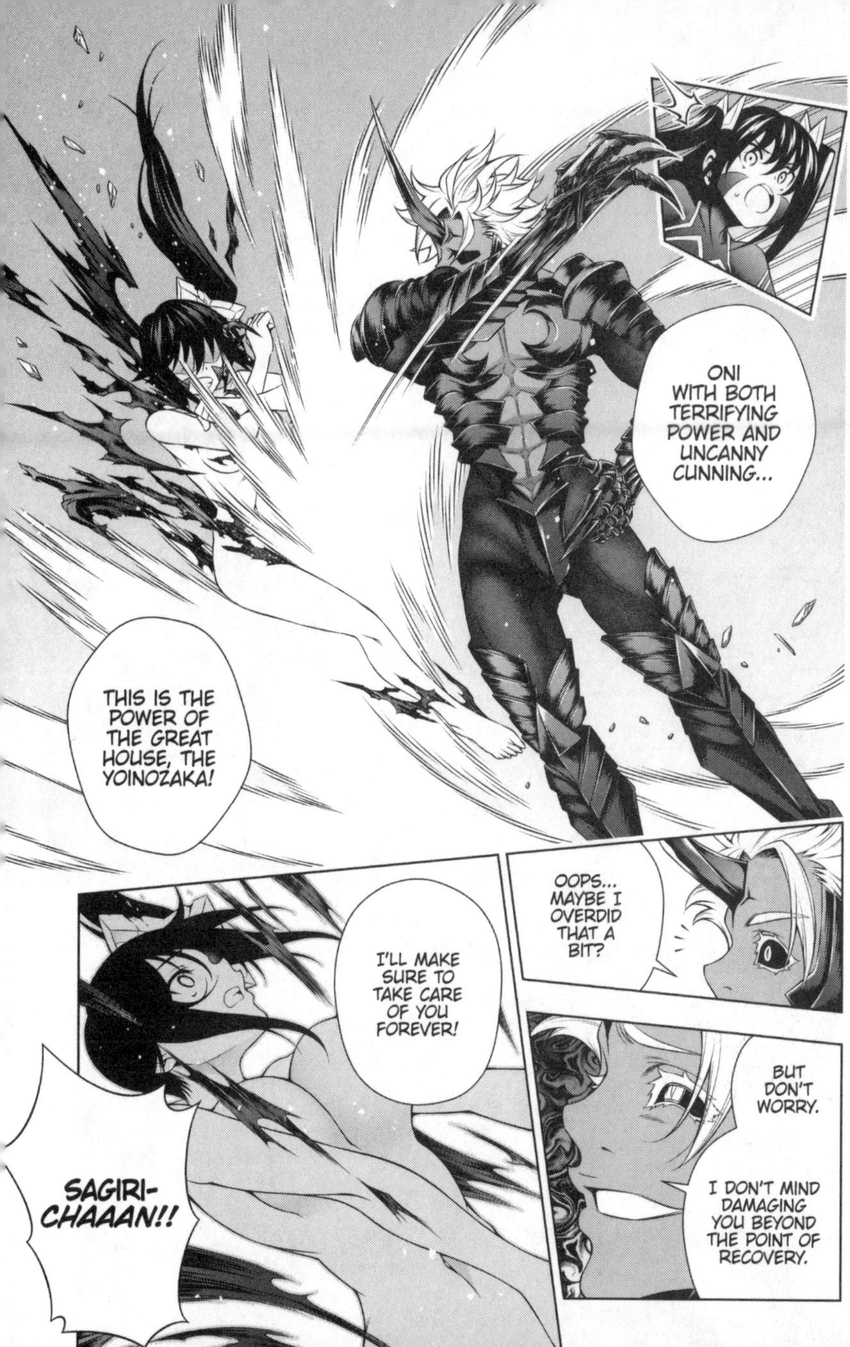
ONI WITH BOTH TERRIFYING POWER AND UNCANNY CUNNING...
THIS IS THE POWER OF THE GREAT HOUSE, THE YOINOZAKA!
OOPS... MAYBE I OVERDID THAT A BIT?
BUT DON'T WORRY.
I DON'T MIND DAMAGING YOU BEYOND THE POINT OF RECOVERY.
I'LL MAKE SURE TO TAKE CARE OF YOU FOREVER!
SAGIRI-CHAAAN!!

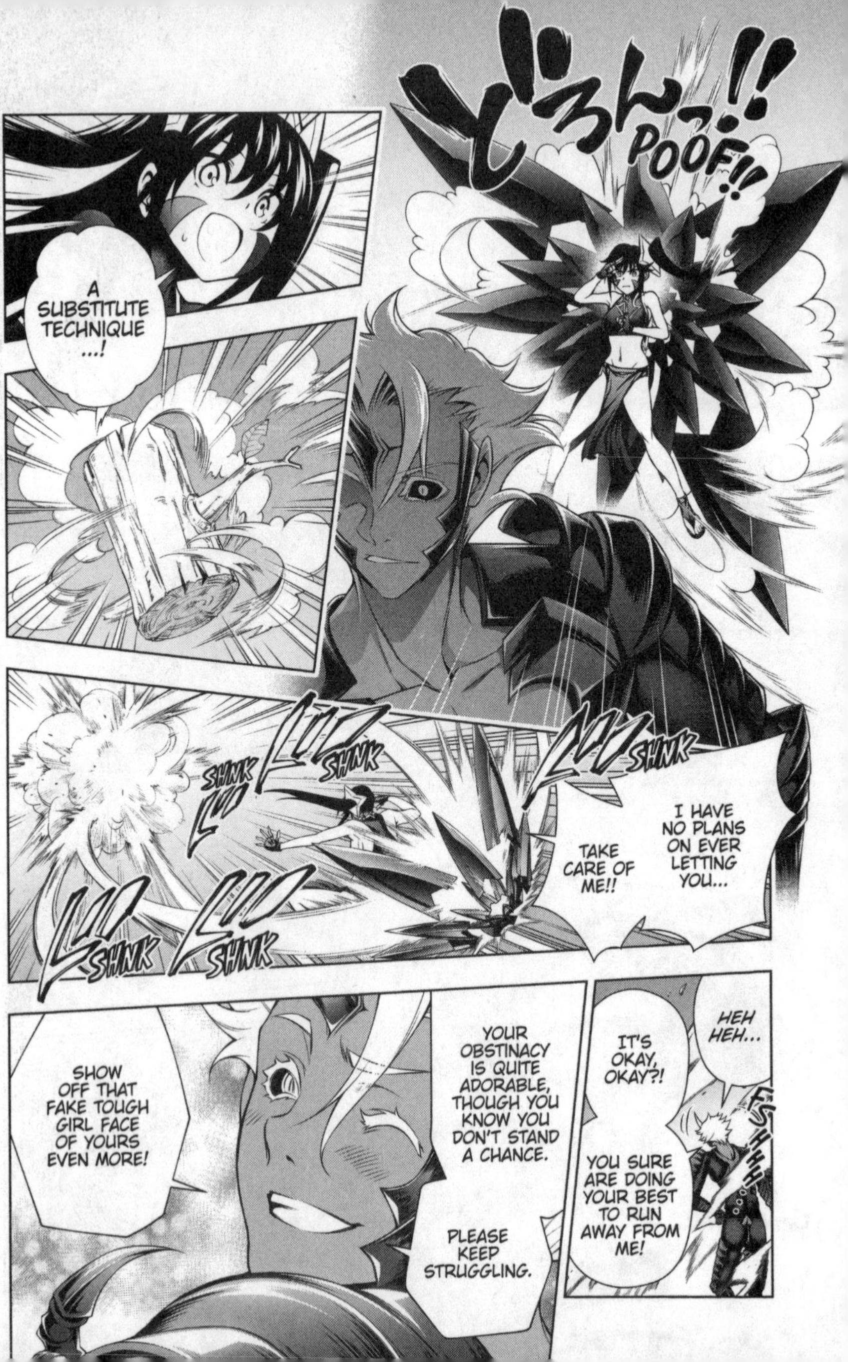
どろんっ!!
POOF!!
A SUBSTITUTE TECHNIQUE ...!
SHNK
SHNK
SHNK
I HAVE NO PLANS ON EVER LETTING YOU...
TAKE CARE OF ME!!
SHNK
SHNK
HEH HEH...
IT'S OKAY, OKAY?!
FSHHHH
YOU SURE ARE DOING YOUR BEST TO RUN AWAY FROM ME!
YOUR OBSTINACY IS QUITE ADORABLE, THOUGH YOU KNOW YOU DON'T STAND A CHANCE.
PLEASE KEEP STRUGGLING.
SHOW OFF THAT FAKE TOUGH GIRL FACE OF YOURS EVEN MORE!

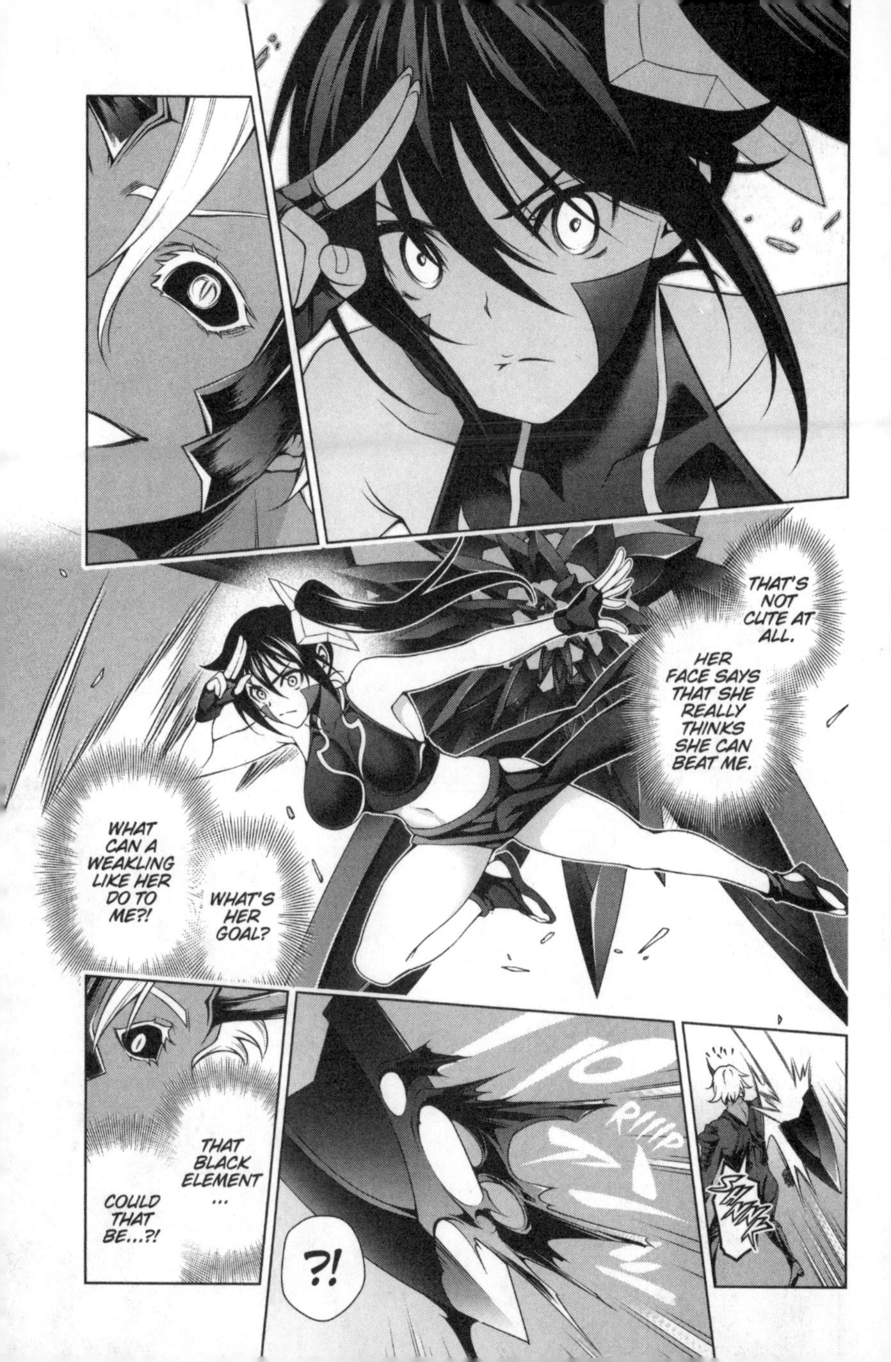
THAT'S NOT CUTE AT ALL.
HER FACE SAYS THAT SHE REALLY THINKS SHE CAN BEAT ME.
WHAT'S HER GOAL?
WHAT CAN A WEAKLING LIKE HER DO TO ME?!
RIIIP
?!
THAT BLACK ELEMENT ...
COULD THAT BE...?!

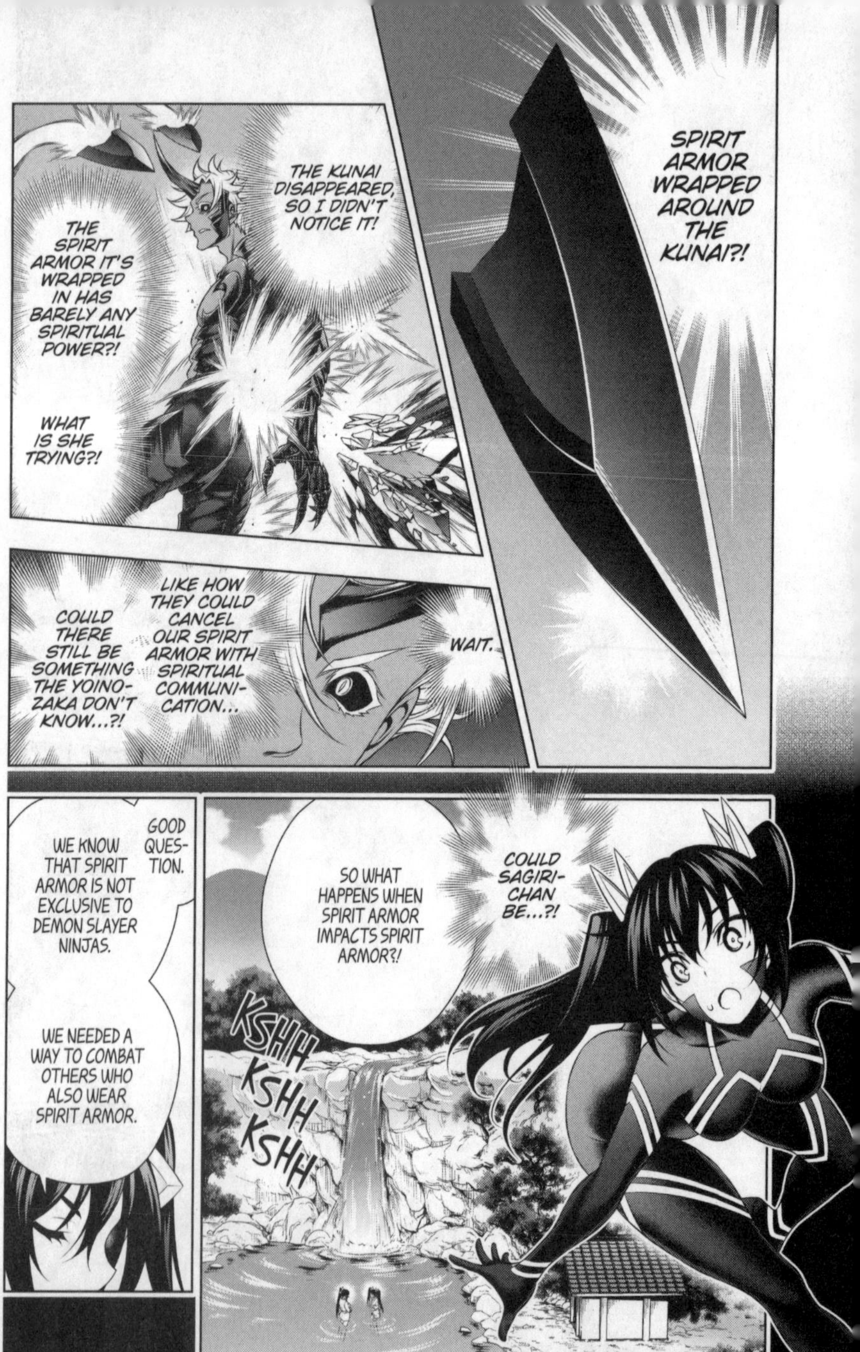

SPIRIT ARMOR WRAPPED AROUND THE KUNAI?!
THE KUNAI DISAPPEARED, SO I DIDN'T NOTICE IT!
THE SPIRIT ARMOR IT'S WRAPPED IN HAS BARELY ANY SPIRITUAL POWER?!
WHAT IS SHE TRYING?!
WAIT.
LIKE HOW THEY COULD CANCEL OUR SPIRIT ARMOR WITH SPIRITUAL COMMUNI-CATION...
COULD THERE STILL BE SOMETHING THE YOINO-ZAKA DON'T KNOW...?!
COULD SAGIRI-CHAN BE...?!
SO WHAT HAPPENS WHEN SPIRIT ARMOR IMPACTS SPIRIT ARMOR?!
KSHH KSHH KSHH
GOOD QUES-TION.
WE KNOW THAT SPIRIT ARMOR IS NOT EXCLUSIVE TO DEMON SLAYER NINJAS.
WE NEEDED A WAY TO COMBAT OTHERS WHO ALSO WEAR SPIRIT ARMOR.

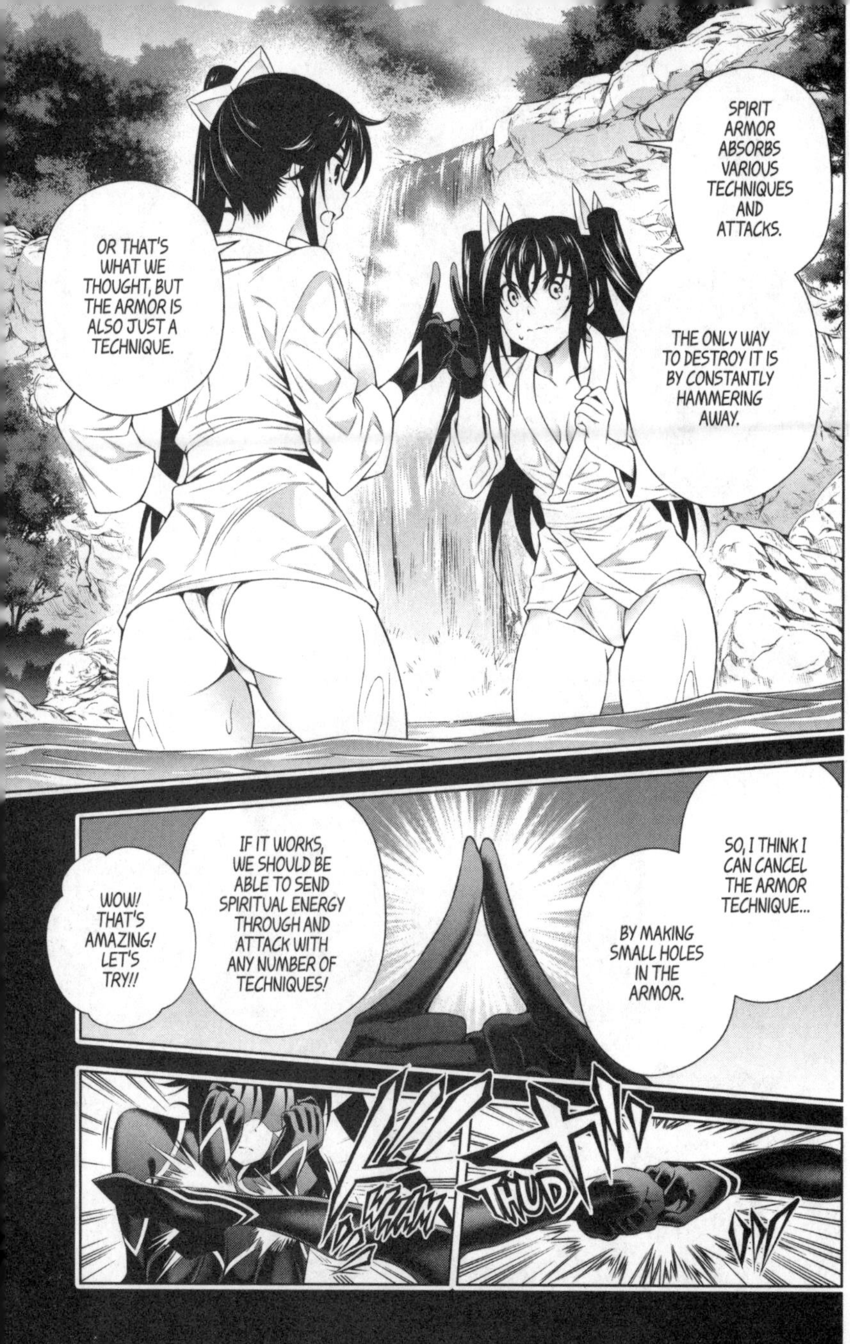
SPIRIT ARMOR ABSORBS VARIOUS TECHNIQUES AND ATTACKS.
THE ONLY WAY TO DESTROY IT IS BY CONSTANTLY HAMMERING AWAY.
OR THAT'S WHAT WE THOUGHT, BUT THE ARMOR IS ALSO JUST A TECHNIQUE.
SO, I THINK I CAN CANCEL THE ARMOR TECHNIQUE...
BY MAKING SMALL HOLES IN THE ARMOR.
IF IT WORKS, WE SHOULD BE ABLE TO SEND SPIRITUAL ENERGY THROUGH AND ATTACK WITH ANY NUMBER OF TECHNIQUES!
WOW! THAT'S AMAZING! LET'S TRY!!
THUD
WHAM

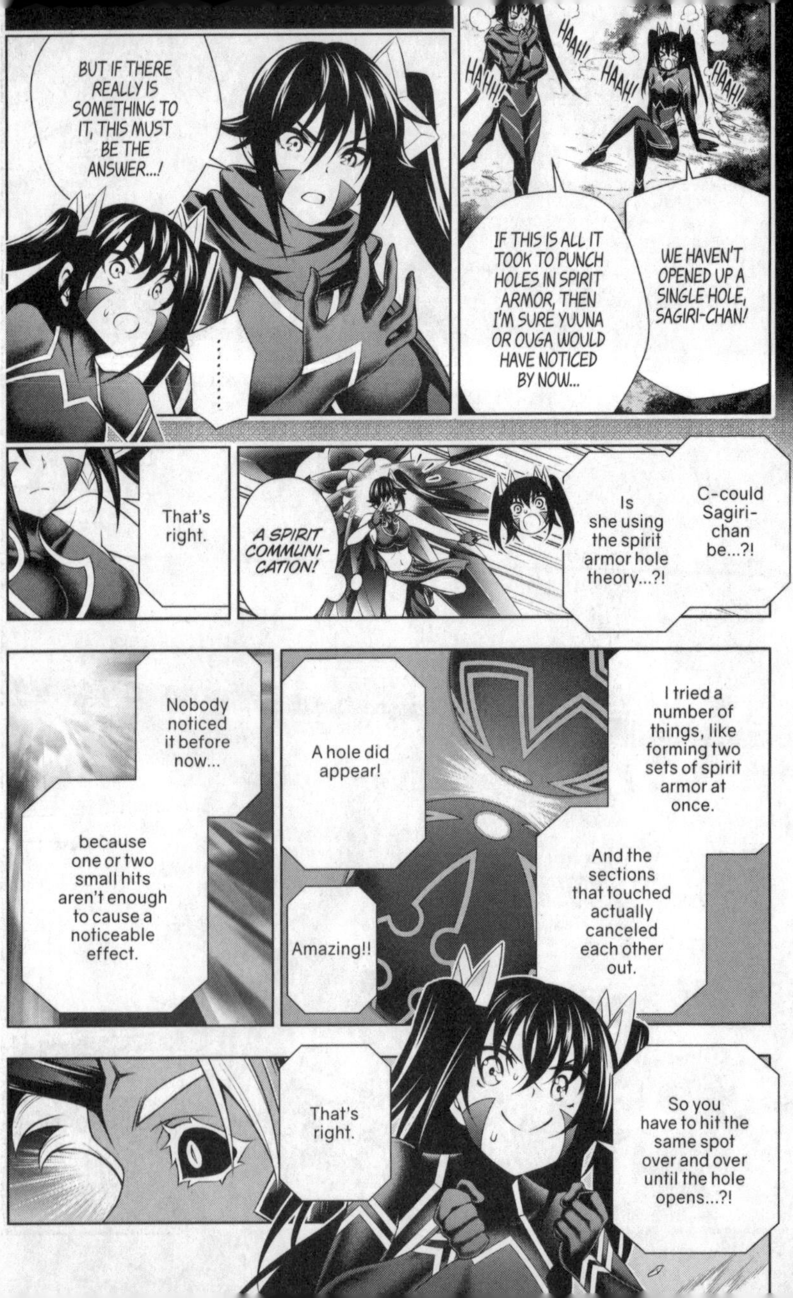
HAAH! HAAH!
HAAH!
HAAH!
WE HAVEN'T OPENED UP A SINGLE HOLE, SAGIRI-CHAN!
IF THIS IS ALL IT TOOK TO PUNCH HOLES IN SPIRIT ARMOR, THEN I'M SURE YUUNA OR OUGA WOULD HAVE NOTICED BY NOW...
BUT IF THERE REALLY IS SOMETHING TO IT, THIS MUST BE THE ANSWER...!
......
C-could Sagiri-chan be...?!
Is she using the spirit armor hole theory...?!
A SPIRIT COMMUNICATION!
That's right.
I tried a number of things, like forming two sets of spirit armor at once.
And the sections that touched actually canceled each other out.
A hole did appear!
Amazing!!
Nobody noticed it before now...
because one or two small hits aren't enough to cause a noticeable effect.
So you have to hit the same spot over and over until the hole opens...?!
That's right.

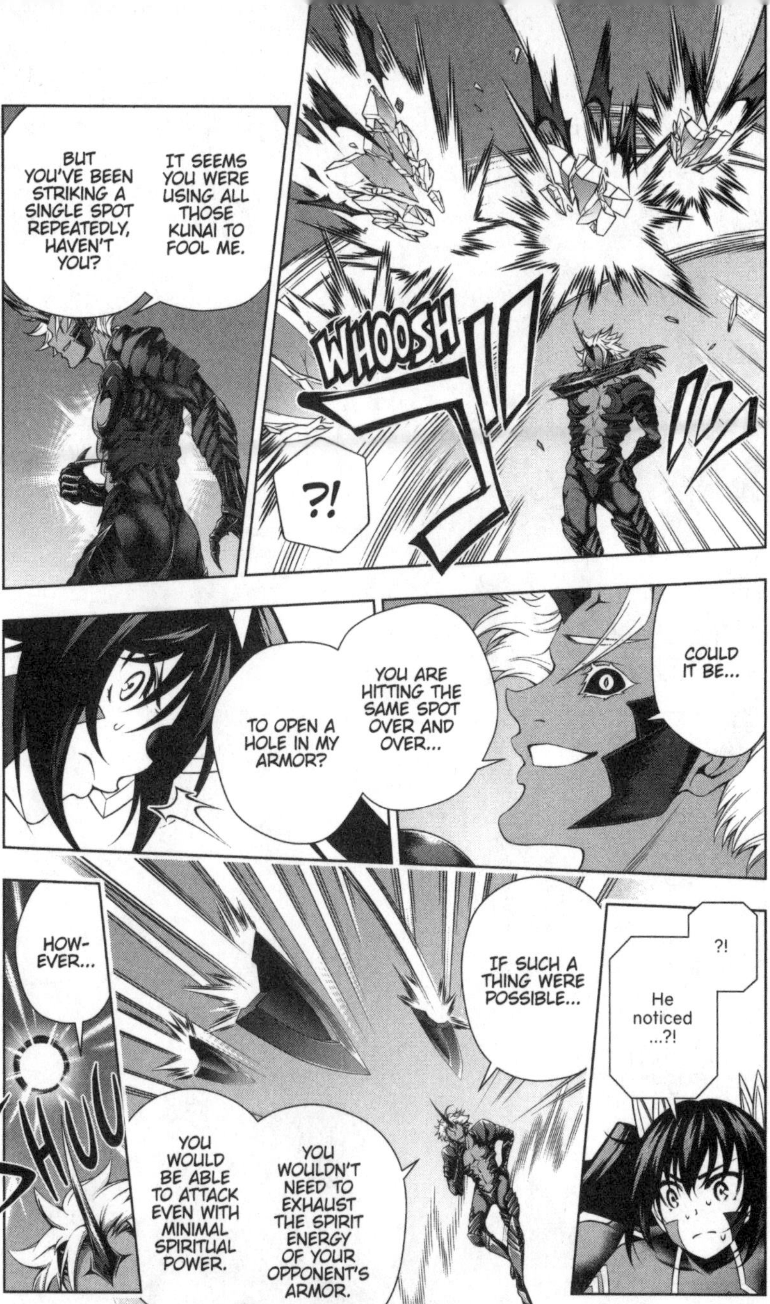
WHOOSH
?!
IT SEEMS YOU WERE USING ALL THOSE KUNAI TO FOOL ME.
BUT YOU'VE BEEN STRIKING A SINGLE SPOT REPEATEDLY, HAVEN'T YOU?
COULD IT BE...
YOU ARE HITTING THE SAME SPOT OVER AND OVER...
TO OPEN A HOLE IN MY ARMOR?
?!
He noticed ...?!
IF SUCH A THING WERE POSSIBLE...
YOU WOULDN'T NEED TO EXHAUST THE SPIRIT ENERGY OF YOUR OPPONENT'S ARMOR.
YOU WOULD BE ABLE TO ATTACK EVEN WITH MINIMAL SPIRITUAL POWER.
HOW-EVER...
SHUU

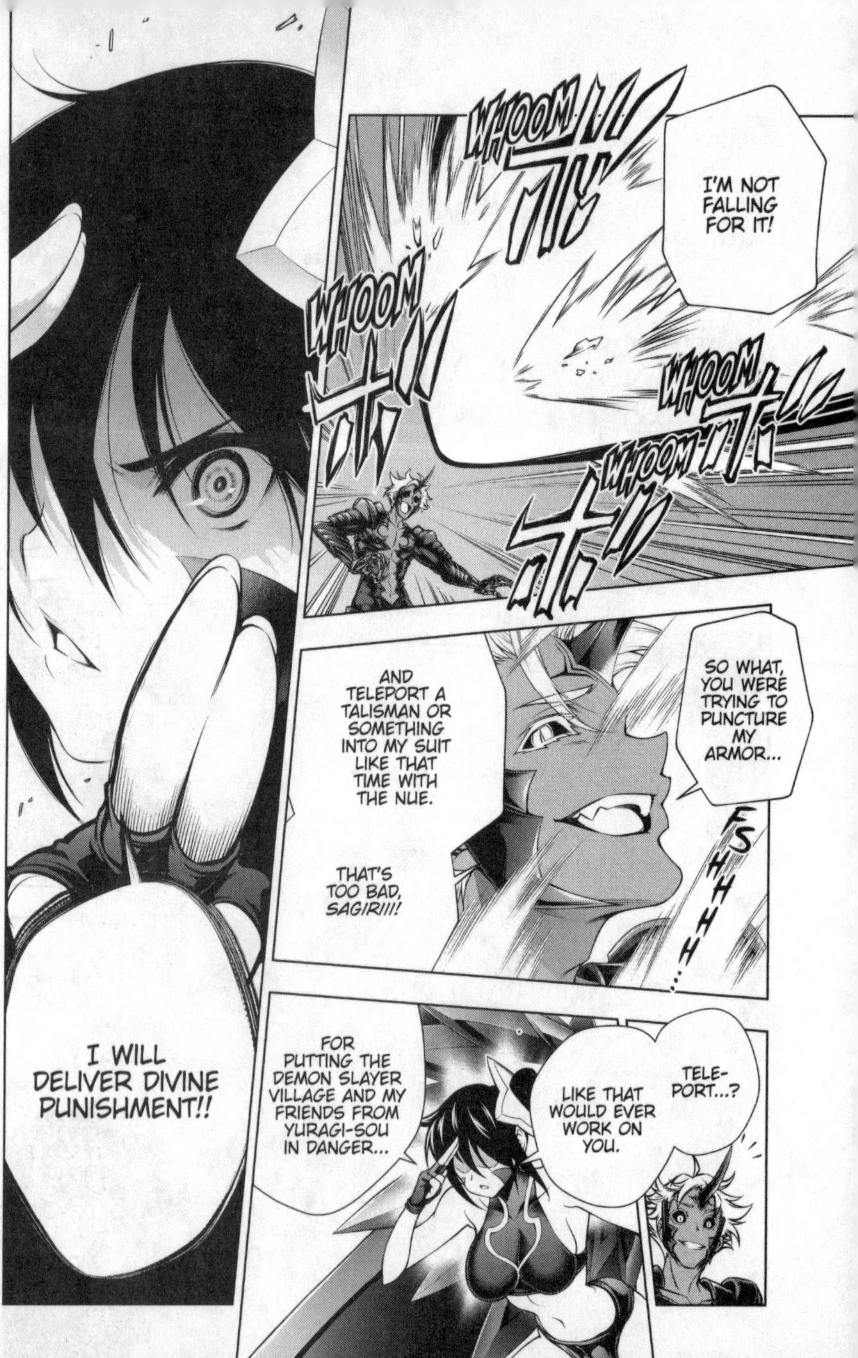
I'M NOT FALLING FOR IT!
WHOOM
WHOOM
WHOOM
WHOOM
SO WHAT, YOU WERE TRYING TO PUNCTURE MY ARMOR...
AND TELEPORT A TALISMAN OR SOMETHING INTO MY SUIT LIKE THAT TIME WITH THE NUE.
THAT'S TOO BAD, SAGIRIII!
FSHHHHH...
TELE-PORT...?
LIKE THAT WOULD EVER WORK ON YOU.
FOR PUTTING THE DEMON SLAYER VILLAGE AND MY FRIENDS FROM YURAGI-SOU IN DANGER...
I WILL DELIVER DIVINE PUNISHMENT!!

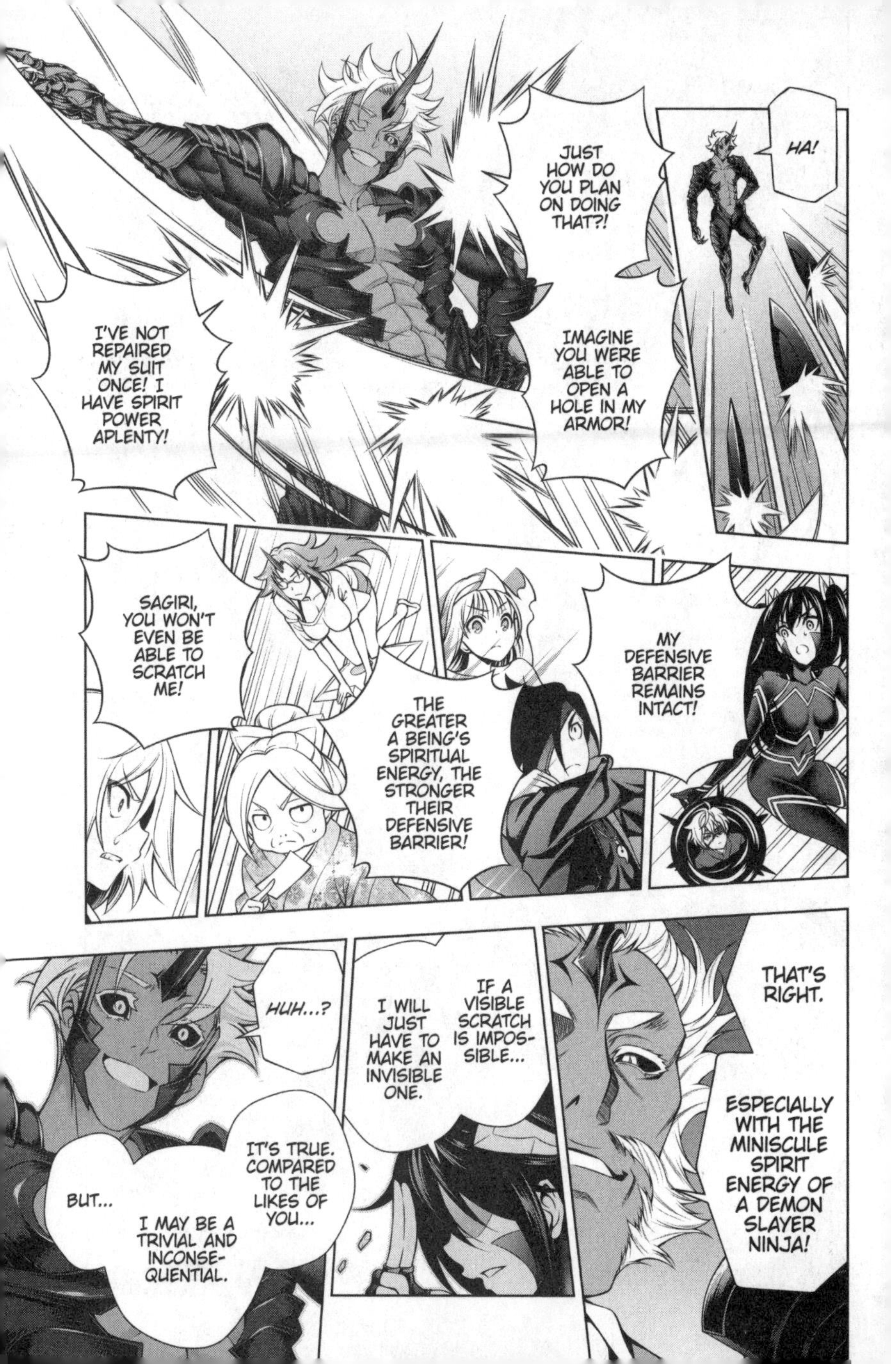
HA!
JUST HOW DO YOU PLAN ON DOING THAT?!
IMAGINE YOU WERE ABLE TO OPEN A HOLE IN MY ARMOR!
I'VE NOT REPAIRED MY SUIT ONCE! I HAVE SPIRIT POWER APLENTY!
MY DEFENSIVE BARRIER REMAINS INTACT!
THE GREATER A BEING'S SPIRITUAL ENERGY, THE STRONGER THEIR DEFENSIVE BARRIER!
SAGIRI, YOU WON'T EVEN BE ABLE TO SCRATCH ME!
THAT'S RIGHT.
ESPECIALLY WITH THE MINISCULE SPIRIT ENERGY OF A DEMON SLAYER NINJA!
IT'S TRUE. COMPARED TO THE LIKES OF YOU...
I MAY BE A TRIVIAL AND INCONSE-QUENTIAL.
BUT...
IF A VISIBLE SCRATCH IS IMPOS-SIBLE...
I WILL JUST HAVE TO MAKE AN INVISIBLE ONE.
HUH...?

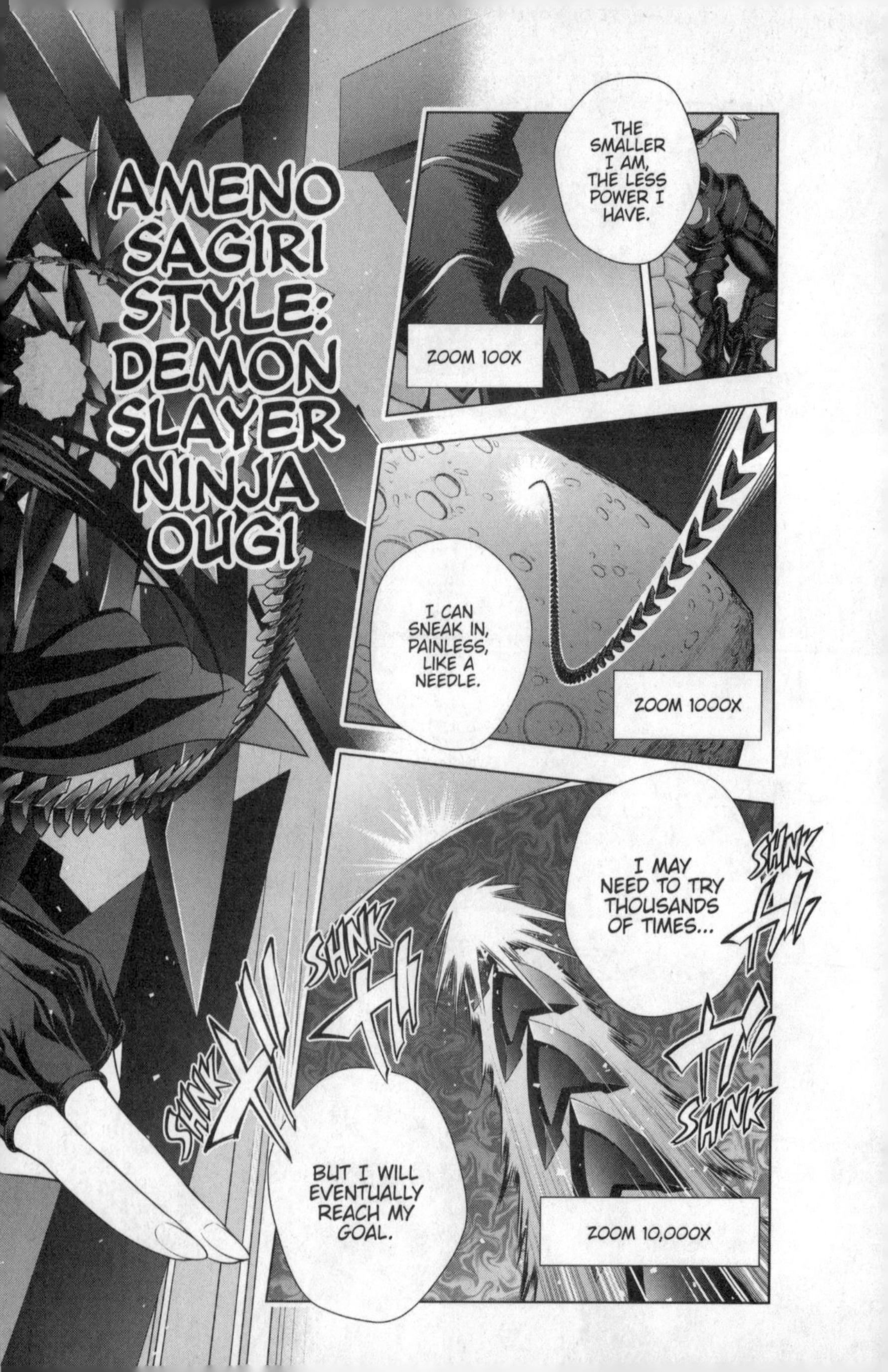
THE SMALLER I AM, THE LESS POWER I HAVE.
ZOOM 100X
I CAN SNEAK IN, PAINLESS, LIKE A NEEDLE.
ZOOM 1000X
I MAY NEED TO TRY THOUSANDS OF TIMES...
SHNK
SHNK
BUT I WILL EVENTUALLY REACH MY GOAL.
ZOOM 10,000X
SHNK
SHNK
AMENO SAGIRI STYLE: DEMON SLAYER NINJA OUGI

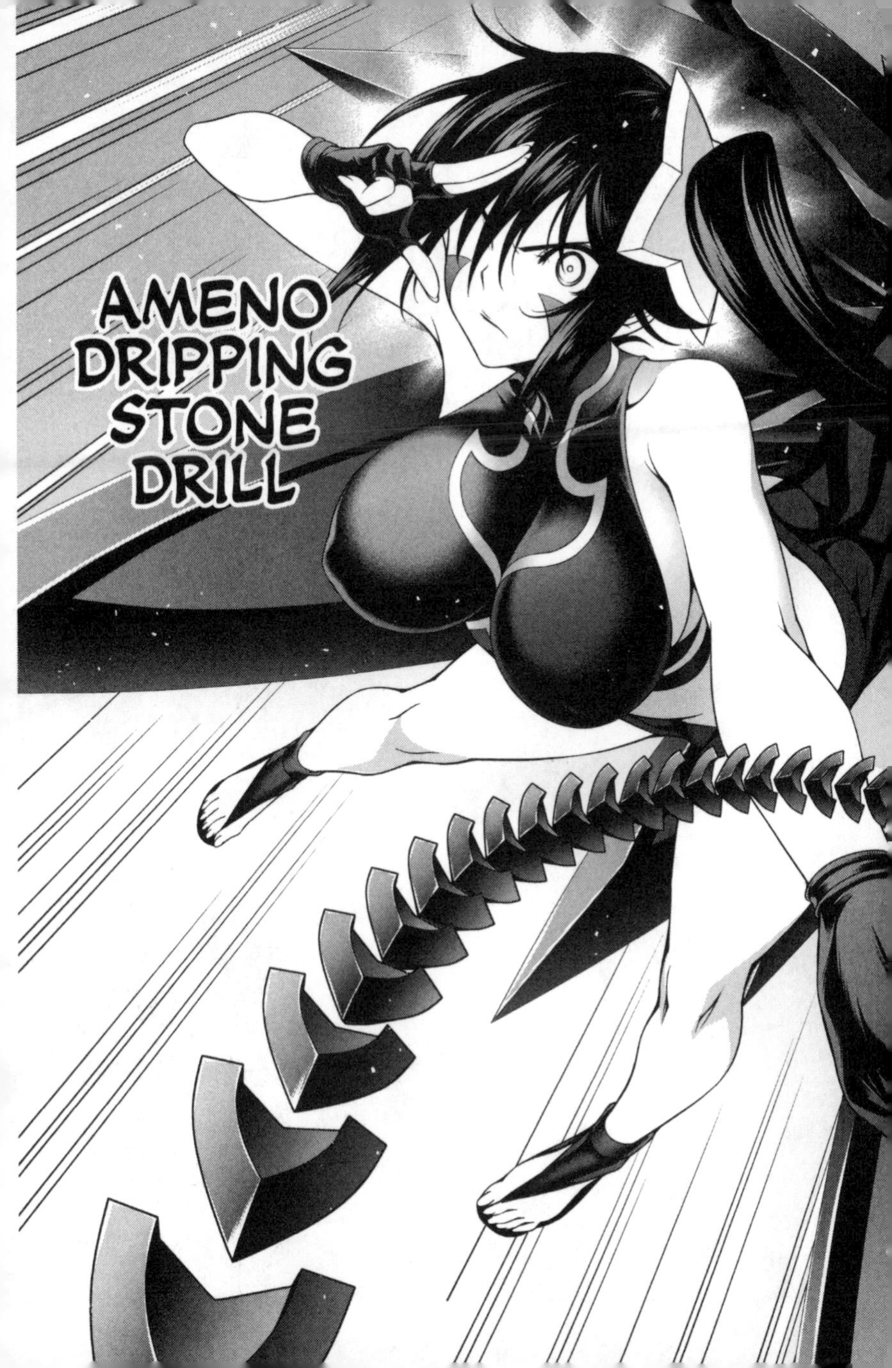
AMENO DRIPPING STONE DRILL

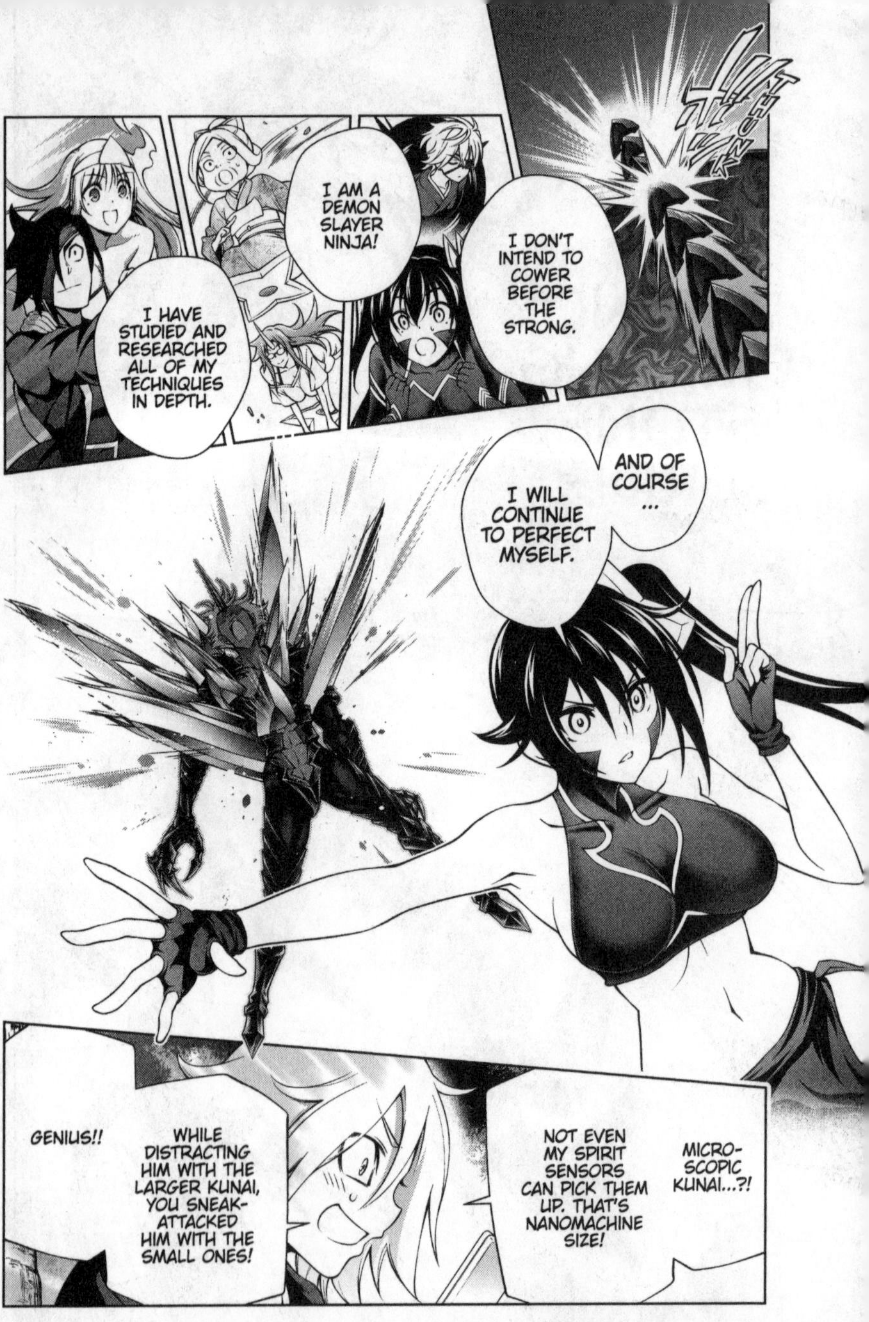
THUNK
I DON'T INTEND TO COWER BEFORE THE STRONG.
I AM A DEMON SLAYER NINJA!
I HAVE STUDIED AND RESEARCHED ALL OF MY TECHNIQUES IN DEPTH.
AND OF COURSE ...
I WILL CONTINUE TO PERFECT MYSELF.
MICRO-SCOPIC KUNAI...?!
NOT EVEN MY SPIRIT SENSORS CAN PICK THEM UP. THAT'S NANOMACHINE SIZE!
WHILE DISTRACTING HIM WITH THE LARGER KUNAI, YOU SNEAK-ATTACKED HIM WITH THE SMALL ONES!
GENIUS!!

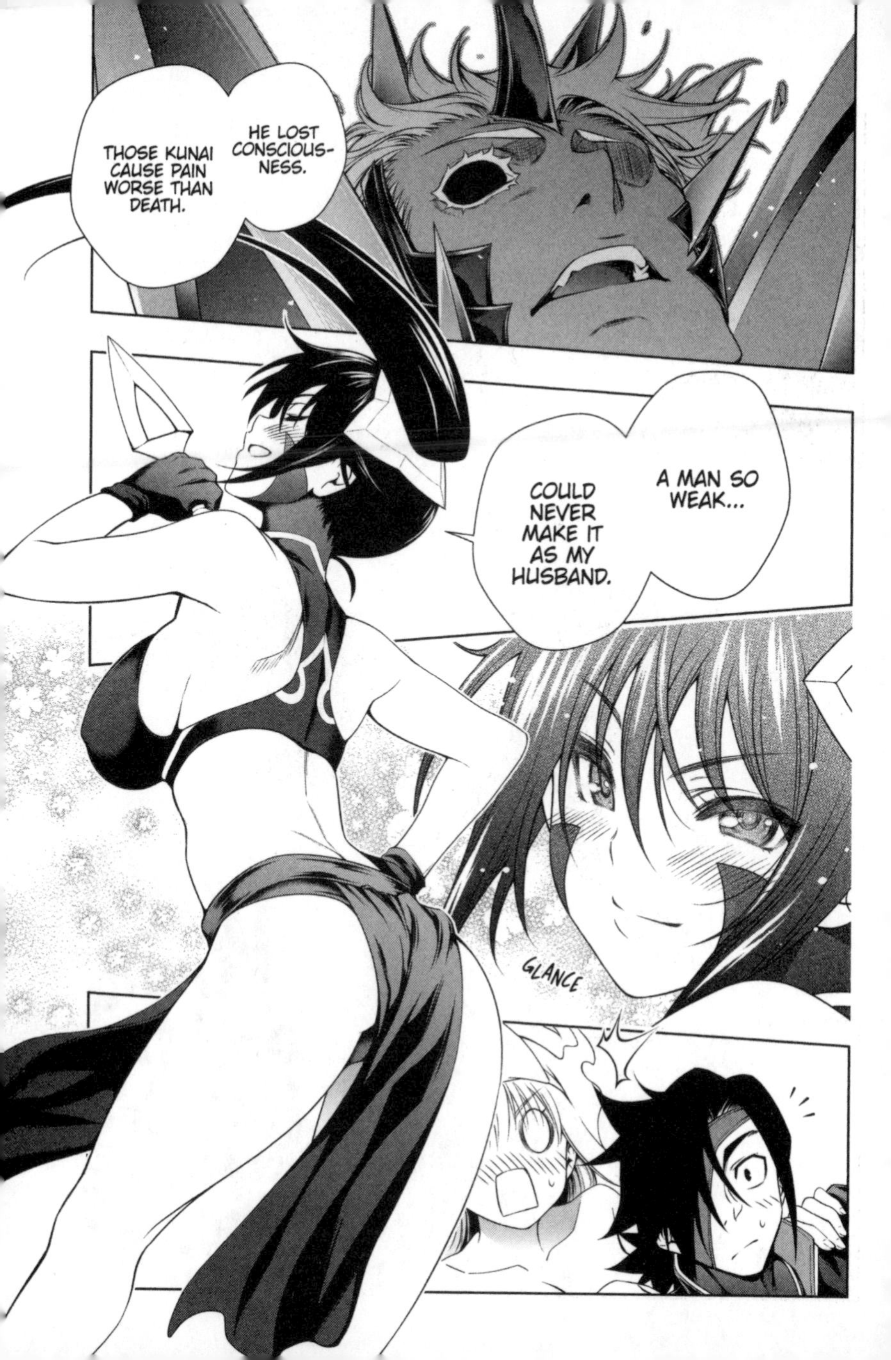
HE LOST CONSCIOUS-NESS.
THOSE KUNAI CAUSE PAIN WORSE THAN DEATH.
A MAN SO WEAK...
COULD NEVER MAKE IT AS MY HUSBAND.
GLANCE

Yuuna
and the
Haunted
Hot
Springs

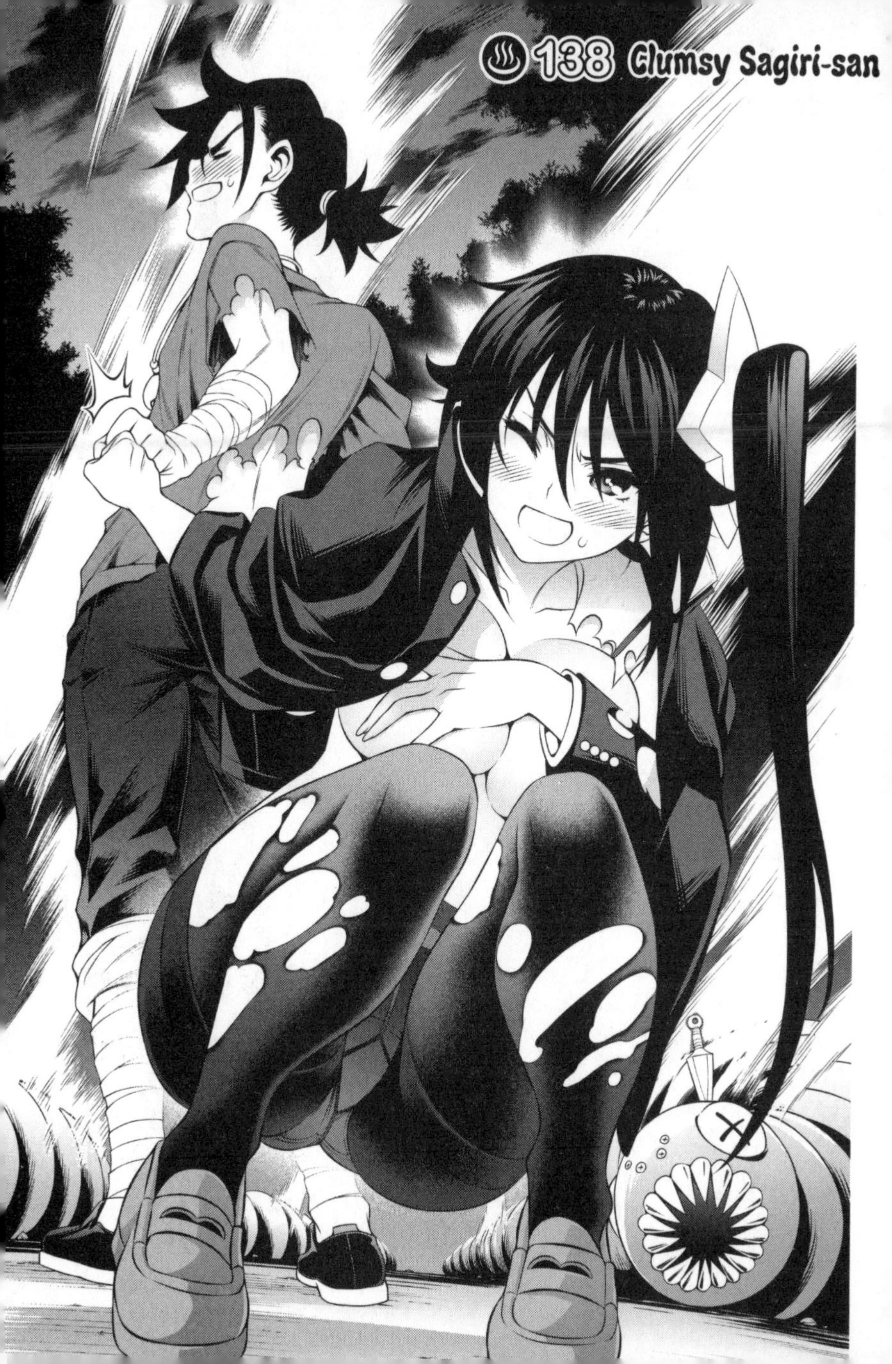
138 Clumsy Sagiri-san

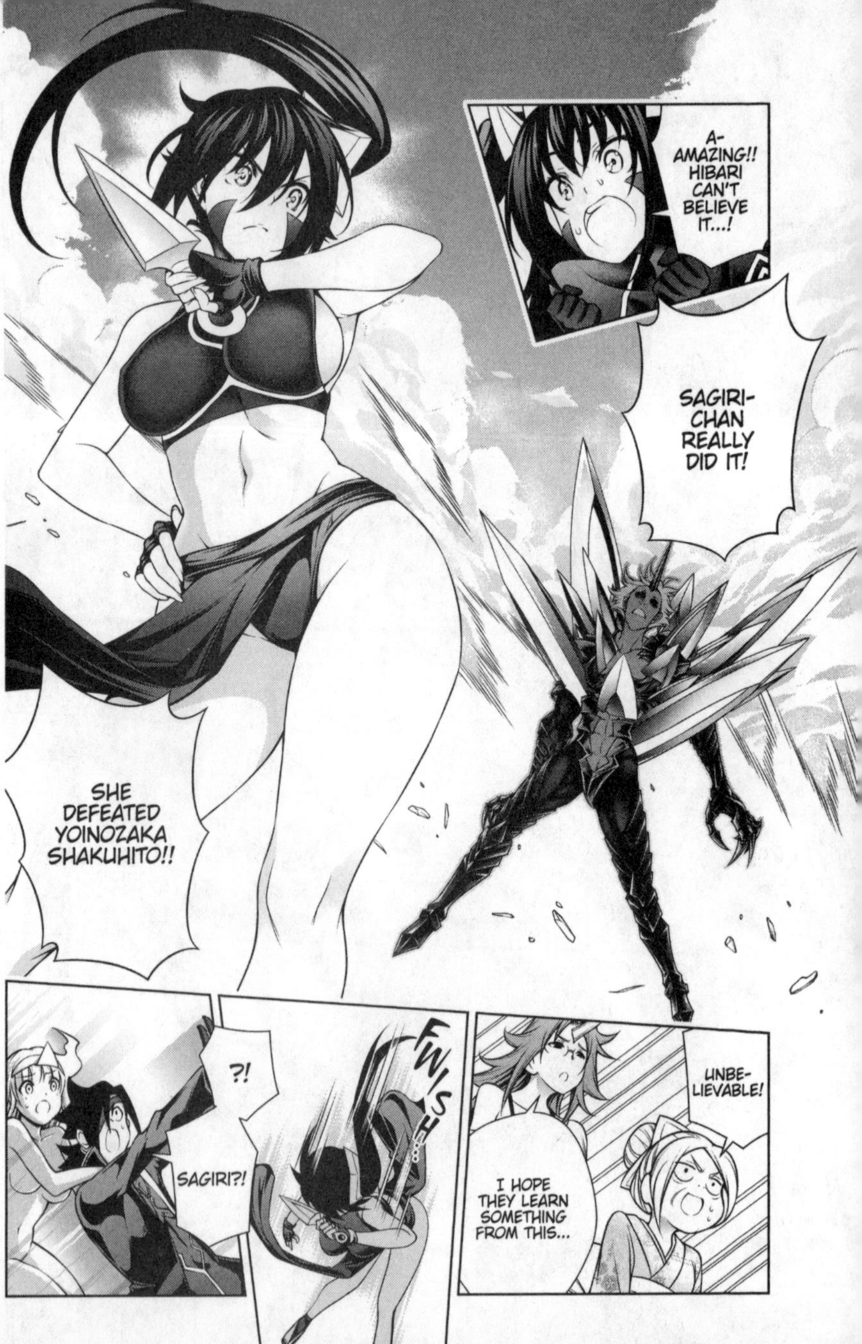
A-AMAZING!! HIBARI CAN'T BELIEVE IT...!
SAGIRI-CHAN REALLY DID IT!
SHE DEFEATED YOINOZAKA SHAKUHITO!!
UNBE-LIEVABLE!
I HOPE THEY LEARN SOMETHING FROM THIS...
FWISH
?!
SAGIRI?!

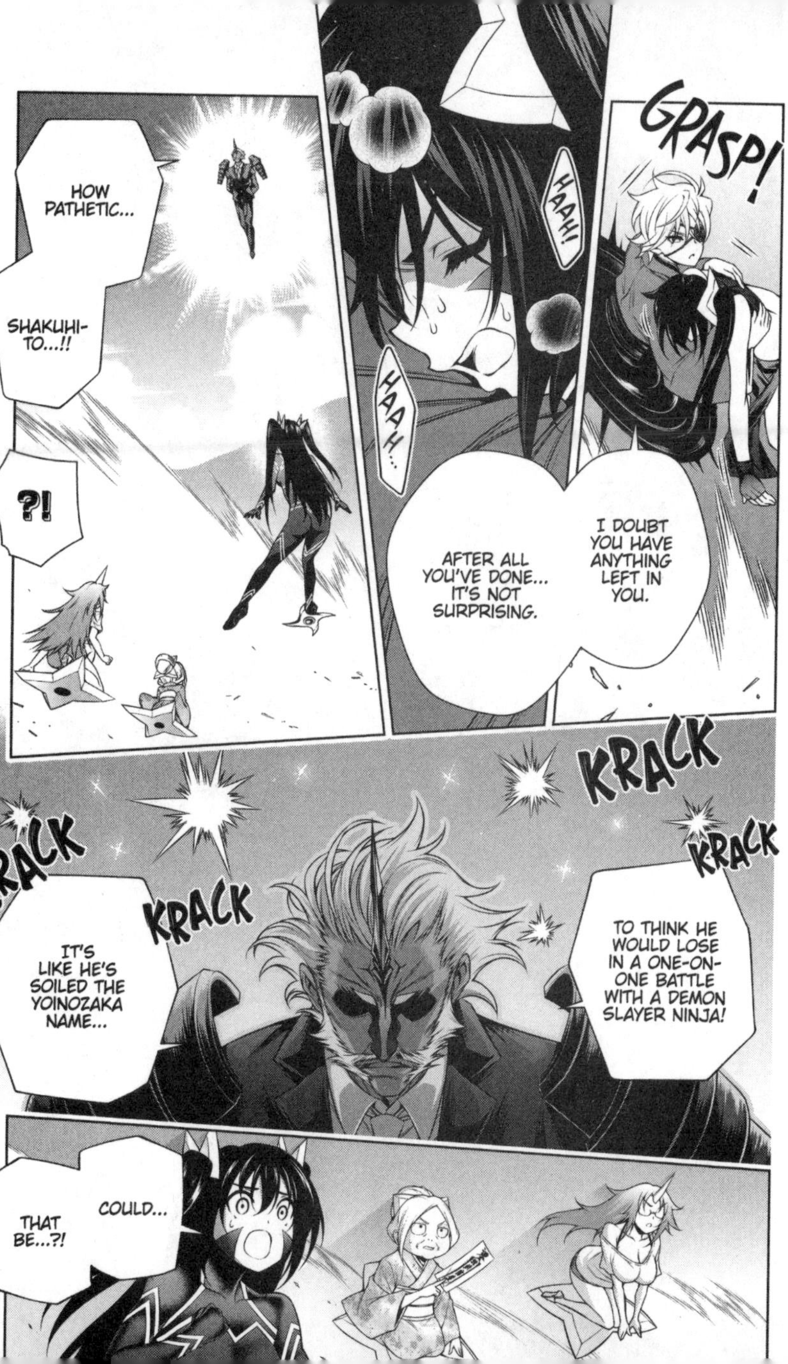
GRASP!
HAAH!
HAAH...
I DOUBT YOU HAVE ANYTHING LEFT IN YOU.
AFTER ALL YOU'VE DONE... IT'S NOT SURPRISING.
HOW PATHETIC...
SHAKUHI-TO...!!
?!
KRACK
KRACK
KRACK
KRACK
TO THINK HE WOULD LOSE IN A ONE-ON-ONE BATTLE WITH A DEMON SLAYER NINJA!
IT'S LIKE HE'S SOILED THE YOINOZAKA NAME...
COULD...
THAT BE...?!

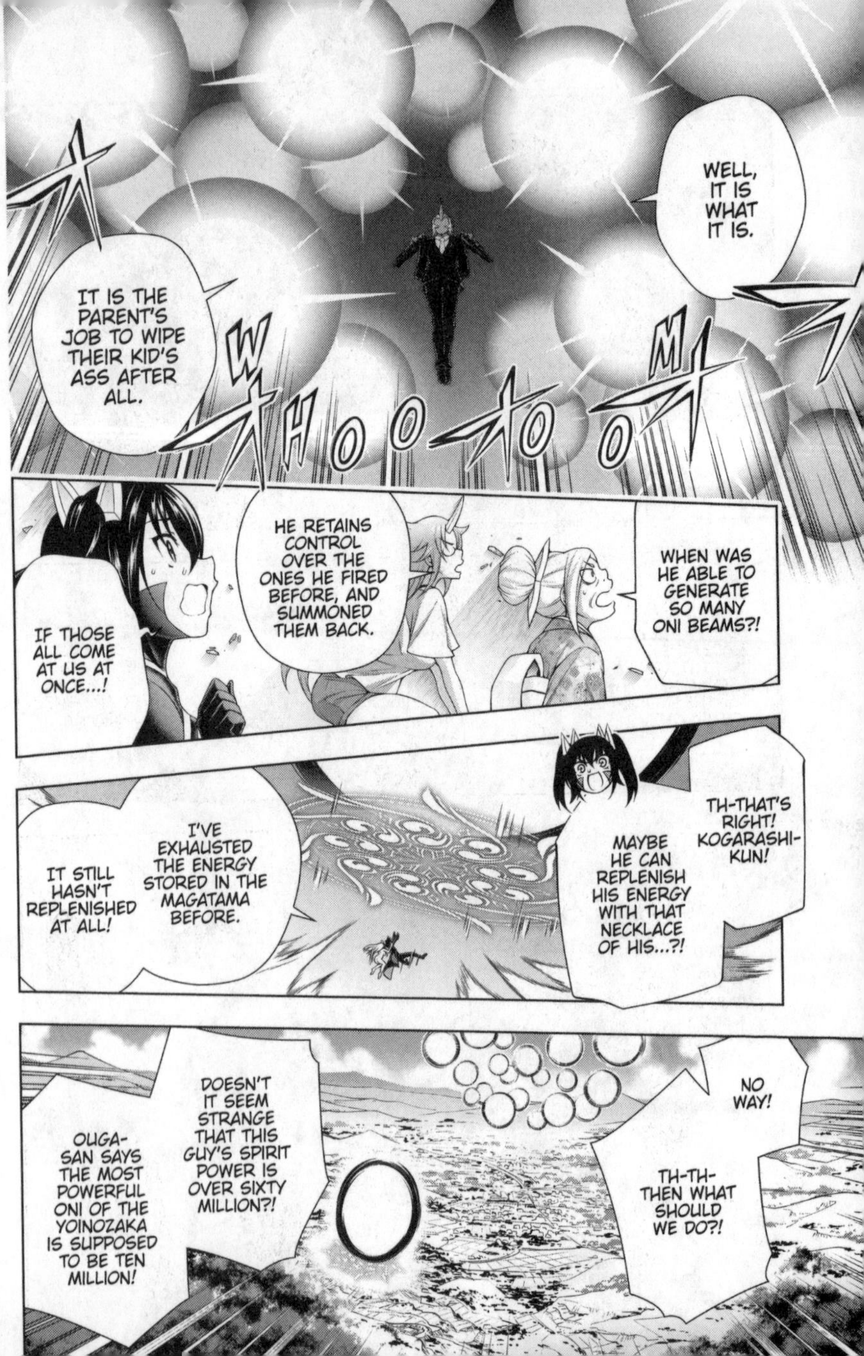
WELL, IT IS WHAT IT IS.
IT IS THE PARENT'S JOB TO WIPE THEIR KID'S ASS AFTER ALL.
WHOOOOM
WHEN WAS HE ABLE TO GENERATE SO MANY ONI BEAMS?!
HE RETAINS CONTROL OVER THE ONES HE FIRED BEFORE, AND SUMMONED THEM BACK.
IF THOSE ALL COME AT US AT ONCE...!
TH-THAT'S RIGHT! KOGARASHI-KUN!
MAYBE HE CAN REPLENISH HIS ENERGY WITH THAT NECKLACE OF HIS...?!
I'VE EXHAUSTED THE ENERGY STORED IN THE MAGATAMA BEFORE.
IT STILL HASN'T REPLENISHED AT ALL!
NO WAY!
TH-TH-THEN WHAT SHOULD WE DO?!
DOESN'T IT SEEM STRANGE THAT THIS GUY'S SPIRIT POWER IS OVER SIXTY MILLION?!
OUGA-SAN SAYS THE MOST POWERFUL ONI OF THE YOINOZAKA IS SUPPOSED TO BE TEN MILLION!

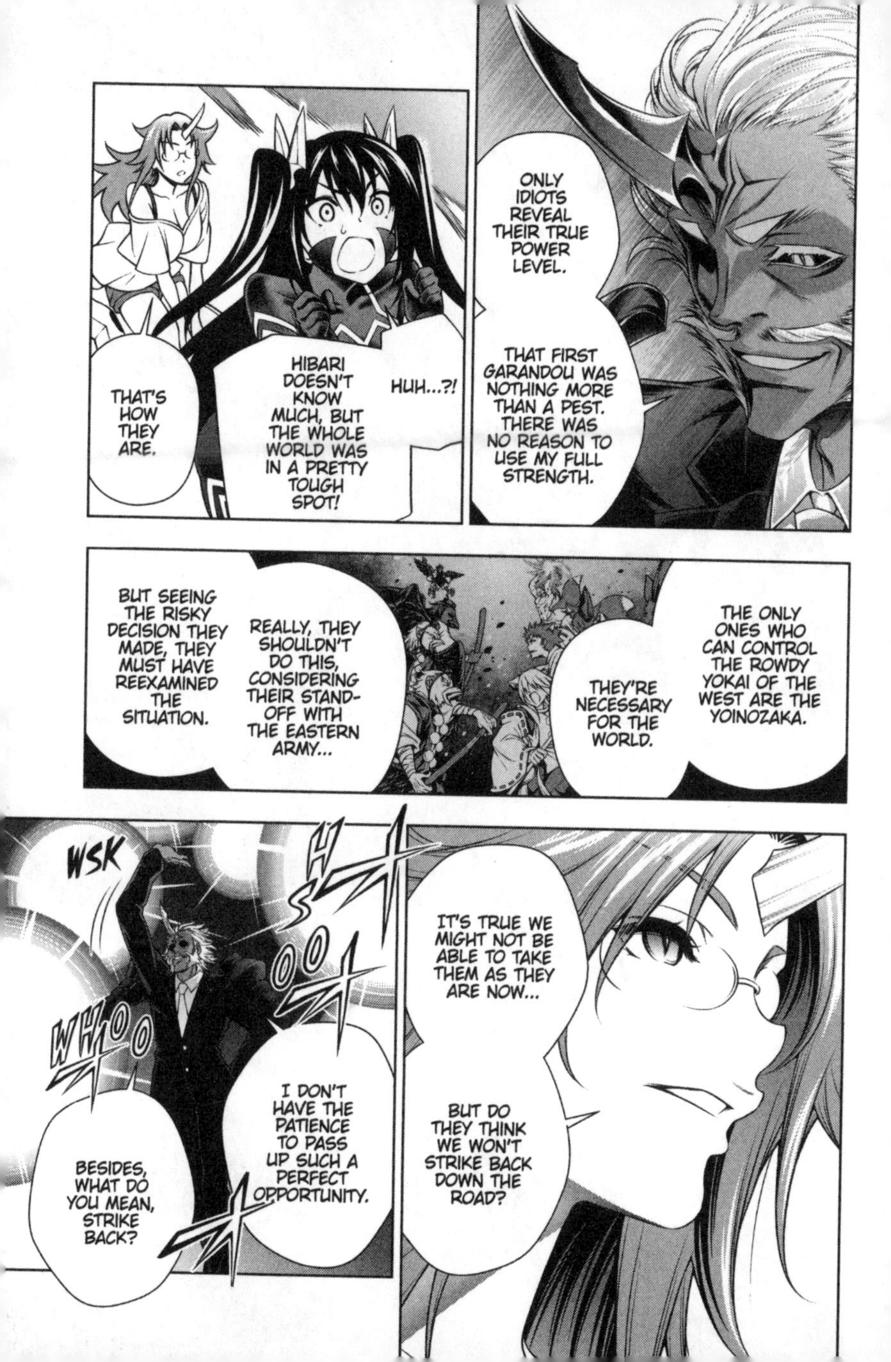
ONLY IDIOTS REVEAL THEIR TRUE POWER LEVEL.
THAT FIRST GARANDOU WAS NOTHING MORE THAN A PEST. THERE WAS NO REASON TO USE MY FULL STRENGTH.
HUH...?!
HIBARI DOESN'T KNOW MUCH, BUT THE WHOLE WORLD WAS IN A PRETTY TOUGH SPOT!
THAT'S HOW THEY ARE.
THE ONLY ONES WHO CAN CONTROL THE ROWDY YOKAI OF THE WEST ARE THE YOINOZAKA.
THEY'RE NECESSARY FOR THE WORLD.
REALLY, THEY SHOULDN'T DO THIS, CONSIDERING THEIR STAND-OFF WITH THE EASTERN ARMY...
BUT SEEING THE RISKY DECISION THEY MADE, THEY MUST HAVE REEXAMINED THE SITUATION.
IT'S TRUE WE MIGHT NOT BE ABLE TO TAKE THEM AS THEY ARE NOW...
BUT DO THEY THINK WE WON'T STRIKE BACK DOWN THE ROAD?
WSK
WHOO
I DON'T HAVE THE PATIENCE TO PASS UP SUCH A PERFECT OPPORTUNITY.
BESIDES, WHAT DO YOU MEAN, STRIKE BACK?

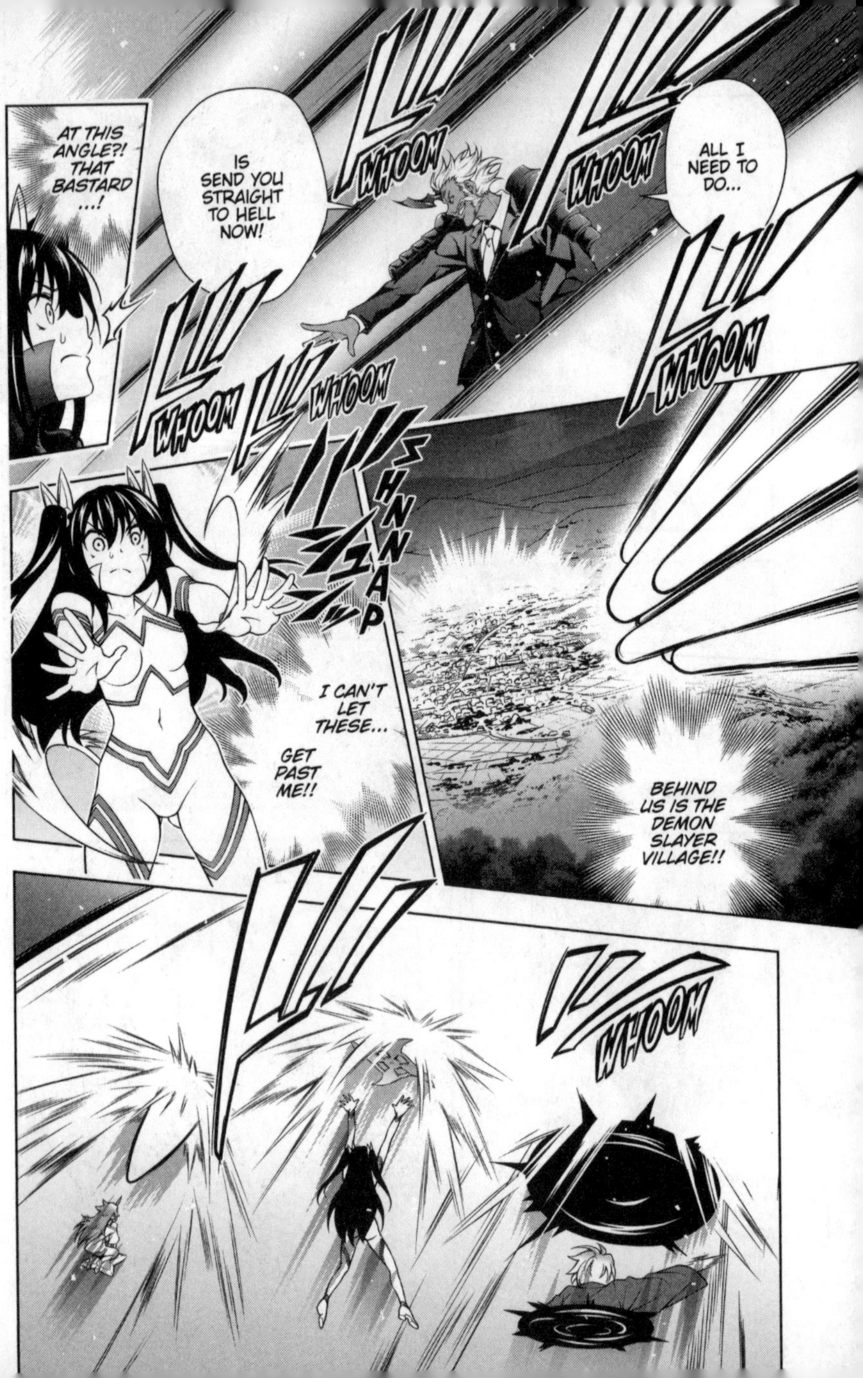

WHOOM
WHOOM
ALL I NEED TO DO...
IS SEND YOU STRAIGHT TO HELL NOW!
WHOOM
WHOOM
WHOOM
AT THIS ANGLE?! THAT BASTARD ...!
BEHIND US IS THE DEMON SLAYER VILLAGE!!
SHNNNAP
I CAN'T LET THESE...
GET PAST ME!!
WHOOM

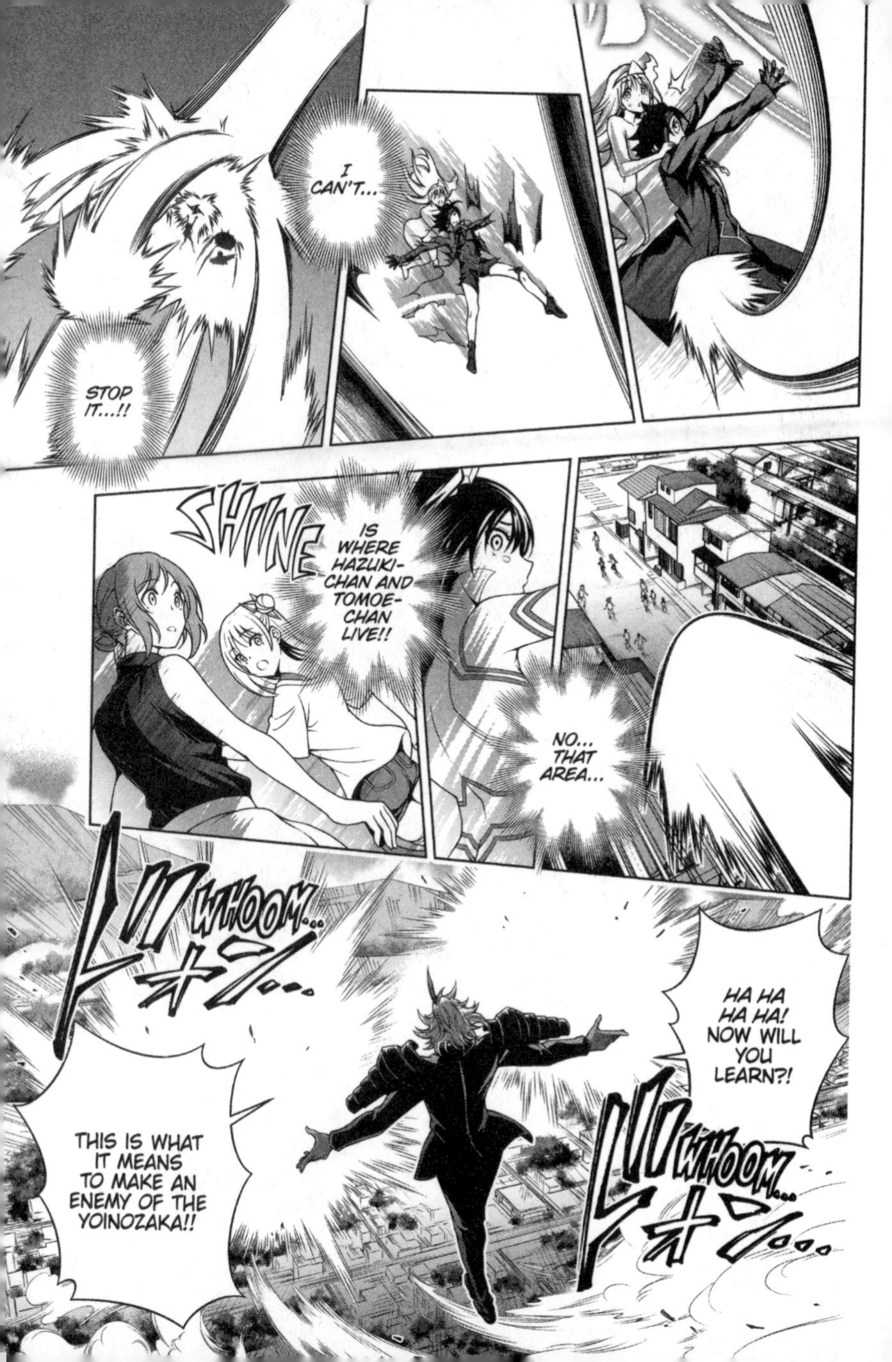
I CAN'T...
STOP IT...!!
NO... THAT AREA...
SHIIINE
IS WHERE HAZUKI-CHAN AND TOMOE-CHAN LIVE!!
WHOOM...
HA HA HA HA! NOW WILL YOU LEARN?!
THIS IS WHAT IT MEANS TO MAKE AN ENEMY OF THE YOINOZAKA!!
WHOOM...

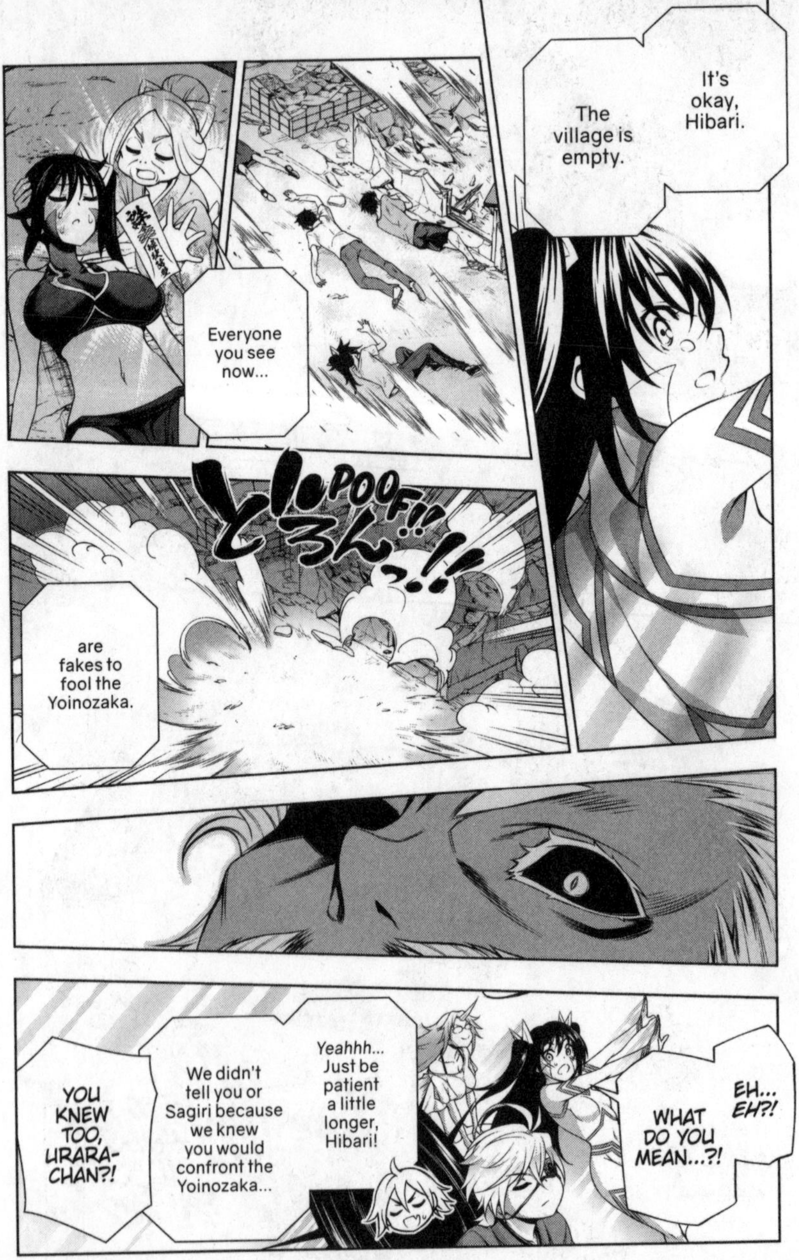
It's okay, Hibari.
The village is empty.
Everyone you see now...
POOF!!
are fakes to fool the Yoinozaka.
EH... EH?!
WHAT DO YOU MEAN...?!
Yeahhh... Just be patient a little longer, Hibari!
We didn't tell you or Sagiri because we knew you would confront the Yoinozaka...
YOU KNEW TOO, URARA-CHAN?!

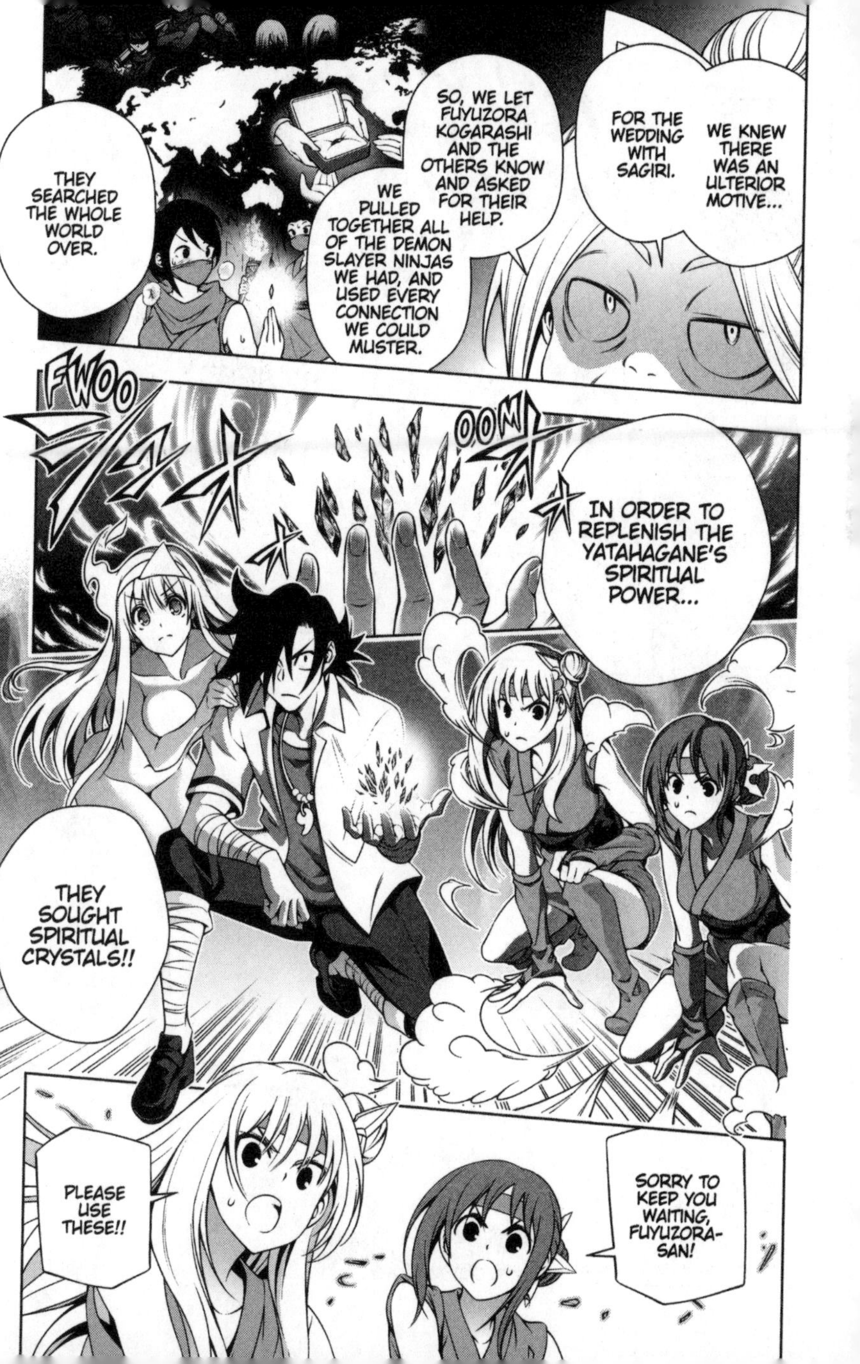
WE KNEW THERE WAS AN ULTERIOR MOTIVE...
FOR THE WEDDING WITH SAGIRI.
SO, WE LET FUYUZORA KOGARASHI AND THE OTHERS KNOW AND ASKED FOR THEIR HELP.
WE PULLED TOGETHER ALL OF THE DEMON SLAYER NINJAS WE HAD, AND USED EVERY CONNECTION WE COULD MUSTER.
THEY SEARCHED THE WHOLE WORLD OVER.
FWOO
OOM
IN ORDER TO REPLENISH THE YATAHAGANE'S SPIRITUAL POWER...
THEY SOUGHT SPIRITUAL CRYSTALS!!
SORRY TO KEEP YOU WAITING, FUYUZORA-SAN!
PLEASE USE THESE!!

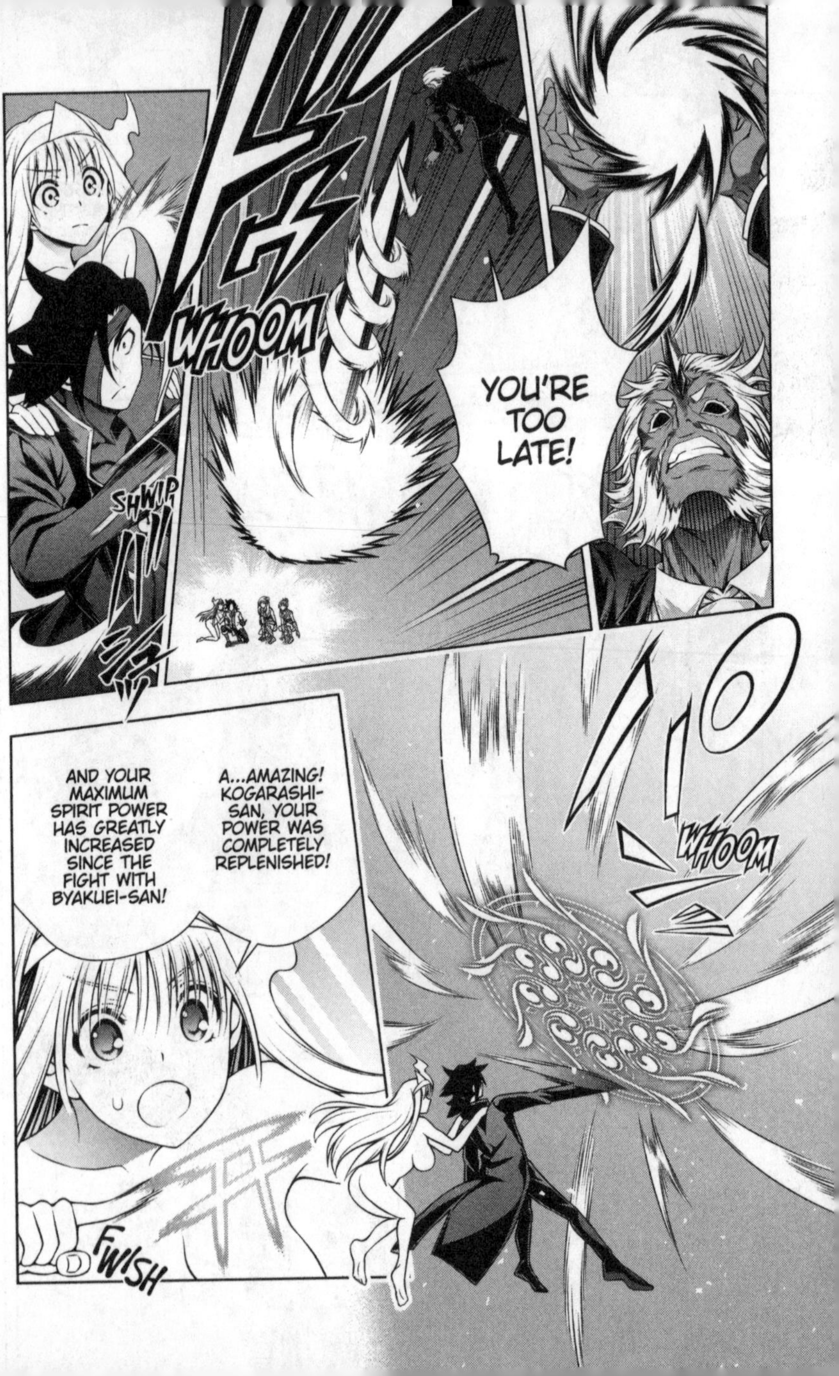
YOU'RE TOO LATE!
WHOOM
SHWIP
WHOOM
A...AMAZING! KOGARASHI-SAN, YOUR POWER WAS COMPLETELY REPLENISHED!
AND YOUR MAXIMUM SPIRIT POWER HAS GREATLY INCREASED SINCE THE FIGHT WITH BYAKUEI-SAN!
FWISH

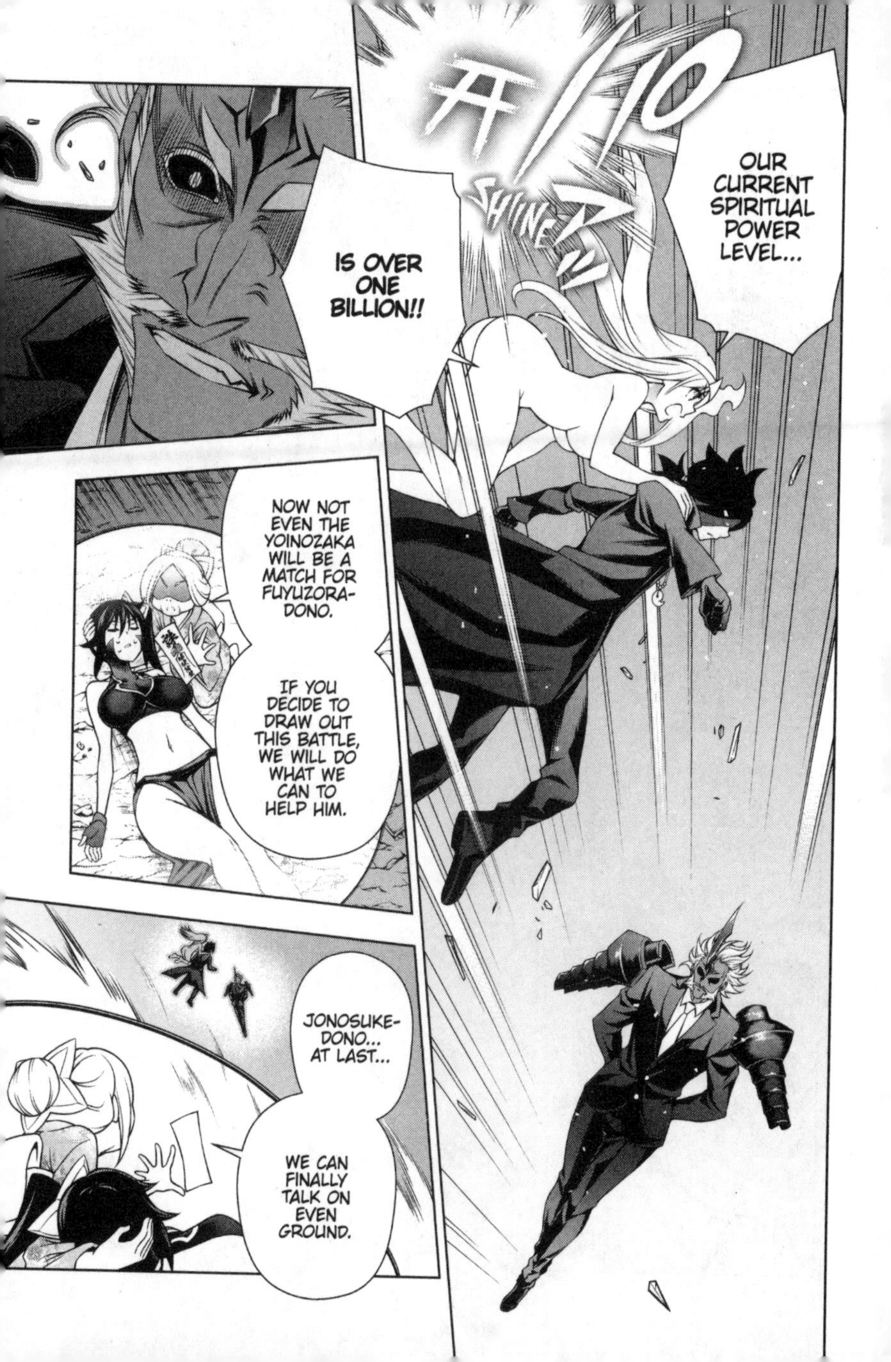
OUR CURRENT SPIRITUAL POWER LEVEL...
SHINE
IS OVER ONE BILLION!!
NOW NOT EVEN THE YOINOZAKA WILL BE A MATCH FOR FUYUZORA-DONO.
IF YOU DECIDE TO DRAW OUT THIS BATTLE, WE WILL DO WHAT WE CAN TO HELP HIM.
JONOSUKE-DONO... AT LAST...
WE CAN FINALLY TALK ON EVEN GROUND.

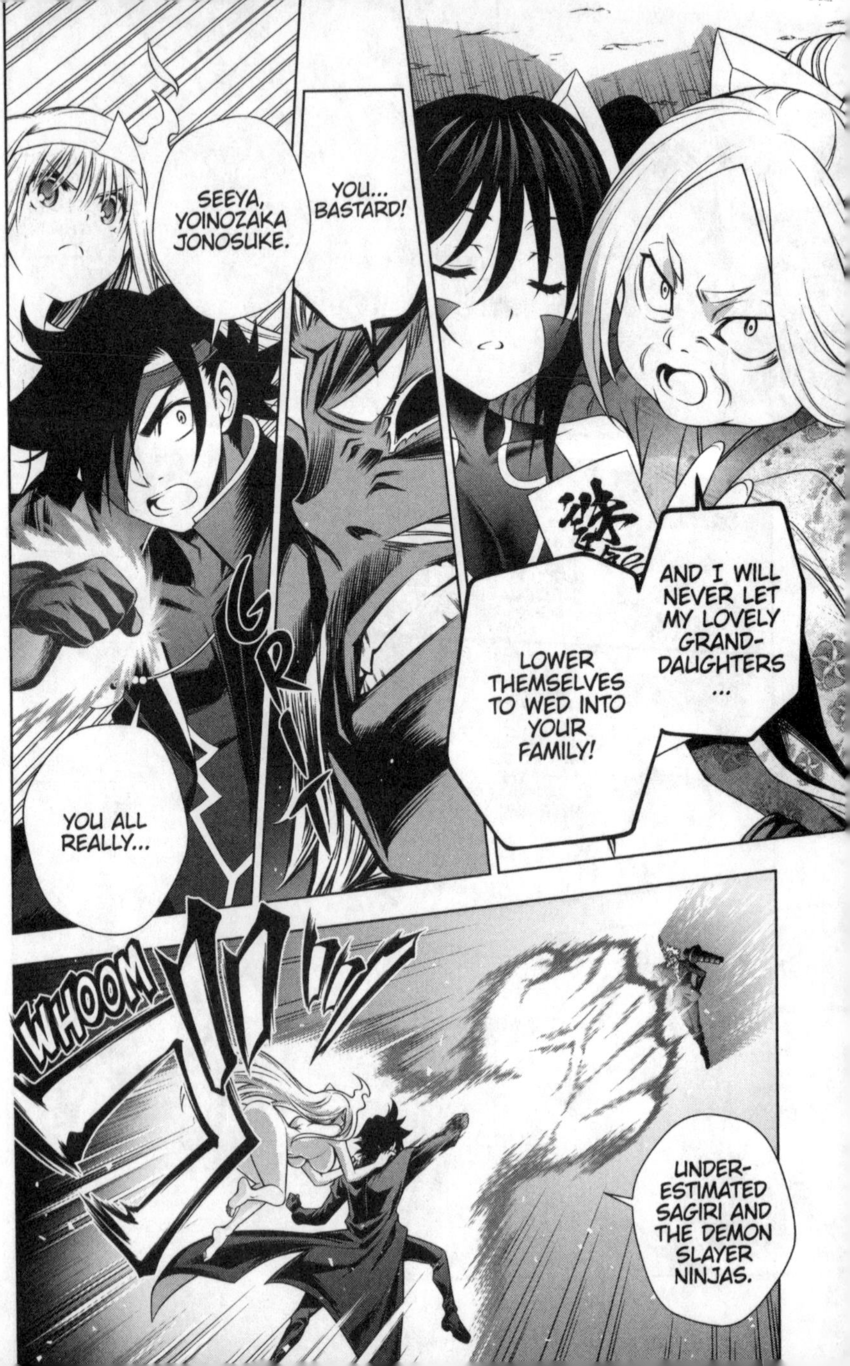
AND I WILL NEVER LET MY LOVELY GRAND-DAUGHTERS ...
LOWER THEMSELVES TO WED INTO YOUR FAMILY!
YOU... BASTARD!
SEEYA, YOINOZAKA JONOSUKE.
YOU ALL REALLY...
UNDER-ESTIMATED SAGIRI AND THE DEMON SLAYER NINJAS.
WHOOM

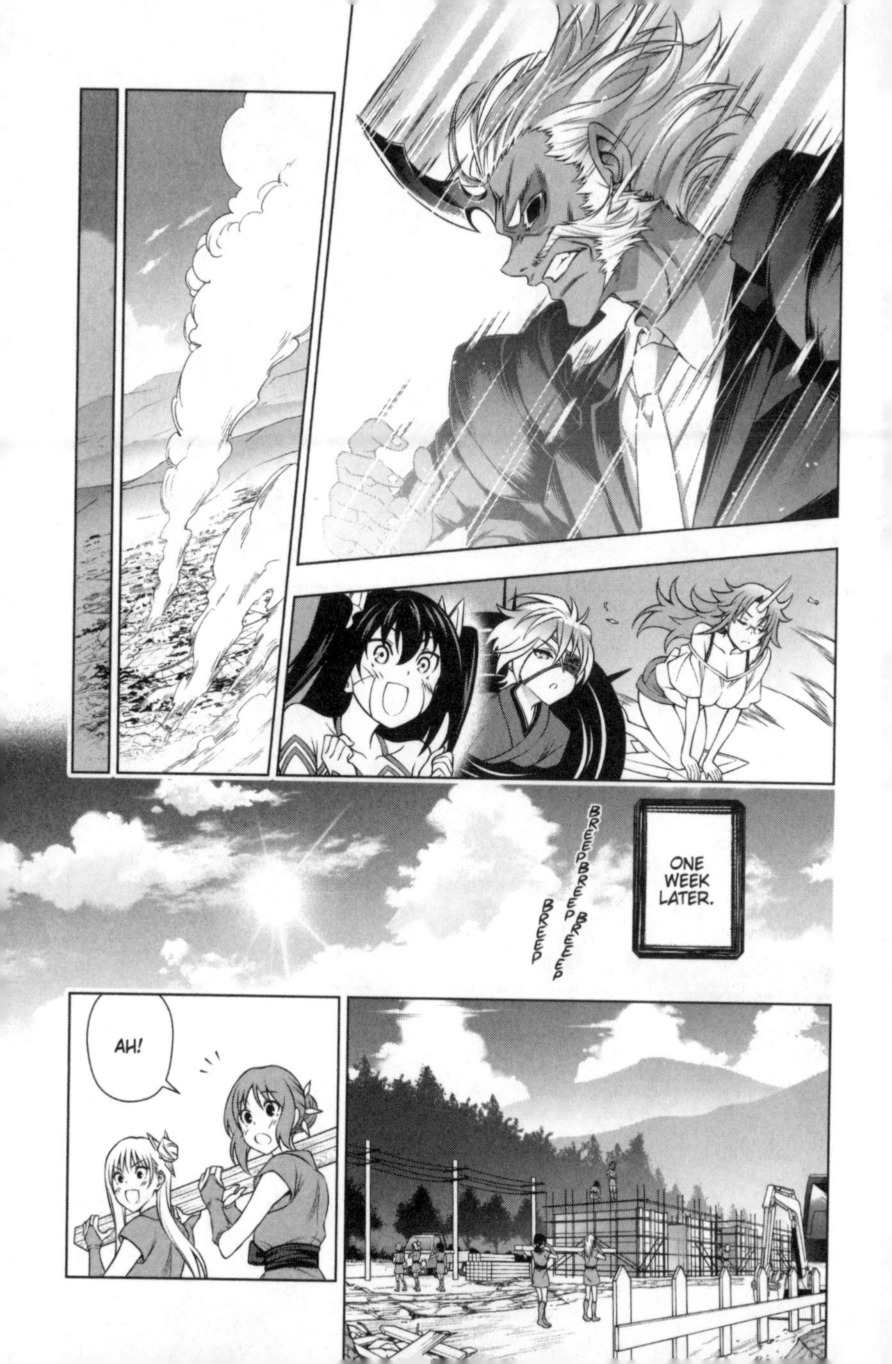
ONE WEEK LATER.
BREEP BREEP BREEP BREEEP BREEP
AH!

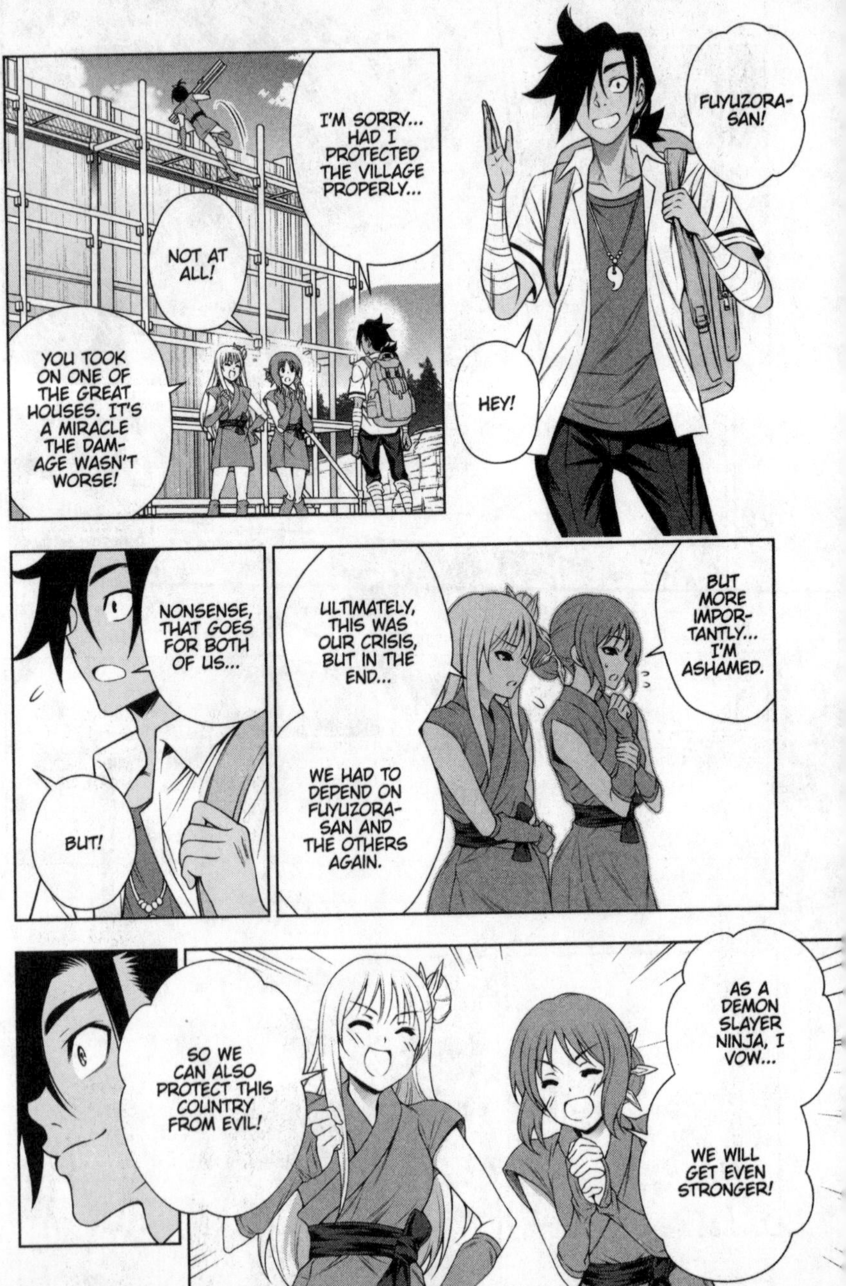
FUYUZORA-SAN!
HEY!
I'M SORRY... HAD I PROTECTED THE VILLAGE PROPERLY...
NOT AT ALL!
YOU TOOK ON ONE OF THE GREAT HOUSES. IT'S A MIRACLE THE DAMAGE WASN'T WORSE!
BUT MORE IMPORTANTLY... I'M ASHAMED.
ULTIMATELY, THIS WAS OUR CRISIS, BUT IN THE END...
WE HAD TO DEPEND ON FUYUZORA-SAN AND THE OTHERS AGAIN.
NONSENSE, THAT GOES FOR BOTH OF US...
BUT!
AS A DEMON SLAYER NINJA, I VOW...
WE WILL GET EVEN STRONGER!
SO WE CAN ALSO PROTECT THIS COUNTRY FROM EVIL!

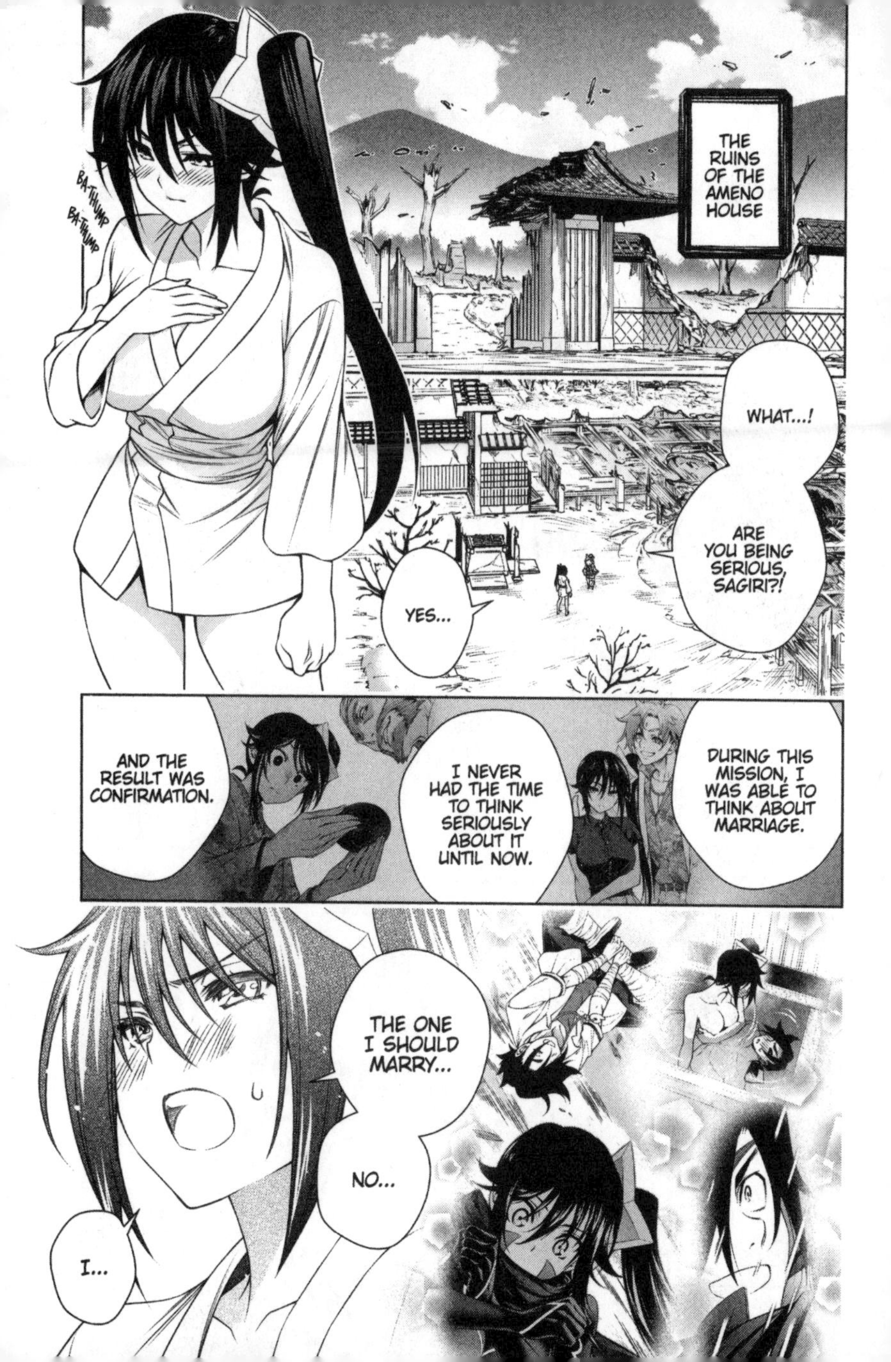
THE RUINS OF THE AMENO HOUSE
WHAT...! ARE YOU BEING SERIOUS, SAGIRI?!
YES...
BA-THUMP BA-THUMP
DURING THIS MISSION, I WAS ABLE TO THINK ABOUT MARRIAGE.
I NEVER HAD THE TIME TO THINK SERIOUSLY ABOUT IT UNTIL NOW.
AND THE RESULT WAS CONFIRMATION.
THE ONE I SHOULD MARRY... NO...
I...

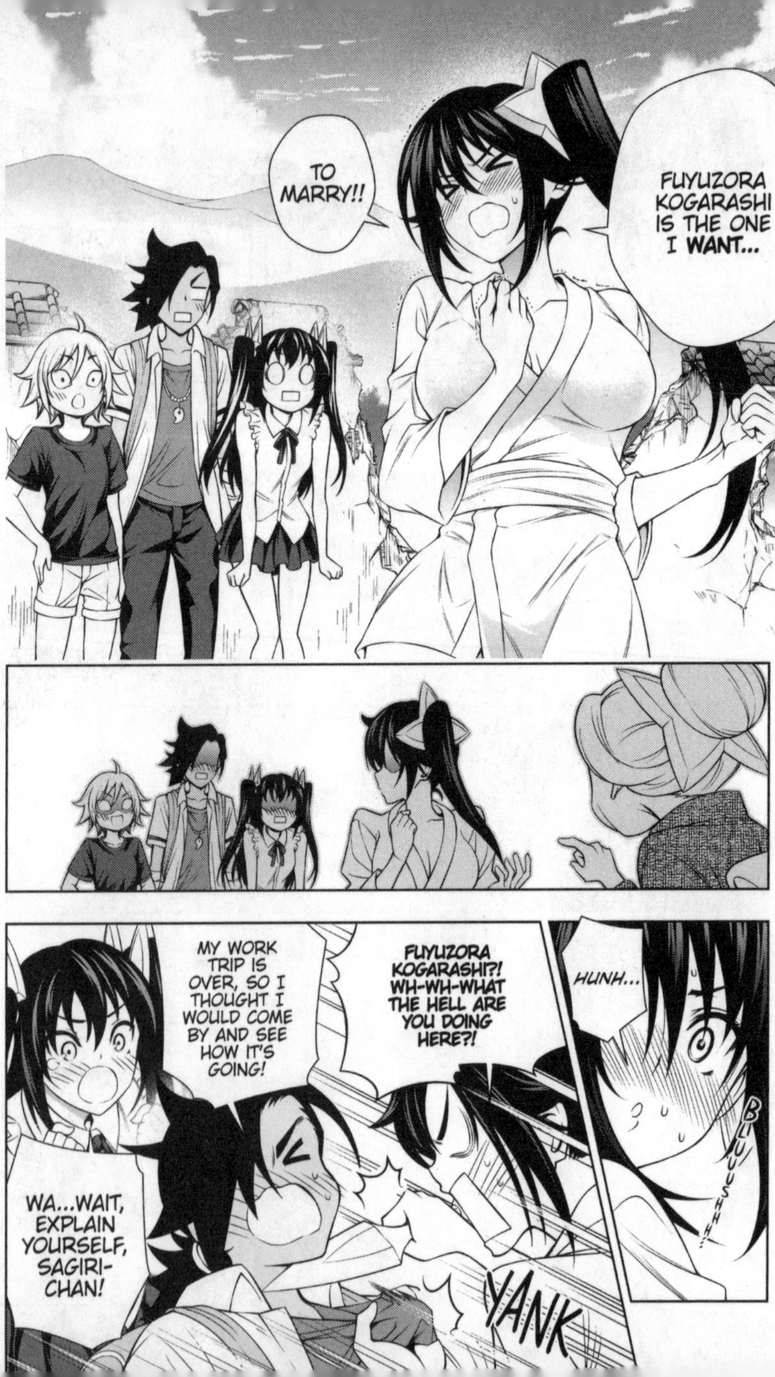
FUYUZORA KOGARASHI IS THE ONE I WANT...
TO MARRY!!
HUNH...
FUYUZORA KOGARASHI?! WH-WH-WHAT THE HELL ARE YOU DOING HERE?!
MY WORK TRIP IS OVER, SO I THOUGHT I WOULD COME BY AND SEE HOW IT'S GOING!
YANK
WA...WAIT, EXPLAIN YOURSELF, SAGIRI-CHAN!

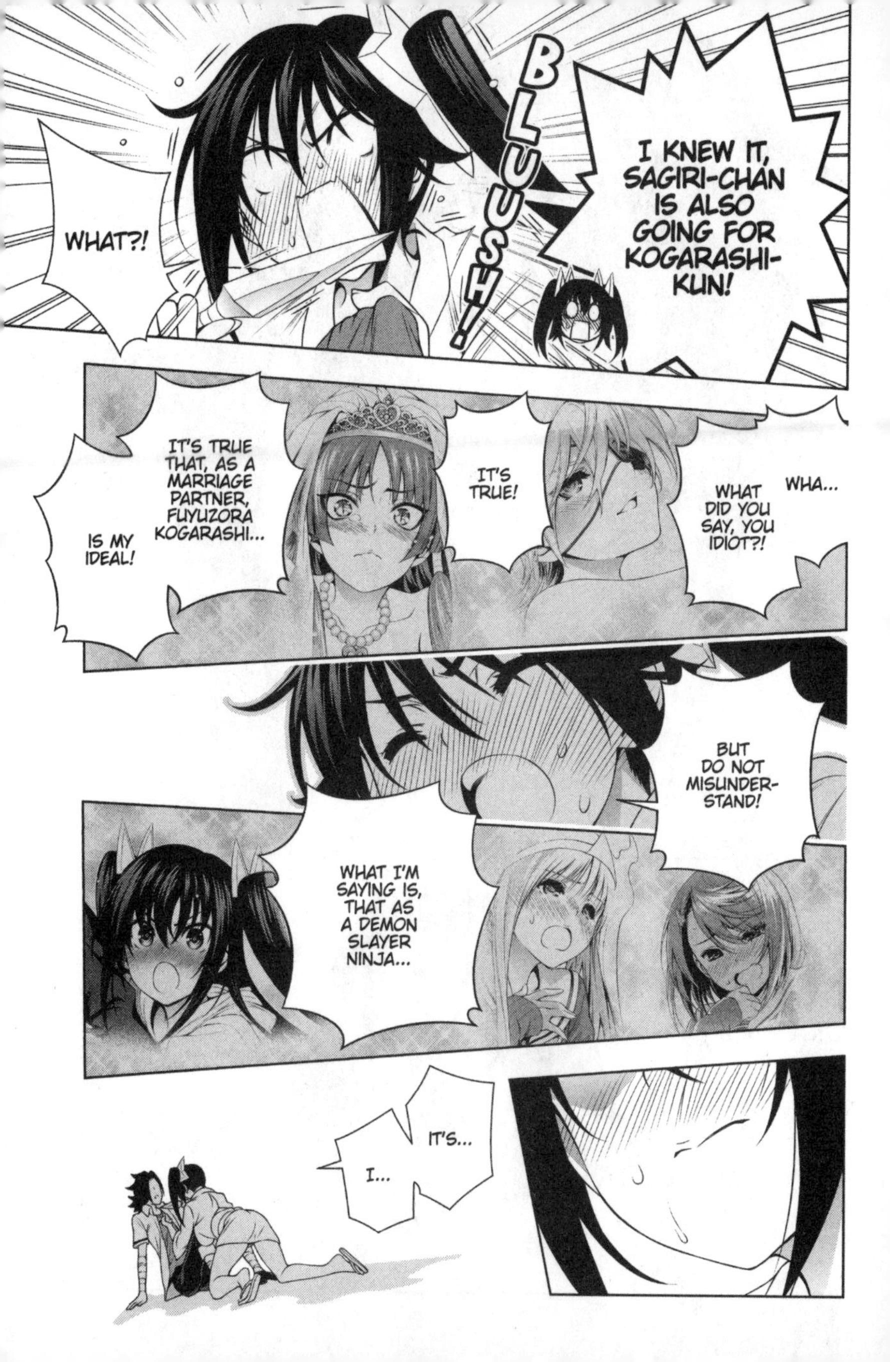
I KNEW IT, SAGIRI-CHAN IS ALSO GOING FOR KOGARASHI-KUN!
BLUUUSH!
WHAT?!
WHA...
WHAT DID YOU SAY, YOU IDIOT?!
IT'S TRUE!
IT'S TRUE THAT, AS A MARRIAGE PARTNER, FUYUZORA KOGARASHI...
IS MY IDEAL!
BUT DO NOT MISUNDER-STAND!
WHAT I'M SAYING IS, THAT AS A DEMON SLAYER NINJA...
IT'S...
I...

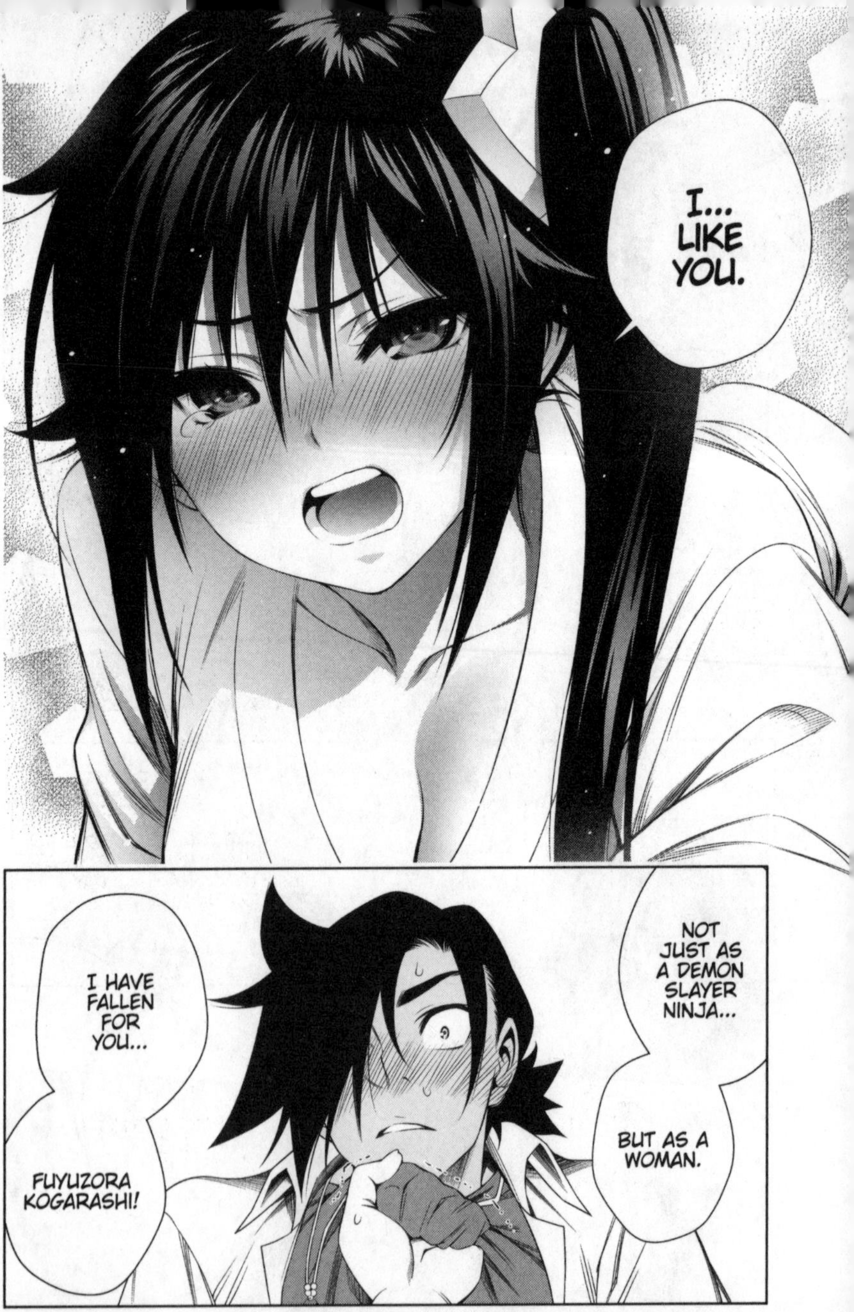
I... LIKE YOU.
NOT JUST AS A DEMON SLAYER NINJA...
BUT AS A WOMAN.
I HAVE FALLEN FOR YOU...
FUYUZORA KOGARASHI!

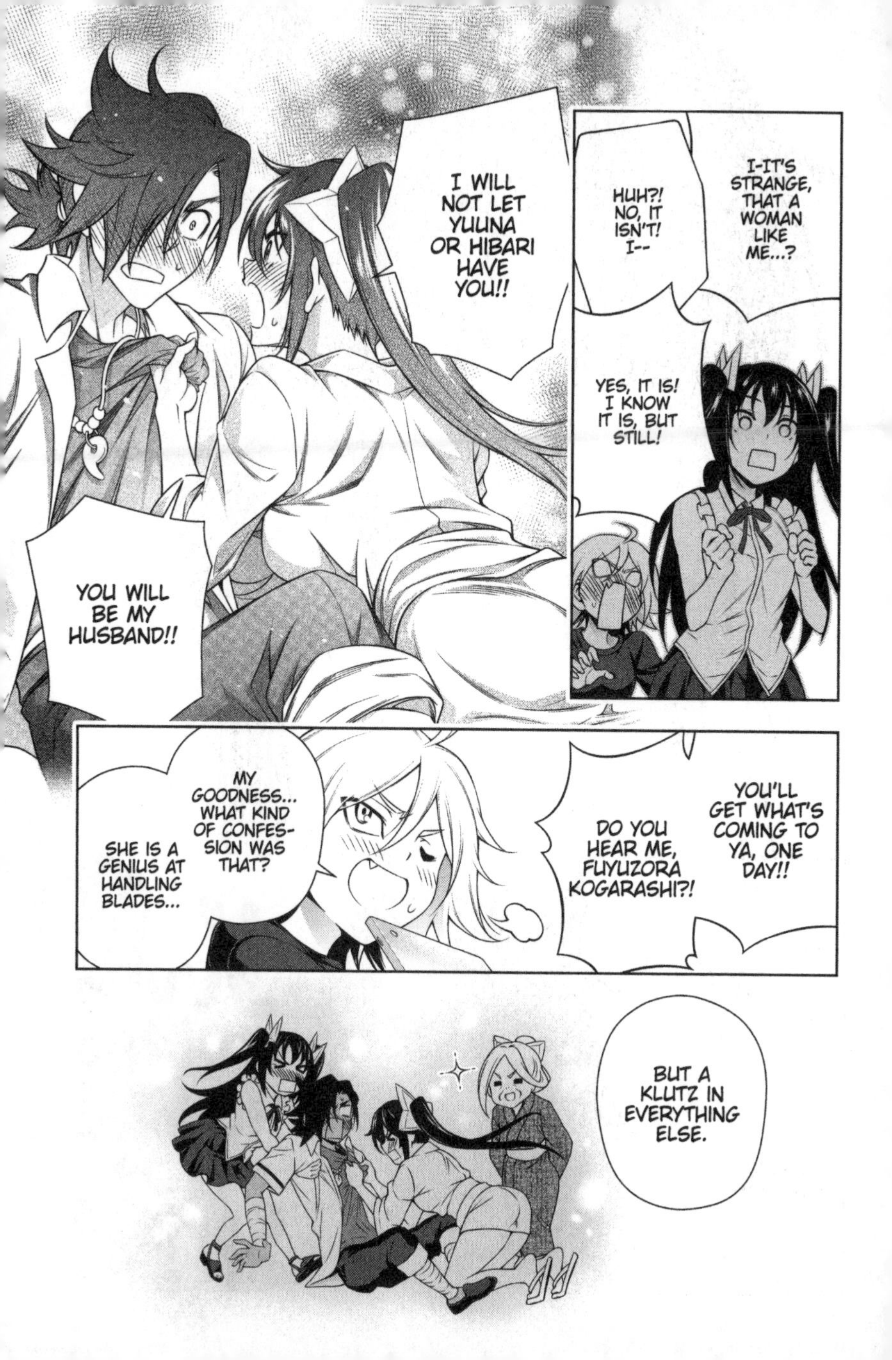
I-IT'S STRANGE, THAT A WOMAN LIKE ME...?
HUH?! NO, IT ISN'T! I--
YES, IT IS! I KNOW IT IS, BUT STILL!
I WILL NOT LET YUUNA OR HIBARI HAVE YOU!!
YOU WILL BE MY HUSBAND!!
YOU'LL GET WHAT'S COMING TO YA, ONE DAY!!
DO YOU HEAR ME, FUYUZORA KOGARASHI?!
MY GOODNESS... WHAT KIND OF CONFES-SION WAS THAT?
SHE IS A GENIUS AT HANDLING BLADES...
BUT A KLUTZ IN EVERYTHING ELSE.

Yuuna
and the
Haunted
Hot
Springs

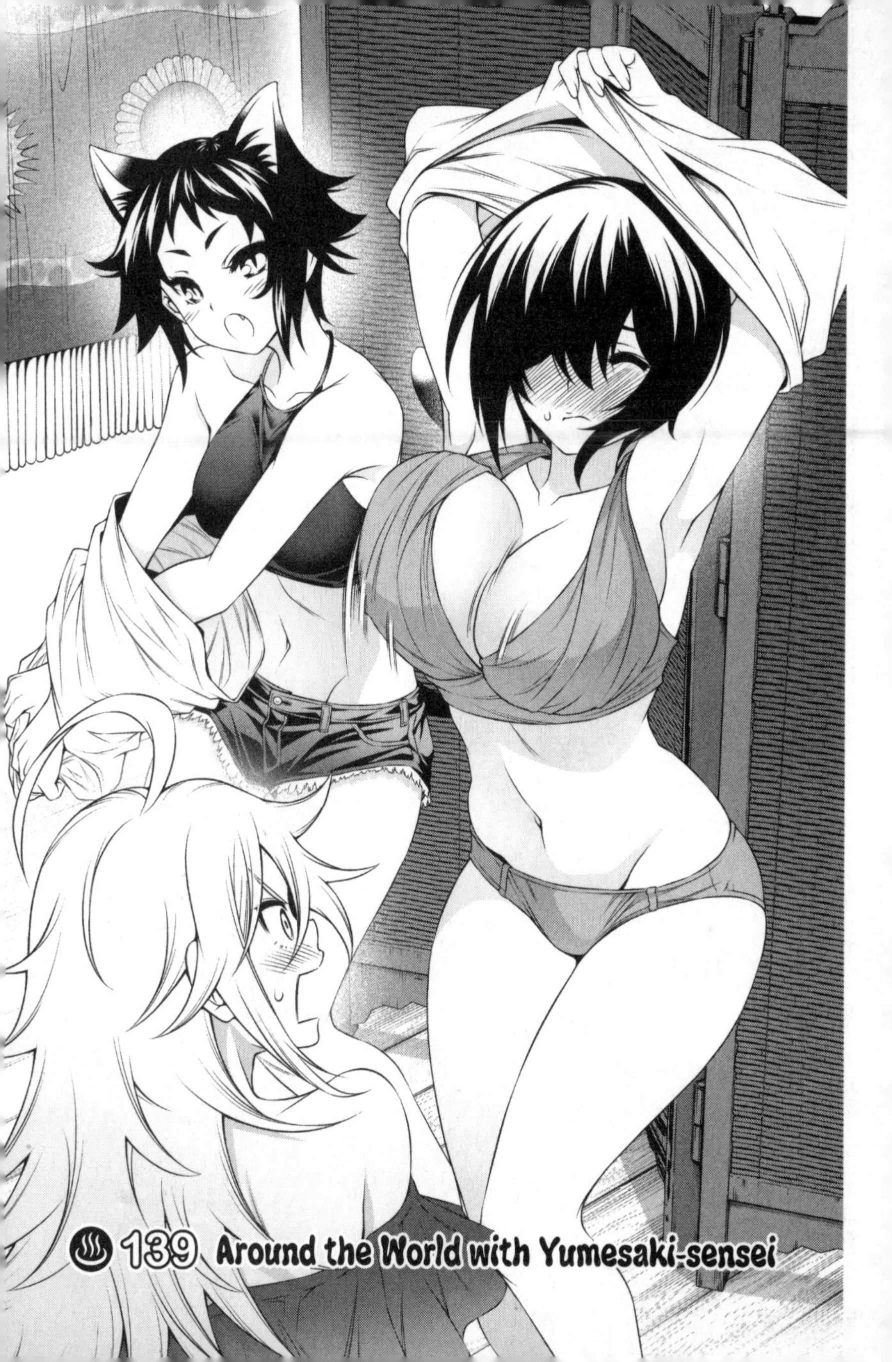
139 Around the World with Yumesaki-sensei

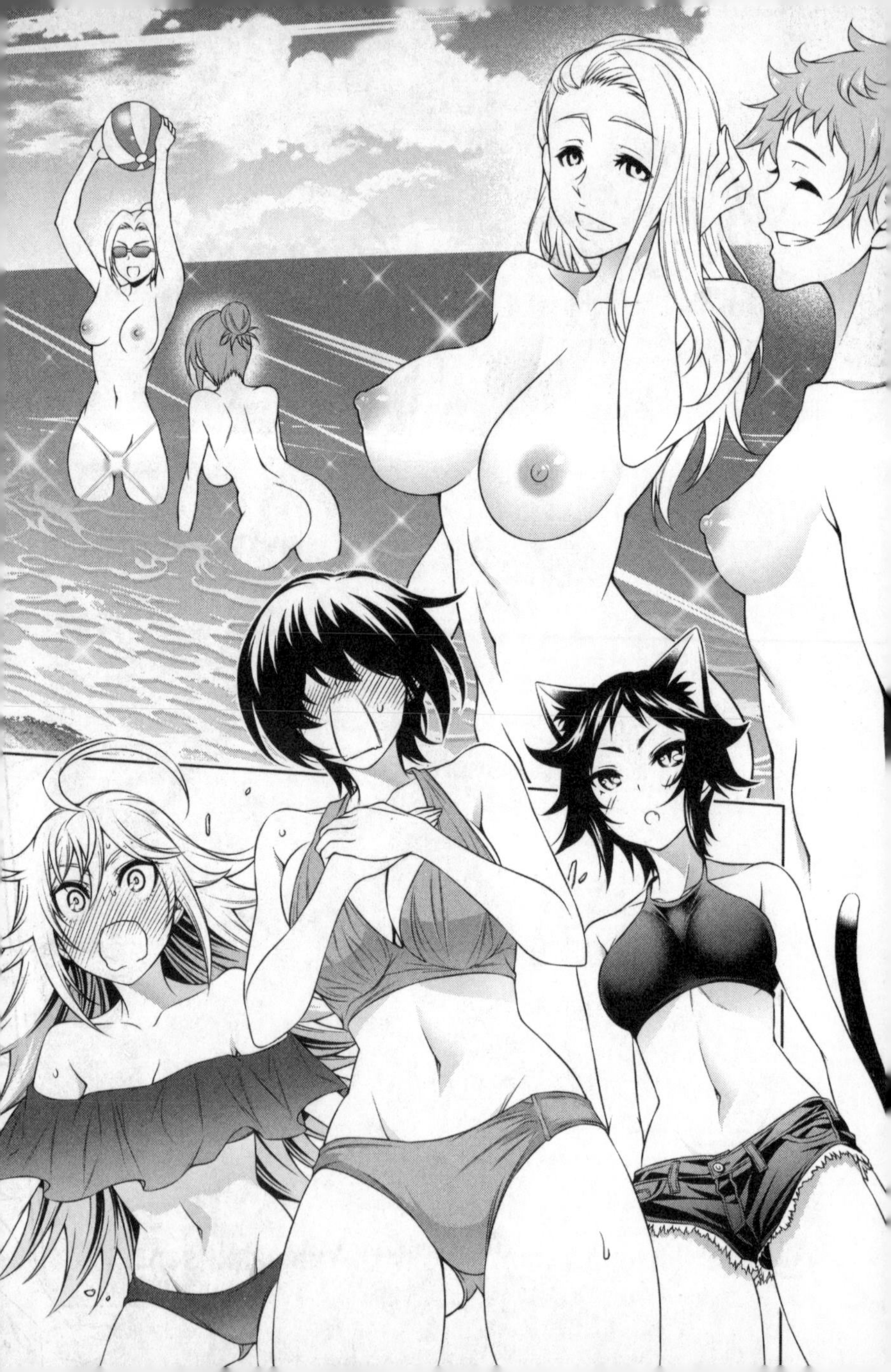

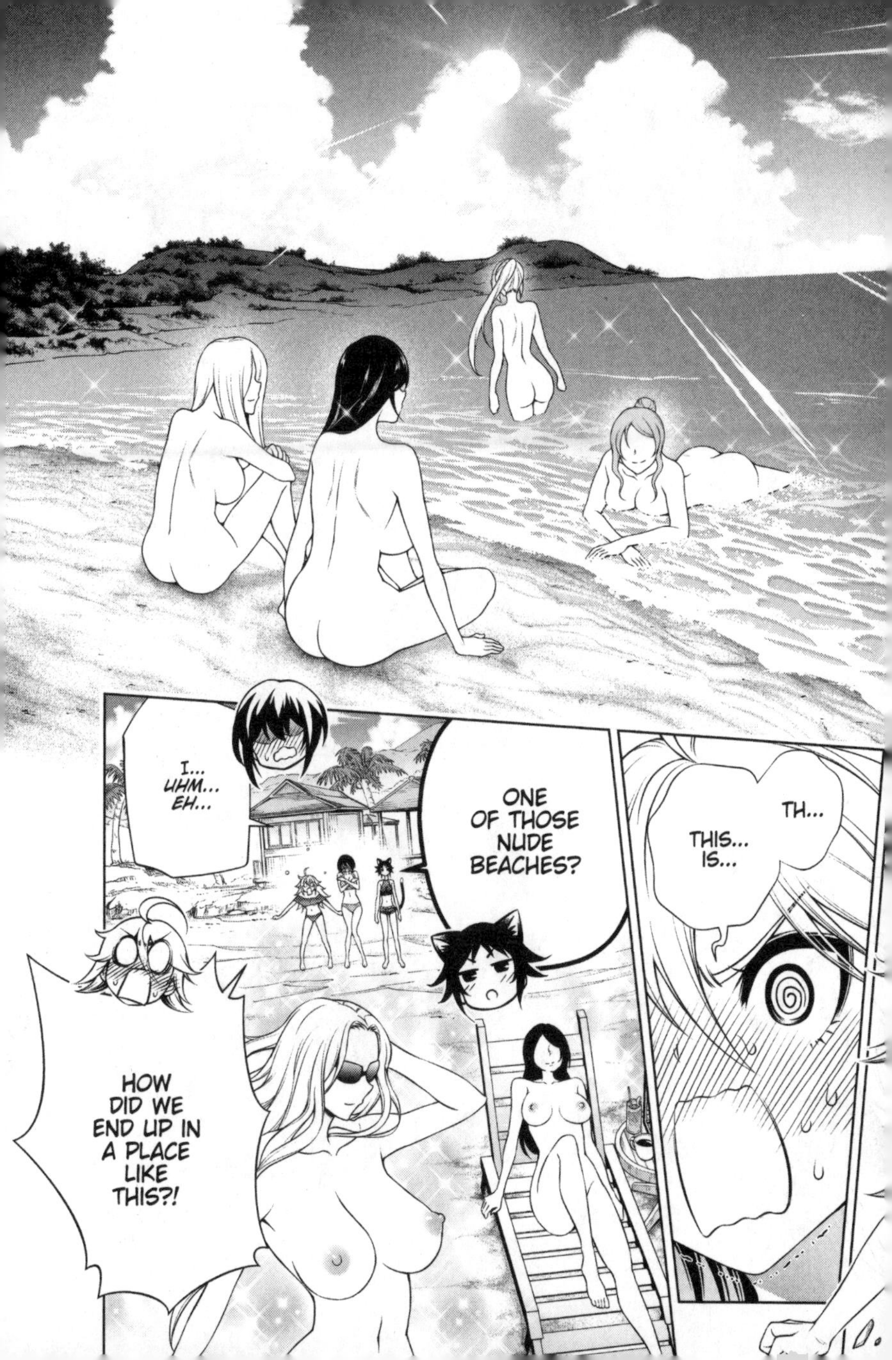
TH...
THIS... IS...
ONE OF THOSE NUDE BEACHES?
I... UHM... EH...
HOW DID WE END UP IN A PLACE LIKE THIS?!

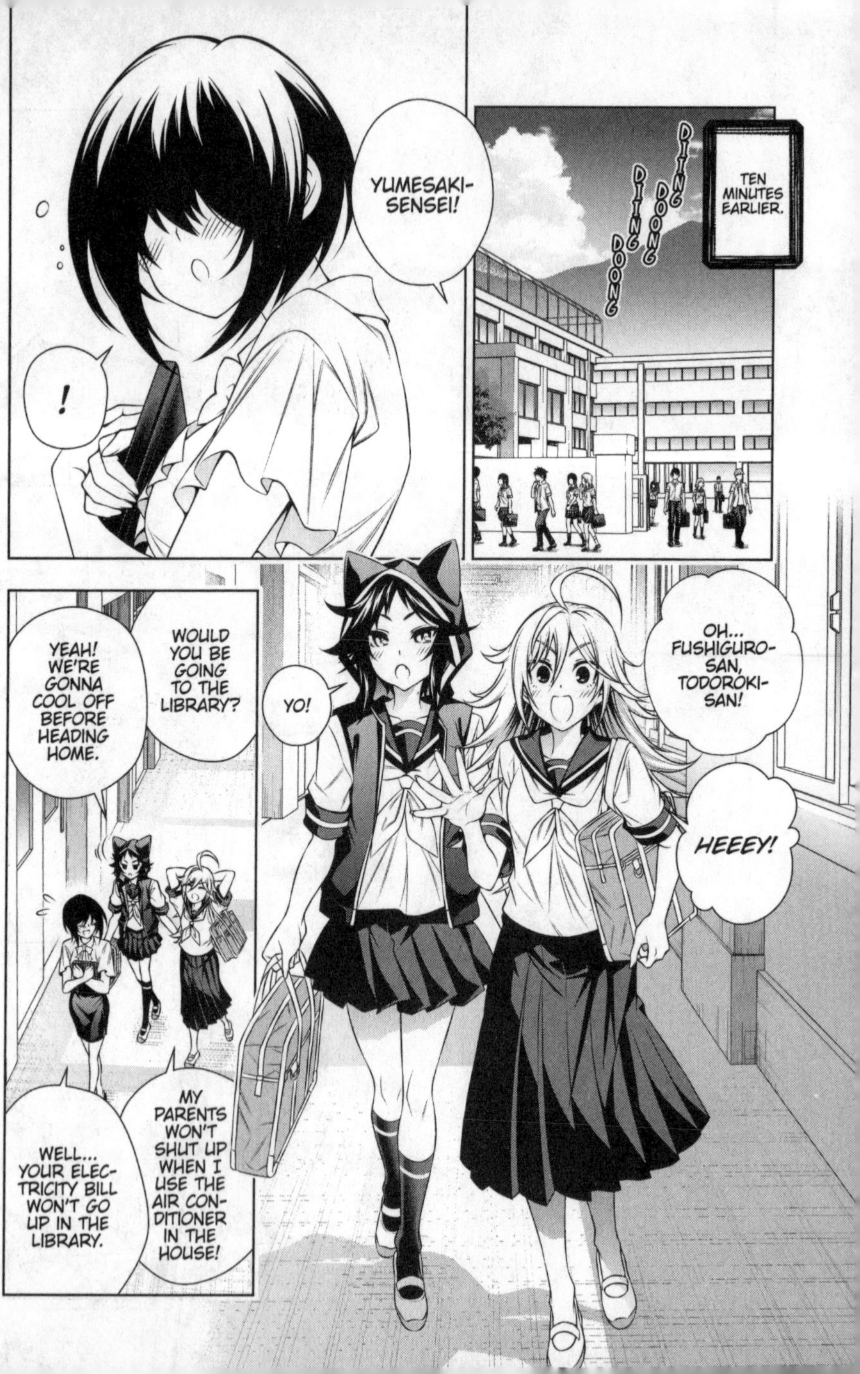
TEN MINUTES EARLIER.
DITING DOONG
DITING DOONG
YUMESAKI-SENSEI!
!
OH... FUSHIGURO-SAN, TODOROKI-SAN!
HEEEY!
YO!
WOULD YOU BE GOING TO THE LIBRARY?
YEAH! WE'RE GONNA COOL OFF BEFORE HEADING HOME.
MY PARENTS WON'T SHUT UP WHEN I USE THE AIR CONDITIONER IN THE HOUSE!
WELL... YOUR ELECTRICITY BILL WON'T GO UP IN THE LIBRARY.

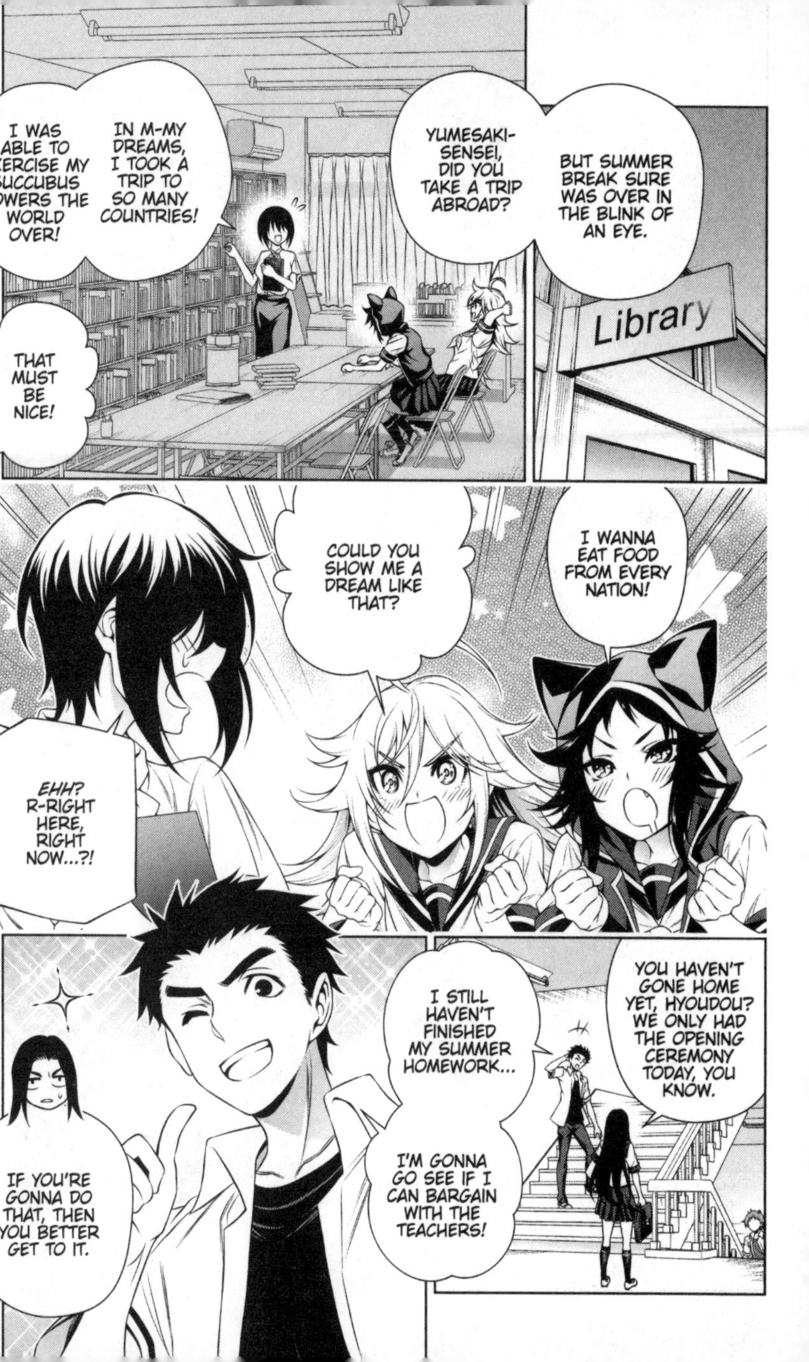
Library
BUT SUMMER BREAK SURE WAS OVER IN THE BLINK OF AN EYE.
YUMESAKI-SENSEI, DID YOU TAKE A TRIP ABROAD?
IN M-MY DREAMS, I TOOK A TRIP TO SO MANY COUNTRIES!
I WAS ABLE TO EXERCISE MY SUCCUBUS POWERS THE WORLD OVER!
THAT MUST BE NICE!
I WANNA EAT FOOD FROM EVERY NATION!
COULD YOU SHOW ME A DREAM LIKE THAT?
EHH? R-RIGHT HERE, RIGHT NOW...?!
YOU HAVEN'T GONE HOME YET, HYOUDOU? WE ONLY HAD THE OPENING CEREMONY TODAY, YOU KNOW.
I STILL HAVEN'T FINISHED MY SUMMER HOMEWORK...
I'M GONNA GO SEE IF I CAN BARGAIN WITH THE TEACHERS!
IF YOU'RE GONNA DO THAT, THEN YOU BETTER GET TO IT.

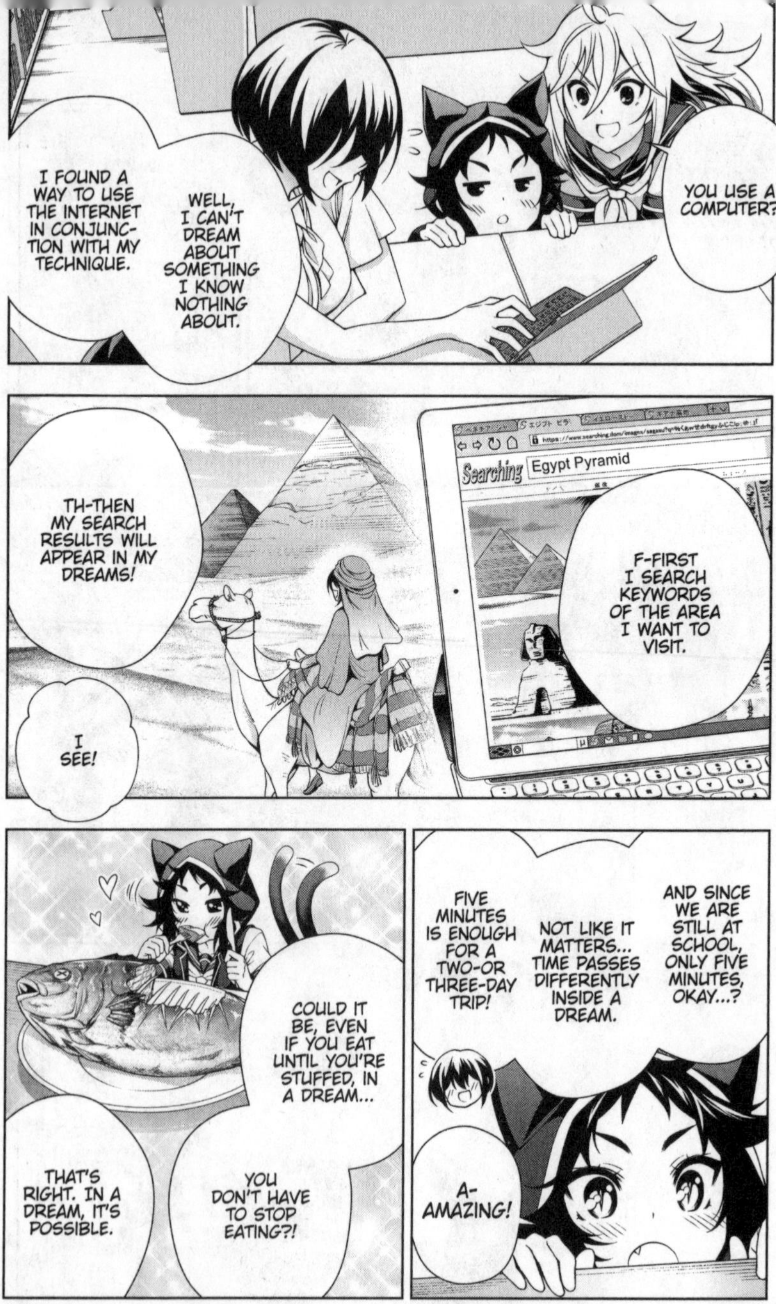
YOU USE A COMPUTER?
WELL, I CAN'T DREAM ABOUT SOMETHING I KNOW NOTHING ABOUT.
I FOUND A WAY TO USE THE INTERNET IN CONJUNCTION WITH MY TECHNIQUE.
Searching
Egypt Pyramid
F-FIRST I SEARCH KEYWORDS OF THE AREA I WANT TO VISIT.
TH-THEN MY SEARCH RESULTS WILL APPEAR IN MY DREAMS!
I SEE!
AND SINCE WE ARE STILL AT SCHOOL, ONLY FIVE MINUTES, OKAY...?
NOT LIKE IT MATTERS... TIME PASSES DIFFERENTLY INSIDE A DREAM.
FIVE MINUTES IS ENOUGH FOR A TWO-OR THREE-DAY TRIP!
A-AMAZING!
COULD IT BE, EVEN IF YOU EAT UNTIL YOU'RE STUFFED, IN A DREAM...
YOU DON'T HAVE TO STOP EATING?!
THAT'S RIGHT. IN A DREAM, IT'S POSSIBLE.

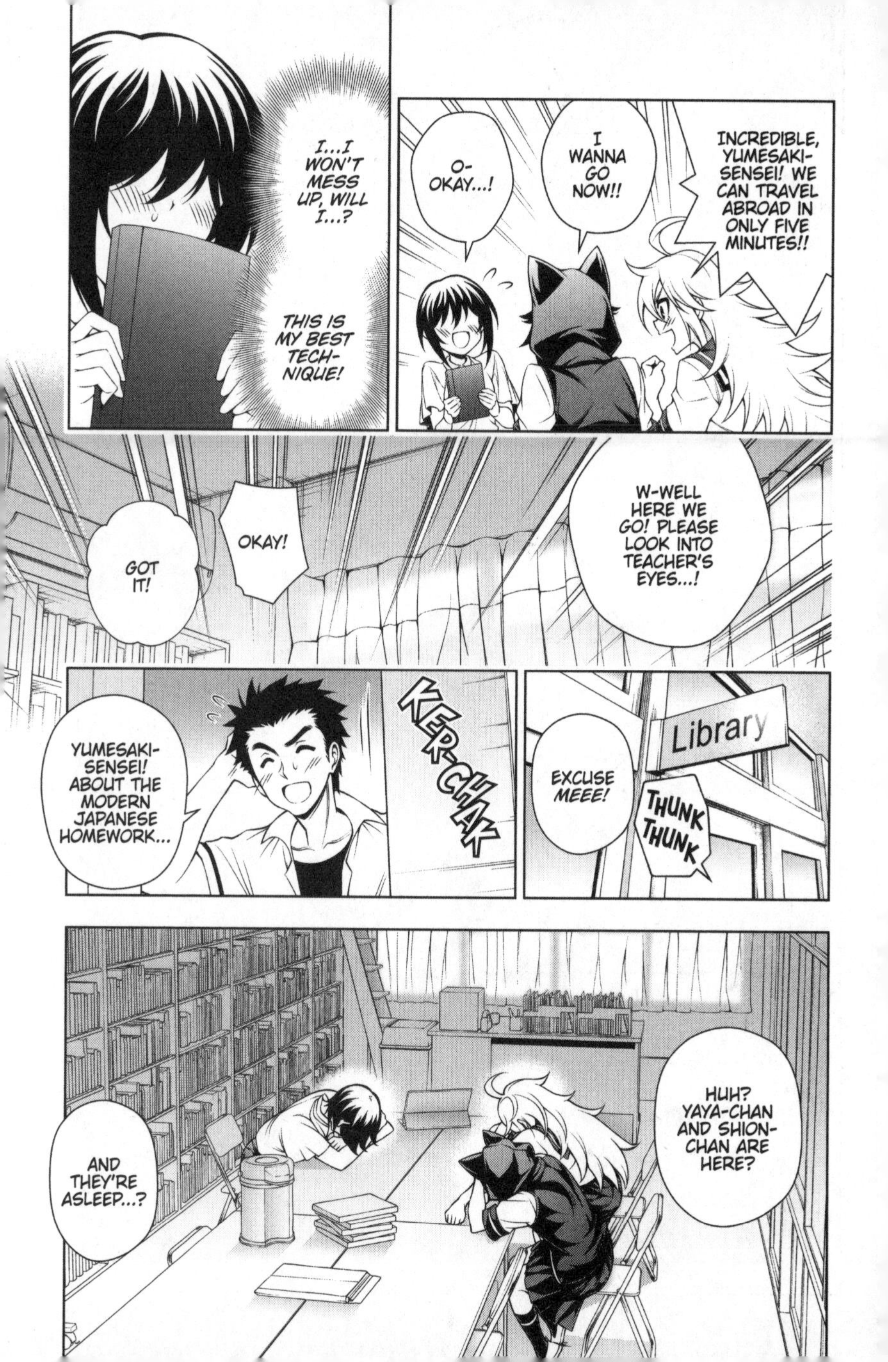
INCREDIBLE, YUMESAKI-SENSEI! WE CAN TRAVEL ABROAD IN ONLY FIVE MINUTES!!
I WANNA GO NOW!!
O-OKAY...!
I...I WON'T MESS UP, WILL I...?
THIS IS MY BEST TECH-NIQUE!
W-WELL HERE WE GO! PLEASE LOOK INTO TEACHER'S EYES...!
OKAY!
GOT IT!
Library
THUNK THUNK
EXCUSE MEEE!
KER-CHAK
YUMESAKI-SENSEI! ABOUT THE MODERN JAPANESE HOMEWORK...
HUH? YAYA-CHAN AND SHION-CHAN ARE HERE?
AND THEY'RE ASLEEP...?

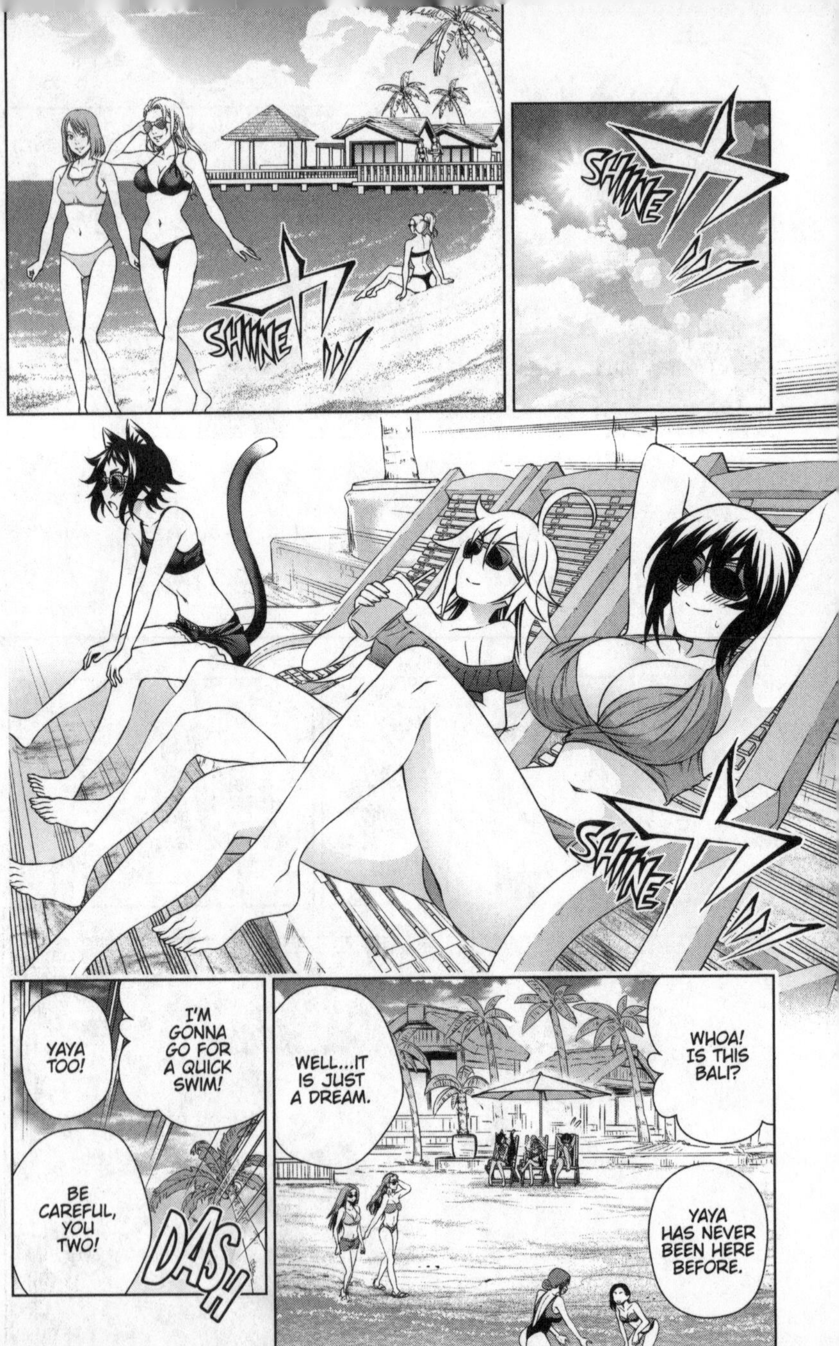
SHINE
SHINE
SHINE
WHOA! IS THIS BALI?
YAYA HAS NEVER BEEN HERE BEFORE.
WELL...IT IS JUST A DREAM.
I'M GONNA GO FOR A QUICK SWIM!
YAYA TOO!
BE CAREFUL, YOU TWO!
DASH

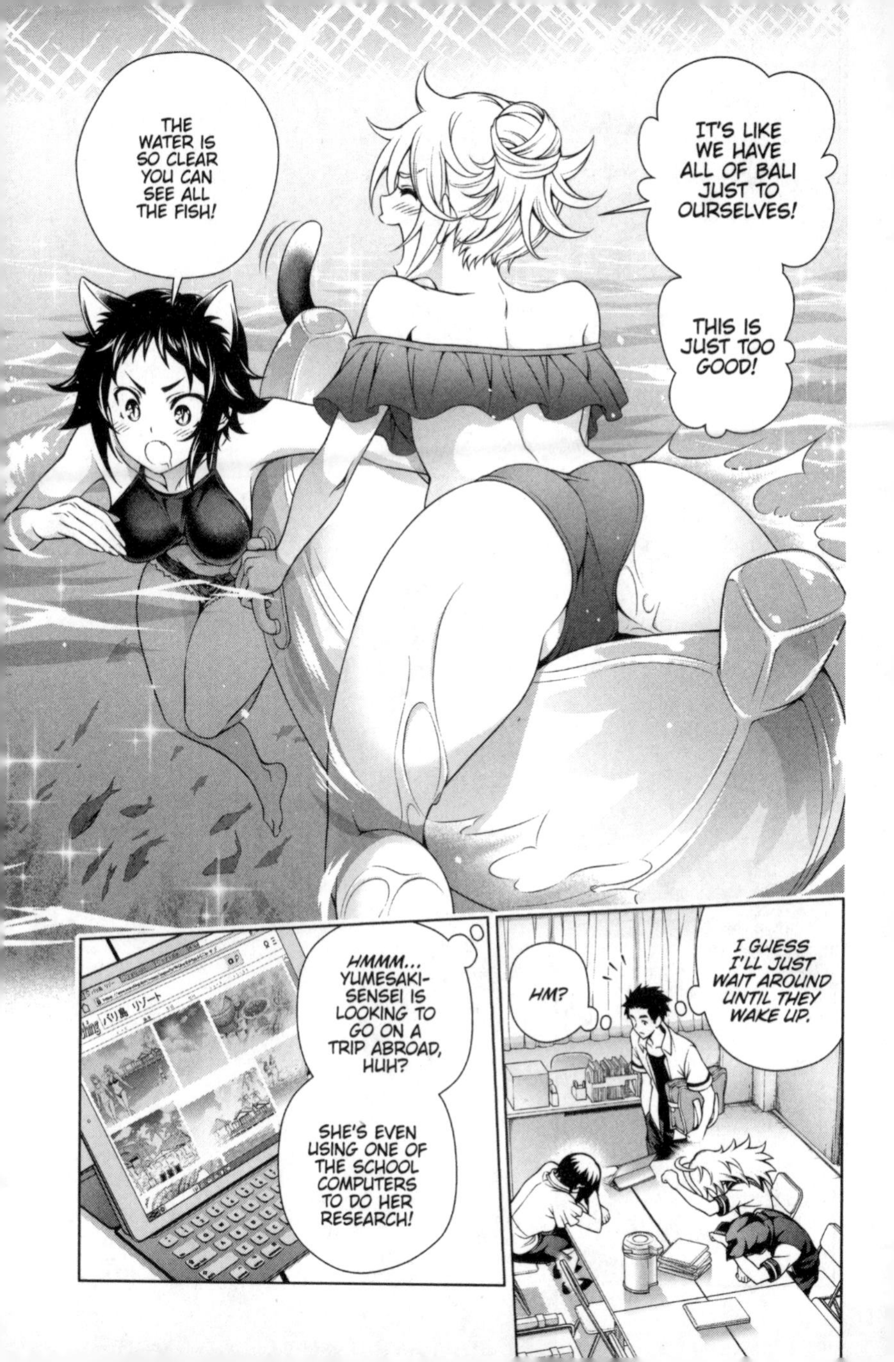
IT'S LIKE WE HAVE ALL OF BALI JUST TO OURSELVES!
THIS IS JUST TOO GOOD!
THE WATER IS SO CLEAR YOU CAN SEE ALL THE FISH!
I GUESS I'LL JUST WAIT AROUND UNTIL THEY WAKE UP.
HM?
HMMM... YUMESAKI-SENSEI IS LOOKING TO GO ON A TRIP ABROAD, HUH?
SHE'S EVEN USING ONE OF THE SCHOOL COMPUTERS TO DO HER RESEARCH!
バリ島 リゾート

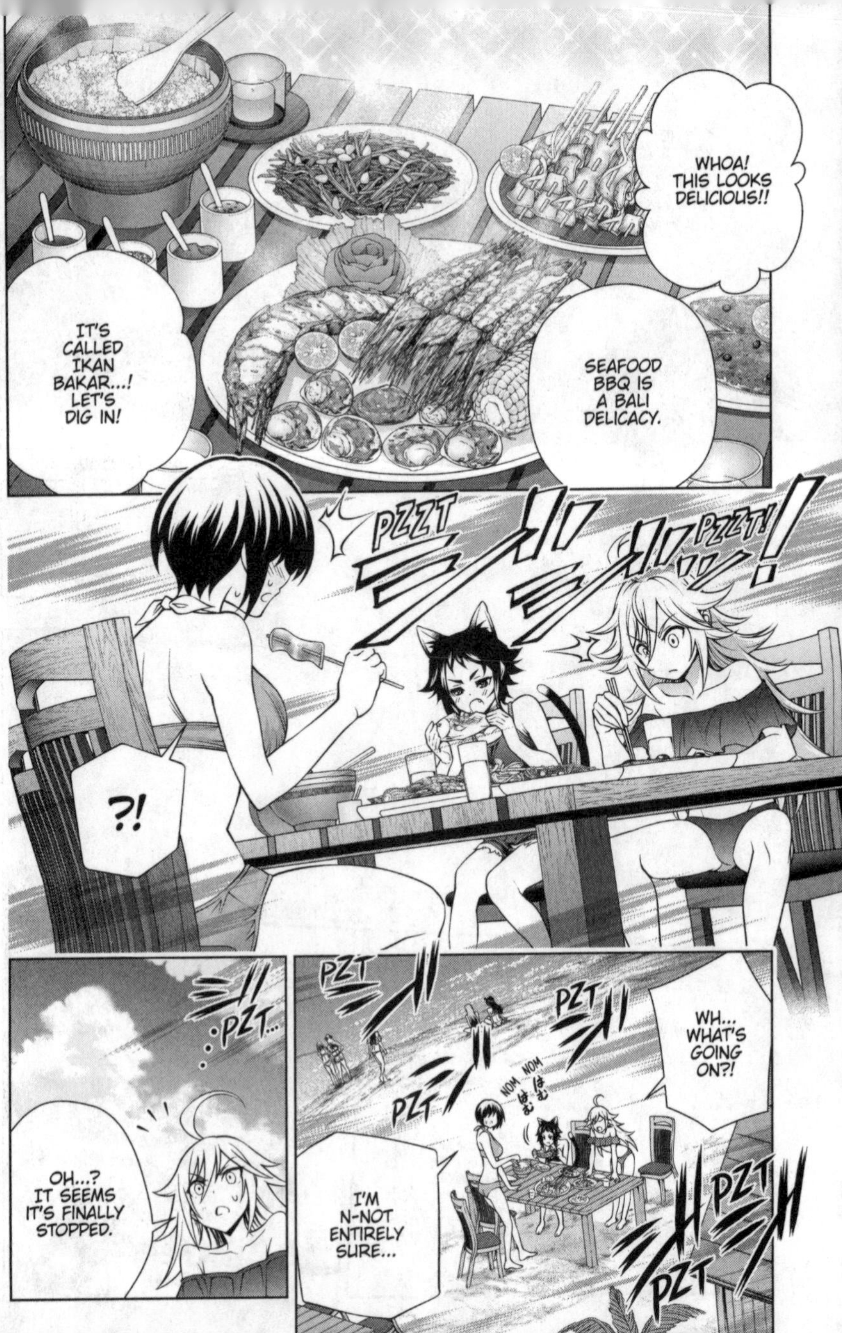
WHOA! THIS LOOKS DELICIOUS!!
SEAFOOD BBQ IS A BALI DELICACY.
IT'S CALLED IKAN BAKAR...! LET'S DIG IN!
PZZT!
PZZT
?!
PZT
PZT
WH... WHAT'S GOING ON?!
NOM NOM
はむはむ
PZT
I'M N-NOT ENTIRELY SURE...
PZT
PZT
PZT...
OH...? IT SEEMS IT'S FINALLY STOPPED.

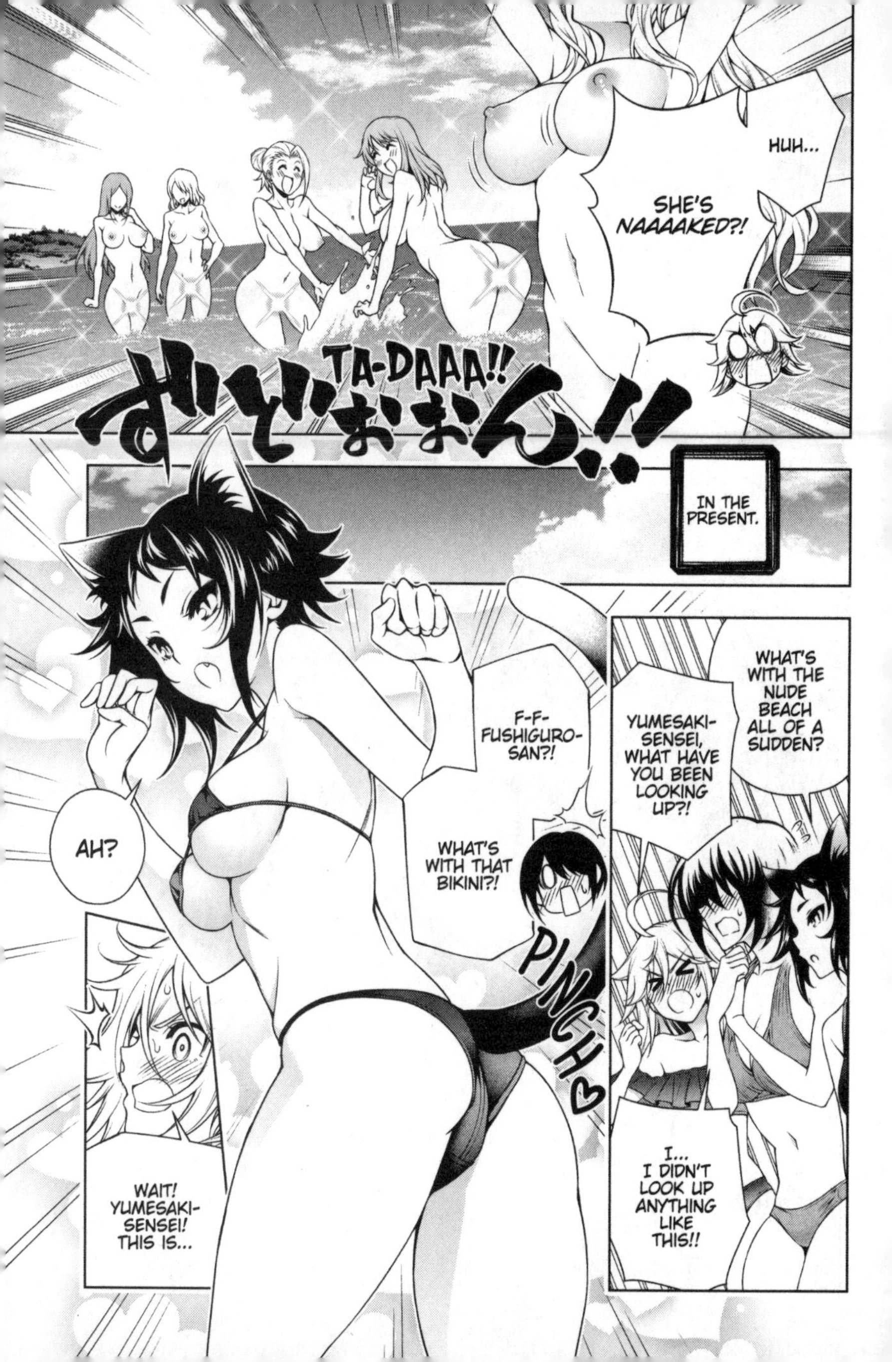
HUH...
SHE'S NAAAAKED?!
TA-DAAA!!
IN THE PRESENT.
WHAT'S WITH THE NUDE BEACH ALL OF A SUDDEN?
YUMESAKI-SENSEI, WHAT HAVE YOU BEEN LOOKING UP?!
F-F-FUSHIGURO-SAN?!
WHAT'S WITH THAT BIKINI?!
AH?
PINCH♥
I... I DIDN'T LOOK UP ANYTHING LIKE THIS!!
WAIT! YUMESAKI-SENSEI! THIS IS...

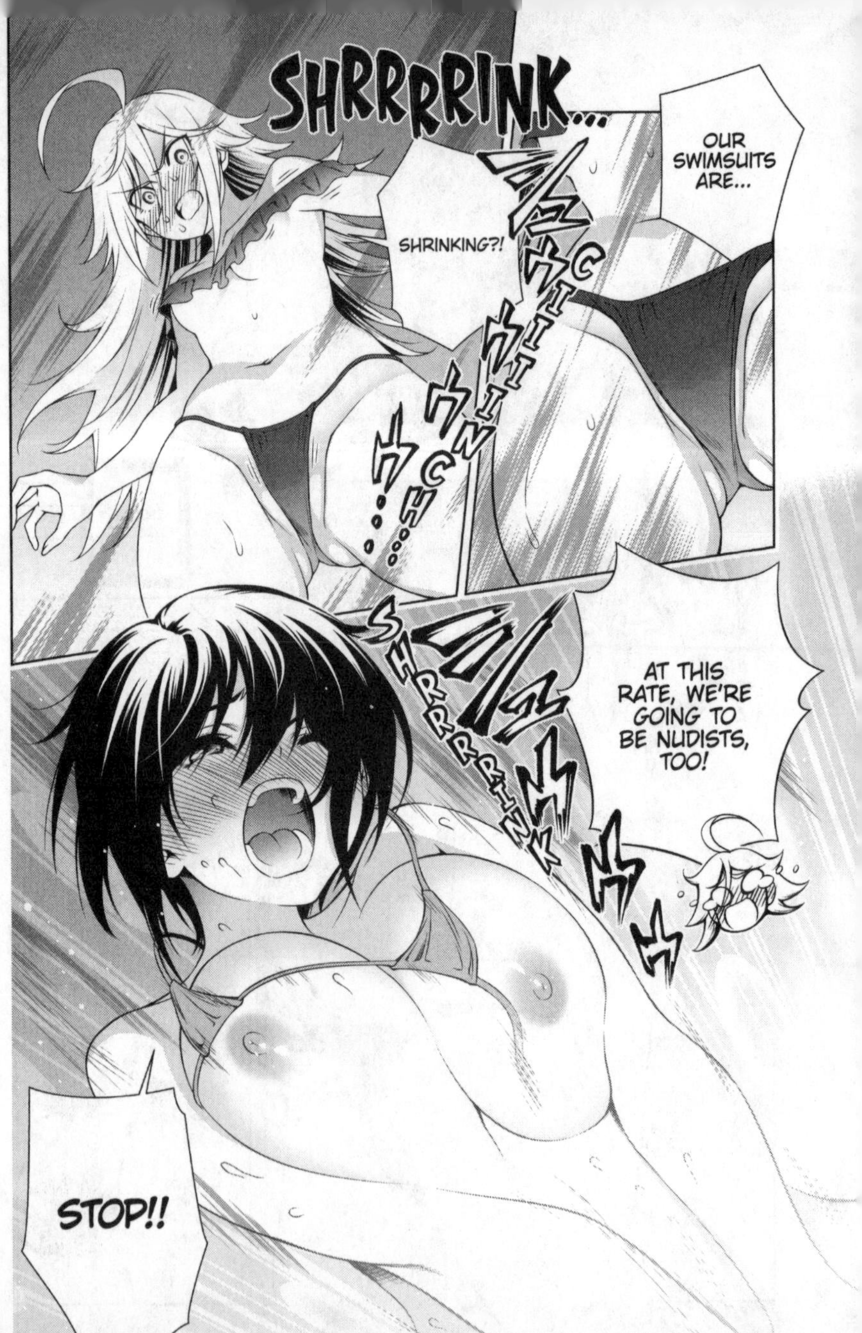
SHRRRRINK...
OUR SWIMSUITS ARE...
SHRINKING?!
CIIIINCH...
SHRRRRRINK
AT THIS RATE, WE'RE GOING TO BE NUDISTS, TOO!
STOP!!

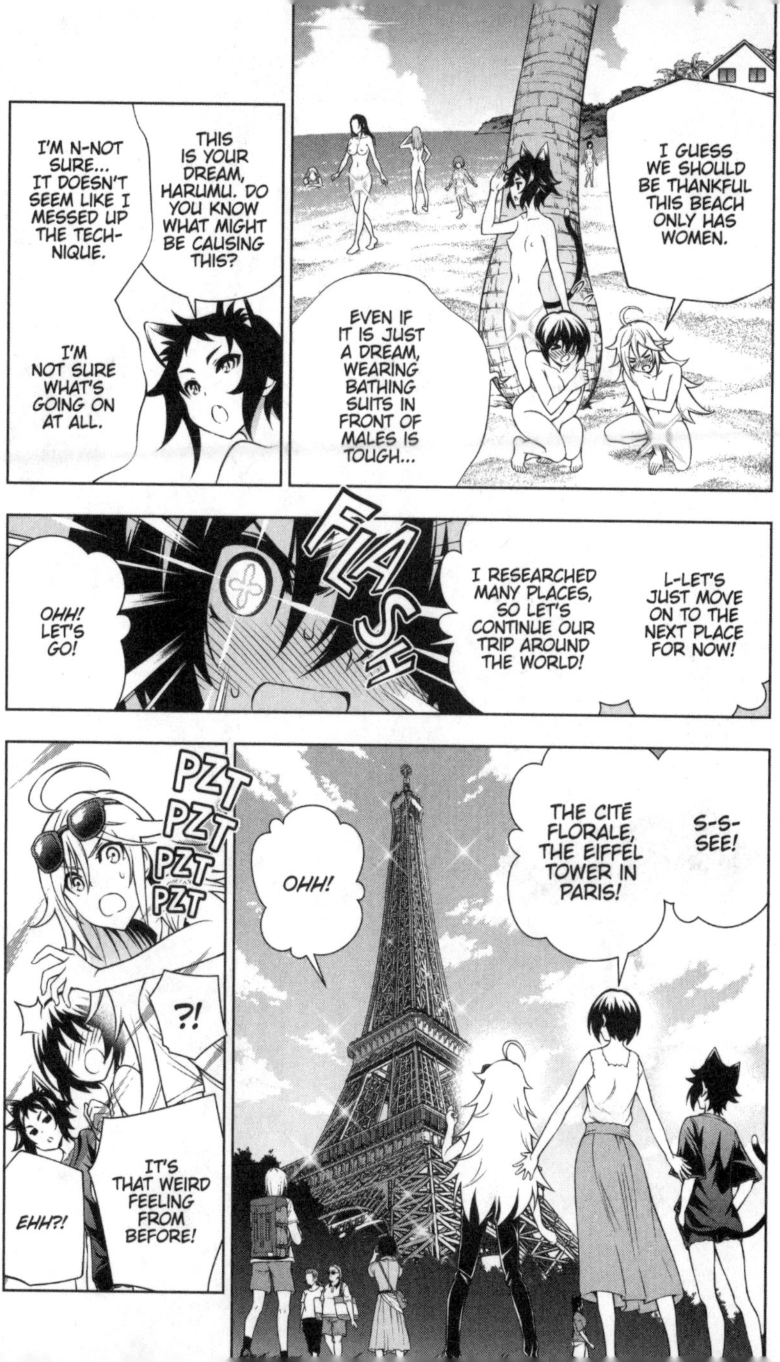
I GUESS WE SHOULD BE THANKFUL THIS BEACH ONLY HAS WOMEN.
EVEN IF IT IS JUST A DREAM, WEARING BATHING SUITS IN FRONT OF MALES IS TOUGH...
THIS IS YOUR DREAM, HARUMU. DO YOU KNOW WHAT MIGHT BE CAUSING THIS?
I'M N-NOT SURE... IT DOESN'T SEEM LIKE I MESSED UP THE TECH-NIQUE.
I'M NOT SURE WHAT'S GOING ON AT ALL.
L-LET'S JUST MOVE ON TO THE NEXT PLACE FOR NOW!
I RESEARCHED MANY PLACES, SO LET'S CONTINUE OUR TRIP AROUND THE WORLD!
FLASH
OHH! LET'S GO!
S-S-SEE!
THE CITÉ FLORALE, THE EIFFEL TOWER IN PARIS!
OHH!
PZT PZT PZT PZT
?!
IT'S THAT WEIRD FEELING FROM BEFORE!
EHH?!

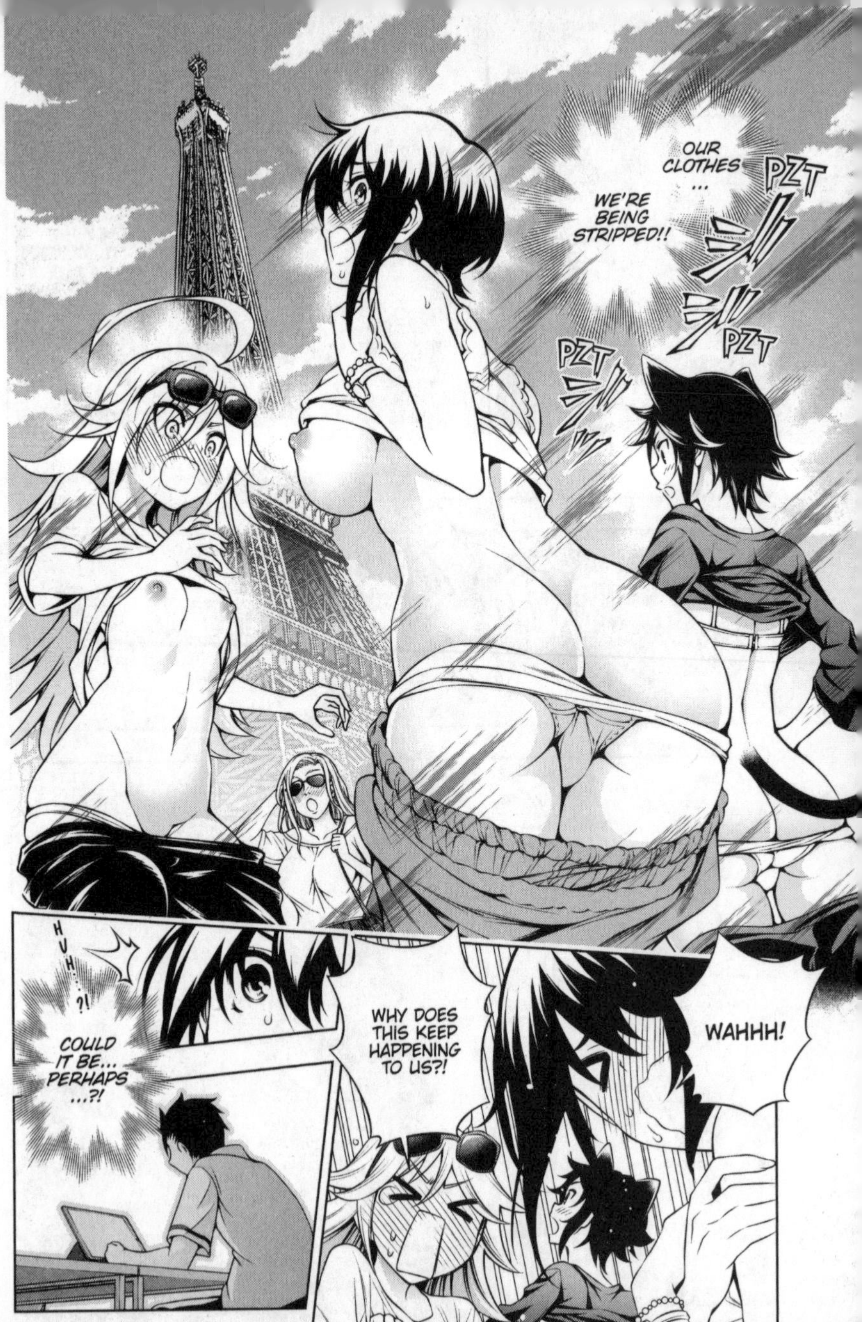
OUR CLOTHES ...
WE'RE BEING STRIPPED!!
PZT
PZT
PZT
WAHHH!
WHY DOES THIS KEEP HAPPENING TO US?!
HUH...?!
COULD IT BE... PERHAPS ...?!

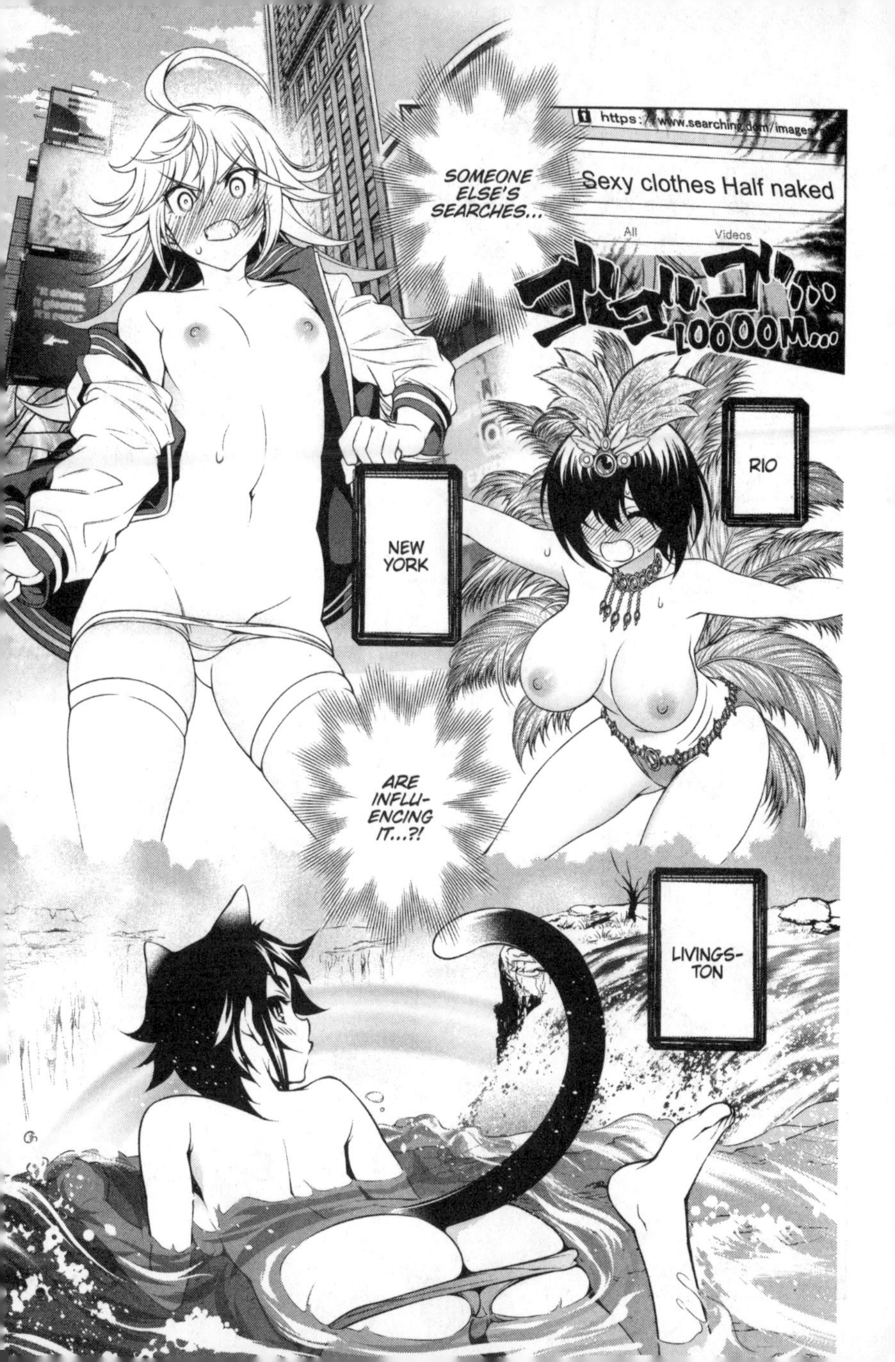

https://www.searching.com/images
Sexy clothes Half naked
All
Videos
SOMEONE ELSE'S SEARCHES...
LOOOOM...
RIO
NEW YORK
ARE INFLU-ENCING IT...?!
LIVINGS-TON

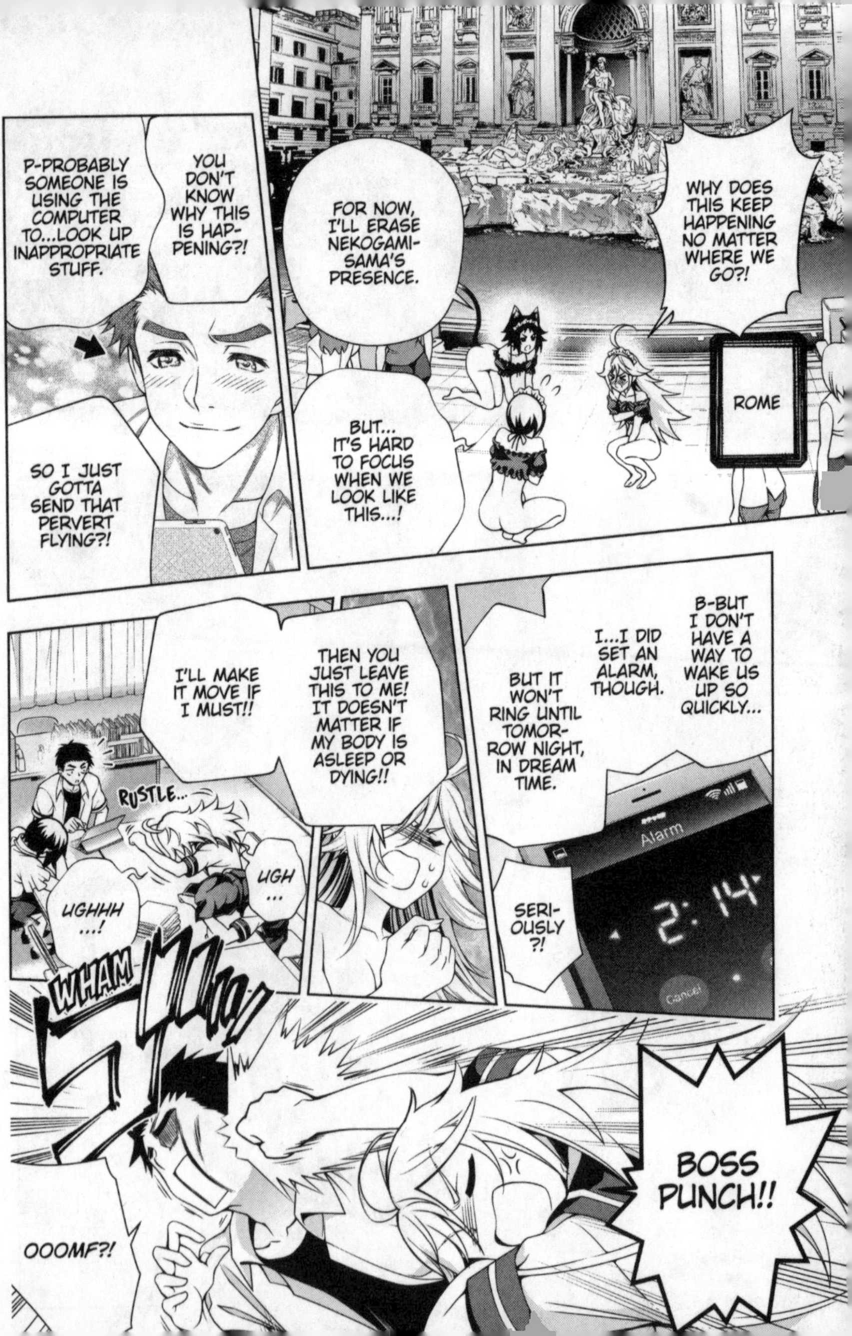
ROME
WHY DOES THIS KEEP HAPPENING NO MATTER WHERE WE GO?!
FOR NOW, I'LL ERASE NEKOGAMI-SAMA'S PRESENCE.
BUT... IT'S HARD TO FOCUS WHEN WE LOOK LIKE THIS...!
YOU DON'T KNOW WHY THIS IS HAP-PENING?!
P-PROBABLY SOMEONE IS USING THE COMPUTER TO...LOOK UP INAPPROPRIATE STUFF.
SO I JUST GOTTA SEND THAT PERVERT FLYING?!
B-BUT I DON'T HAVE A WAY TO WAKE US UP SO QUICKLY...
I...I DID SET AN ALARM, THOUGH.
BUT IT WON'T RING UNTIL TOMOR-ROW NIGHT, IN DREAM TIME.
Alarm
2:14
Cancel
SERI-OUSLY?!
THEN YOU JUST LEAVE THIS TO ME! IT DOESN'T MATTER IF MY BODY IS ASLEEP OR DYING!!
UGH...
I'LL MAKE IT MOVE IF I MUST!!
RUSTLE...
UGHHH...!
WHAM
BOSS PUNCH!!
OOOMF?!

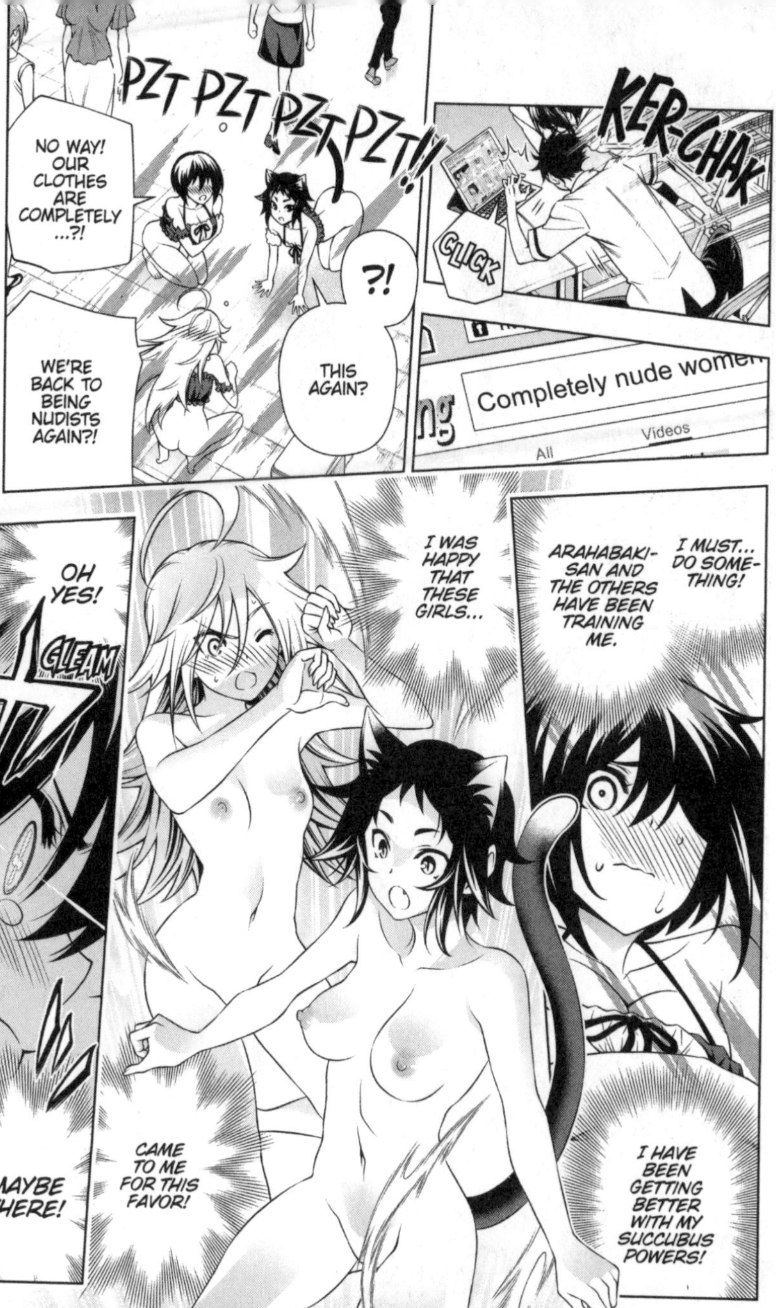
KER-CHAK
CLICK
Completely nude women
Videos
All
PZT PZT PZT PZT!!
?!
NO WAY! OUR CLOTHES ARE COMPLETELY ...?!
THIS AGAIN?
WE'RE BACK TO BEING NUDISTS AGAIN?!
I MUST... DO SOME-THING!
ARAHABAKI-SAN AND THE OTHERS HAVE BEEN TRAINING ME.
I HAVE BEEN GETTING BETTER WITH MY SUCCUBUS POWERS!
I WAS HAPPY THAT THESE GIRLS...
CAME TO ME FOR THIS FAVOR!
OH YES!
GLEAM
MAYBE THERE!

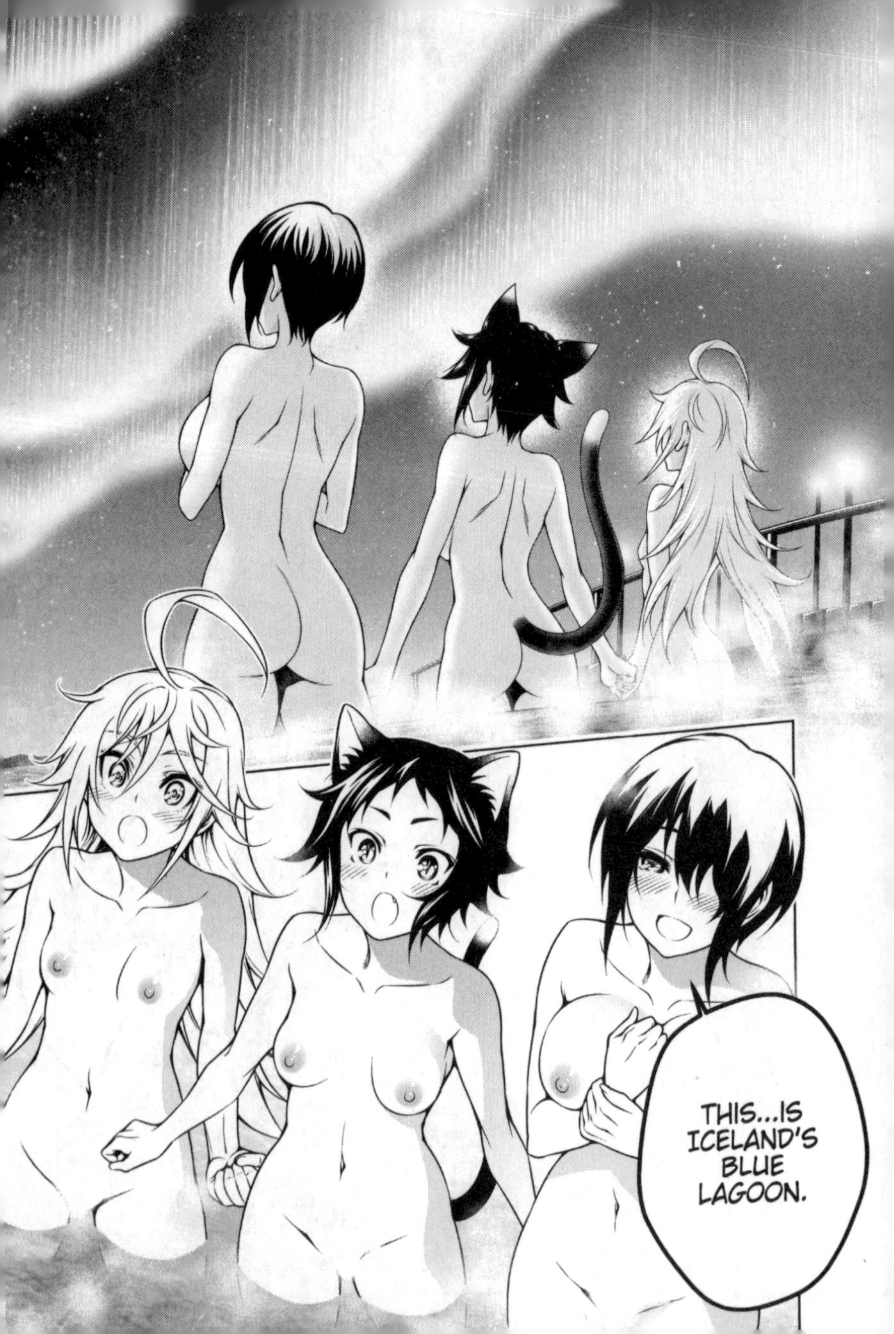
THIS...IS ICELAND'S BLUE LAGOON.

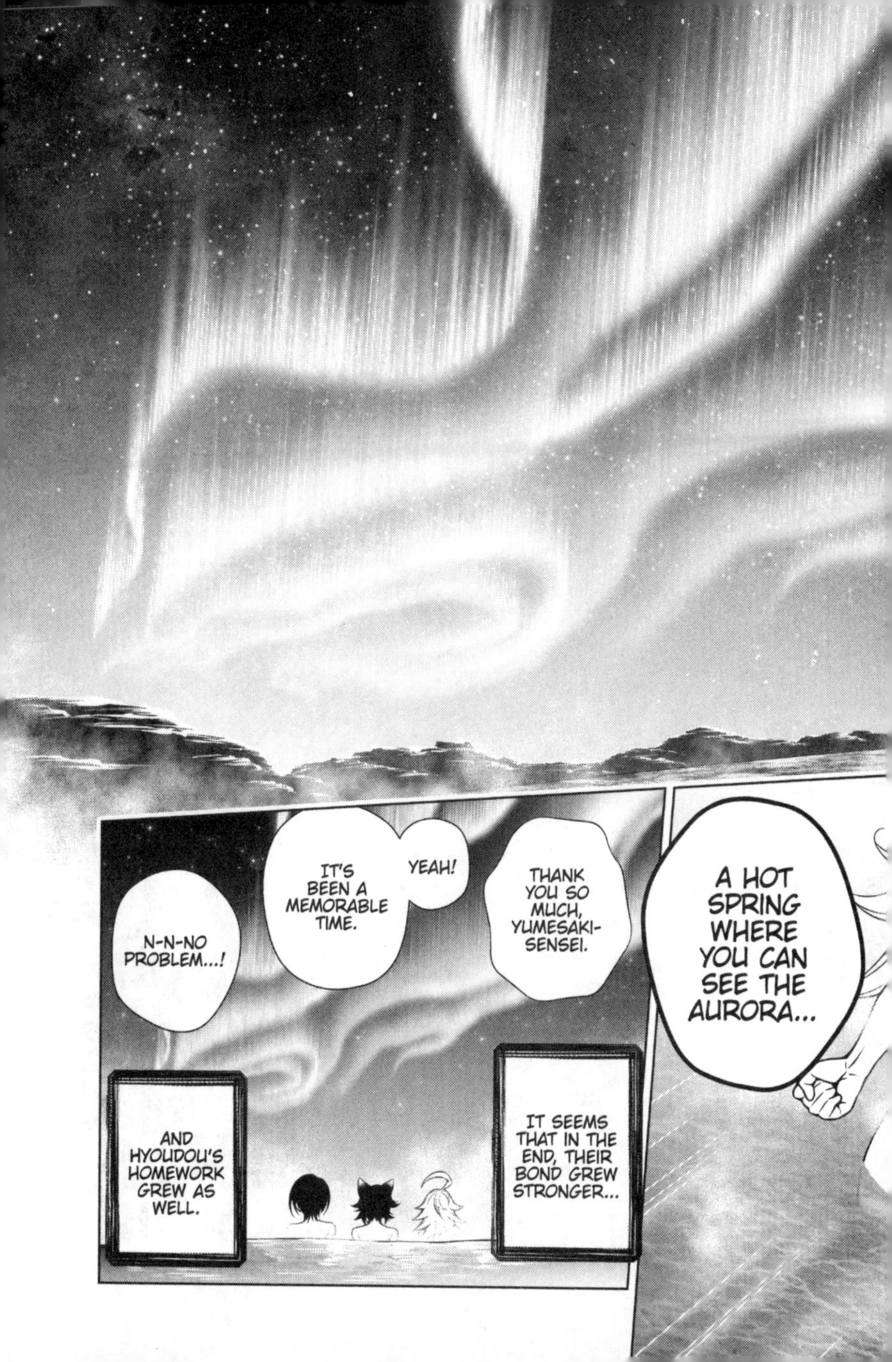
A HOT SPRING WHERE YOU CAN SEE THE AURORA...
THANK YOU SO MUCH, YUMESAKI-SENSEI.
YEAH!
IT'S BEEN A MEMORABLE TIME.
N-N-NO PROBLEM...!
IT SEEMS THAT IN THE END, THEIR BOND GREW STRONGER...
AND HYOUDOU'S HOMEWORK GREW AS WELL.

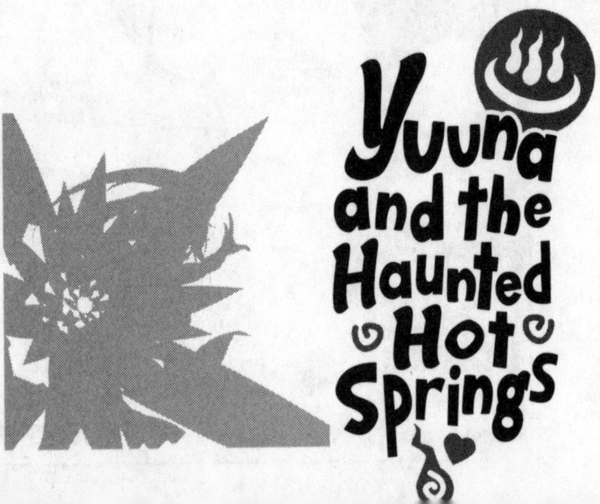

Yuuna and the Haunted Hot Springs

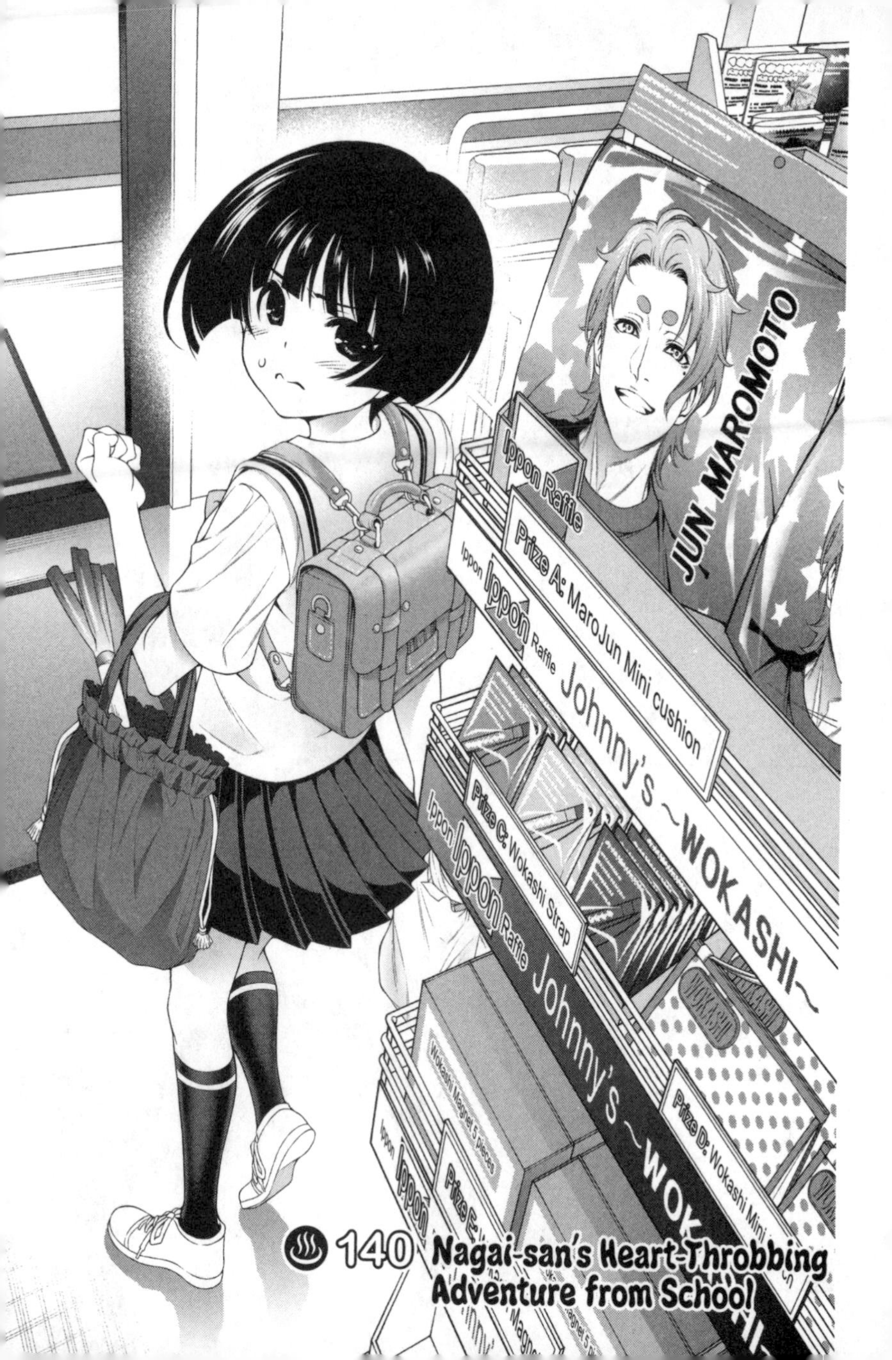
JUN MAROMOTO
Ippon Raffle
Prize A: MaroJun Mini cushion
Ippon Ippon Raffle Johnny's ~WOKASHI~
Prize C: Wokashi Strap
Ippon Ippon Raffle
WOKASHI
Prize D: Wokashi Mini
Wokashi Magnet 5 pieces
140 Nagai-san's Heart-Throbbing Adventure from School

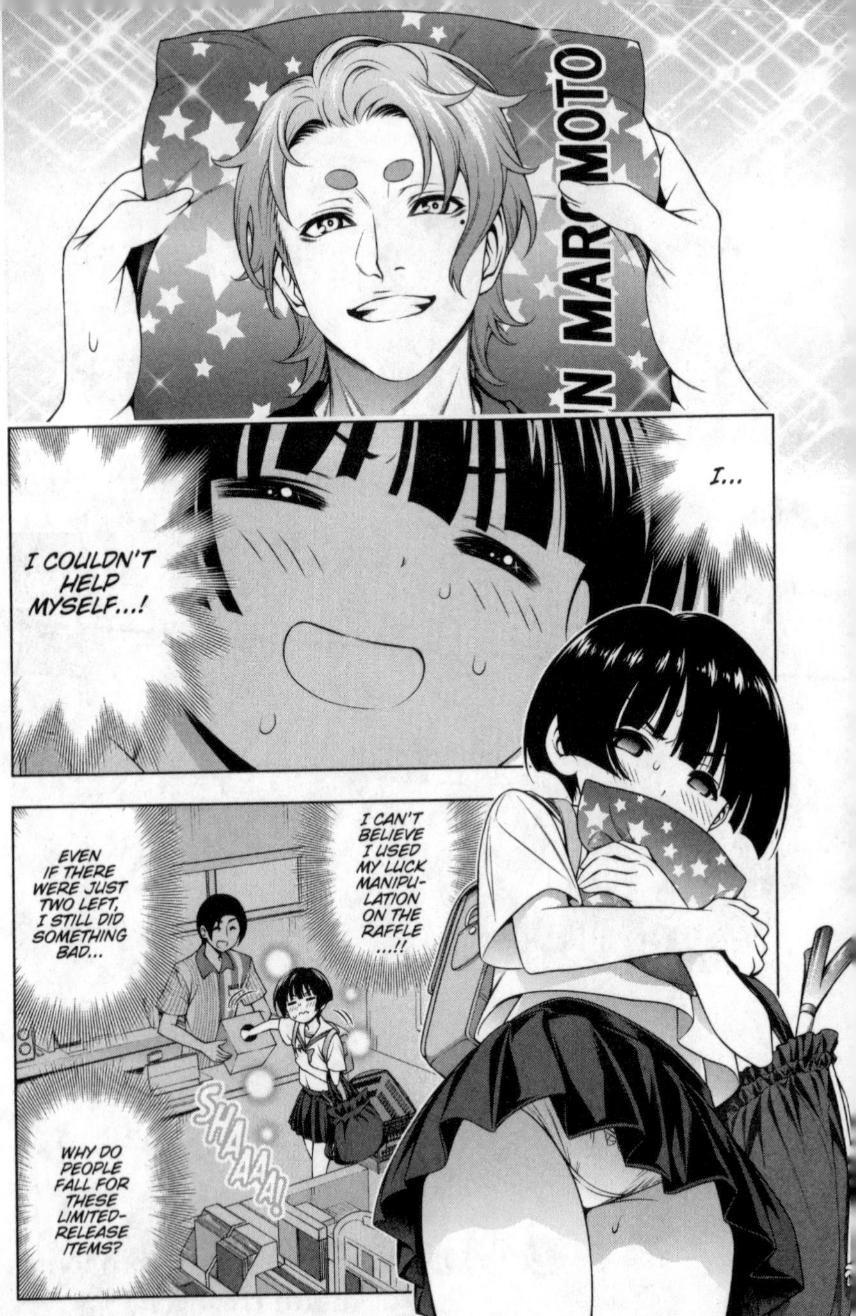

N MAROMOTO
I...
I COULDN'T HELP MYSELF...!
I CAN'T BELIEVE I USED MY LUCK MANIPULATION ON THE RAFFLE...!!
EVEN IF THERE WERE JUST TWO LEFT, I STILL DID SOMETHING BAD...
SHAAAA!
WHY DO PEOPLE FALL FOR THESE LIMITED-RELEASE ITEMS?

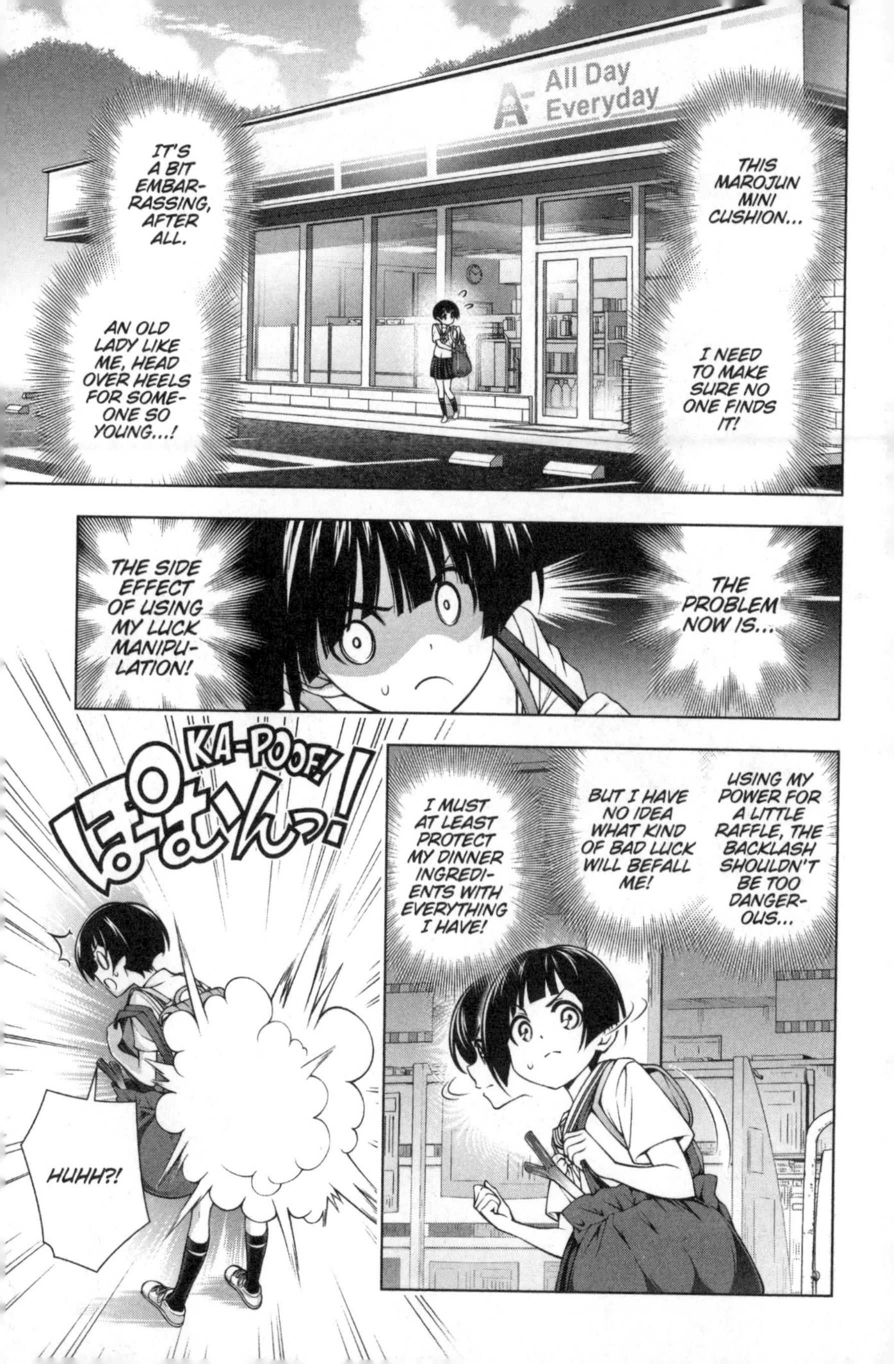
All Day Everyday
THIS MAROJUN MINI CUSHION...
I NEED TO MAKE SURE NO ONE FINDS IT!
IT'S A BIT EMBARRASSING, AFTER ALL.
AN OLD LADY LIKE ME, HEAD OVER HEELS FOR SOMEONE SO YOUNG...!
THE PROBLEM NOW IS...
THE SIDE EFFECT OF USING MY LUCK MANIPULATION!
USING MY POWER FOR A LITTLE RAFFLE, THE BACKLASH SHOULDN'T BE TOO DANGEROUS...
BUT I HAVE NO IDEA WHAT KIND OF BAD LUCK WILL BEFALL ME!
I MUST AT LEAST PROTECT MY DINNER INGREDIENTS WITH EVERYTHING I HAVE!
ぽふんっ!
KA-POOF!
HUHH?!

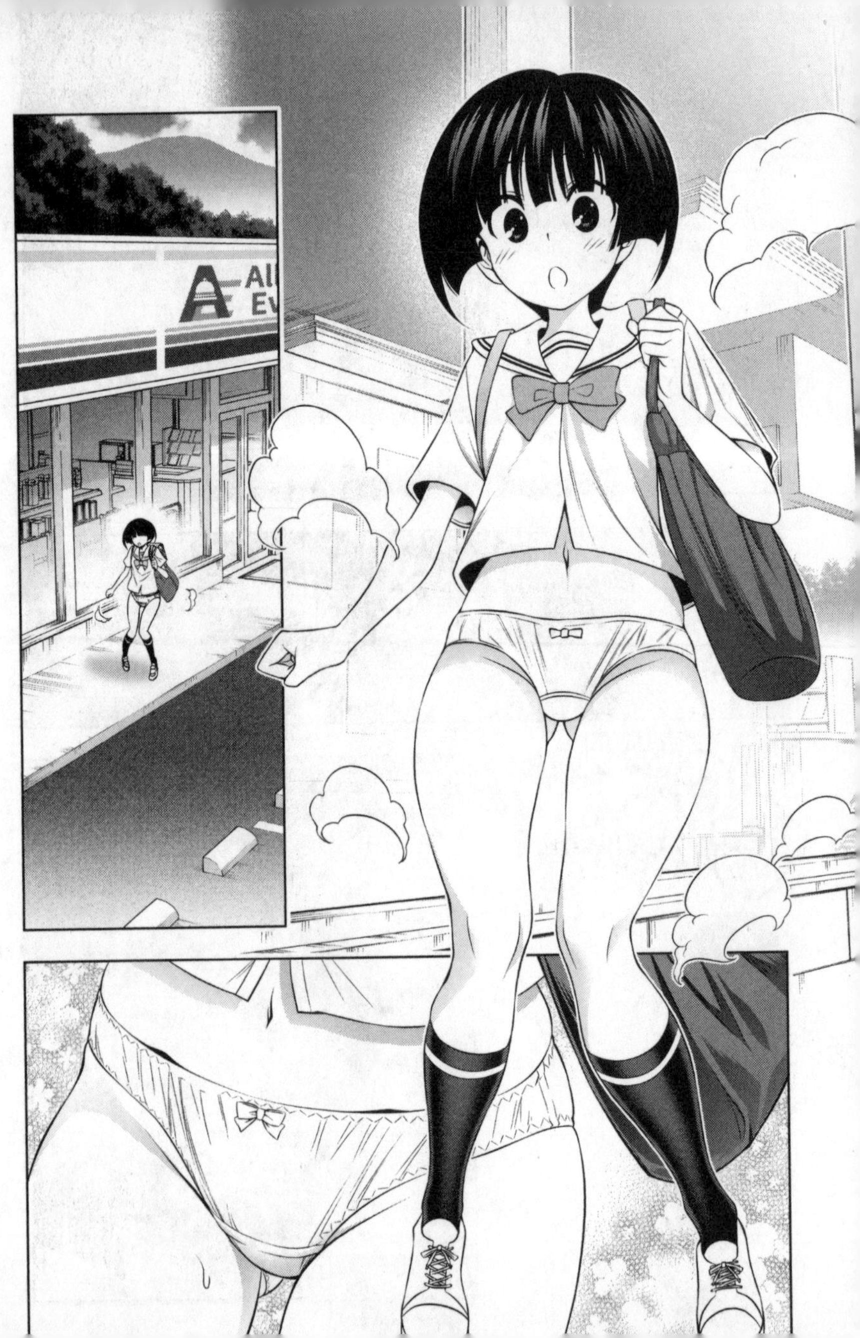

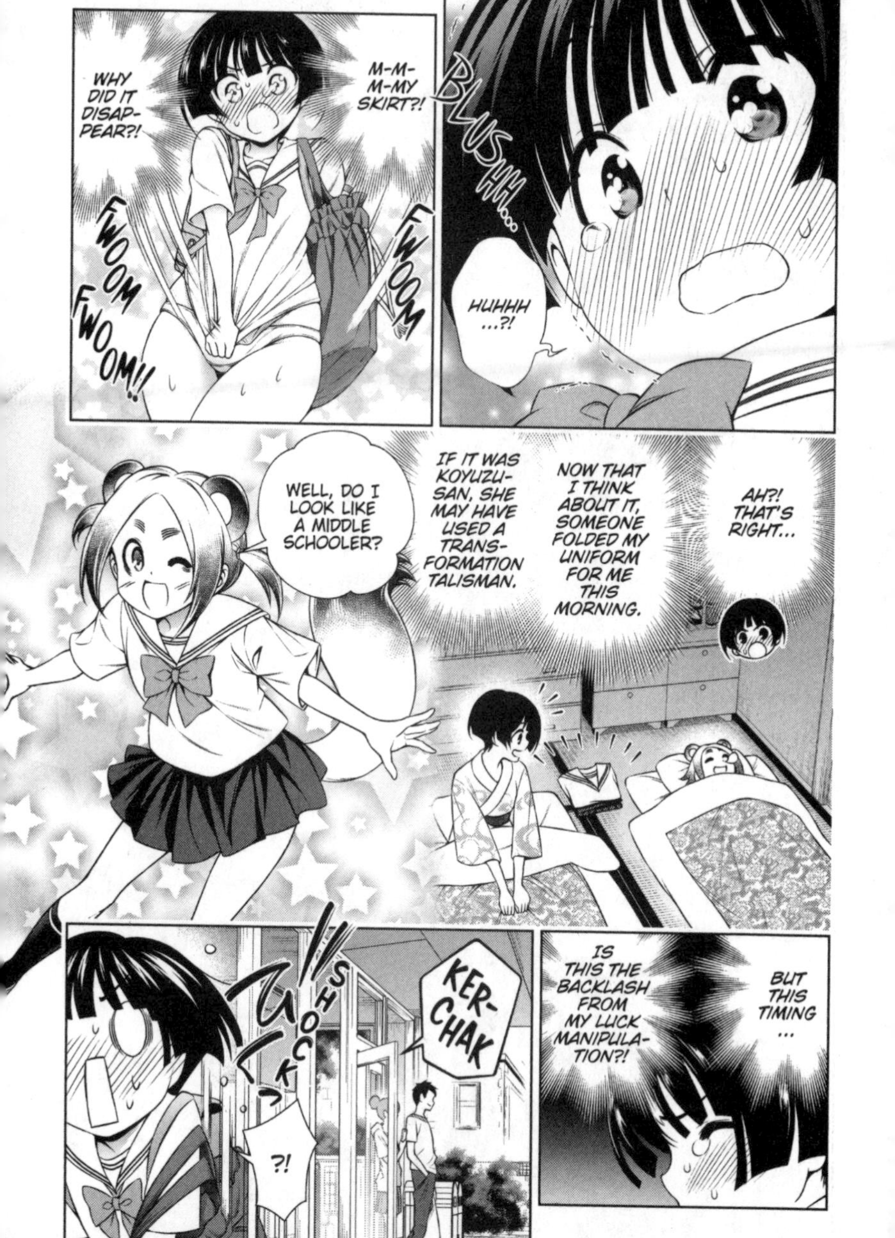
BLUSHH...
HUHHH ...?!
M-M-M-MY SKIRT?!
WHY DID IT DISAPPEAR?!
FWOOM
FWOOM FWOOM!!
AH?! THAT'S RIGHT...
NOW THAT I THINK ABOUT IT, SOMEONE FOLDED MY UNIFORM FOR ME THIS MORNING.
IF IT WAS KOYUZU-SAN, SHE MAY HAVE USED A TRANSFORMATION TALISMAN.
WELL, DO I LOOK LIKE A MIDDLE SCHOOLER?
IS THIS THE BACKLASH FROM MY LUCK MANIPULATION?!
BUT THIS TIMING ...
KER-CHAK
SHOCK
?!

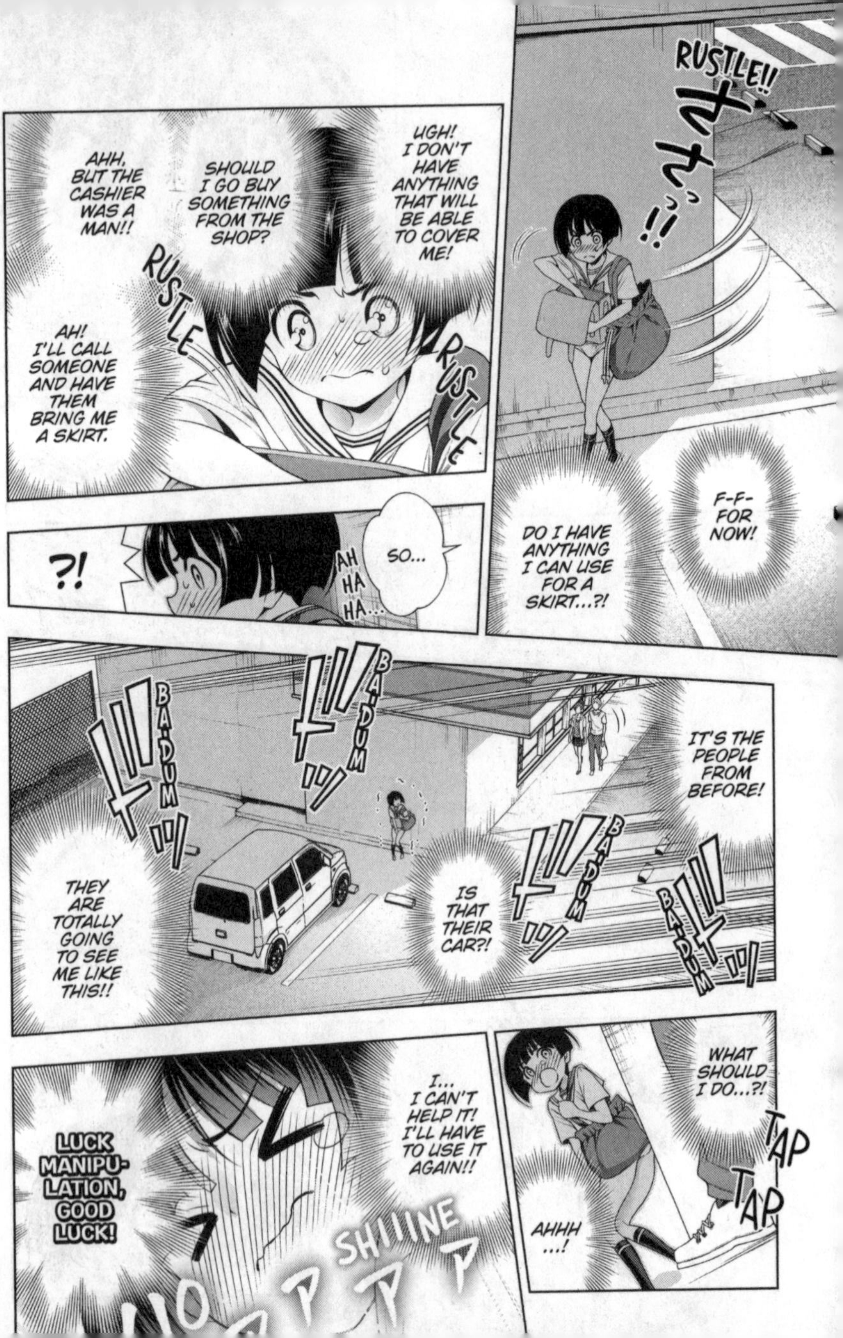
RUSTLE!!
さ さっ!!
F-F-FOR NOW!
DO I HAVE ANYTHING I CAN USE FOR A SKIRT...?!
UGH! I DON'T HAVE ANYTHING THAT WILL BE ABLE TO COVER ME!
SHOULD I GO BUY SOMETHING FROM THE SHOP?
AHH, BUT THE CASHIER WAS A MAN!!
RUSTLE
RUSTLE
AH! I'LL CALL SOMEONE AND HAVE THEM BRING ME A SKIRT.
SO...
AH HA HA...
?!
IT'S THE PEOPLE FROM BEFORE!
BA-DUM
BA-DUM
IS THAT THEIR CAR?!
BA-DUM
BA-DUM
THEY ARE TOTALLY GOING TO SEE ME LIKE THIS!!
WHAT SHOULD I DO...?!
TAP
TAP
AHHH ...!
I... I CAN'T HELP IT! I'LL HAVE TO USE IT AGAIN!!
LUCK MANIPULATION, GOOD LUCK!
SHIIINE

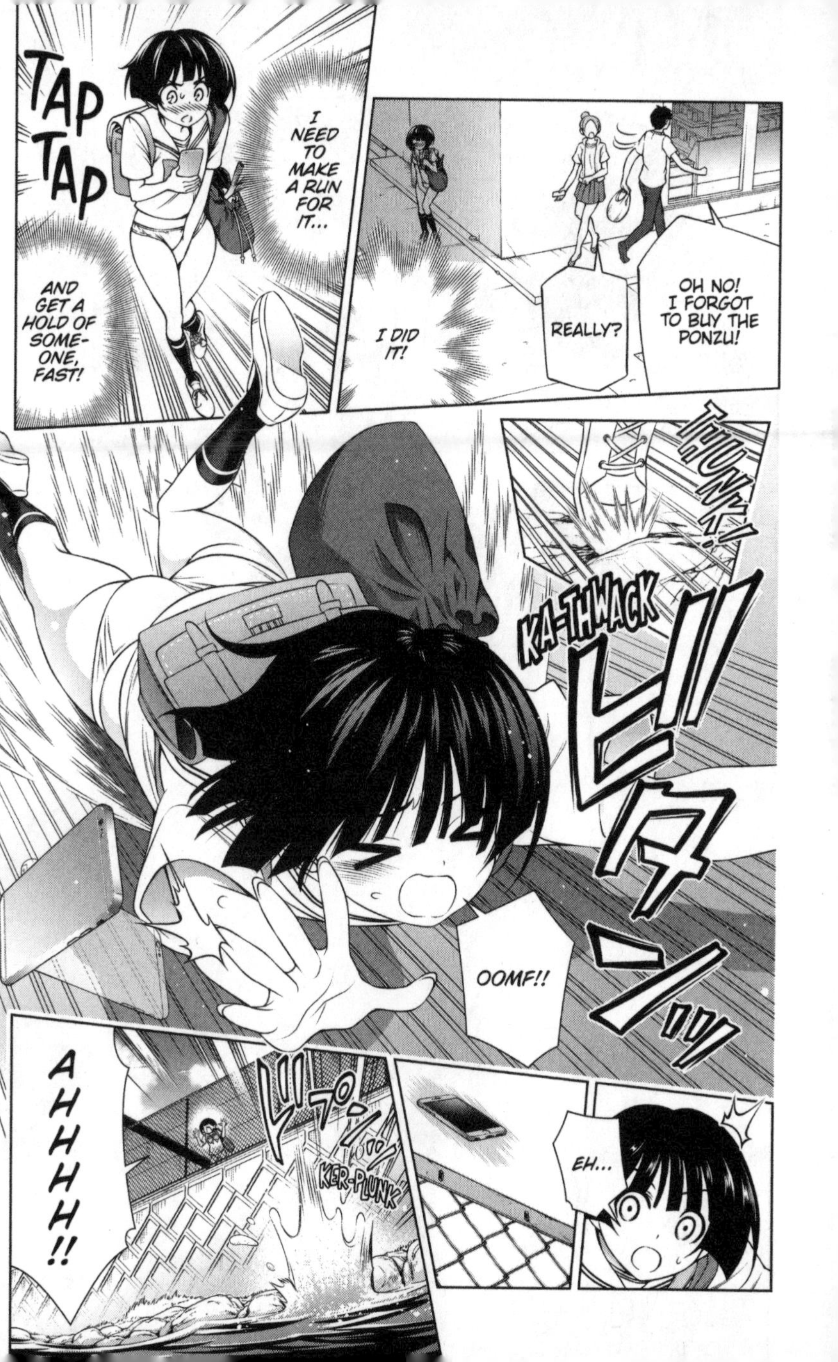

OH NO! I FORGOT TO BUY THE PONZU!
REALLY?
I DID IT!
I NEED TO MAKE A RUN FOR IT...
AND GET A HOLD OF SOME-ONE, FAST!
TAP TAP
THUNK!!
KA-THWACK
OOMF!!
EH...
KER-PLUNK
AHHHHH!!

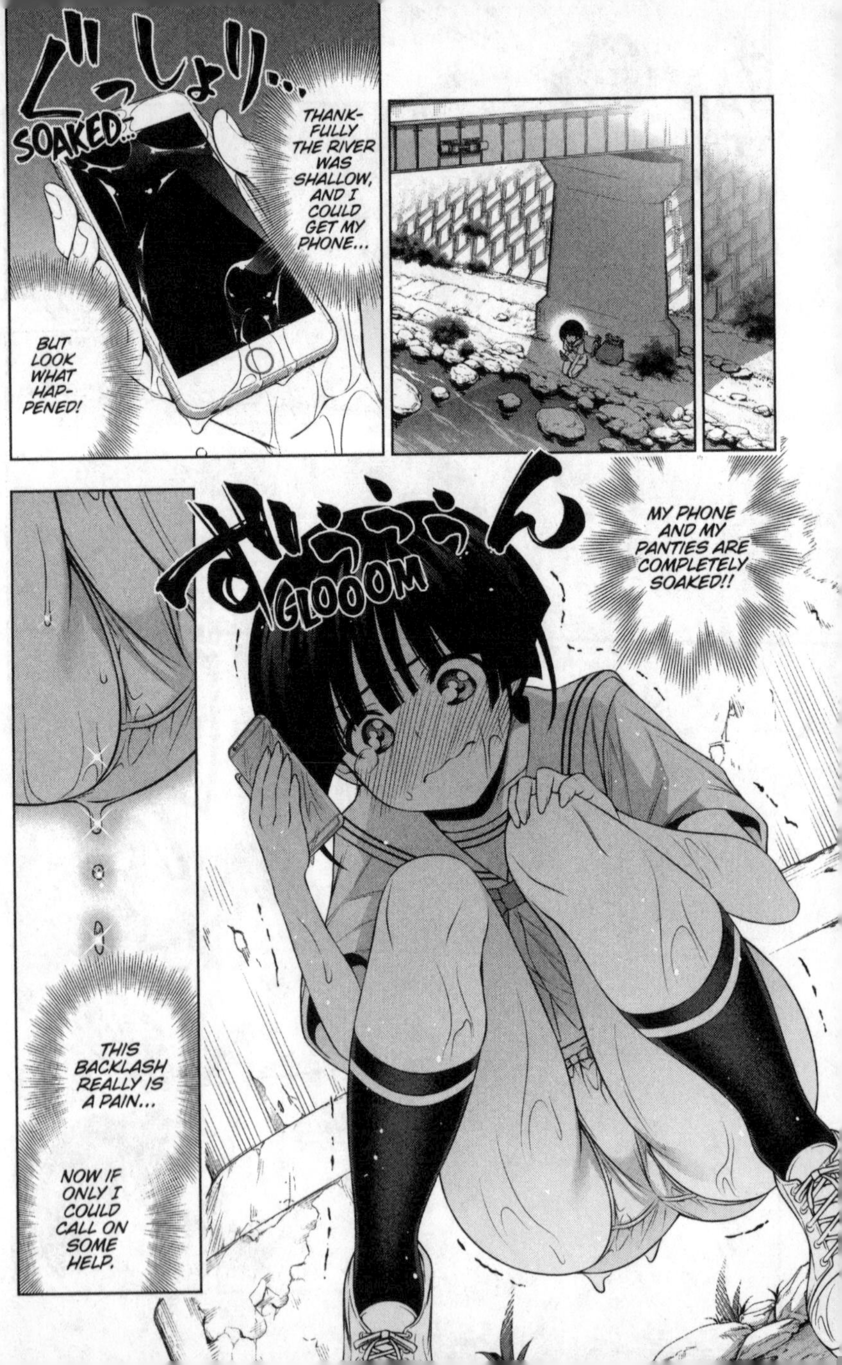

ぐっしょり…
SOAKED…
THANK-FULLY THE RIVER WAS SHALLOW, AND I COULD GET MY PHONE…
BUT LOOK WHAT HAP-PENED!
GLOOOM
MY PHONE AND MY PANTIES ARE COMPLETELY SOAKED!!
THIS BACKLASH REALLY IS A PAIN…
NOW IF ONLY I COULD CALL ON SOME HELP.

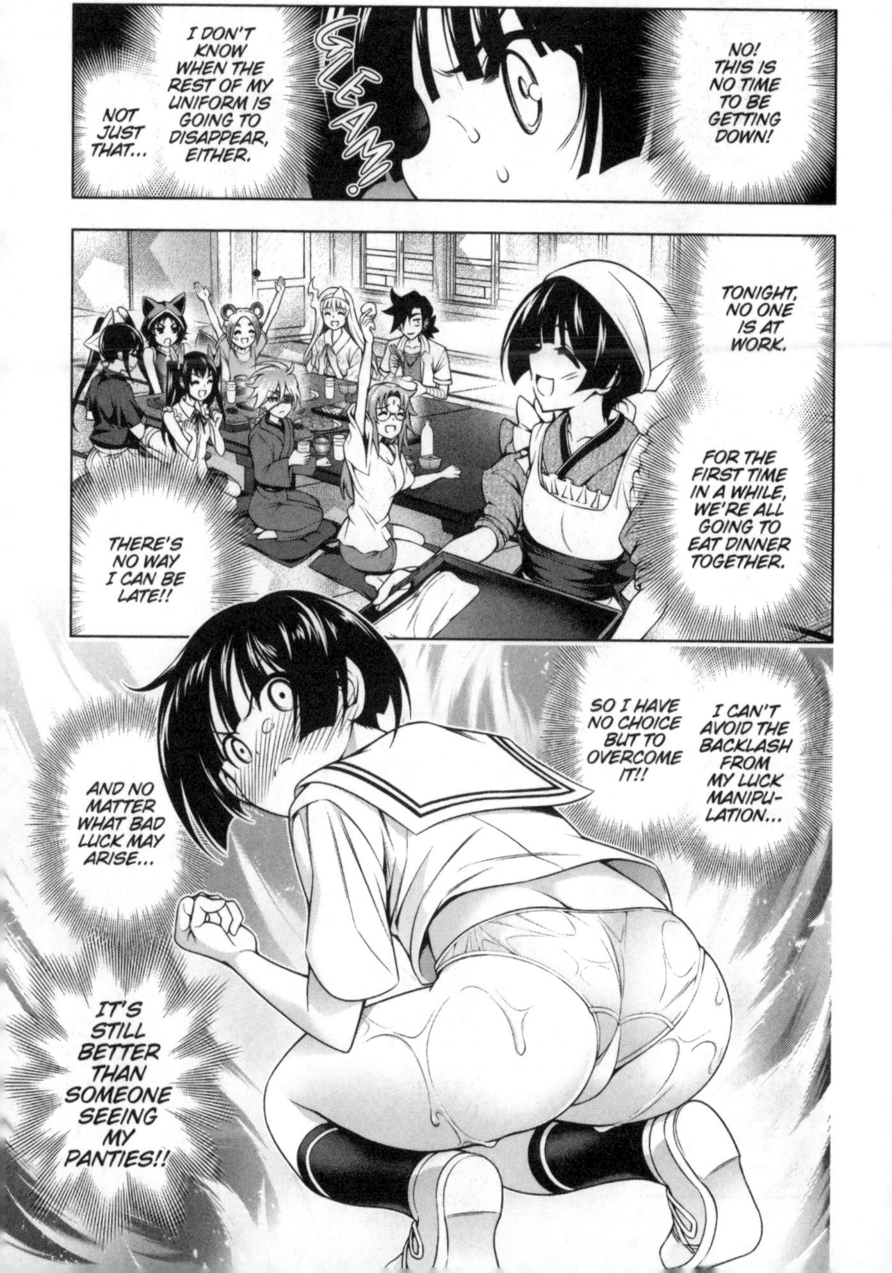
NO! THIS IS NO TIME TO BE GETTING DOWN!
GLEAM!
I DON'T KNOW WHEN THE REST OF MY UNIFORM IS GOING TO DISAPPEAR, EITHER.
NOT JUST THAT...
TONIGHT, NO ONE IS AT WORK.
FOR THE FIRST TIME IN A WHILE, WE'RE ALL GOING TO EAT DINNER TOGETHER.
THERE'S NO WAY I CAN BE LATE!!
I CAN'T AVOID THE BACKLASH FROM MY LUCK MANIPULATION...
SO I HAVE NO CHOICE BUT TO OVERCOME IT!!
AND NO MATTER WHAT BAD LUCK MAY ARISE...
IT'S STILL BETTER THAN SOMEONE SEEING MY PANTIES!!

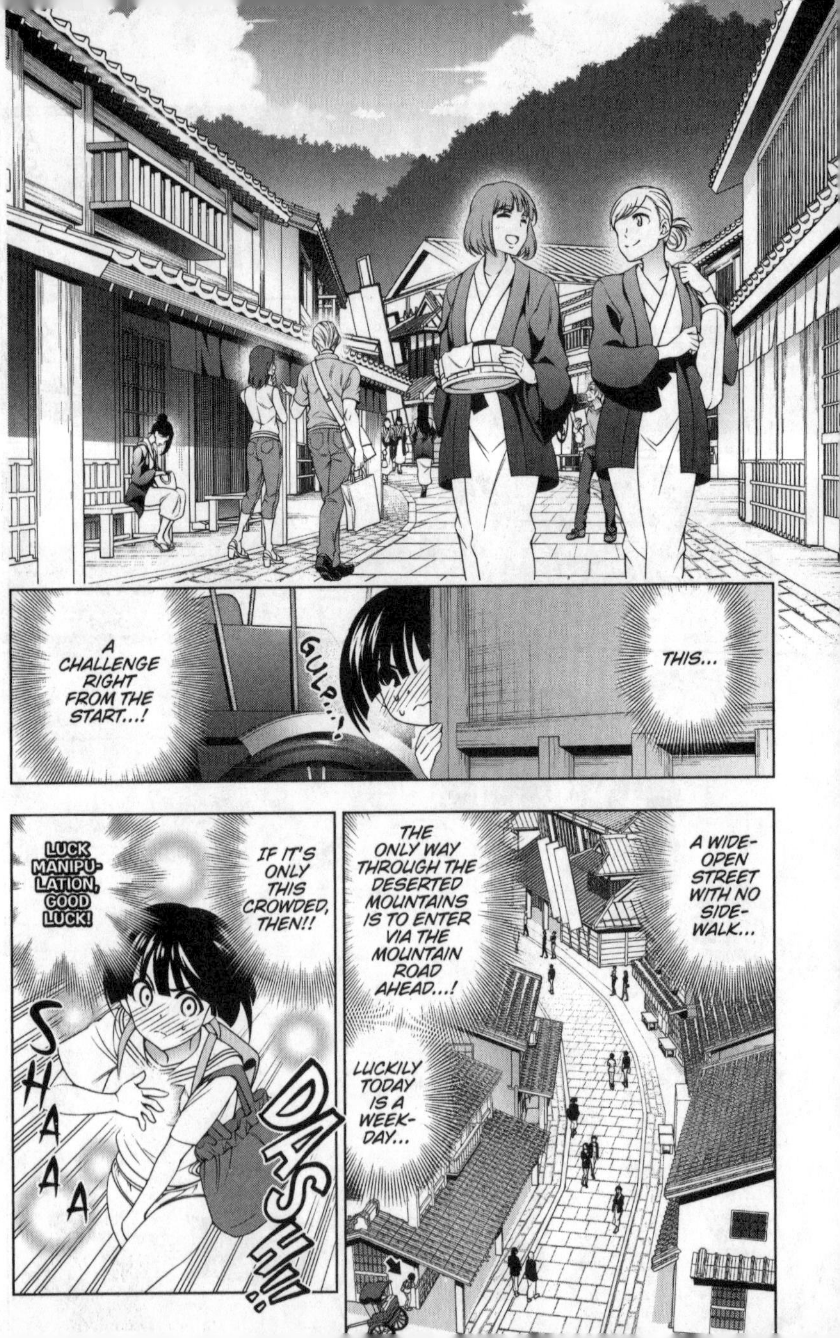
THIS...
GULP...!
A CHALLENGE RIGHT FROM THE START...!
A WIDE-OPEN STREET WITH NO SIDEWALK...
THE ONLY WAY THROUGH THE DESERTED MOUNTAINS IS TO ENTER VIA THE MOUNTAIN ROAD AHEAD...!
LUCKILY TODAY IS A WEEKDAY...
IF IT'S ONLY THIS CROWDED, THEN!!
LUCK MANIPULATION, GOOD LUCK!
DASH!!
SHAAA

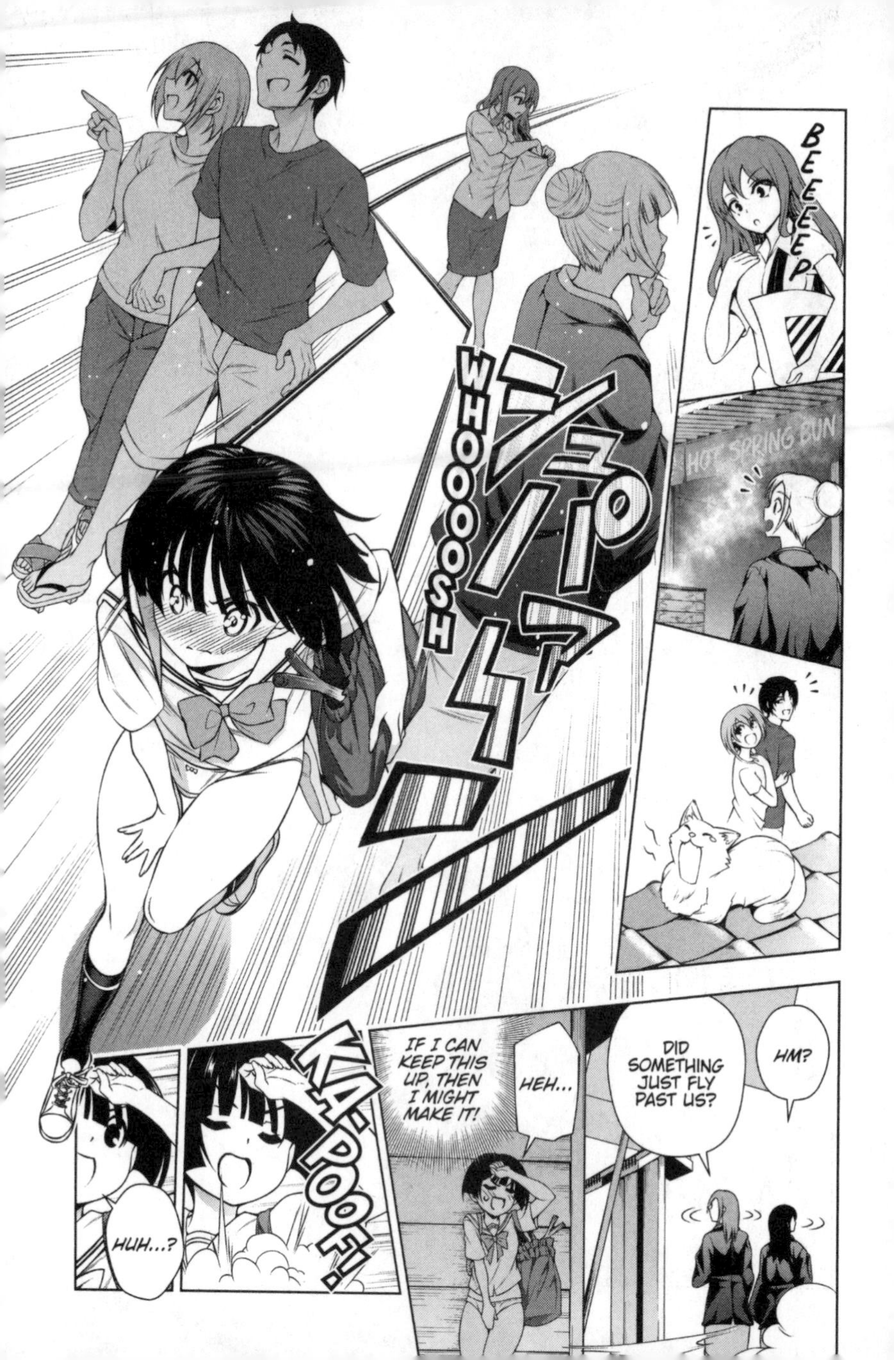
BEEEEP
HOT SPRING BUN
WHOOOOOSH
HM?
DID SOMETHING JUST FLY PAST US?
HEH...
IF I CAN KEEP THIS UP, THEN I MIGHT MAKE IT!
KA-POOF!
HUH...?

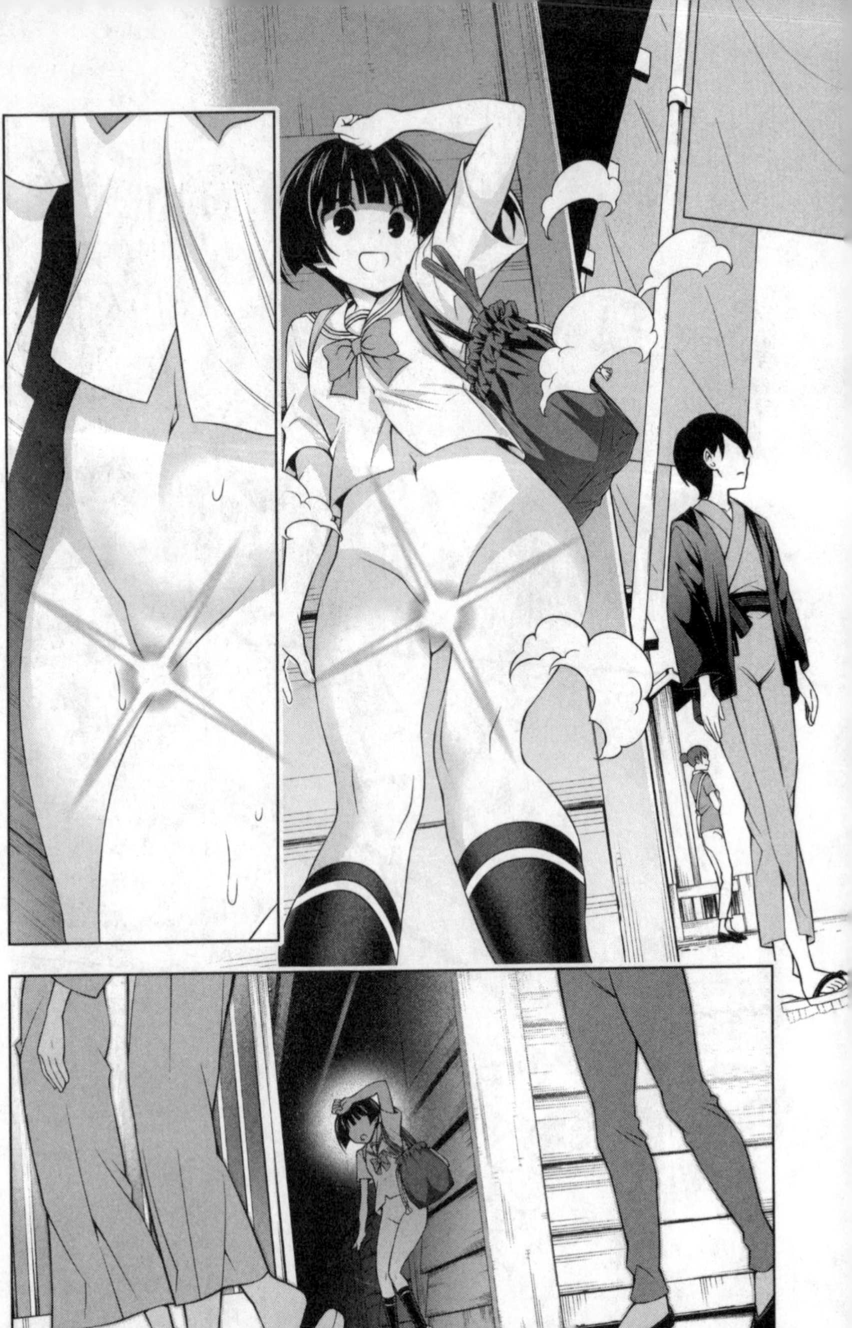

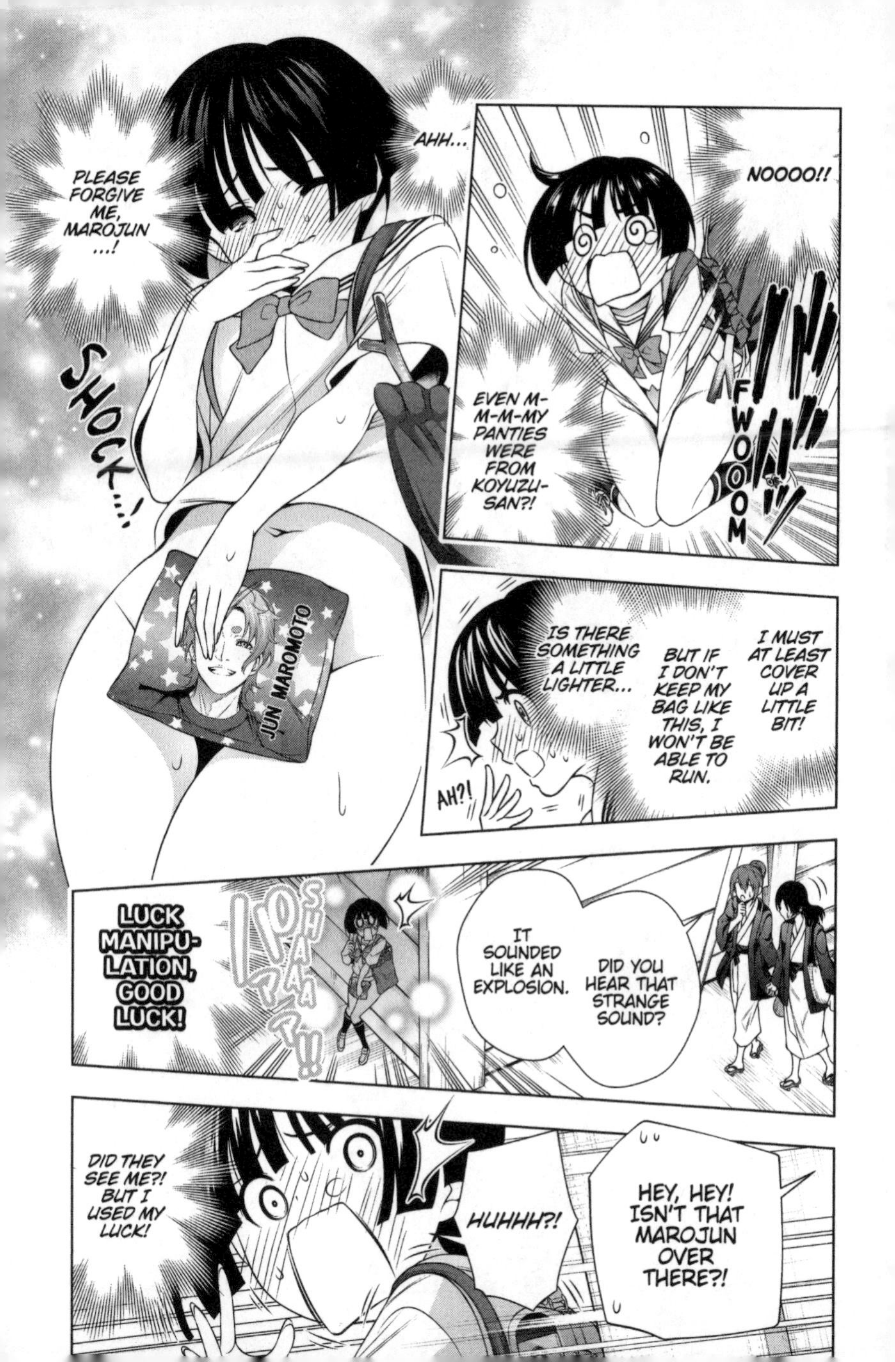
NOOOO!!
FWOOOOM
EVEN M-M-M-MY PANTIES WERE FROM KOYUZU-SAN?!
AHH...
PLEASE FORGIVE ME, MAROJUN ...!
SHOCK...!
JUN MAROMOTO
I MUST AT LEAST COVER UP A LITTLE BIT!
BUT IF I DON'T KEEP MY BAG LIKE THIS, I WON'T BE ABLE TO RUN.
IS THERE SOMETHING A LITTLE LIGHTER...
AH?!
DID YOU HEAR THAT STRANGE SOUND?
IT SOUNDED LIKE AN EXPLOSION.
SHAAAA
LUCK MANIPULATION, GOOD LUCK!
HEY, HEY! ISN'T THAT MAROJUN OVER THERE?!
HUHHH?!
DID THEY SEE ME?! BUT I USED MY LUCK!

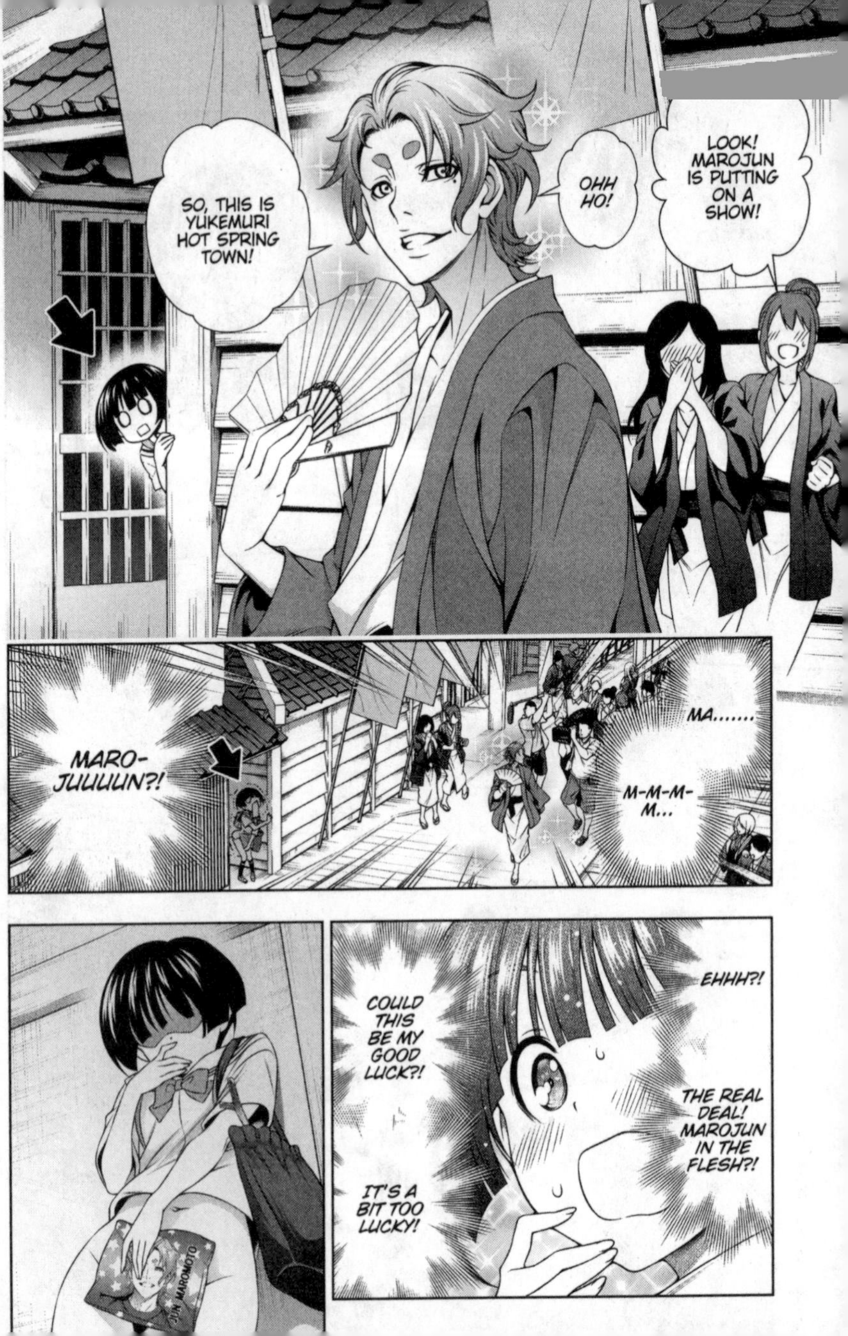
LOOK! MAROJUN IS PUTTING ON A SHOW!
OHH HO!
SO, THIS IS YUKEMURI HOT SPRING TOWN!
MA.......
M-M-M-M...
MARO-JUUUUN?!
EHHH?!
THE REAL DEAL! MAROJUN IN THE FLESH?!
COULD THIS BE MY GOOD LUCK?!
IT'S A BIT TOO LUCKY!
JUN MAROMOTO

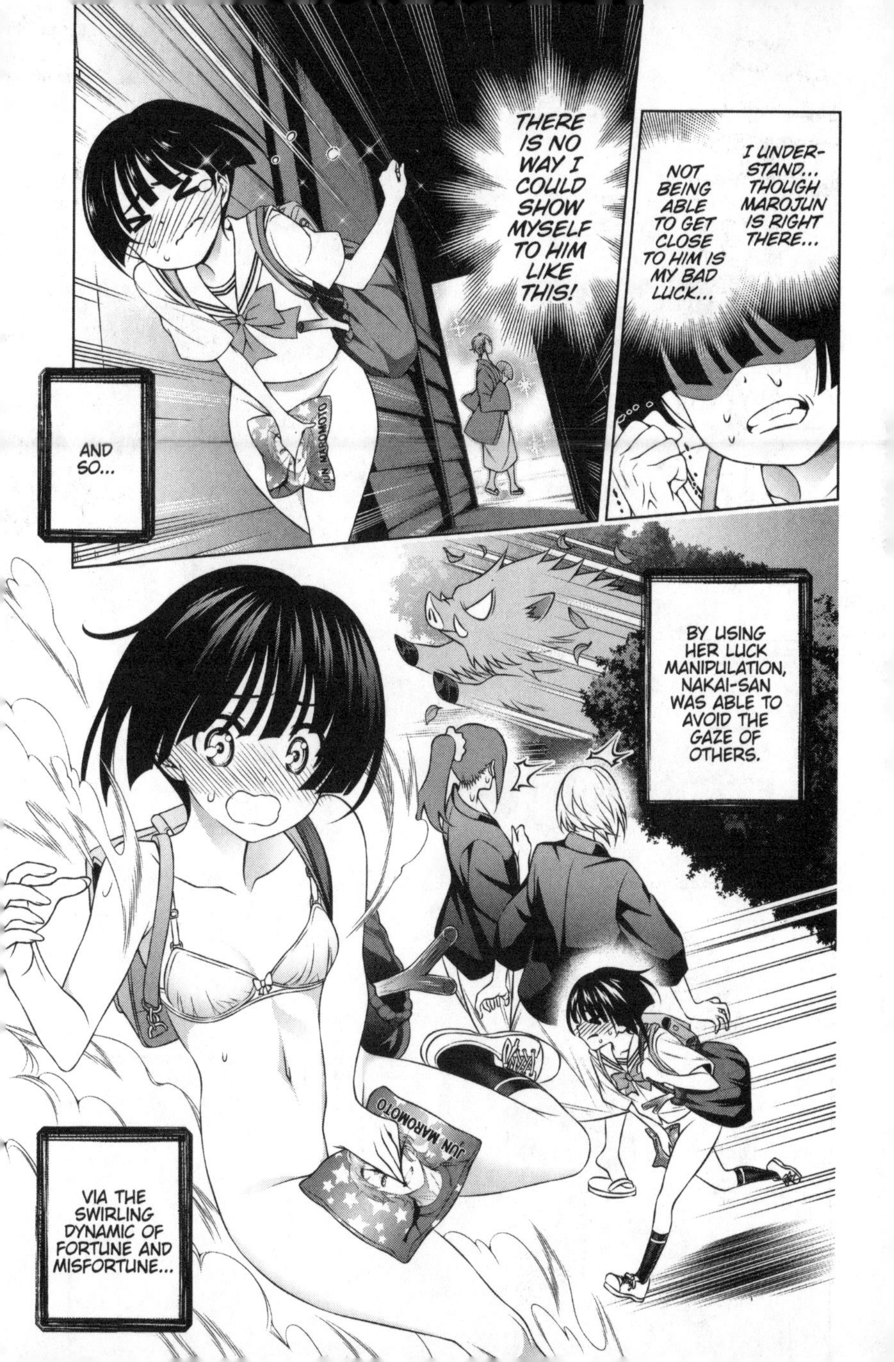
I UNDERSTAND... THOUGH MAROJUN IS RIGHT THERE...
NOT BEING ABLE TO GET CLOSE TO HIM IS MY BAD LUCK...
THERE IS NO WAY I COULD SHOW MYSELF TO HIM LIKE THIS!
JUN MAROMOTO
AND SO...
BY USING HER LUCK MANIPULATION, NAKAI-SAN WAS ABLE TO AVOID THE GAZE OF OTHERS.
JUN MAROMOTO
VIA THE SWIRLING DYNAMIC OF FORTUNE AND MISFORTUNE...

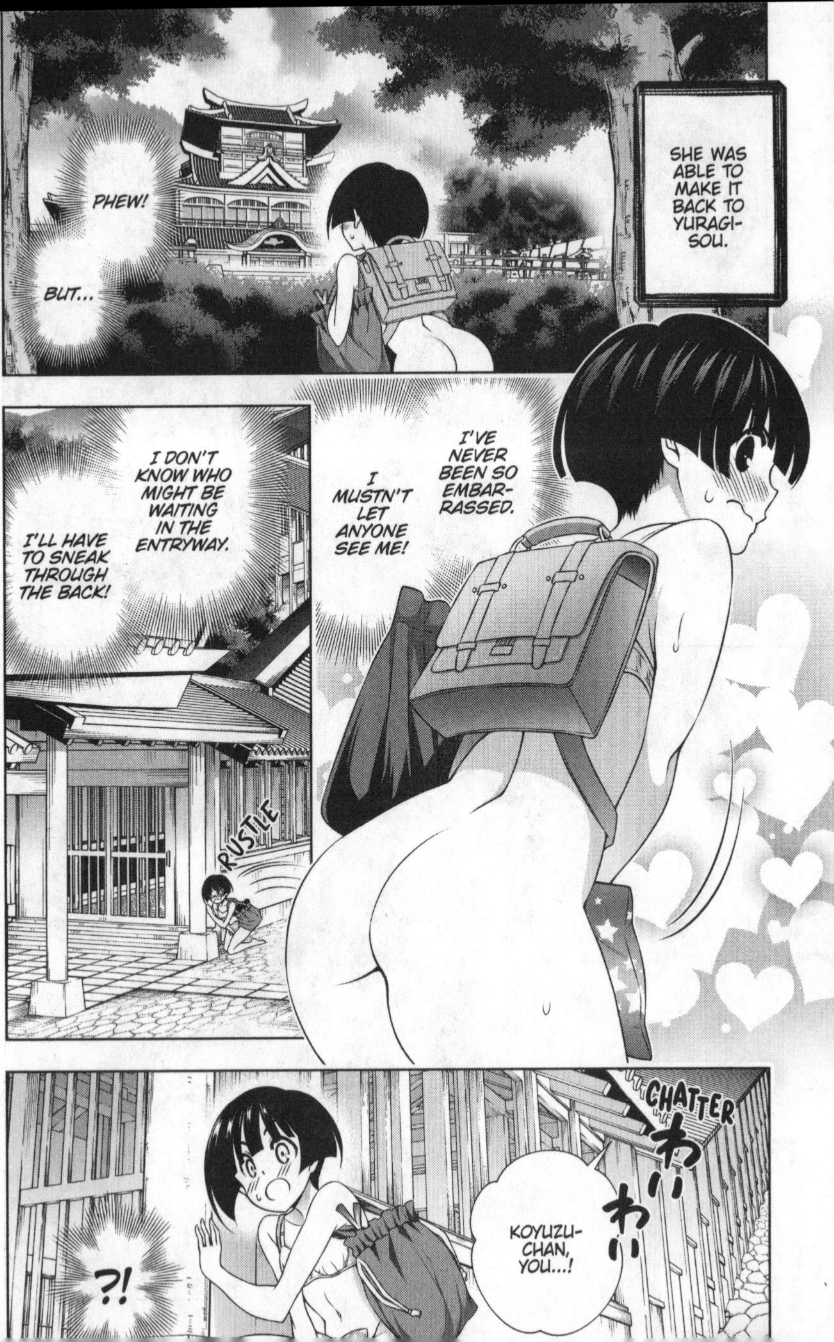
SHE WAS ABLE TO MAKE IT BACK TO YURAGI-SOU.
PHEW!
BUT...
I'VE NEVER BEEN SO EMBARRASSED.
I MUSTN'T LET ANYONE SEE ME!
I DON'T KNOW WHO MIGHT BE WAITING IN THE ENTRYWAY.
I'LL HAVE TO SNEAK THROUGH THE BACK!
RUSTLE
CHATTER
わいわい
KOYUZU-CHAN, YOU...!
?!

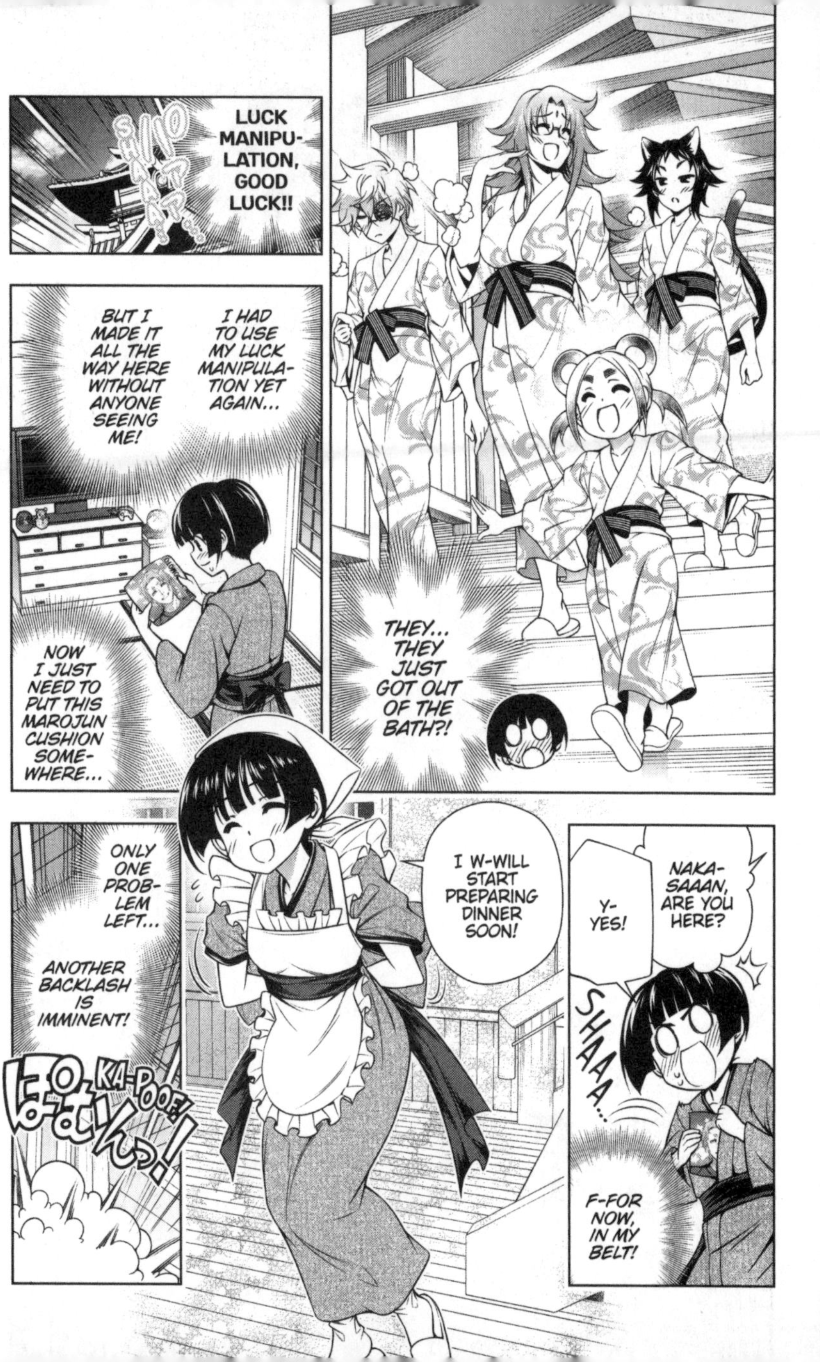
SHIAAA...
LUCK MANIPU-LATION, GOOD LUCK!!
I HAD TO USE MY LUCK MANIPULA-TION YET AGAIN...
BUT I MADE IT ALL THE WAY HERE WITHOUT ANYONE SEEING ME!
NOW I JUST NEED TO PUT THIS MAROJUN CUSHION SOME-WHERE...
THEY... THEY JUST GOT OUT OF THE BATH?!
NAKA-SAAAN, ARE YOU HERE?
Y-YES!
SHAAA...
F-FOR NOW, IN MY BELT!
I W-WILL START PREPARING DINNER SOON!
ONLY ONE PROB-LEM LEFT...
ANOTHER BACKLASH IS IMMINENT!
KA-POOF!

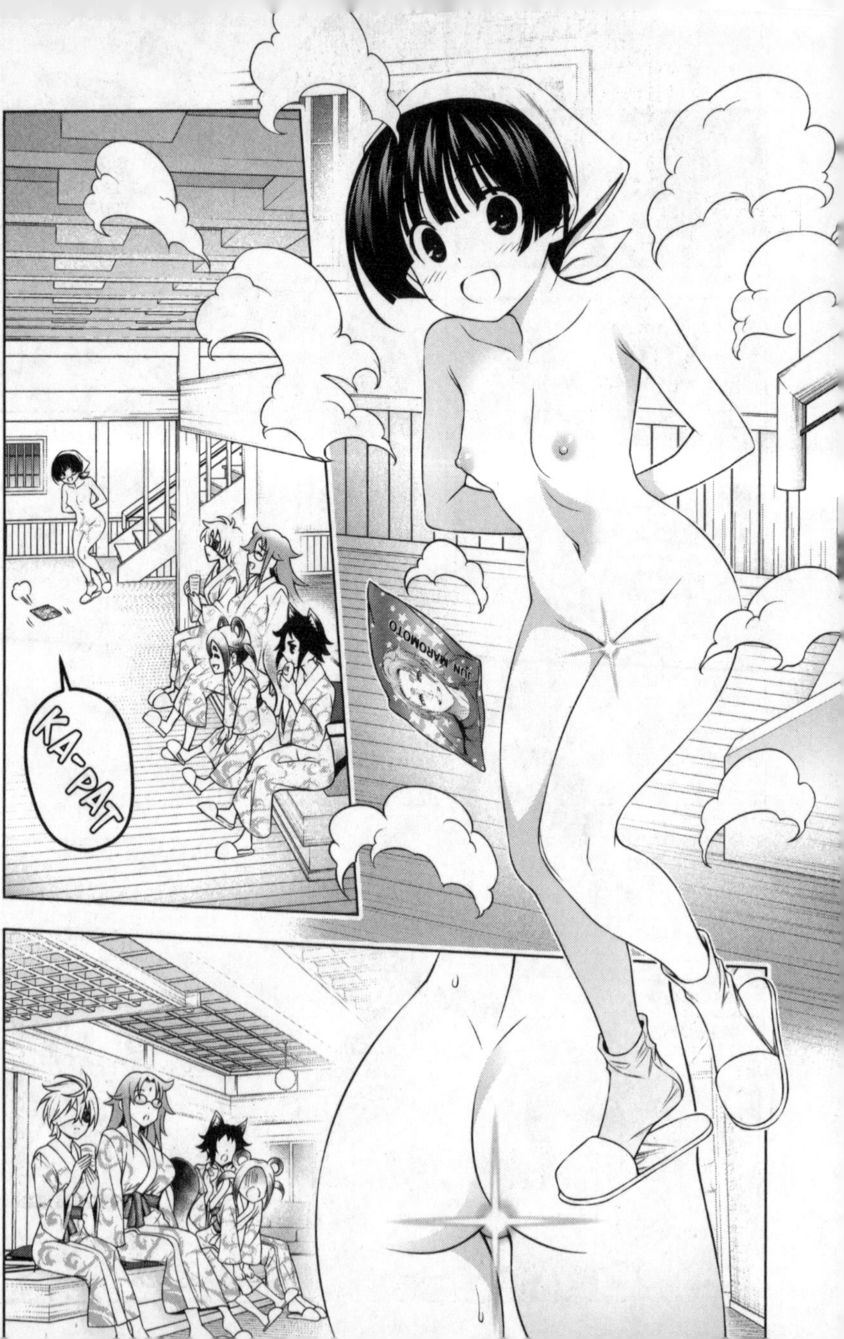
KA-PAT
JUN MAROMOTO

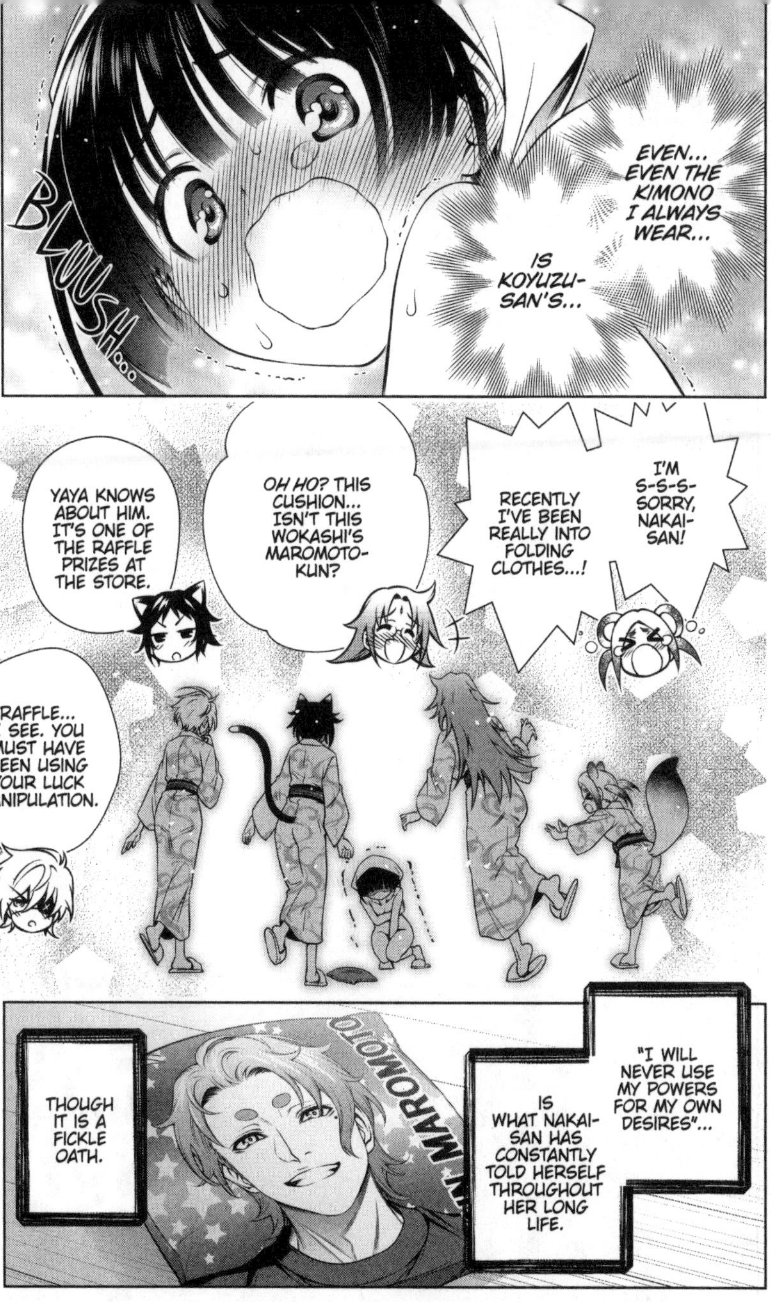
EVEN... EVEN THE KIMONO I ALWAYS WEAR...
IS KOYUZU-SAN'S...
BLUUSH...
I'M S-S-S-SORRY, NAKAI-SAN!
RECENTLY I'VE BEEN REALLY INTO FOLDING CLOTHES...!
OH HO? THIS CUSHION... ISN'T THIS WOKASHI'S MAROMOTO-KUN?
YAYA KNOWS ABOUT HIM. IT'S ONE OF THE RAFFLE PRIZES AT THE STORE.
RAFFLE... I SEE. YOU MUST HAVE BEEN USING YOUR LUCK MANIPULATION.
"I WILL NEVER USE MY POWERS FOR MY OWN DESIRES"...
IS WHAT NAKAI-SAN HAS CONSTANTLY TOLD HERSELF THROUGHOUT HER LONG LIFE.
THOUGH IT IS A FICKLE OATH.
MAROMOTO

Yuuna
and the
Haunted
Hot
Springs

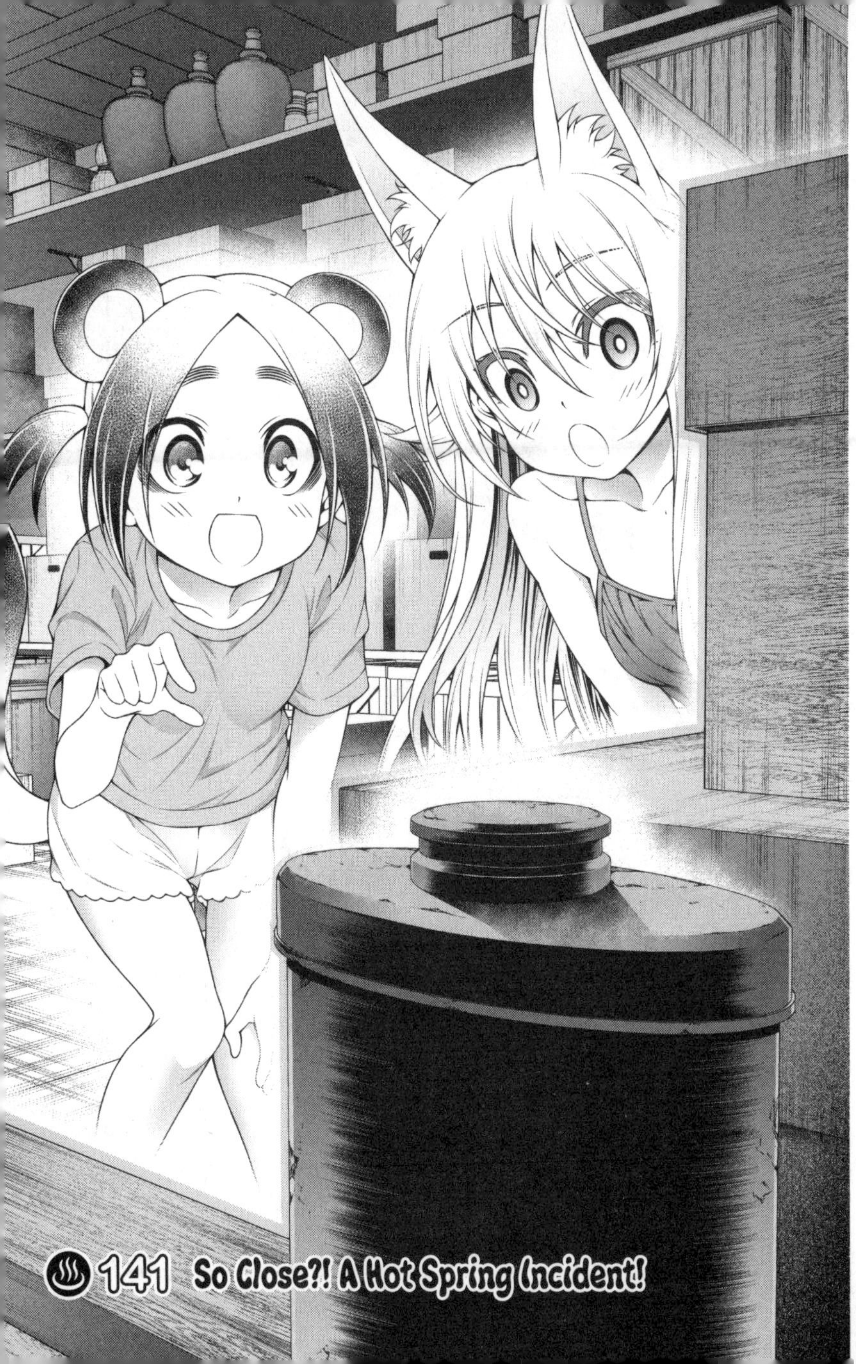
141 So Close?! A Hot Spring Incident!

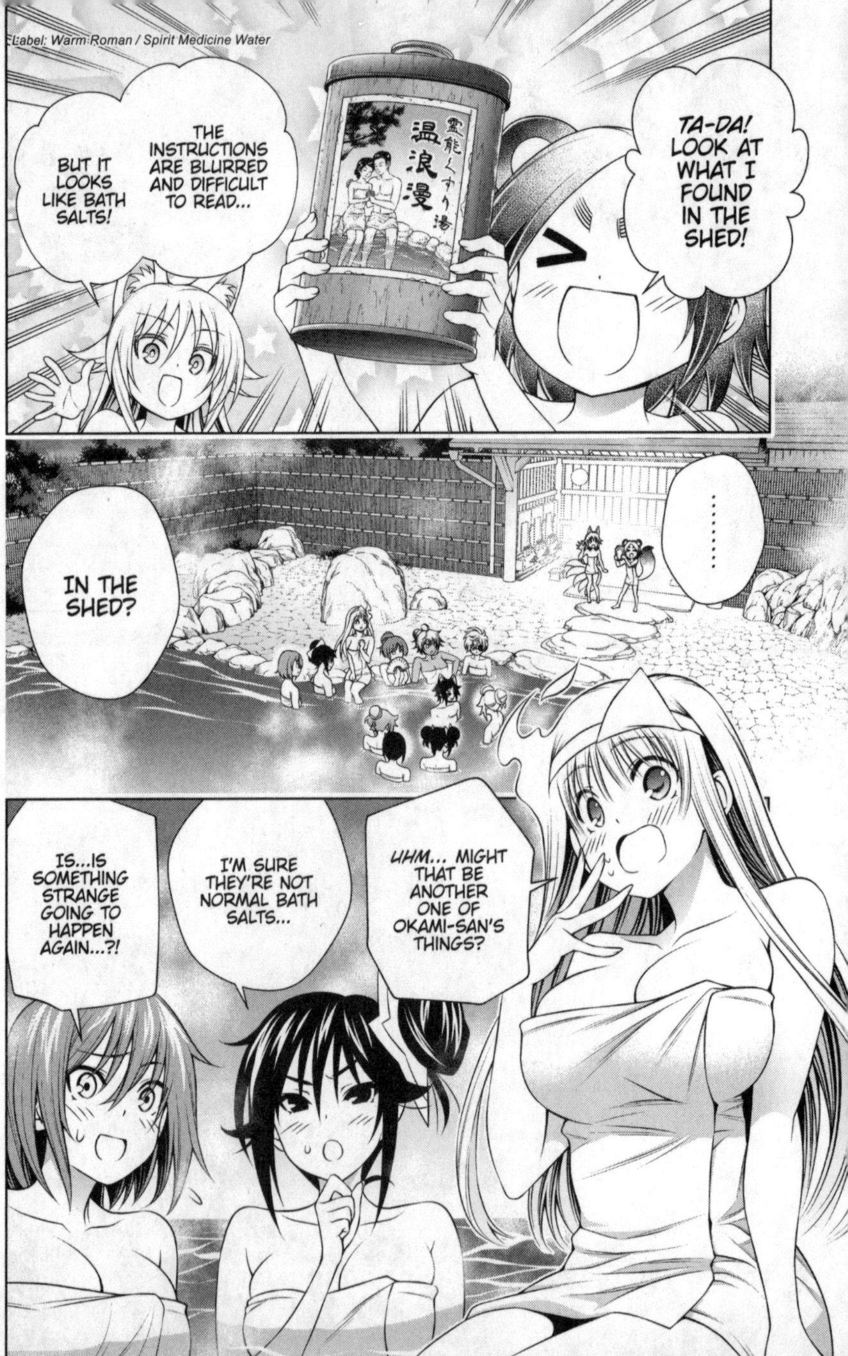
Label: Warm Roman / Spirit Medicine Water
TA-DA! LOOK AT WHAT I FOUND IN THE SHED!
霊能くすり湯
温浪漫
THE INSTRUCTIONS ARE BLURRED AND DIFFICULT TO READ...
BUT IT LOOKS LIKE BATH SALTS!
......
IN THE SHED?
UHM... MIGHT THAT BE ANOTHER ONE OF OKAMI-SAN'S THINGS?
I'M SURE THEY'RE NOT NORMAL BATH SALTS...
IS...IS SOMETHING STRANGE GOING TO HAPPEN AGAIN...?!

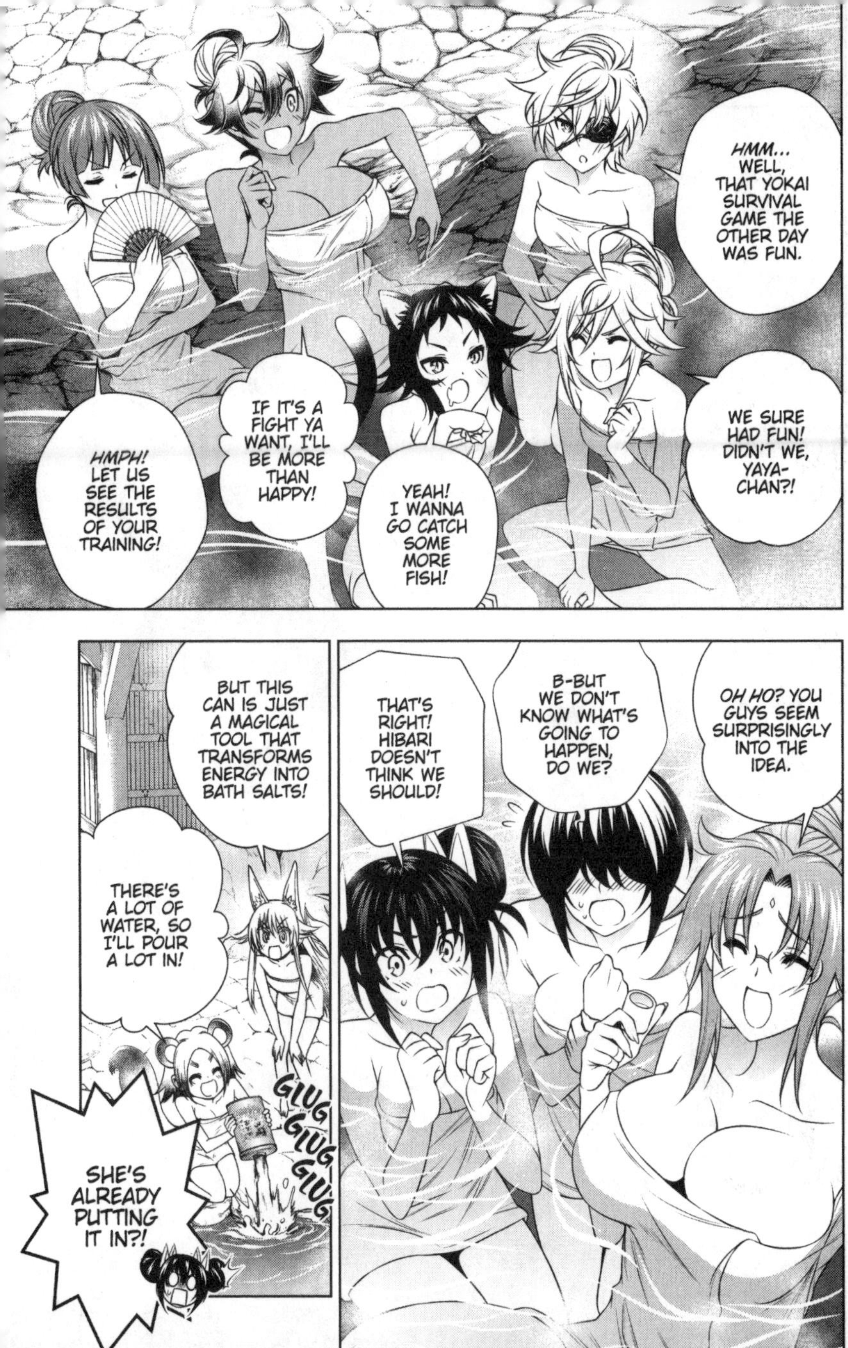
HMM... WELL, THAT YOKAI SURVIVAL GAME THE OTHER DAY WAS FUN.
WE SURE HAD FUN! DIDN'T WE, YAYA-CHAN?!
YEAH! I WANNA GO CATCH SOME MORE FISH!
IF IT'S A FIGHT YA WANT, I'LL BE MORE THAN HAPPY!
HMPH! LET US SEE THE RESULTS OF YOUR TRAINING!
OH HO? YOU GUYS SEEM SURPRISINGLY INTO THE IDEA.
B-BUT WE DON'T KNOW WHAT'S GOING TO HAPPEN, DO WE?
THAT'S RIGHT! HIBARI DOESN'T THINK WE SHOULD!
BUT THIS CAN IS JUST A MAGICAL TOOL THAT TRANSFORMS ENERGY INTO BATH SALTS!
THERE'S A LOT OF WATER, SO I'LL POUR A LOT IN!
GLUG GLUG GLUG GLUG
SHE'S ALREADY PUTTING IT IN?!

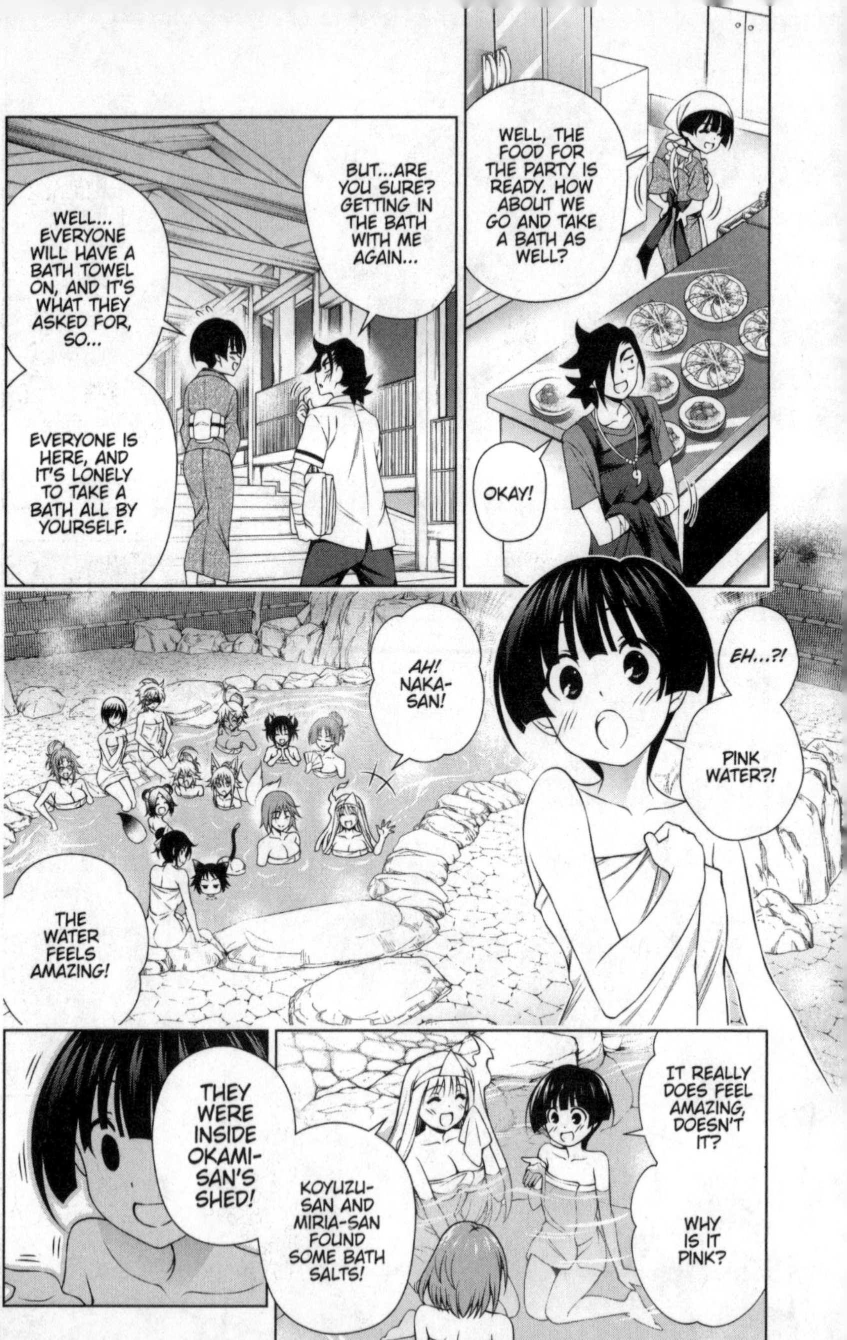
WELL, THE FOOD FOR THE PARTY IS READY. HOW ABOUT WE GO AND TAKE A BATH AS WELL?
OKAY!
BUT...ARE YOU SURE? GETTING IN THE BATH WITH ME AGAIN...
WELL... EVERYONE WILL HAVE A BATH TOWEL ON, AND IT'S WHAT THEY ASKED FOR, SO...
EVERYONE IS HERE, AND IT'S LONELY TO TAKE A BATH ALL BY YOURSELF.
EH...?!
PINK WATER?!
AH! NAKA-SAN!
THE WATER FEELS AMAZING!
IT REALLY DOES FEEL AMAZING, DOESN'T IT?
WHY IS IT PINK?
KOYUZU-SAN AND MIRIA-SAN FOUND SOME BATH SALTS!
THEY WERE INSIDE OKAMI-SAN'S SHED!

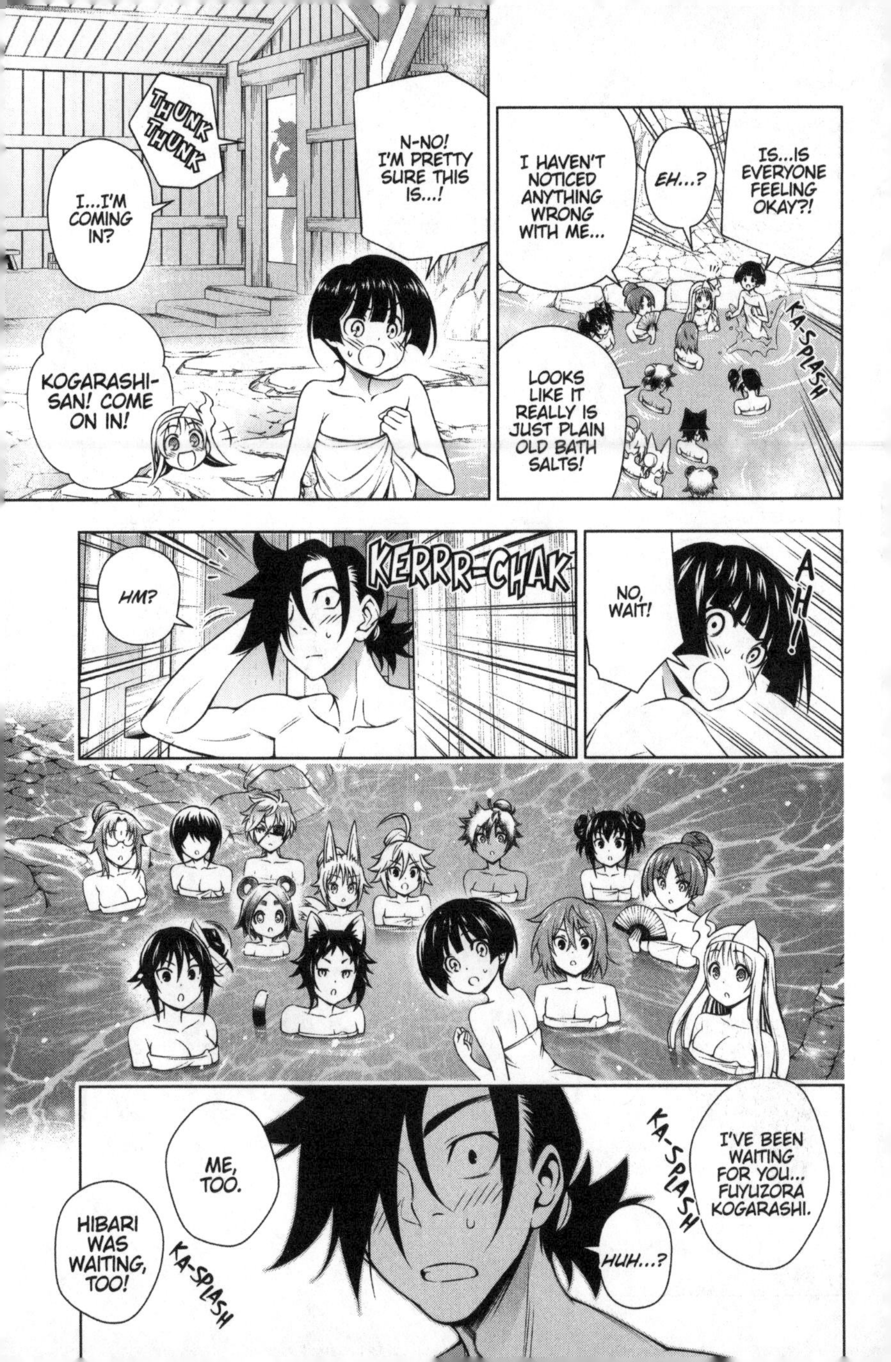
THUNK THUNK
I...I'M COMING IN?
N-NO! I'M PRETTY SURE THIS IS...!
KOGARASHI-SAN! COME ON IN!
I HAVEN'T NOTICED ANYTHING WRONG WITH ME...
EH...?
IS...IS EVERYONE FEELING OKAY?!
KA-SPLASH
LOOKS LIKE IT REALLY IS JUST PLAIN OLD BATH SALTS!
HM?
KERRR-CHAK
NO, WAIT!
AH!
ME, TOO.
HIBARI WAS WAITING, TOO!
KA-SPLASH
KA-SPLASH
I'VE BEEN WAITING FOR YOU... FUYUZORA KOGARASHI.
HUH...?

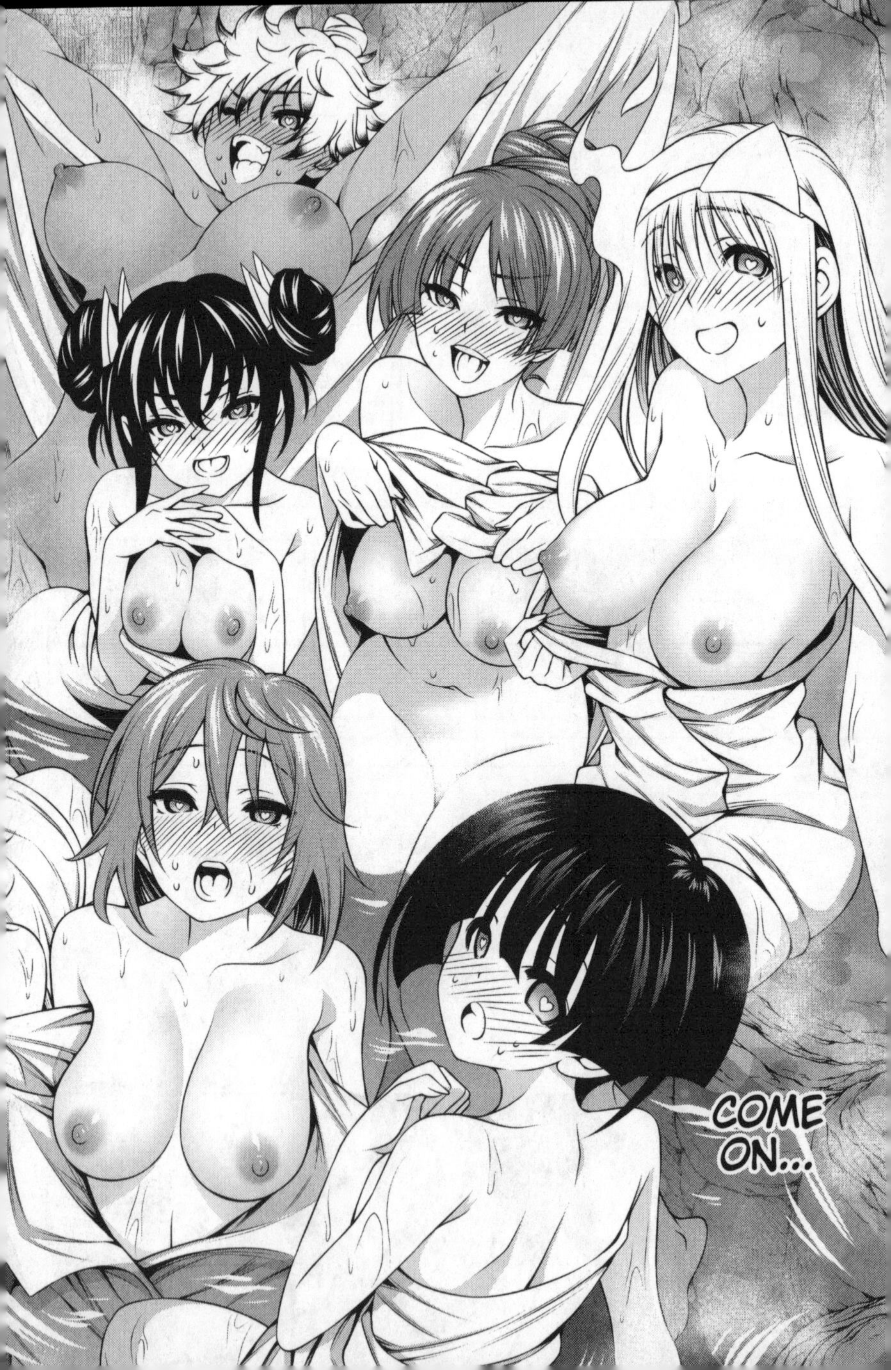
COME ON...

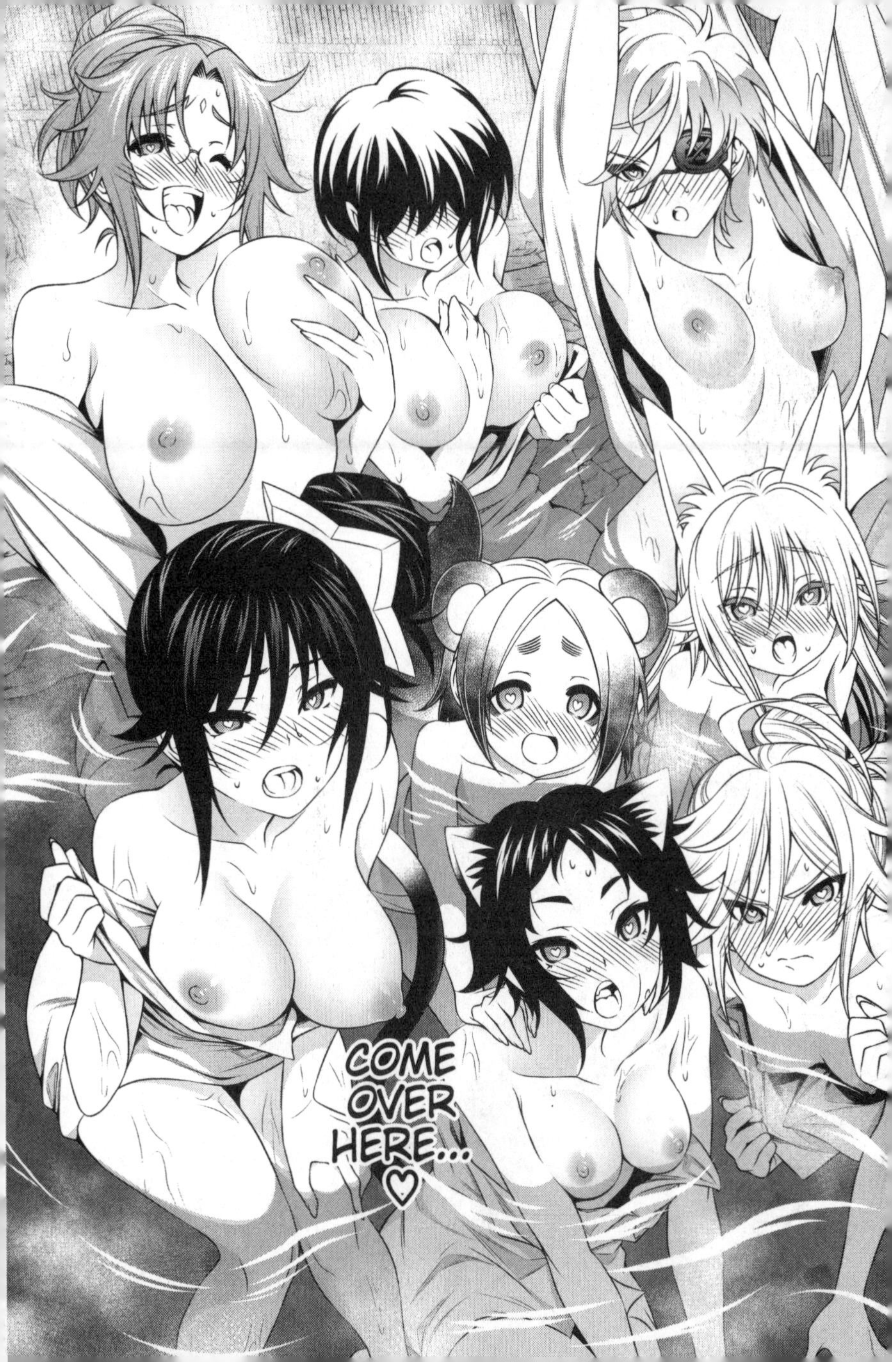
COME OVER HERE...♡

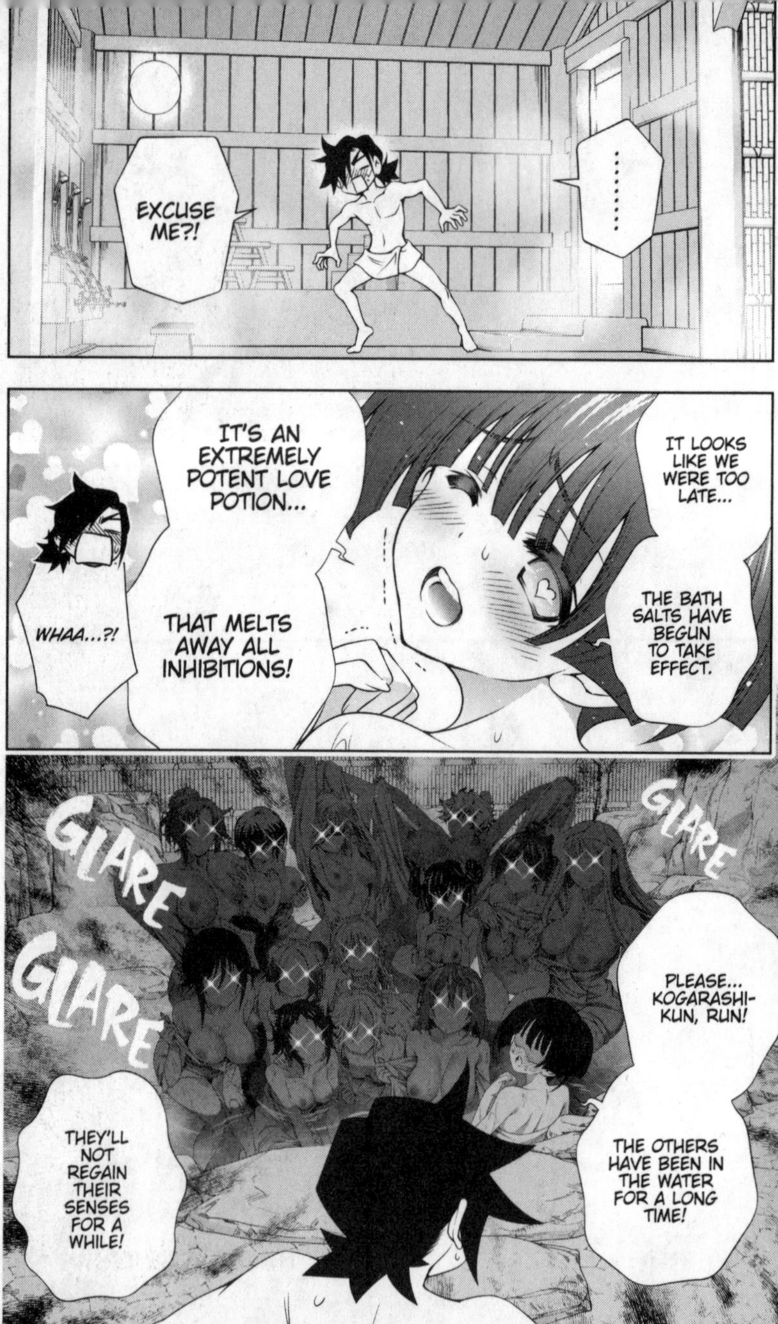

……
EXCUSE ME?!
IT LOOKS LIKE WE WERE TOO LATE...
THE BATH SALTS HAVE BEGUN TO TAKE EFFECT.
IT'S AN EXTREMELY POTENT LOVE POTION...
THAT MELTS AWAY ALL INHIBITIONS!
WHAA...?!
GLARE
PLEASE... KOGARASHI-KUN, RUN!
THE OTHERS HAVE BEEN IN THE WATER FOR A LONG TIME!
THEY'LL NOT REGAIN THEIR SENSES FOR A WHILE!
GLARE
GLARE
GLARE

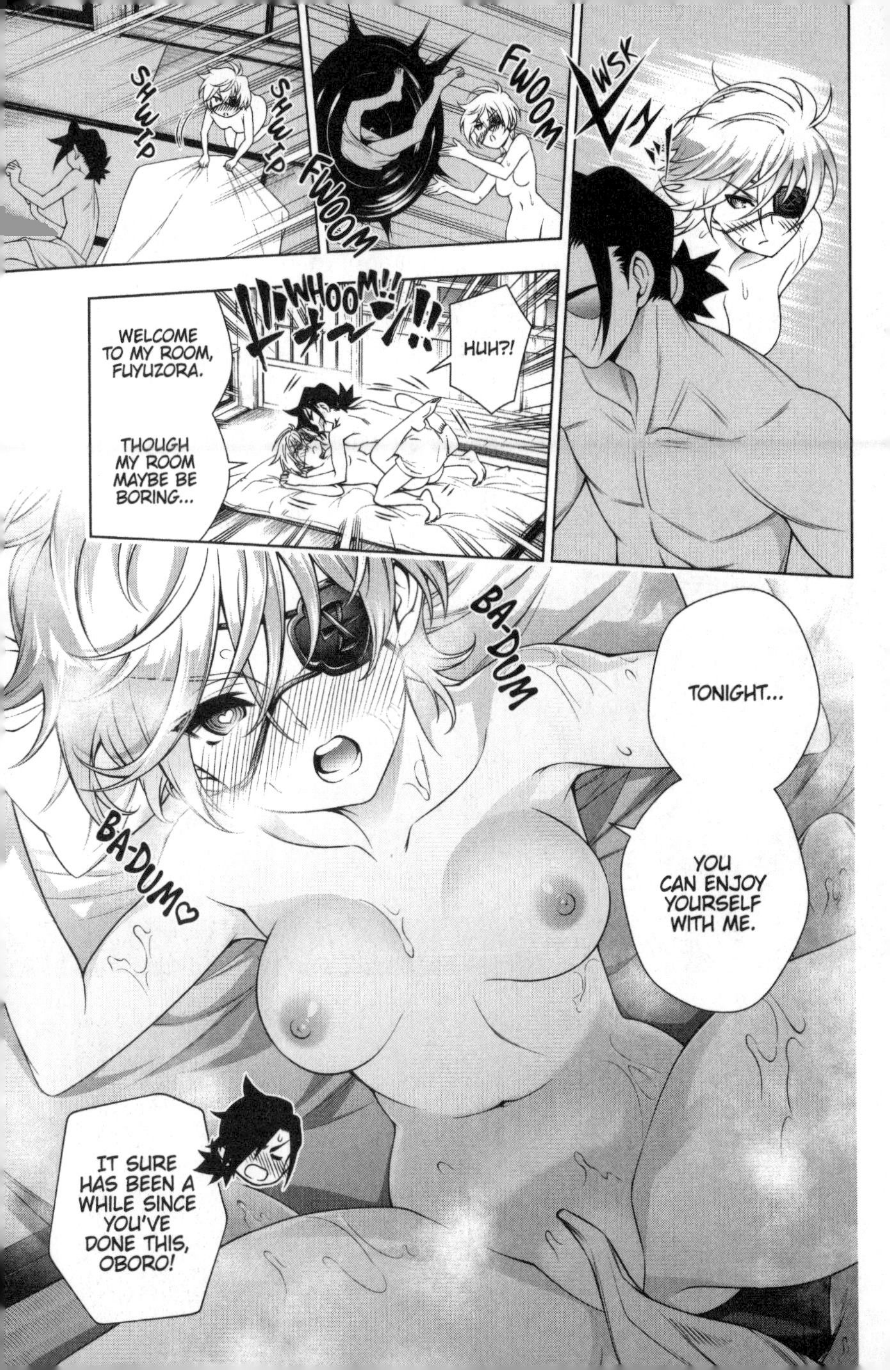
WSK
FWOOM
FWOOM
SHWIP
SHWIP
WHOOM!!
HUH?!
WELCOME TO MY ROOM, FUYUZORA.
THOUGH MY ROOM MAYBE BE BORING...
BA-DUM
BA-DUM
TONIGHT...
YOU CAN ENJOY YOURSELF WITH ME.
IT SURE HAS BEEN A WHILE SINCE YOU'VE DONE THIS, OBORO!

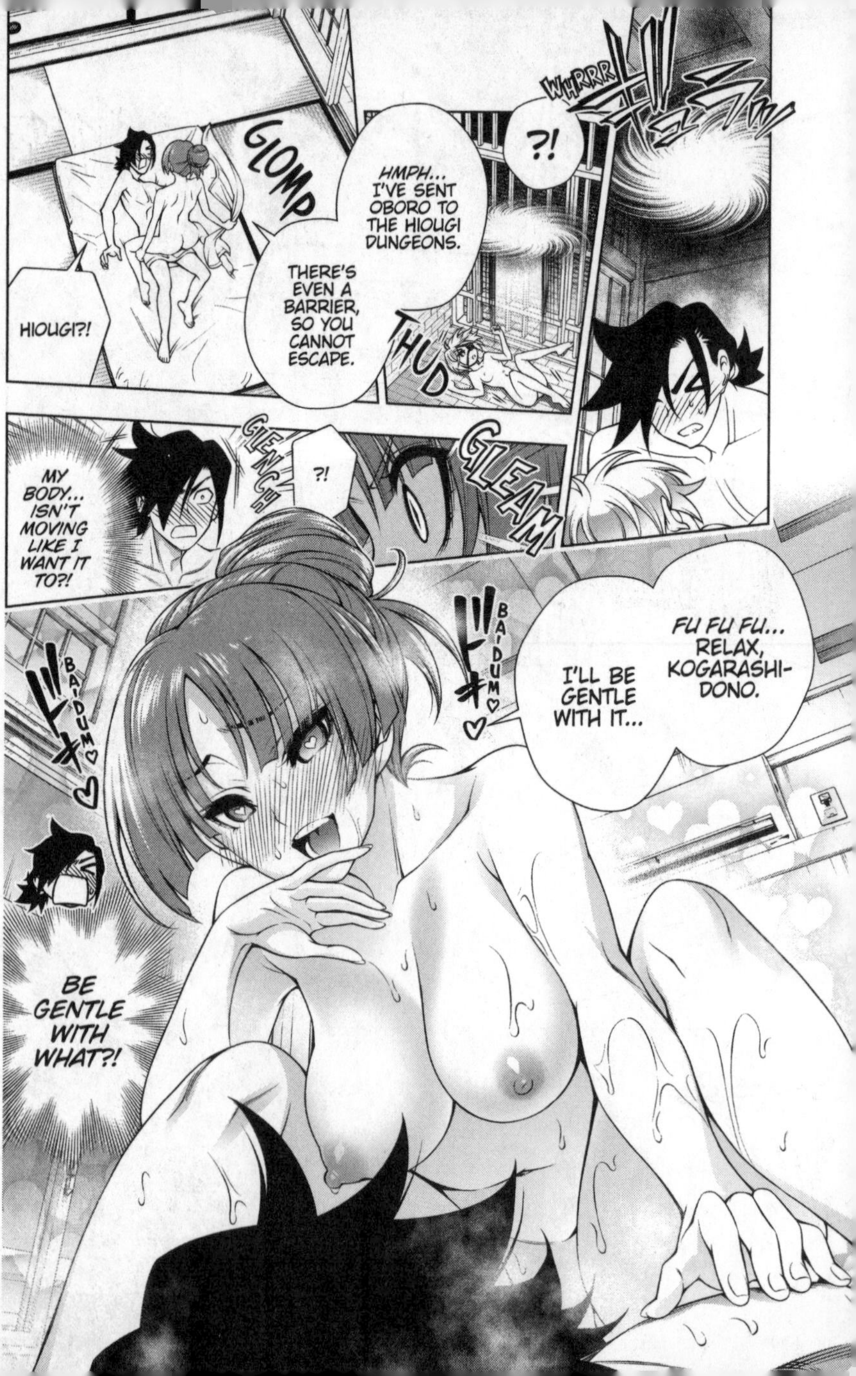
WHRRR
?!
HMPH... I'VE SENT OBORO TO THE HIOUGI DUNGEONS.
THERE'S EVEN A BARRIER, SO YOU CANNOT ESCAPE.
THUD
GLOMP
HIOUGI?!
GLEAM
?!
CLENCH
MY BODY... ISN'T MOVING LIKE I WANT IT TO?!
FU FU FU... RELAX, KOGARASHI-DONO.
I'LL BE GENTLE WITH IT...
BAIDUM♡
BAIDUM♡
BE GENTLE WITH WHAT?!

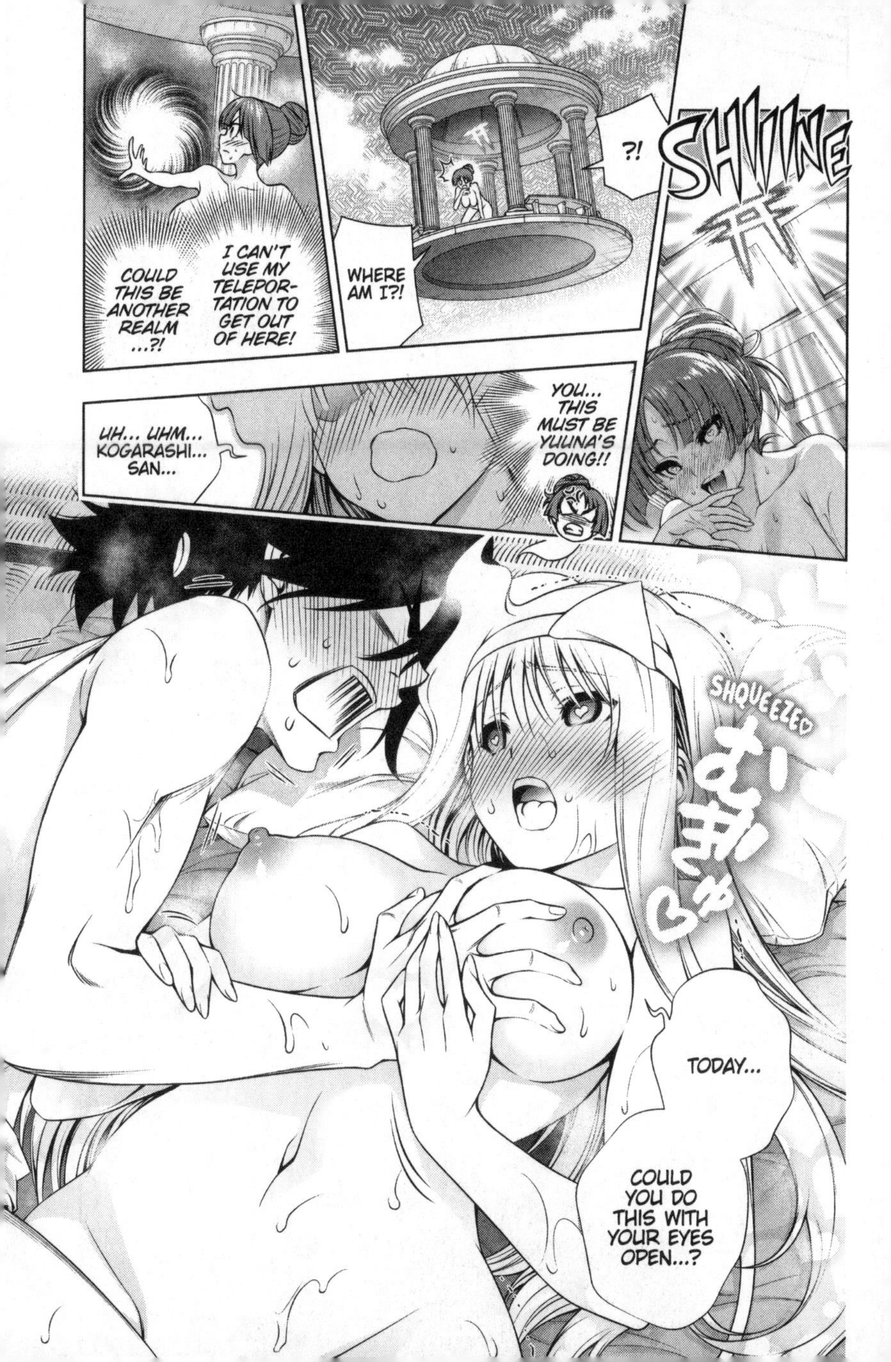
SHIIINE
?!
WHERE AM I?!
I CAN'T USE MY TELEPORTATION TO GET OUT OF HERE!
COULD THIS BE ANOTHER REALM ...?!
YOU... THIS MUST BE YUUNA'S DOING!!
UH... UHM... KOGARASHI... SAN...
SHQUEEZE♥
TODAY...
COULD YOU DO THIS WITH YOUR EYES OPEN...?

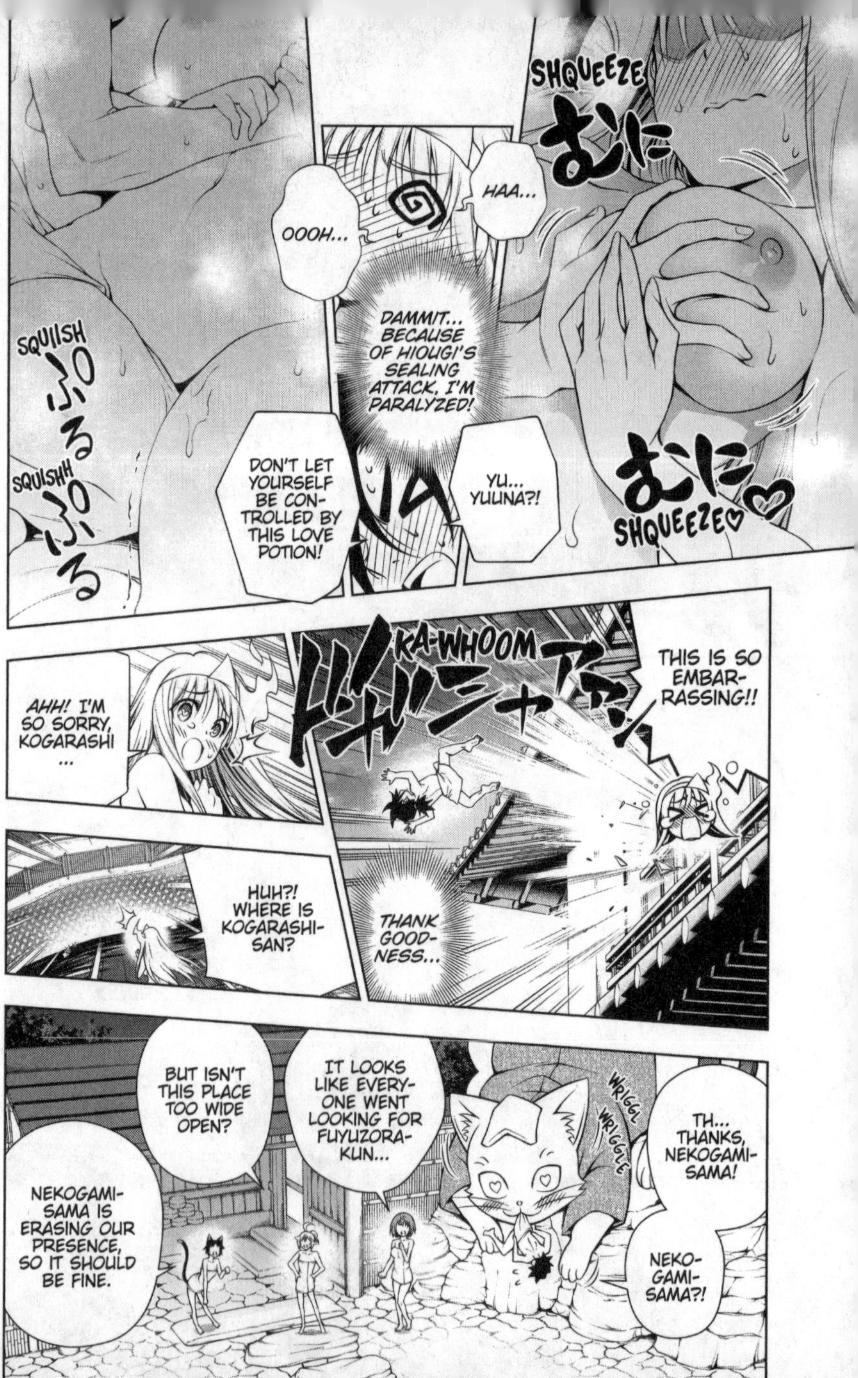
SHQUEEZE
むに
HAA...
OOOH...
DAMMIT... BECAUSE OF HIOUGI'S SEALING ATTACK, I'M PARALYZED!
YU... YUUNA?!
DON'T LET YOURSELF BE CONTROLLED BY THIS LOVE POTION!
SQUIISH
ぷる
SQUISHH
ぷる
むに♡
SHQUEEZE♡
KA-WHOOM
THIS IS SO EMBARRASSING!!
AHH! I'M SO SORRY, KOGARASHI...
THANK GOODNESS...
HUH?! WHERE IS KOGARASHI-SAN?
TH... THANKS, NEKOGAMI-SAMA!
WRIGGL
WRIGGLE
NEKOGAMI-SAMA?!
IT LOOKS LIKE EVERYONE WENT LOOKING FOR FUYUZORA-KUN...
BUT ISN'T THIS PLACE TOO WIDE OPEN?
NEKOGAMI-SAMA IS ERASING OUR PRESENCE, SO IT SHOULD BE FINE.

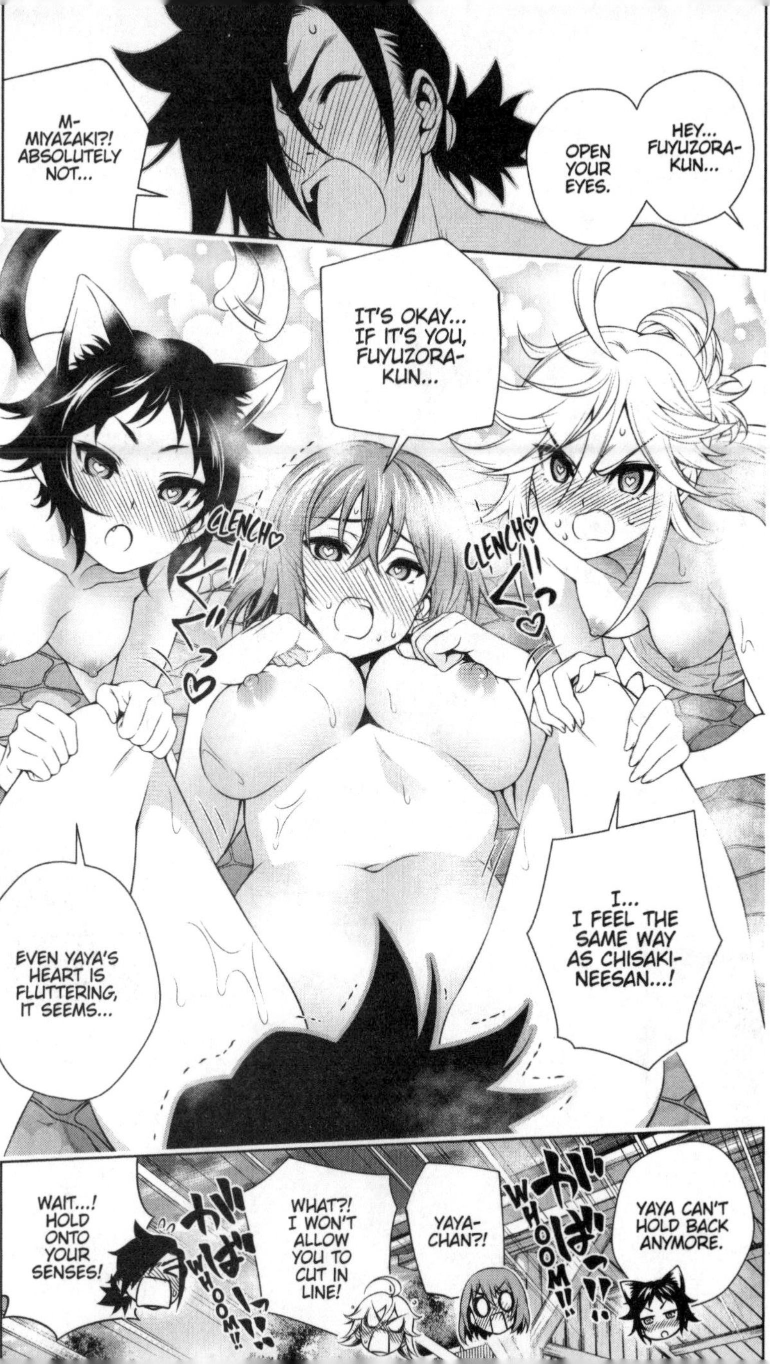
HEY... FUYUZORA-KUN...
OPEN YOUR EYES.
M-MIYAZAKI?! ABSOLUTELY NOT...
IT'S OKAY... IF IT'S YOU, FUYUZORA-KUN...
CLENCH♡
CLENCH♡
I... I FEEL THE SAME WAY AS CHISAKI-NEESAN...!
EVEN YAYA'S HEART IS FLUTTERING, IT SEEMS...
YAYA CAN'T HOLD BACK ANYMORE.
WHOOM!!
YAYA-CHAN?!
WHAT?! I WON'T ALLOW YOU TO CUT IN LINE!
WHOOM!!
WAIT...! HOLD ONTO YOUR SENSES!

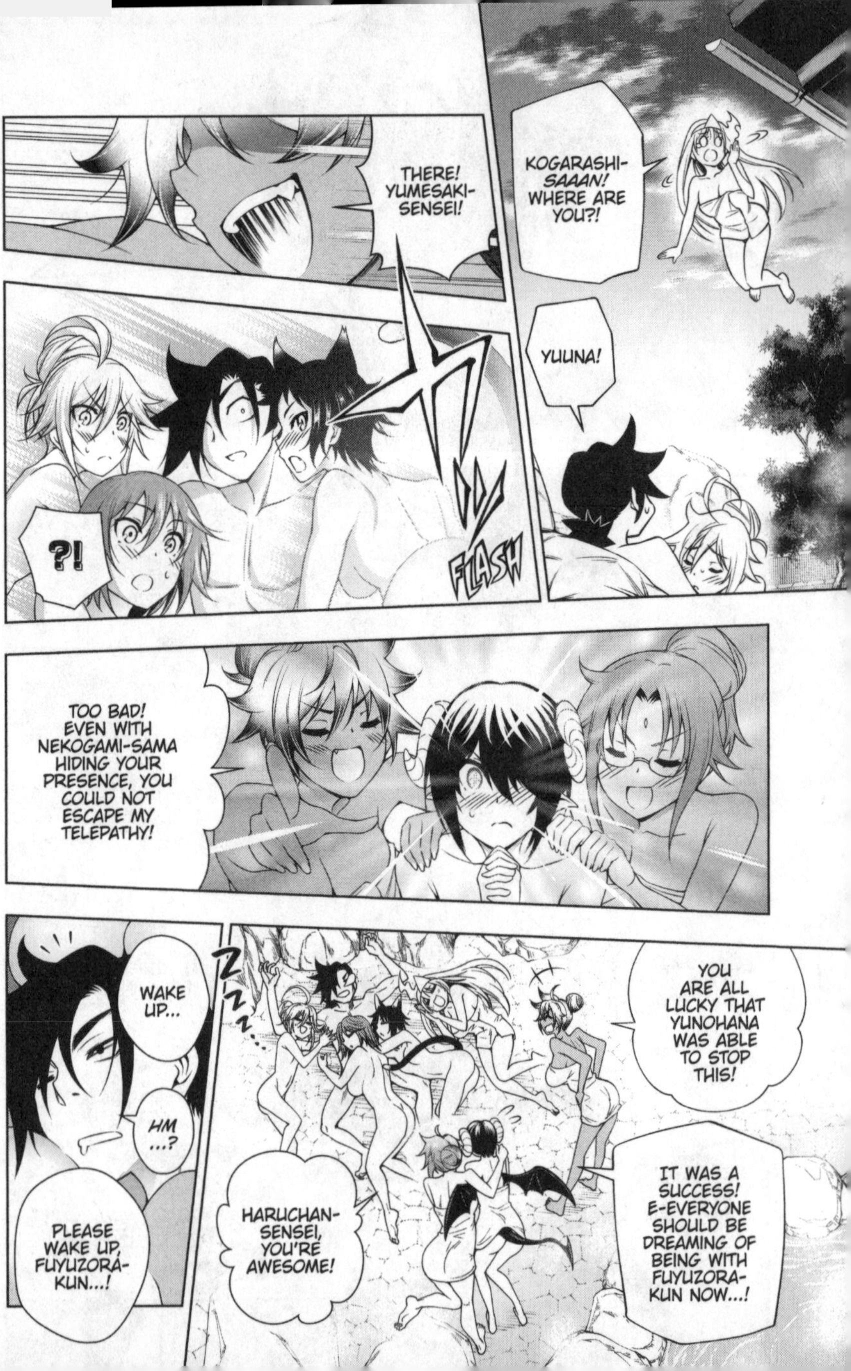
KOGARASHI-SAAAN! WHERE ARE YOU?!
THERE! YUMESAKI-SENSEI!
YUUNA!
FLASH
?!
TOO BAD! EVEN WITH NEKOGAMI-SAMA HIDING YOUR PRESENCE, YOU COULD NOT ESCAPE MY TELEPATHY!
YOU ARE ALL LUCKY THAT YUNOHANA WAS ABLE TO STOP THIS!
IT WAS A SUCCESS! E-EVERYONE SHOULD BE DREAMING OF BEING WITH FUYUZORA-KUN NOW...!
HARUCHAN-SENSEI, YOU'RE AWESOME!
WAKE UP...
HM ...?
PLEASE WAKE UP, FUYUZORA-KUN...!

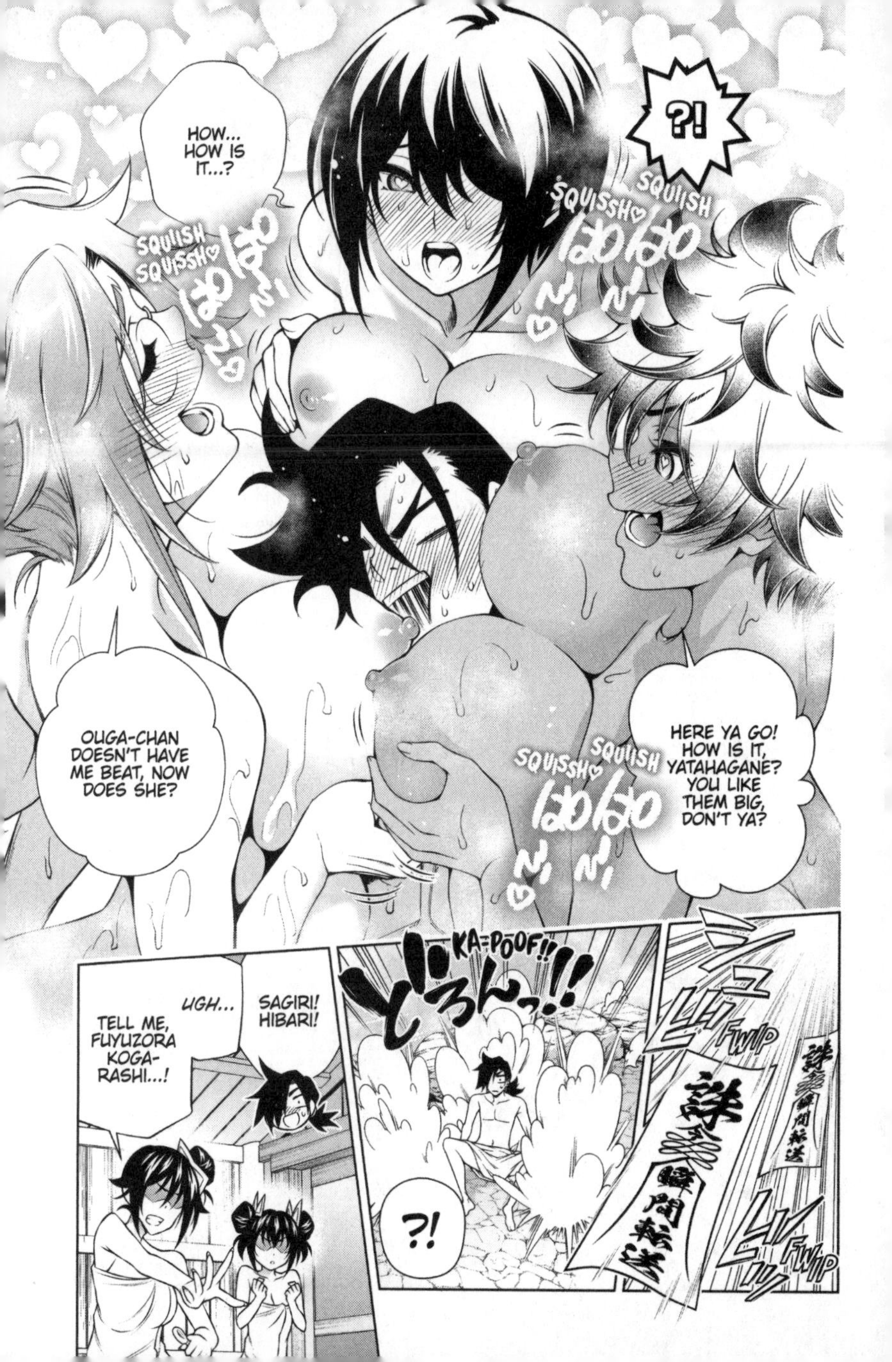
?!
SQUIISH
SQUIISSH♡
HOW... HOW IS IT...?
SQUIISH
SQUIISSH♡
HERE YA GO! HOW IS IT, YATAHAGANE? YOU LIKE THEM BIG, DON'T YA?
SQUIISH
SQUIISSH♡
OUGA-CHAN DOESN'T HAVE ME BEAT, NOW DOES SHE?
FWIP
FWIP
KA=POOF!!
どろんっ!!
?!
SAGIRI! HIBARI!
UGH...
TELL ME, FUYUZORA KOGA-RASHI...!

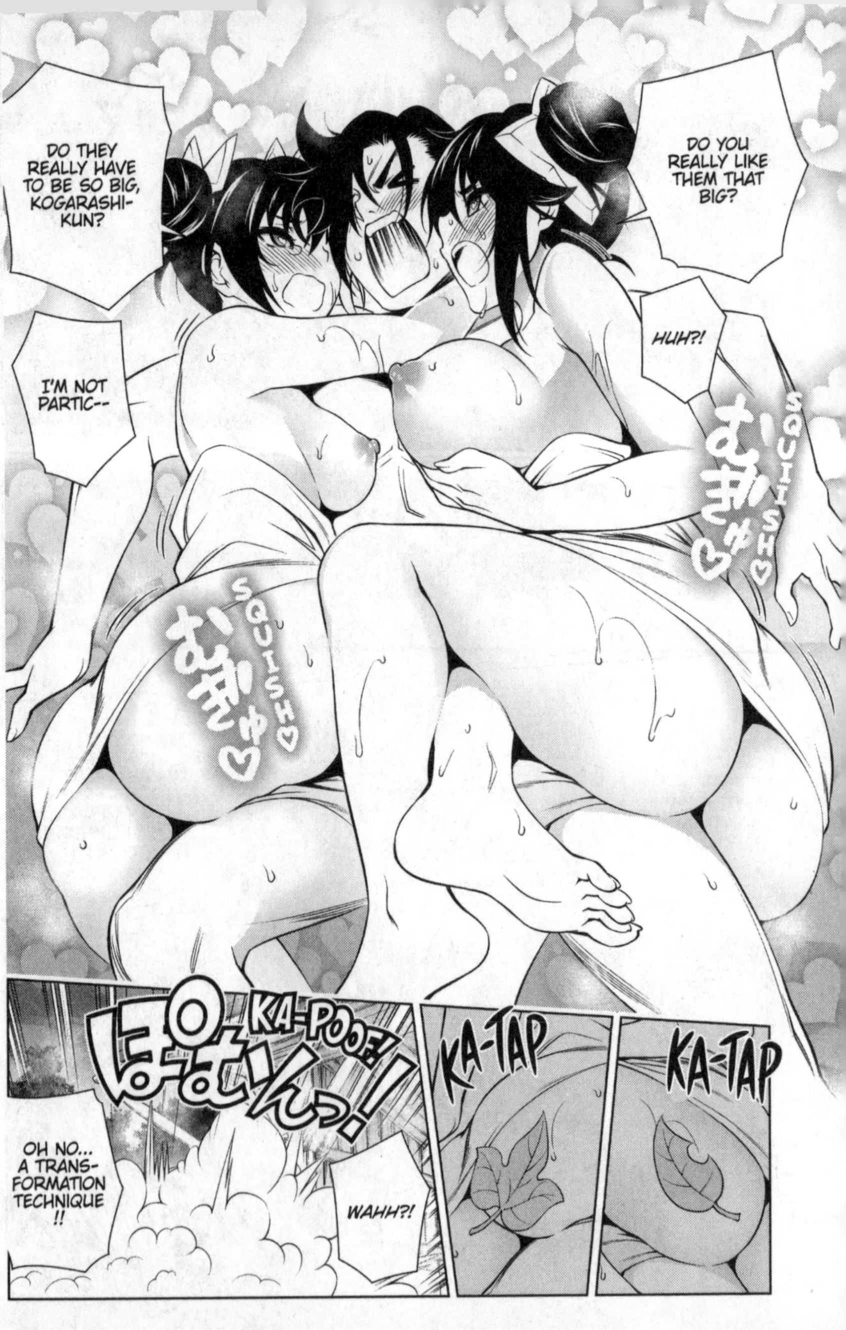
DO YOU REALLY LIKE THEM THAT BIG?
DO THEY REALLY HAVE TO BE SO BIG, KOGARASHI-KUN?
HUH?!
I'M NOT PARTIC--
むぎゅ♡ SQUISH♥
むぎゅ♡ SQUISH♥
KA-TAP
KA-TAP
KA-POOF!
WAHH?!
OH NO... A TRANS-FORMATION TECHNIQUE !!

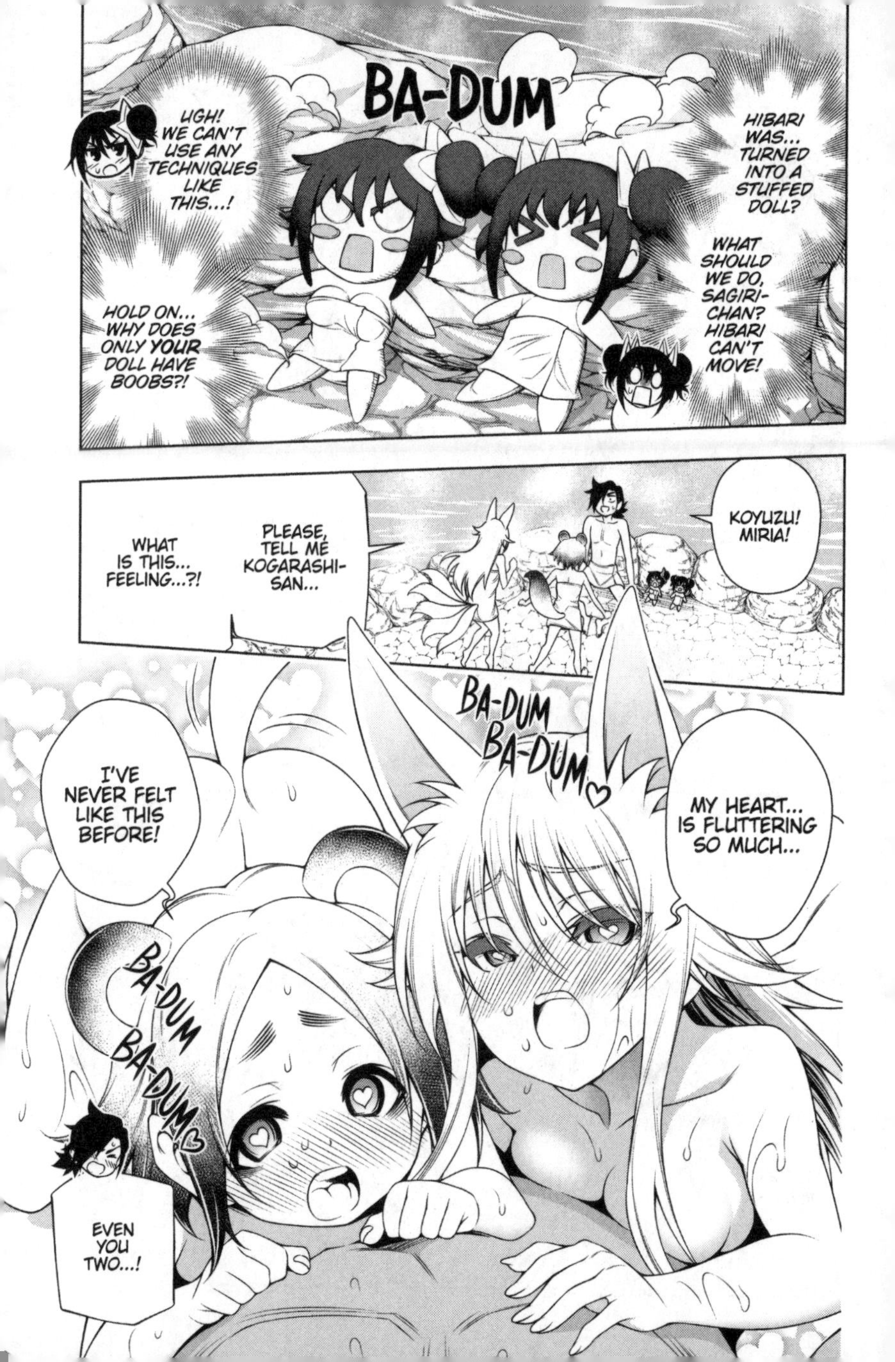
BA-DUM
HIBARI WAS... TURNED INTO A STUFFED DOLL?
WHAT SHOULD WE DO, SAGIRI-CHAN? HIBARI CAN'T MOVE!
UGH! WE CAN'T USE ANY TECHNIQUES LIKE THIS...!
HOLD ON... WHY DOES ONLY YOUR DOLL HAVE BOOBS?!
KOYUZU! MIRIA!
PLEASE, TELL ME KOGARASHI-SAN...
WHAT IS THIS... FEELING...?!
BA-DUM BA-DUM♡
MY HEART... IS FLUTTERING SO MUCH...
I'VE NEVER FELT LIKE THIS BEFORE!
BA-DUM BA-DUM♡
EVEN YOU TWO...!

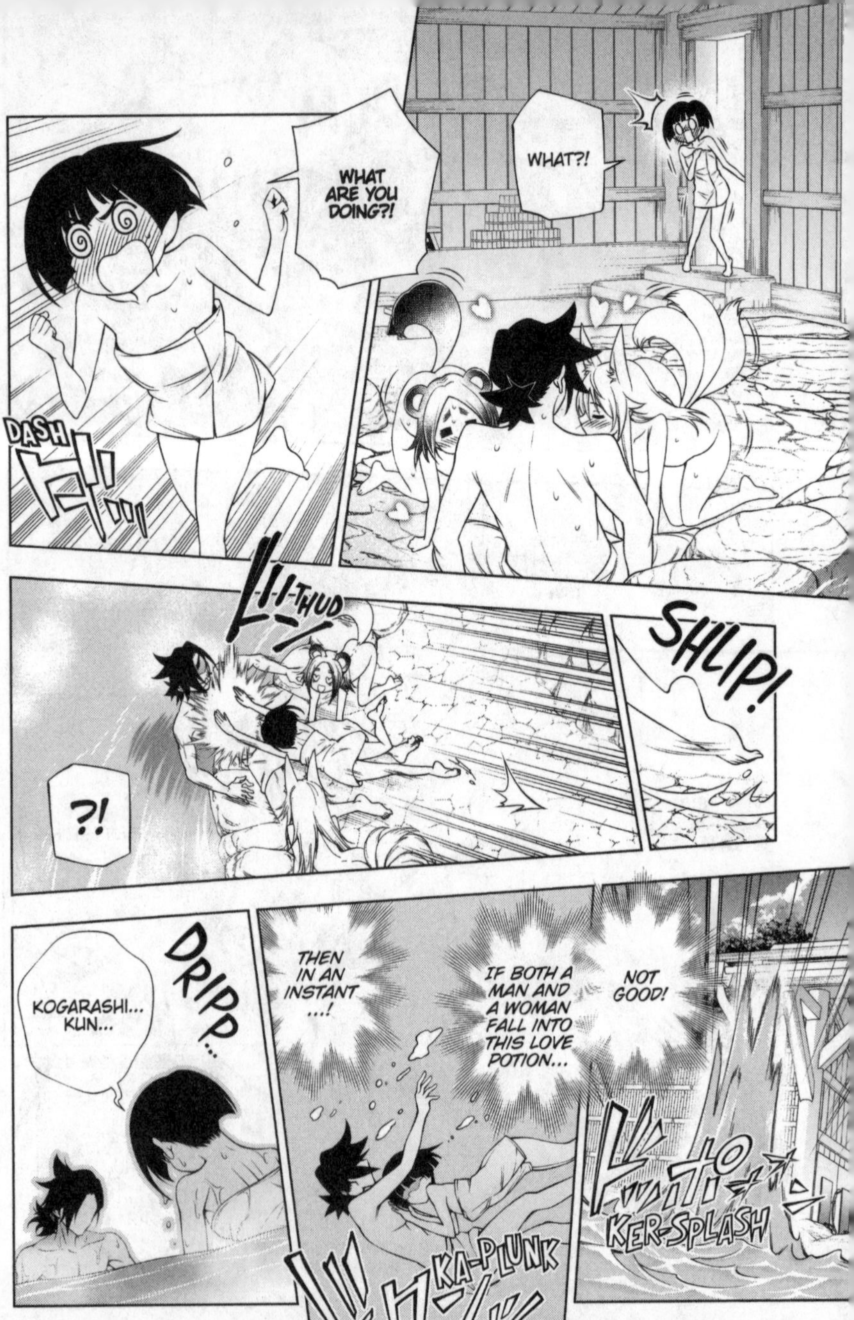

WHAT?!
WHAT ARE YOU DOING?!
DASH
THUD
SHLIP!
?!
NOT GOOD!
IF BOTH A MAN AND A WOMAN FALL INTO THIS LOVE POTION...
THEN IN AN INSTANT ...!
KER-SPLASH
KA-PLUNK
DRIPP...
KOGARASHI... KUN...

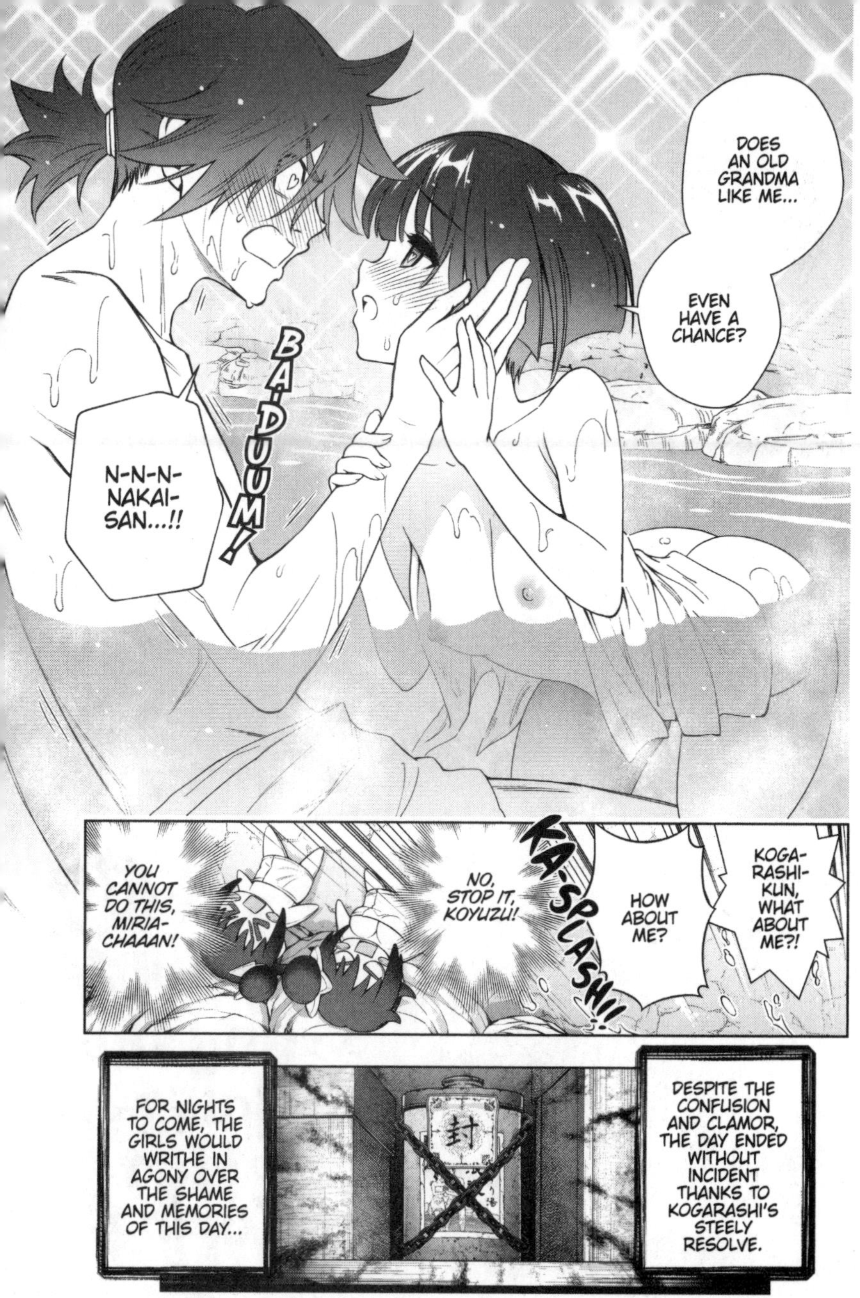
DOES AN OLD GRANDMA LIKE ME...
EVEN HAVE A CHANCE?
BA-DUUM!
N-N-N-NAKAI-SAN...!!
KOGA-RASHI-KUN, WHAT ABOUT ME?!
HOW ABOUT ME?
KA-SPLASH!!
NO, STOP IT, KOYUZU!
YOU CANNOT DO THIS, MIRIA-CHAAAN!
DESPITE THE CONFUSION AND CLAMOR, THE DAY ENDED WITHOUT INCIDENT THANKS TO KOGARASHI'S STEELY RESOLVE.
封
FOR NIGHTS TO COME, THE GIRLS WOULD WRITHE IN AGONY OVER THE SHAME AND MEMORIES OF THIS DAY...

Text: SEAL

Yuuna and the Haunted Hot Springs

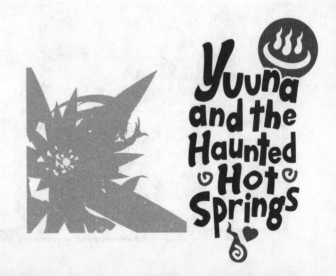

142 Chisaki-san Wants to Close the Distance

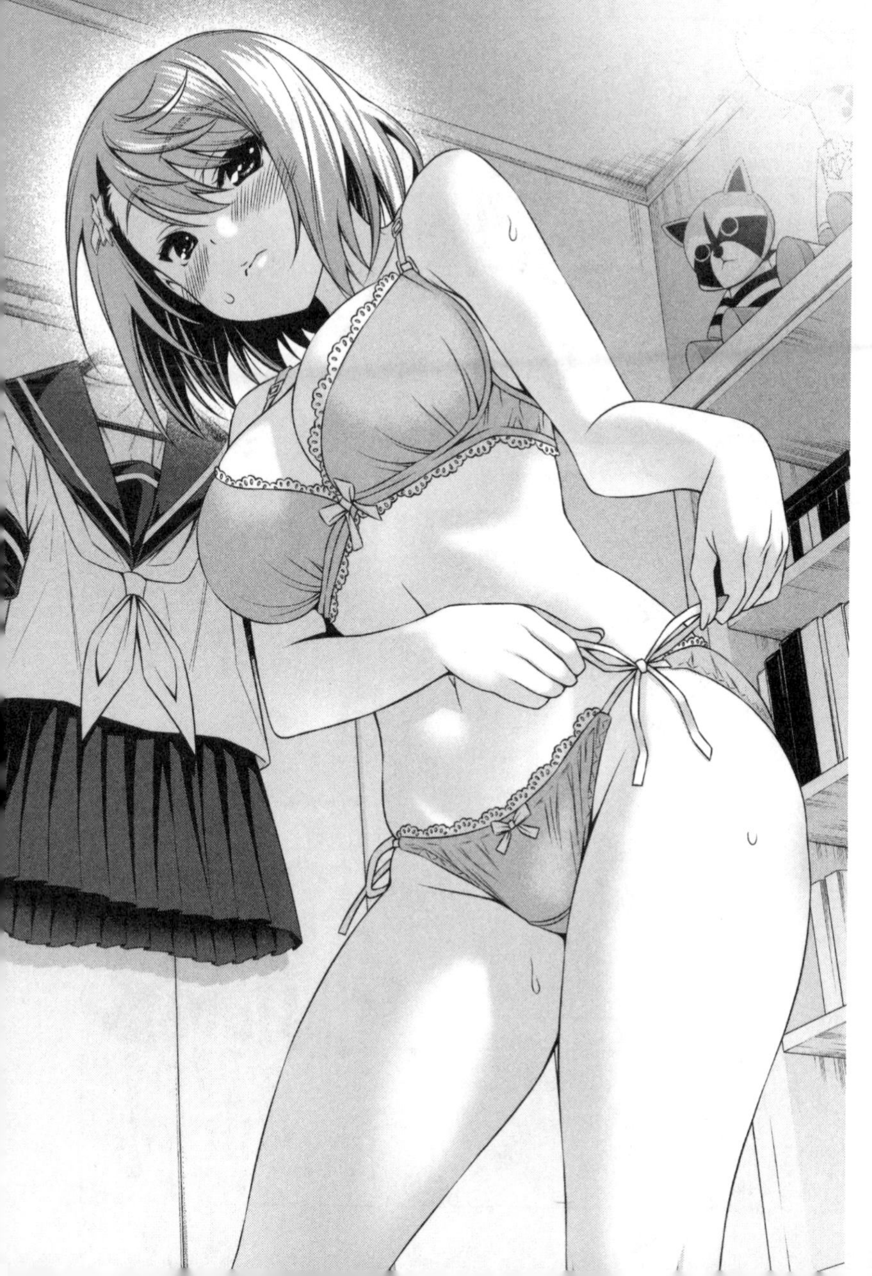

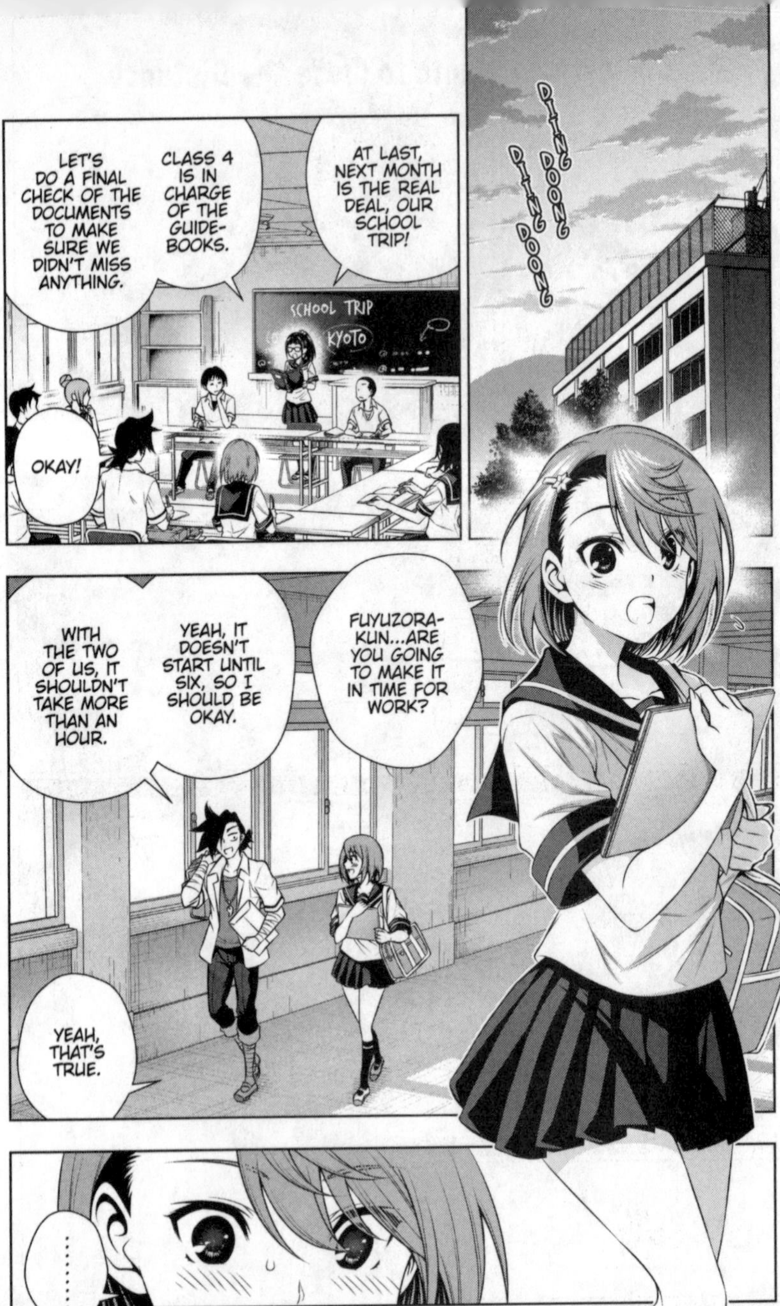
DING DOONG
DING DOONG
AT LAST, NEXT MONTH IS THE REAL DEAL, OUR SCHOOL TRIP!
CLASS 4 IS IN CHARGE OF THE GUIDE-BOOKS.
LET'S DO A FINAL CHECK OF THE DOCUMENTS TO MAKE SURE WE DIDN'T MISS ANYTHING.
SCHOOL TRIP
KYOTO
OKAY!
FUYUZORA-KUN...ARE YOU GOING TO MAKE IT IN TIME FOR WORK?
YEAH, IT DOESN'T START UNTIL SIX, SO I SHOULD BE OKAY.
WITH THE TWO OF US, IT SHOULDN'T TAKE MORE THAN AN HOUR.
YEAH, THAT'S TRUE.
......

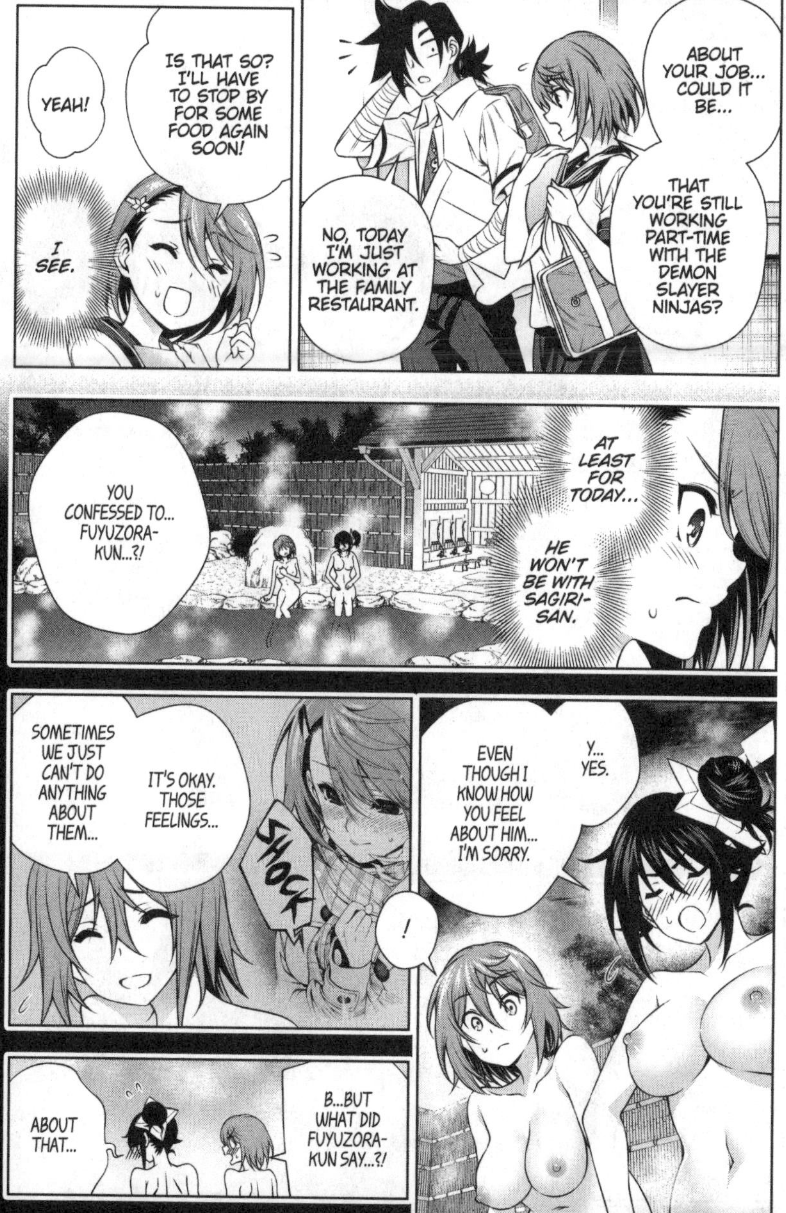
ABOUT YOUR JOB... COULD IT BE...
THAT YOU'RE STILL WORKING PART-TIME WITH THE DEMON SLAYER NINJAS?
NO, TODAY I'M JUST WORKING AT THE FAMILY RESTAURANT.
IS THAT SO? I'LL HAVE TO STOP BY FOR SOME FOOD AGAIN SOON!
YEAH!
I SEE.
AT LEAST FOR TODAY...
HE WON'T BE WITH SAGIRI-SAN.
YOU CONFESSED TO... FUYUZORA-KUN...?!
Y... YES.
EVEN THOUGH I KNOW HOW YOU FEEL ABOUT HIM... I'M SORRY.
!
SHOCK
IT'S OKAY. THOSE FEELINGS...
SOMETIMES WE JUST CAN'T DO ANYTHING ABOUT THEM...
B...BUT WHAT DID FUYUZORA-KUN SAY...?!
ABOUT THAT...

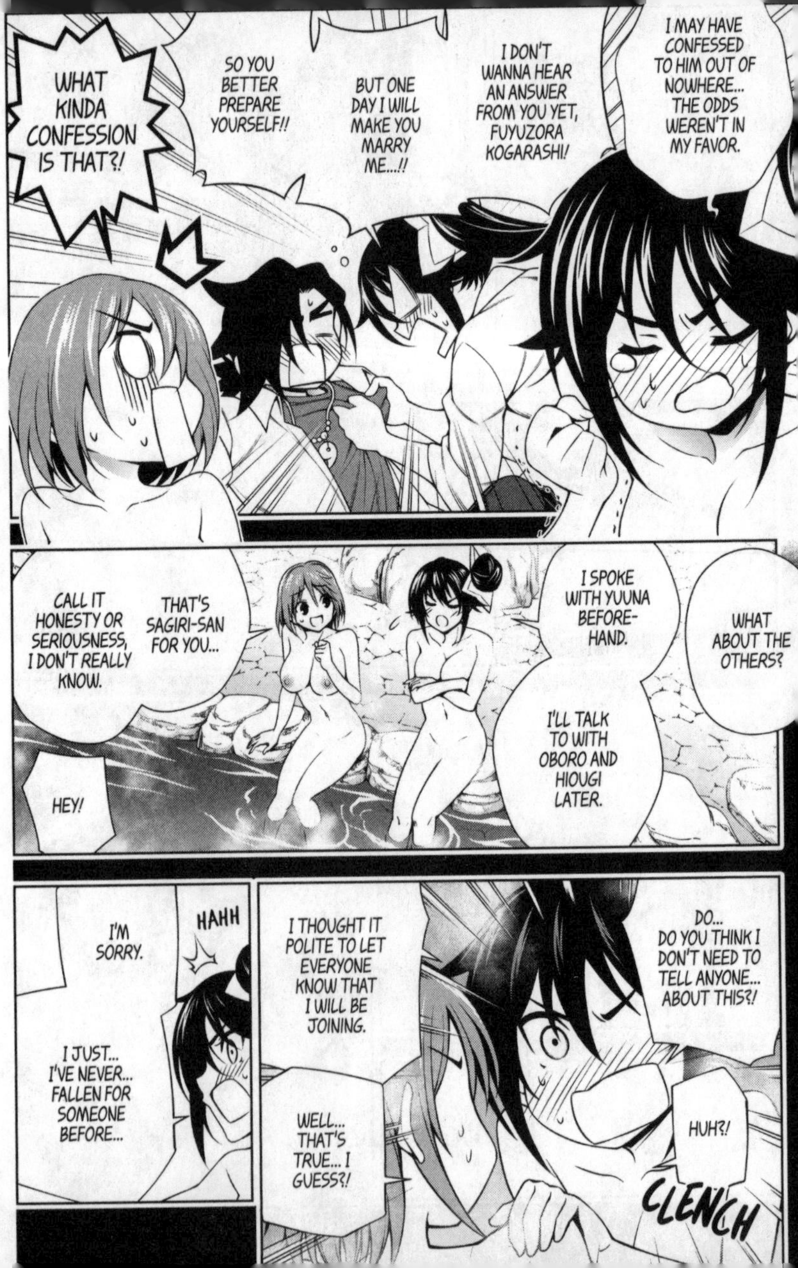
I MAY HAVE CONFESSED TO HIM OUT OF NOWHERE... THE ODDS WEREN'T IN MY FAVOR.
I DON'T WANNA HEAR AN ANSWER FROM YOU YET, FUYUZORA KOGARASHI!
BUT ONE DAY I WILL MAKE YOU MARRY ME...!!
SO YOU BETTER PREPARE YOURSELF!!
WHAT KINDA CONFESSION IS THAT?!
WHAT ABOUT THE OTHERS?
I SPOKE WITH YUUNA BEFORE-HAND.
I'LL TALK TO WITH OBORO AND HIOUGI LATER.
THAT'S SAGIRI-SAN FOR YOU...
CALL IT HONESTY OR SERIOUSNESS, I DON'T REALLY KNOW.
HEY!
DO... DO YOU THINK I DON'T NEED TO TELL ANYONE... ABOUT THIS?!
HUH?!
CLENCH
I THOUGHT IT POLITE TO LET EVERYONE KNOW THAT I WILL BE JOINING.
WELL... THAT'S TRUE... I GUESS?!
HAHH
I'M SORRY.
I JUST... I'VE NEVER... FALLEN FOR SOMEONE BEFORE...

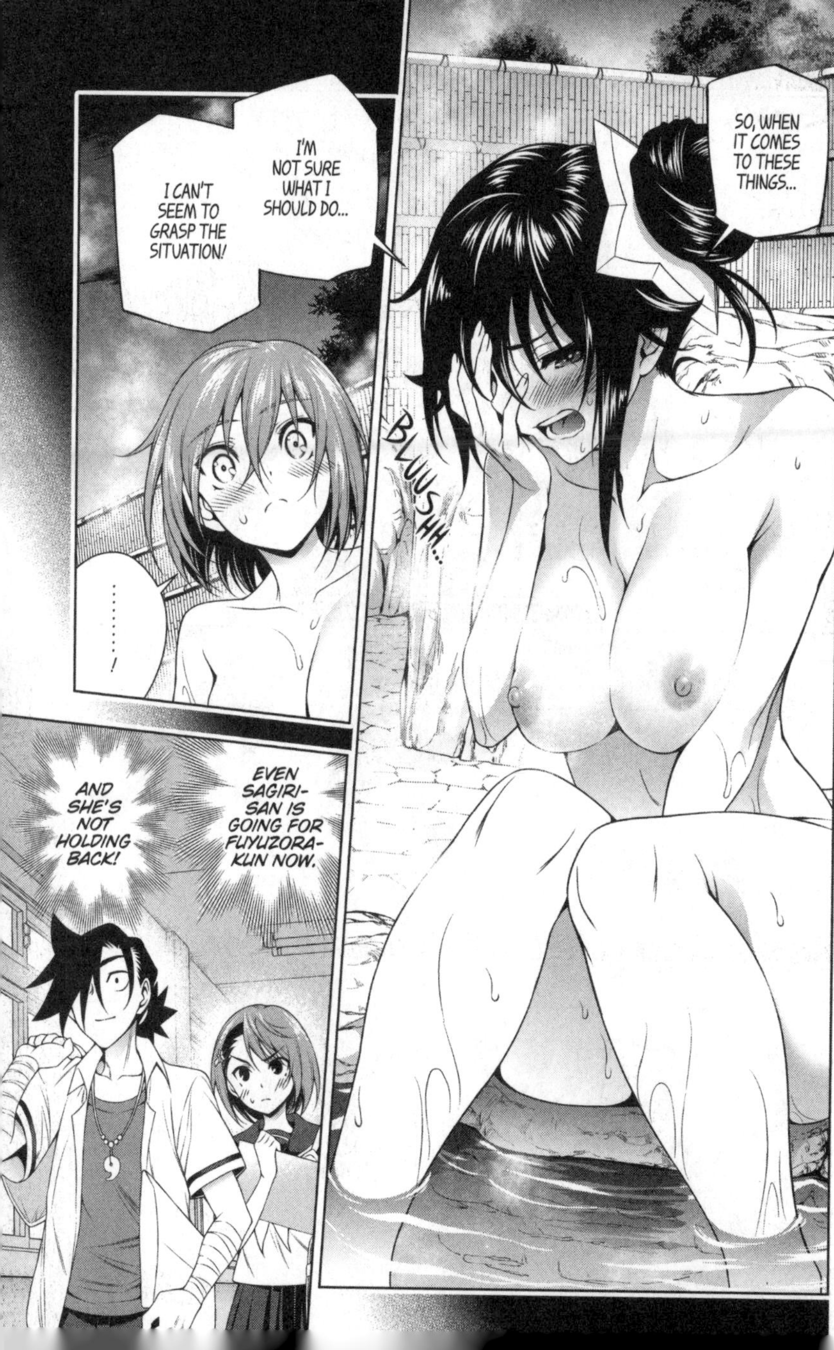
SO, WHEN IT COMES TO THESE THINGS...
I'M NOT SURE WHAT I SHOULD DO...
I CAN'T SEEM TO GRASP THE SITUATION!
BLUUSHH...
......!
EVEN SAGIRI-SAN IS GOING FOR FUYUZORA-KUN NOW.
AND SHE'S NOT HOLDING BACK!

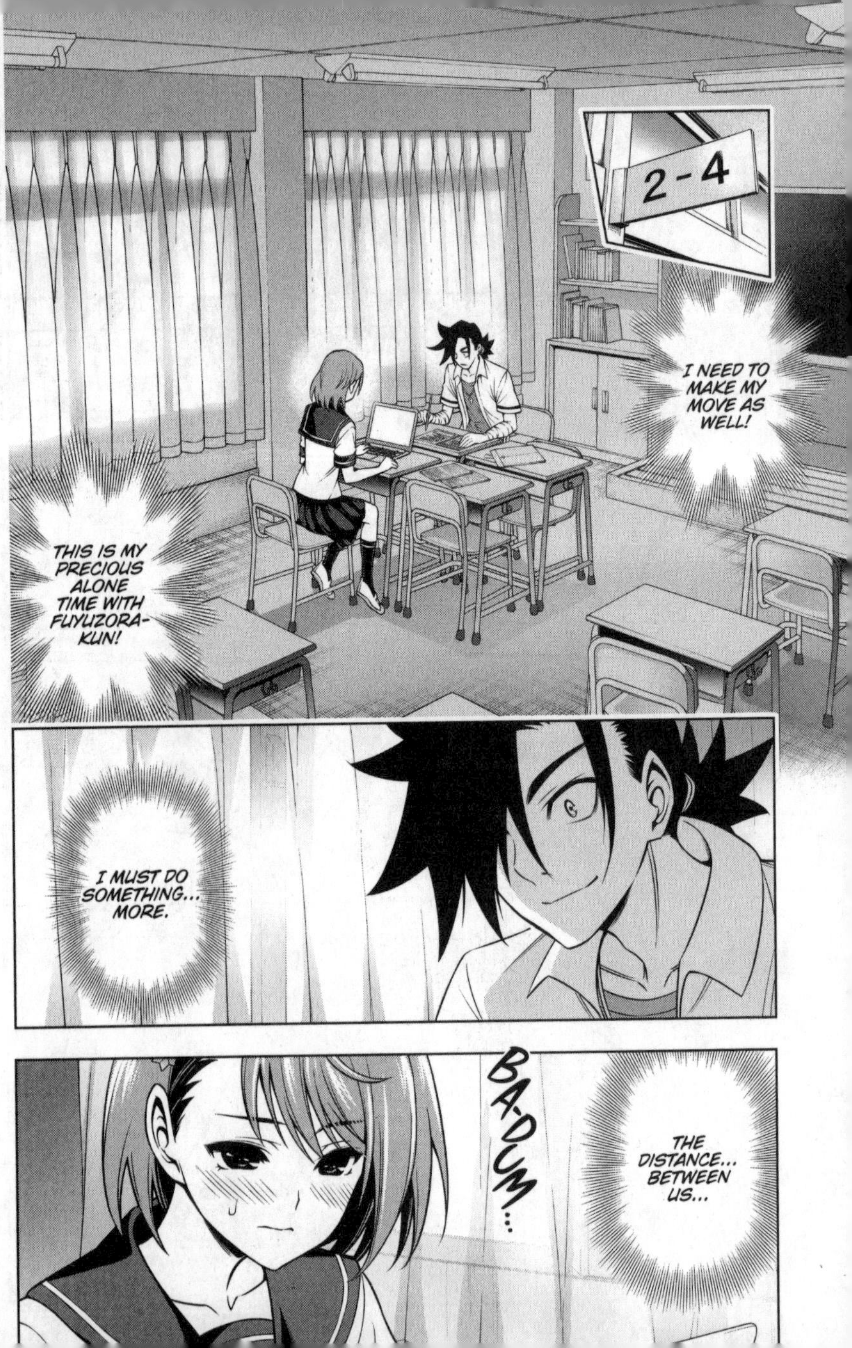
2-4
I NEED TO MAKE MY MOVE AS WELL!
THIS IS MY PRECIOUS ALONE TIME WITH FUYUZORA-KUN!
I MUST DO SOMETHING... MORE.
THE DISTANCE... BETWEEN US...
BA-DUM...

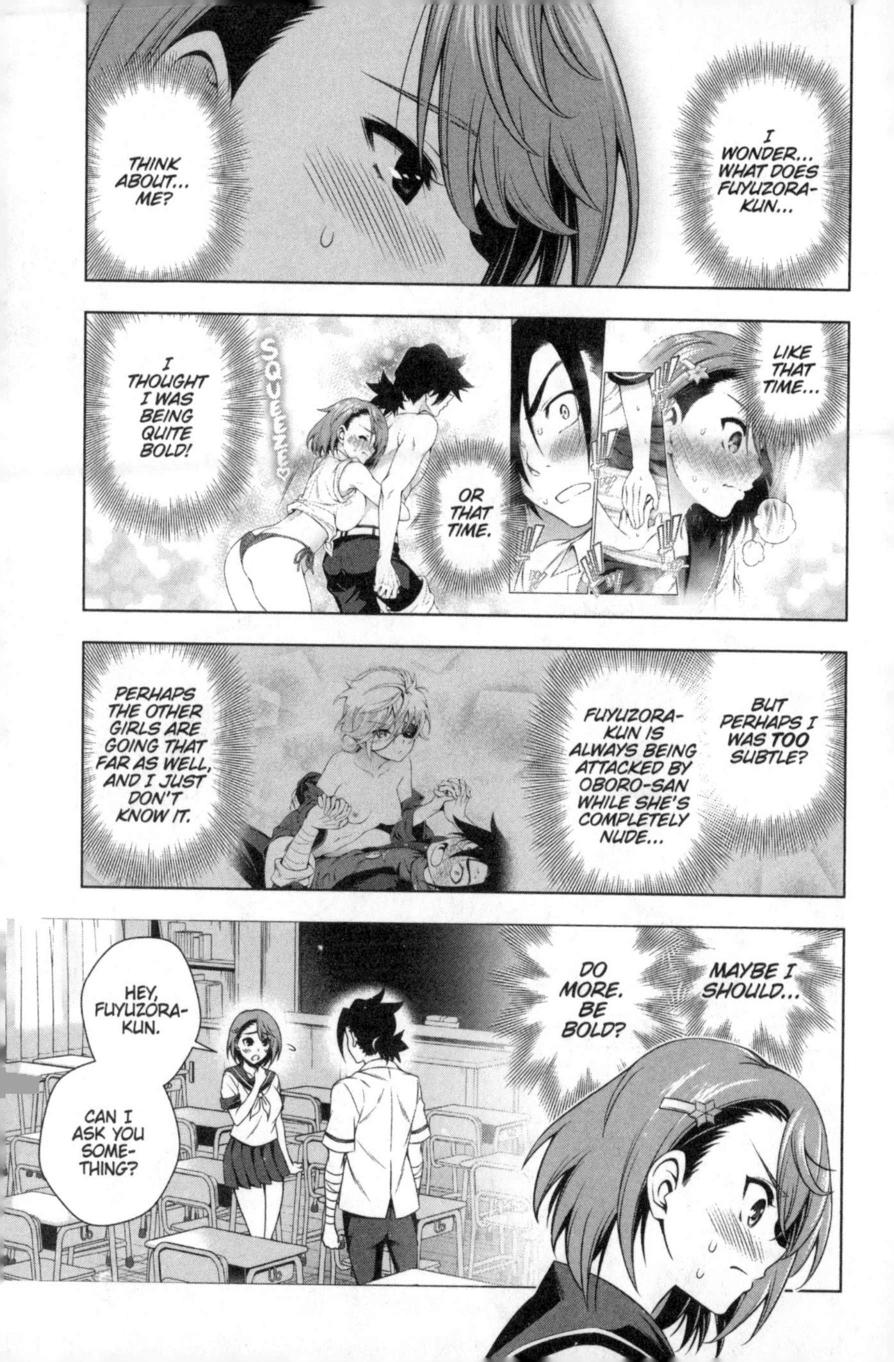
I WONDER... WHAT DOES FUYUZORA-KUN...
THINK ABOUT... ME?
LIKE THAT TIME...
OR THAT TIME.
SQUEEZE
I THOUGHT I WAS BEING QUITE BOLD!
BUT PERHAPS I WAS **TOO** SUBTLE?
FUYUZORA-KUN IS ALWAYS BEING ATTACKED BY OBORO-SAN WHILE SHE'S COMPLETELY NUDE...
PERHAPS THE OTHER GIRLS ARE GOING THAT FAR AS WELL, AND I JUST DON'T KNOW IT.
MAYBE I SHOULD...
DO MORE. BE BOLD?
HEY, FUYUZORA-KUN.
CAN I ASK YOU SOMETHING?

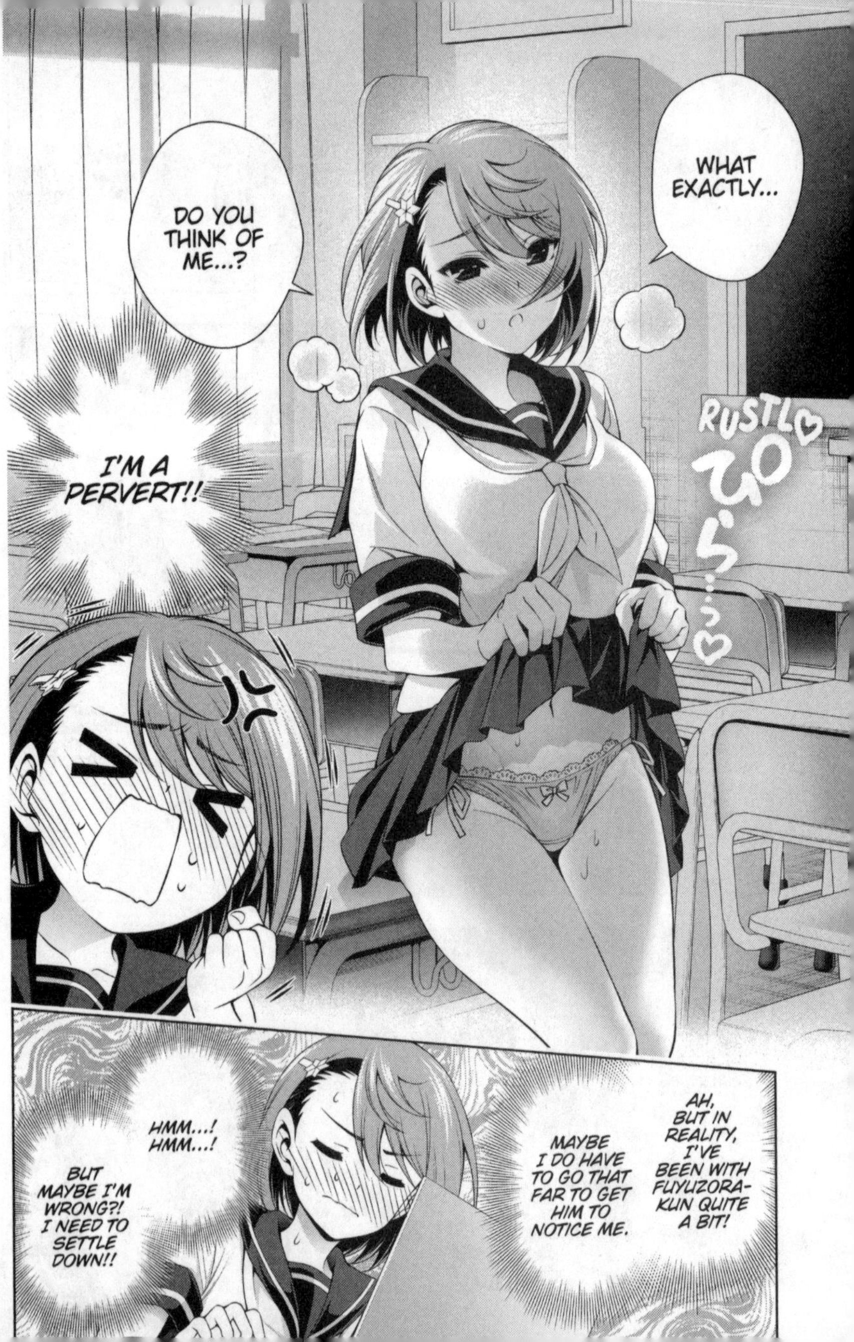
WHAT EXACTLY...
DO YOU THINK OF ME...?
RUSTL♡
ひら…っ♡
I'M A PERVERT!!
AH, BUT IN REALITY, I'VE BEEN WITH FUYUZORA-KUN QUITE A BIT!
MAYBE I DO HAVE TO GO THAT FAR TO GET HIM TO NOTICE ME.
HMM...! HMM...!
BUT MAYBE I'M WRONG?! I NEED TO SETTLE DOWN!!

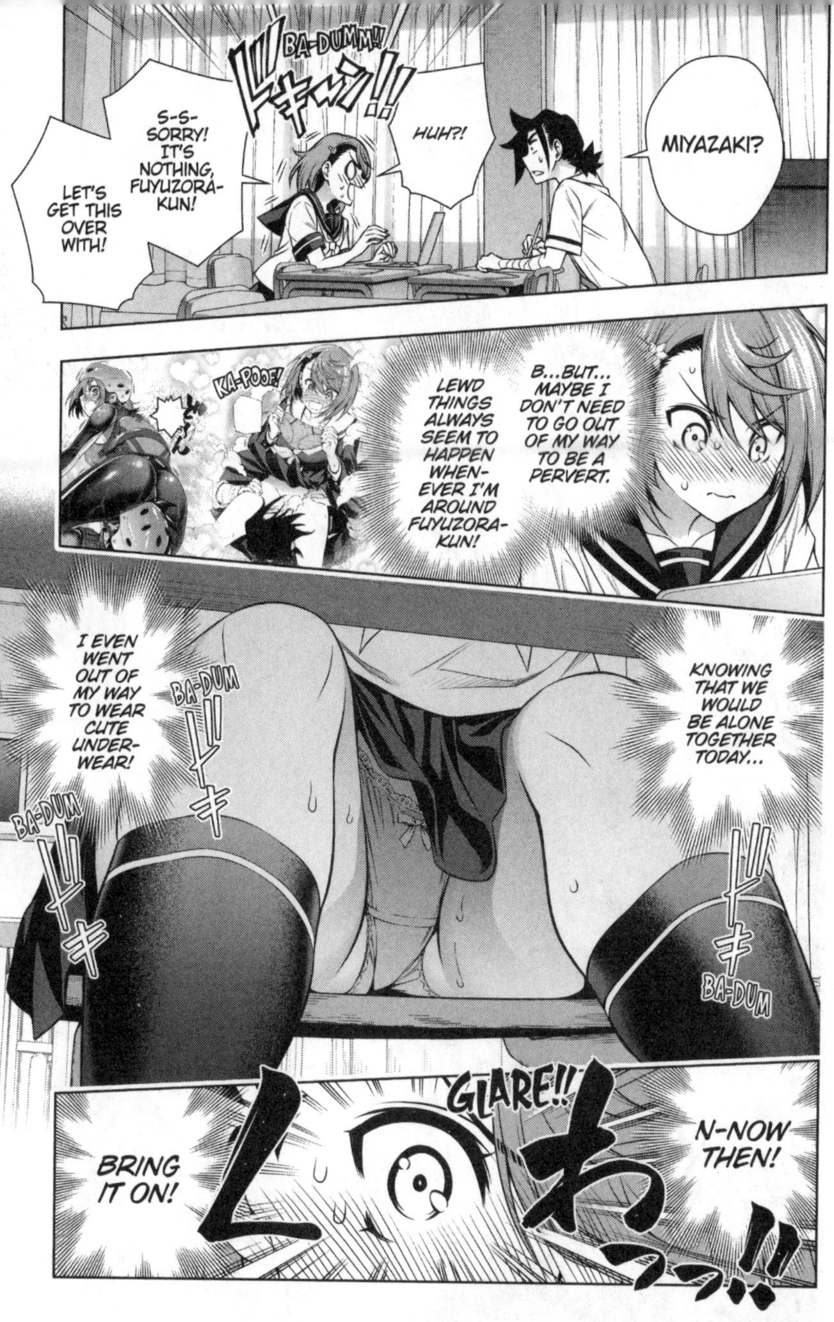
MIYAZAKI?
BA-DUMM!!
HUH?!
S-S-SORRY! IT'S NOTHING, FUYUZORA-KUN!
LET'S GET THIS OVER WITH!
B...BUT... MAYBE I DON'T NEED TO GO OUT OF MY WAY TO BE A PERVERT.
LEWD THINGS ALWAYS SEEM TO HAPPEN WHENEVER I'M AROUND FUYUZORA-KUN!
KA-POOF!
KNOWING THAT WE WOULD BE ALONE TOGETHER TODAY...
BA-DUM
I EVEN WENT OUT OF MY WAY TO WEAR CUTE UNDERWEAR!
BA-DUM
BA-DUM
N-NOW THEN!
GLARE!!
BRING IT ON!

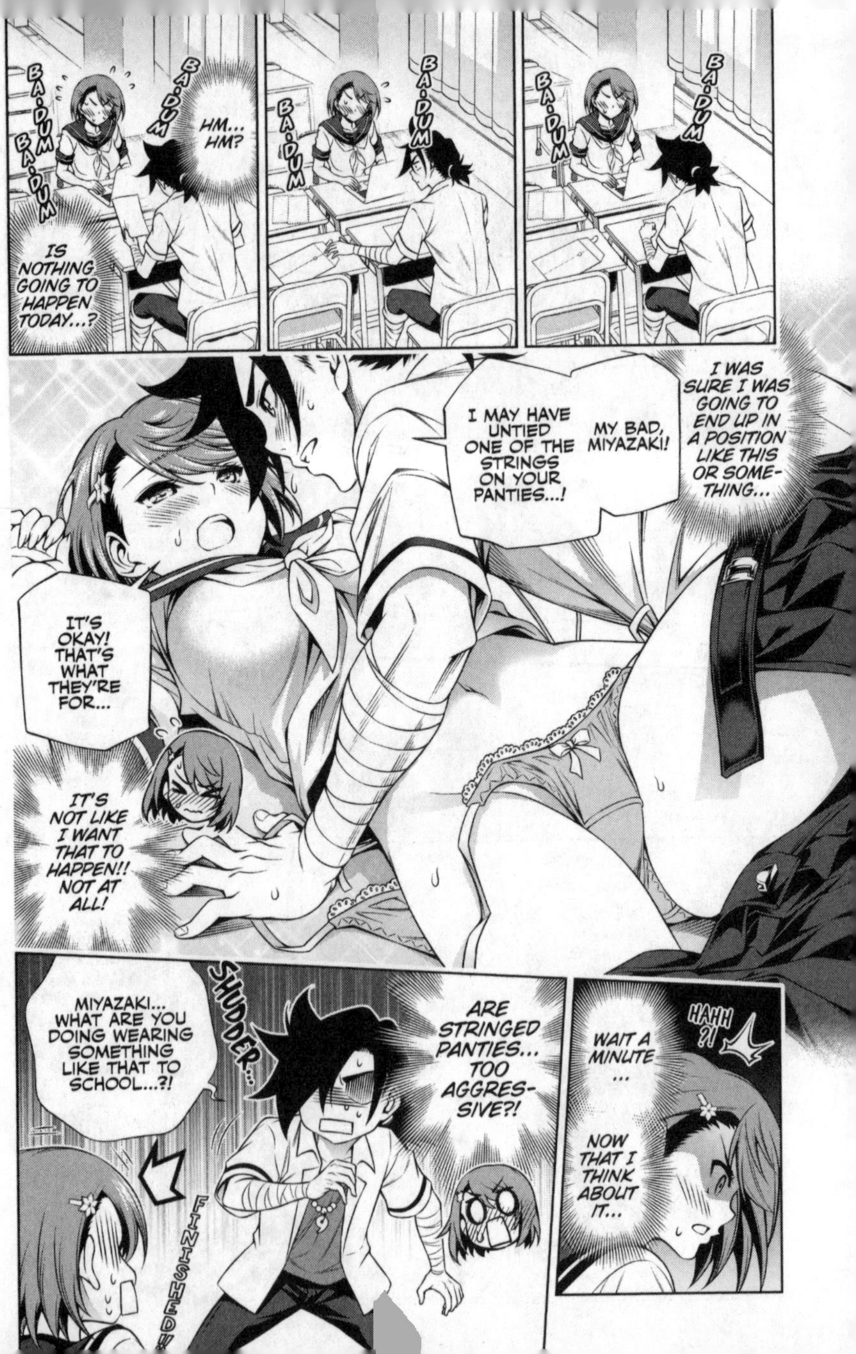
BA-DUM
BA-DUM
BA-DUM
BA-DUM
BA-DUM
HM... HM?
BA-DUM
BA-DUM
IS NOTHING GOING TO HAPPEN TODAY...?
I WAS SURE I WAS GOING TO END UP IN A POSITION LIKE THIS OR SOME-THING...
MY BAD, MIYAZAKI!
I MAY HAVE UNTIED ONE OF THE STRINGS ON YOUR PANTIES...!
IT'S OKAY! THAT'S WHAT THEY'RE FOR...
IT'S NOT LIKE I WANT THAT TO HAPPEN!! NOT AT ALL!
HAHH?!
WAIT A MINUTE...
NOW THAT I THINK ABOUT IT...
ARE STRINGED PANTIES... TOO AGGRES-SIVE?!
SHUDDER...
MIYAZAKI... WHAT ARE YOU DOING WEARING SOMETHING LIKE THAT TO SCHOOL...?!
FINISHED!!

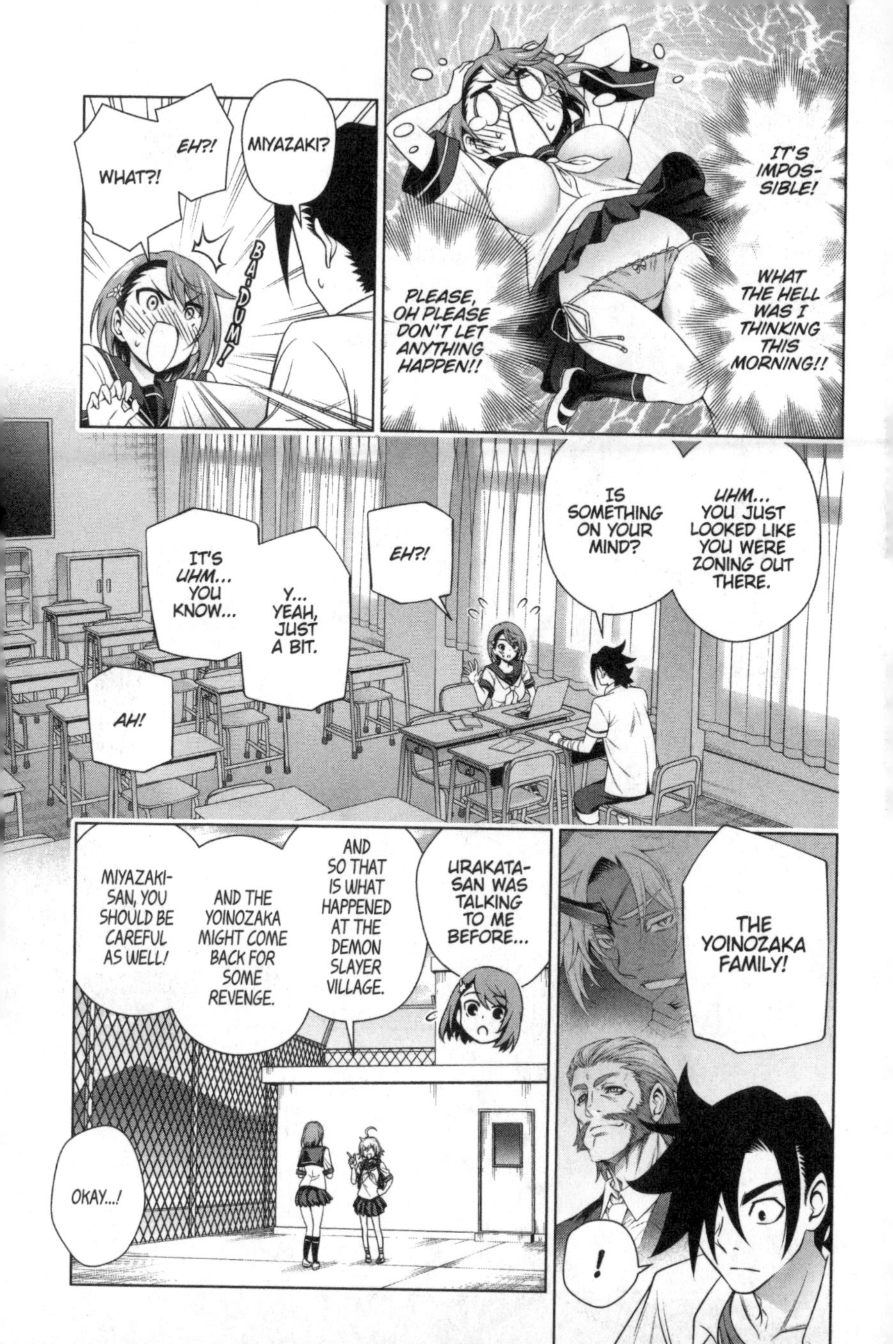
IT'S IMPOSSIBLE!
WHAT THE HELL WAS I THINKING THIS MORNING!!
PLEASE, OH PLEASE DON'T LET ANYTHING HAPPEN!!
MIYAZAKI?
EH?!
WHAT?!
BA-DUM!
UHM... YOU JUST LOOKED LIKE YOU WERE ZONING OUT THERE.
IS SOMETHING ON YOUR MIND?
EH?!
Y... YEAH, JUST A BIT.
IT'S UHM... YOU KNOW...
AH!
THE YOINOZAKA FAMILY!
!
URAKATA-SAN WAS TALKING TO ME BEFORE...
AND SO THAT IS WHAT HAPPENED AT THE DEMON SLAYER VILLAGE.
AND THE YOINOZAKA MIGHT COME BACK FOR SOME REVENGE.
MIYAZAKI-SAN, YOU SHOULD BE CAREFUL AS WELL!
OKAY...!

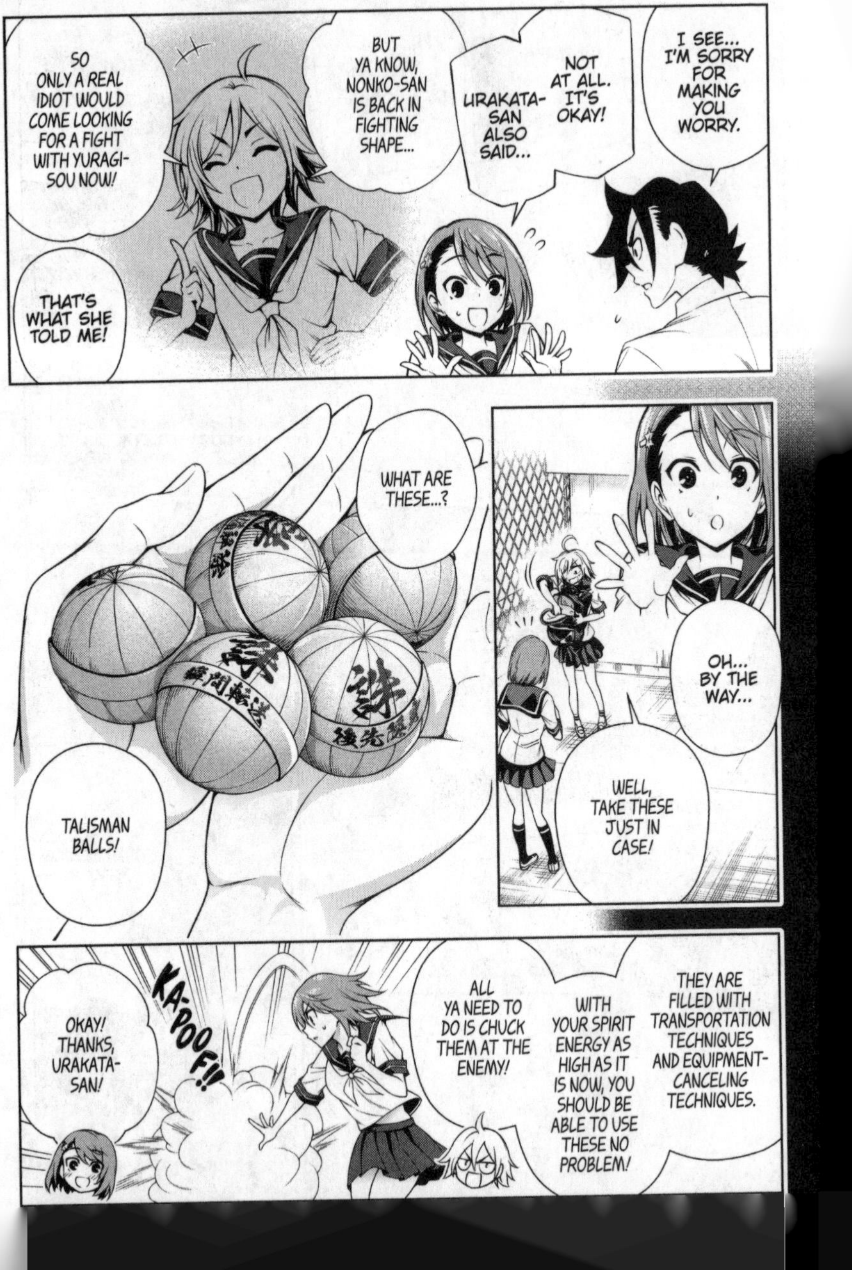
I SEE... I'M SORRY FOR MAKING YOU WORRY.
NOT AT ALL. IT'S OKAY!
URAKATA-SAN ALSO SAID...
BUT YA KNOW, NONKO-SAN IS BACK IN FIGHTING SHAPE...
SO ONLY A REAL IDIOT WOULD COME LOOKING FOR A FIGHT WITH YURAGI-SOU NOW!
THAT'S WHAT SHE TOLD ME!
OH... BY THE WAY...
WELL, TAKE THESE JUST IN CASE!
WHAT ARE THESE...?
TALISMAN BALLS!
THEY ARE FILLED WITH TRANSPORTATION TECHNIQUES AND EQUIPMENT-CANCELING TECHNIQUES.
WITH YOUR SPIRIT ENERGY AS HIGH AS IT IS NOW, YOU SHOULD BE ABLE TO USE THESE NO PROBLEM!
ALL YA NEED TO DO IS CHUCK THEM AT THE ENEMY!
KA-POOF!!
OKAY! THANKS, URAKATA-SAN!

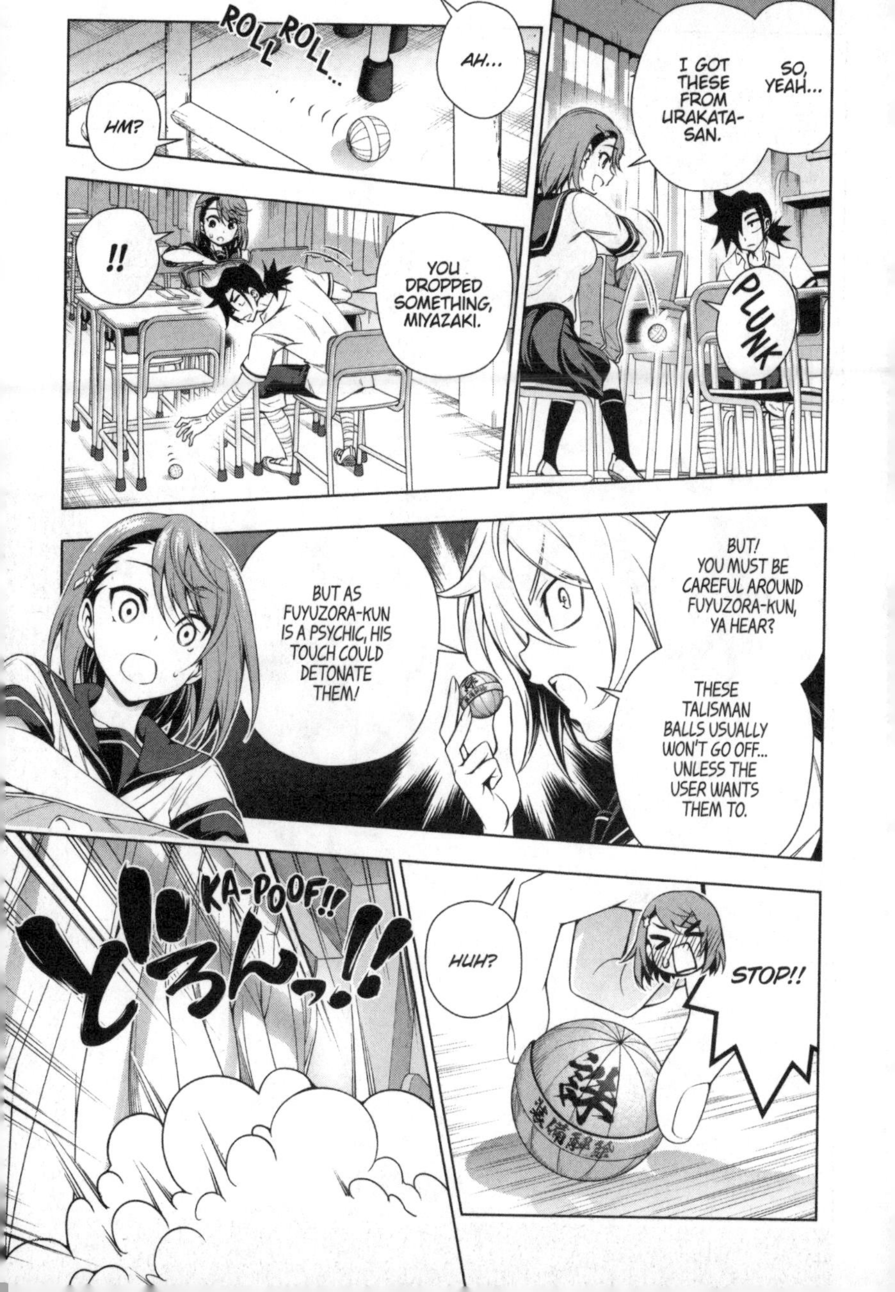
SO, YEAH...
I GOT THESE FROM URAKATA-SAN.
PLUNK
AH...
ROLL ROLL...
HM?
YOU DROPPED SOMETHING, MIYAZAKI.
!!
BUT! YOU MUST BE CAREFUL AROUND FUYUZORA-KUN, YA HEAR?
THESE TALISMAN BALLS USUALLY WON'T GO OFF... UNLESS THE USER WANTS THEM TO.
BUT AS FUYUZORA-KUN IS A PSYCHIC, HIS TOUCH COULD DETONATE THEM!
STOP!!
HUH?
KA-POOF!!
どろんっ!!

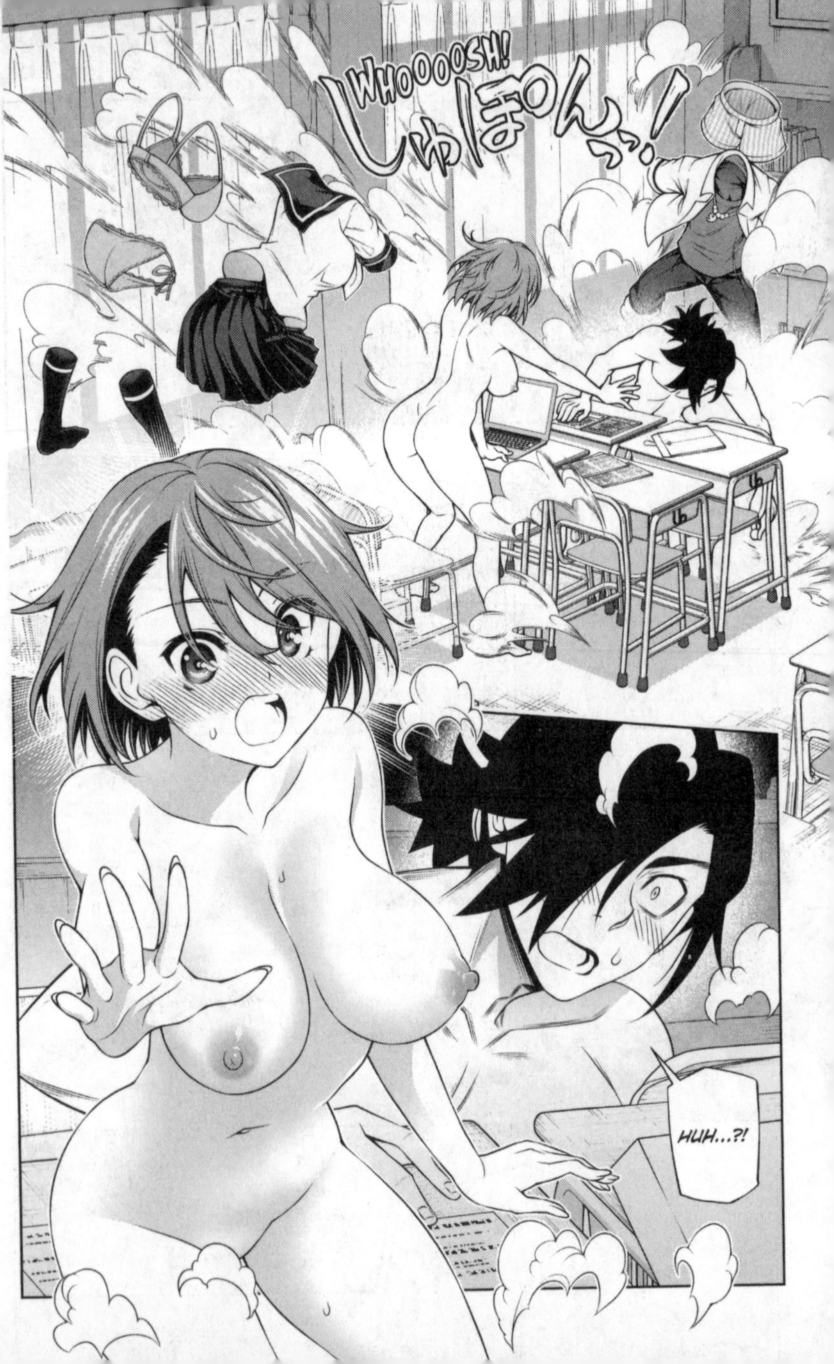
WHOOOOSH!
しゅぽんっっ!
HUH...?!

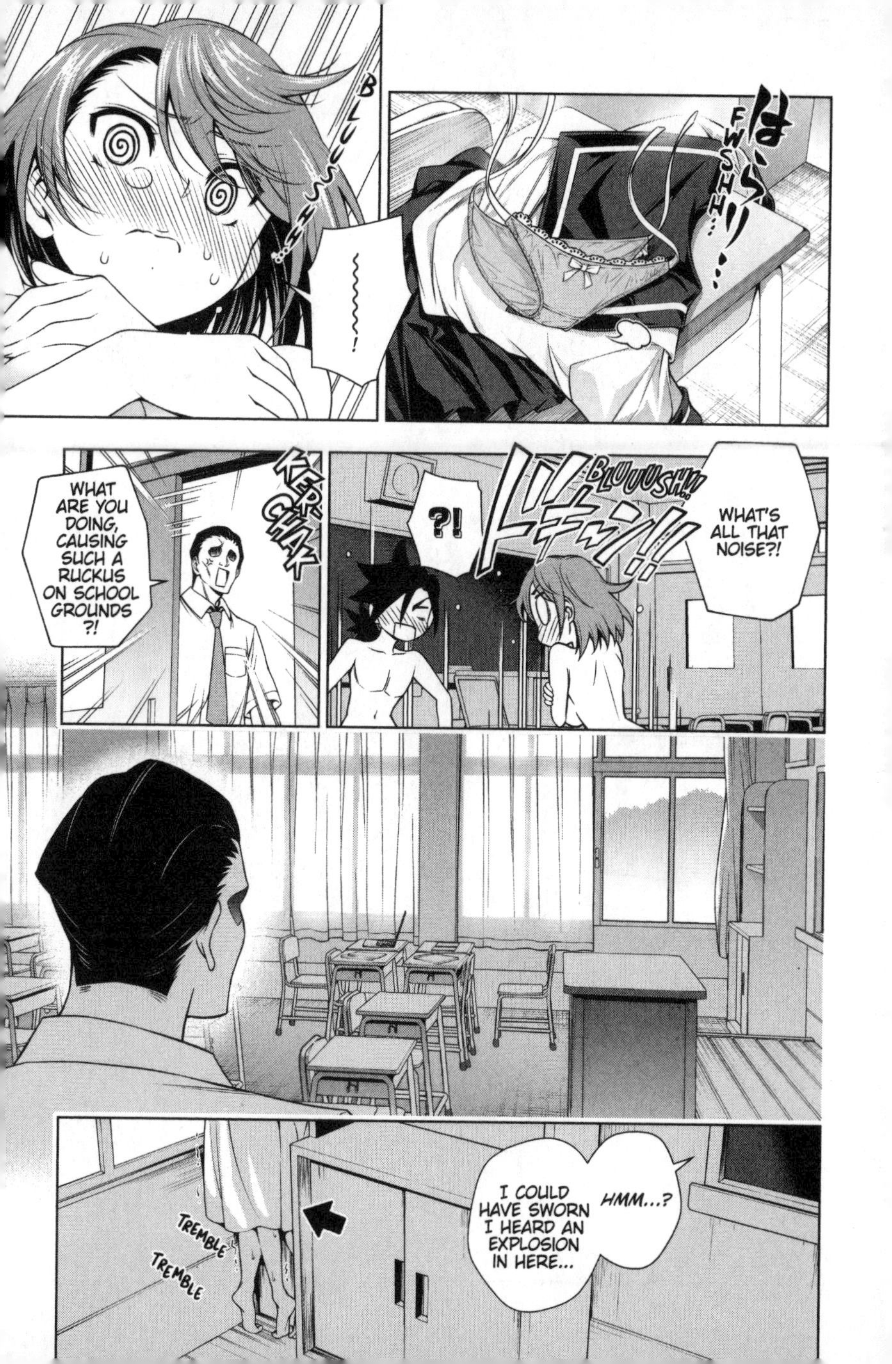

はらり…
FWSHH…
BLUUUSHH…
~~~~~!
WHAT'S ALL THAT NOISE?!
BLUUUSH!!
ドキュン!!
?!
KER-CHAK
WHAT ARE YOU DOING, CAUSING SUCH A RUCKUS ON SCHOOL GROUNDS?!
HMM…?
I COULD HAVE SWORN I HEARD AN EXPLOSION IN HERE…
TREMBLE
TREMBLE
~~~~~

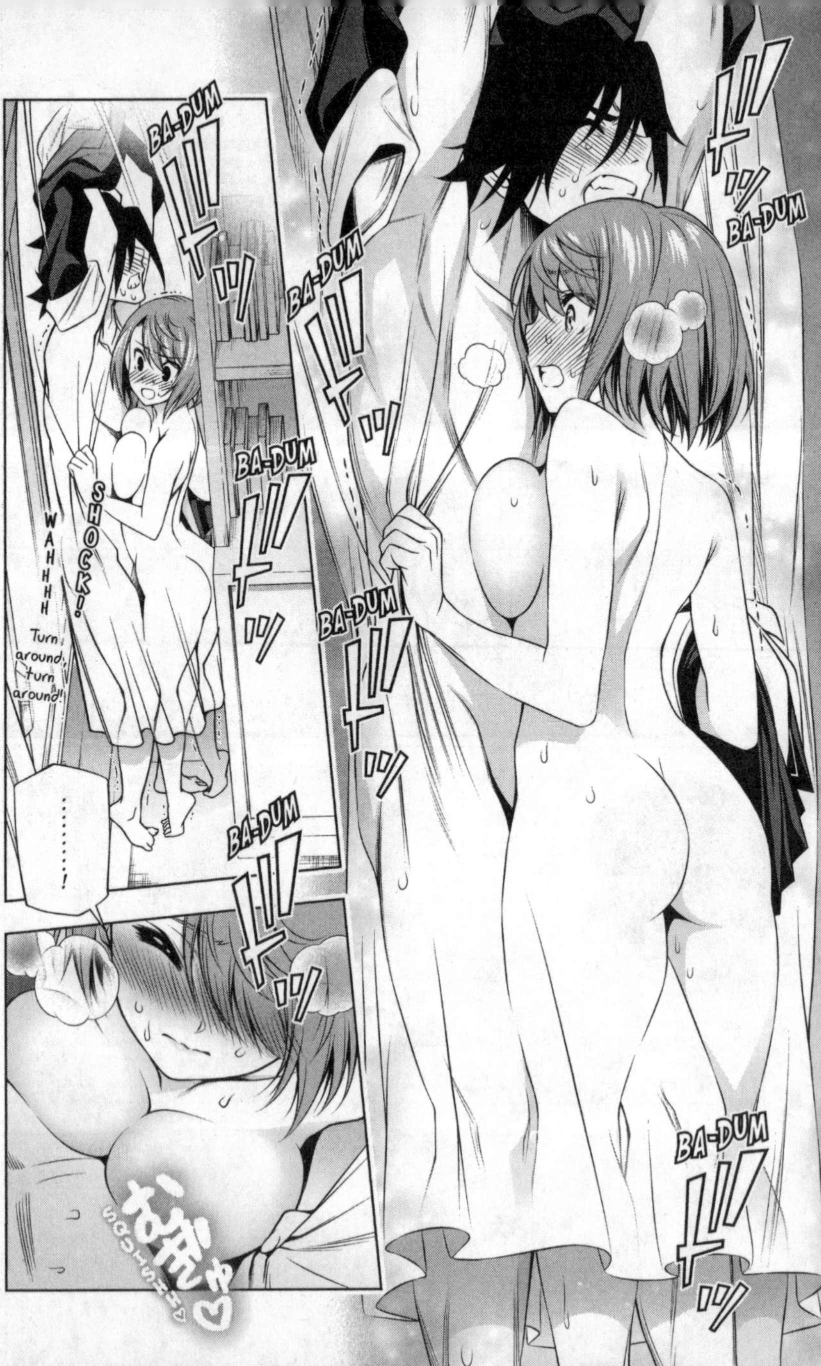
BA-DUM
BA-DUM
BA-DUM
BA-DUM
BA-DUM
BA-DUM
BA-DUM
SHOCK!
WAHHHH
Turn around, turn around!
......!
SQUISH♡

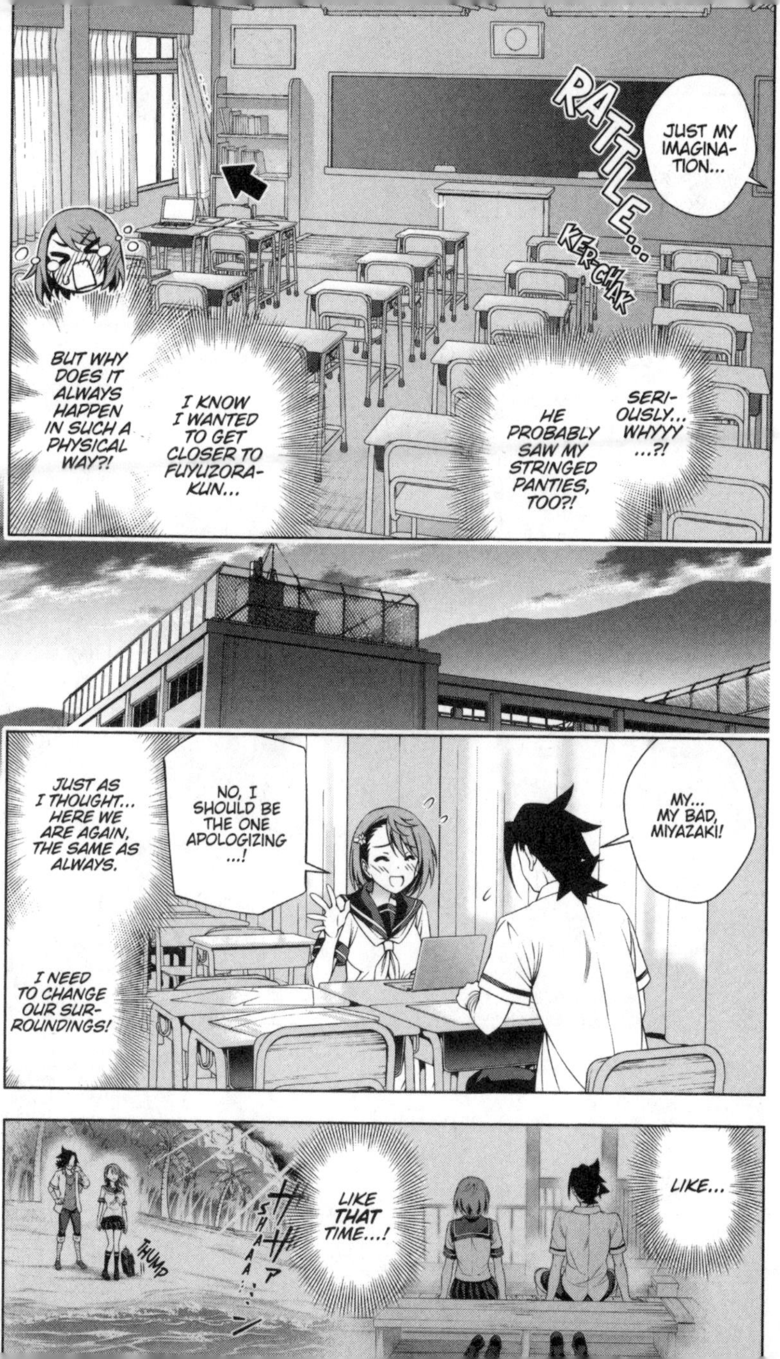

JUST MY IMAGINATION...
RATTLE...
KER-CHAK
SERIOUSLY... WHYYY...?!
HE PROBABLY SAW MY STRINGED PANTIES, TOO?!
I KNOW I WANTED TO GET CLOSER TO FUYUZORA-KUN...
BUT WHY DOES IT ALWAYS HAPPEN IN SUCH A PHYSICAL WAY?!
MY... MY BAD, MIYAZAKI!
NO, I SHOULD BE THE ONE APOLOGIZING...!
JUST AS I THOUGHT... HERE WE ARE AGAIN, THE SAME AS ALWAYS.
I NEED TO CHANGE OUR SURROUNDINGS!
LIKE...
LIKE THAT TIME...!
SHAAA...
THUMP

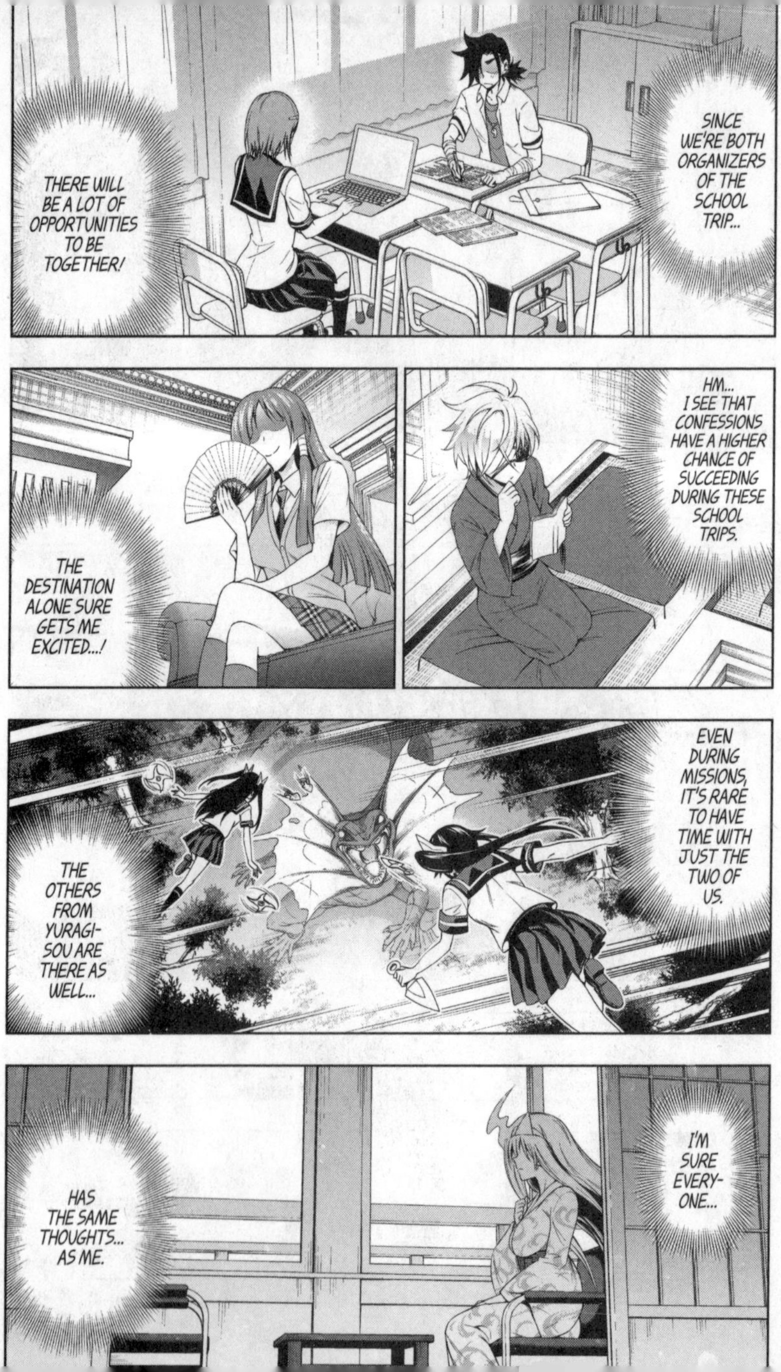
SINCE WE'RE BOTH ORGANIZERS OF THE SCHOOL TRIP...
THERE WILL BE A LOT OF OPPORTUNITIES TO BE TOGETHER!
HM... I SEE THAT CONFESSIONS HAVE A HIGHER CHANCE OF SUCCEEDING DURING THESE SCHOOL TRIPS.
THE DESTINATION ALONE SURE GETS ME EXCITED...!
EVEN DURING MISSIONS, IT'S RARE TO HAVE TIME WITH JUST THE TWO OF US.
THE OTHERS FROM YURAGI-SOU ARE THERE AS WELL...
I'M SURE EVERY-ONE...
HAS THE SAME THOUGHTS... AS ME.

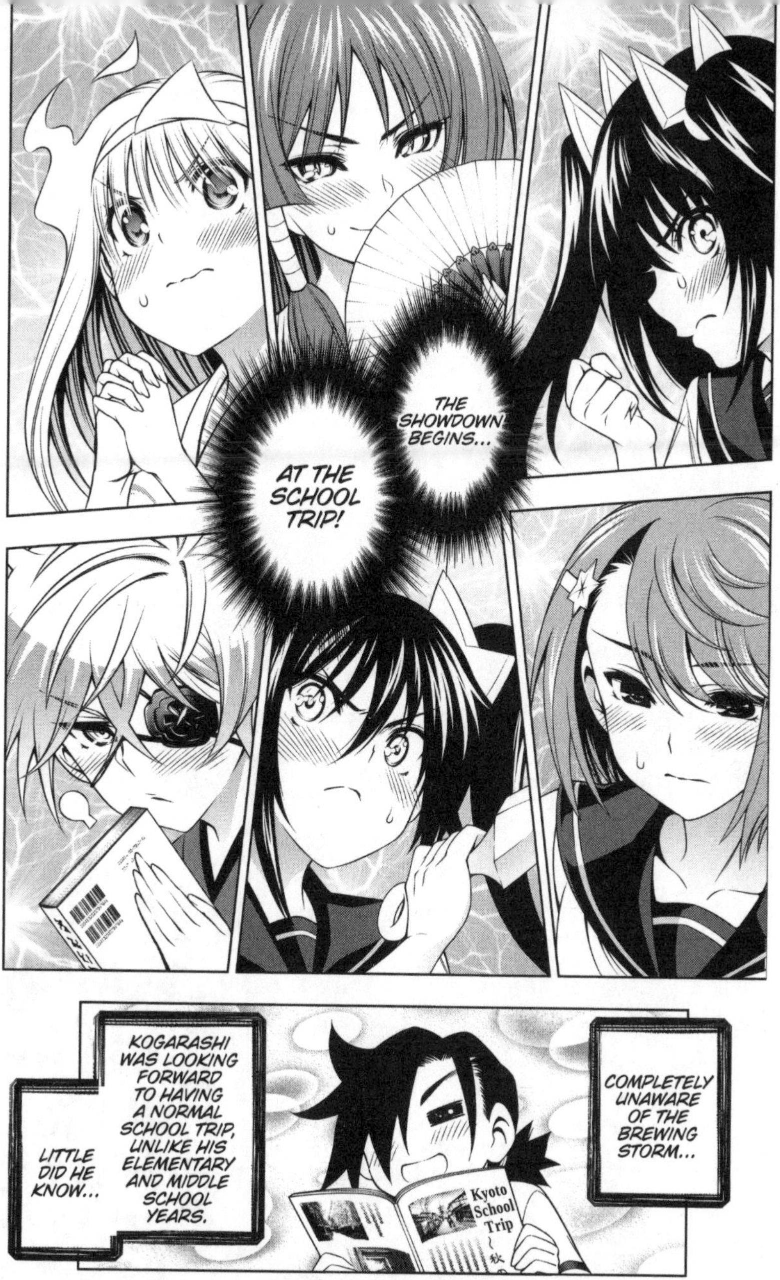
THE SHOWDOWN BEGINS...
AT THE SCHOOL TRIP!
COMPLETELY UNAWARE OF THE BREWING STORM...
KOGARASHI WAS LOOKING FORWARD TO HAVING A NORMAL SCHOOL TRIP, UNLIKE HIS ELEMENTARY AND MIDDLE SCHOOL YEARS.
LITTLE DID HE KNOW...
Kyoto School Trip

16 Clumsy Sagiri-san (End)

Yuuna
and the
Haunted
Hot
Springs

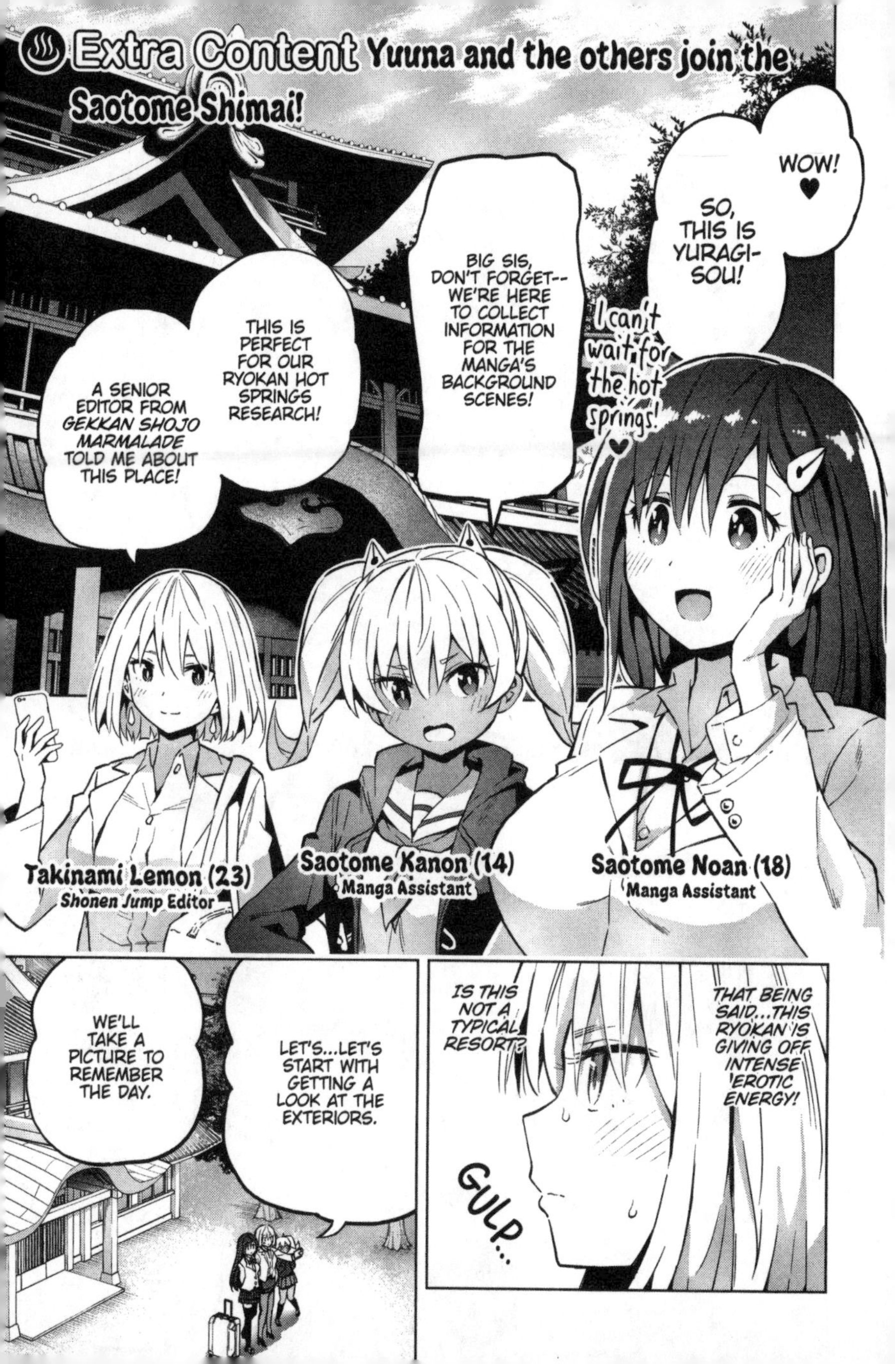
Extra Content Yuuna and the others join the Saotome Shimai!
WOW! ♥
SO, THIS IS YURAGI-SOU!
I can't wait for the hot springs! ♥
BIG SIS, DON'T FORGET-- WE'RE HERE TO COLLECT INFORMATION FOR THE MANGA'S BACKGROUND SCENES!
THIS IS PERFECT FOR OUR RYOKAN HOT SPRINGS RESEARCH!
A SENIOR EDITOR FROM GEKKAN SHOJO MARMALADE TOLD ME ABOUT THIS PLACE!
Saotome Noan (18) Manga Assistant
Saotome Kanon (14) Manga Assistant
Takinami Lemon (23) Shonen Jump Editor
THAT BEING SAID...THIS RYOKAN IS GIVING OFF INTENSE EROTIC ENERGY!
IS THIS NOT A TYPICAL RESORT?
GULP...
LET'S...LET'S START WITH GETTING A LOOK AT THE EXTERIORS.
WE'LL TAKE A PICTURE TO REMEMBER THE DAY.

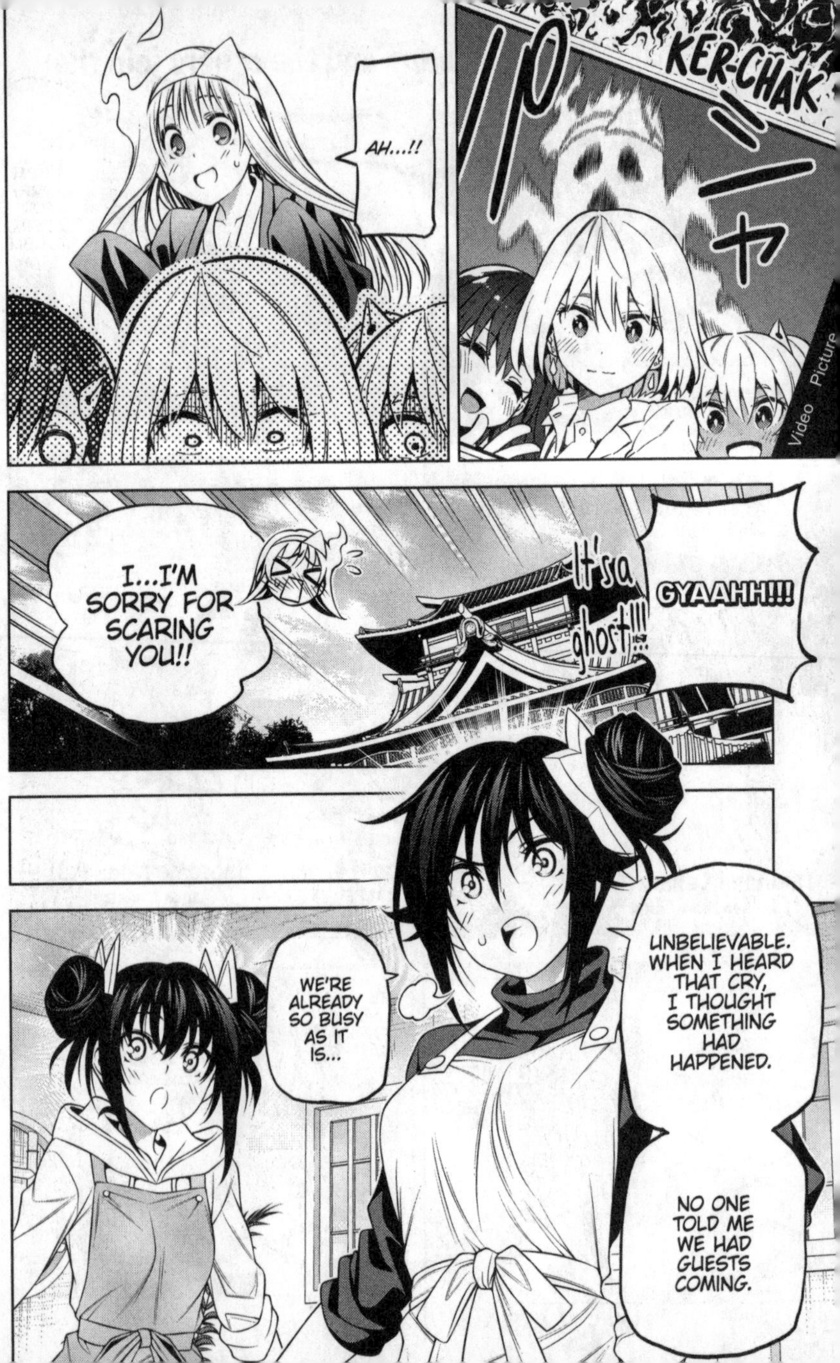
KER-CHAK
AH...!!
GYAAHH!!!
It's a ghost!!!
I...I'M SORRY FOR SCARING YOU!!
UNBELIEVABLE. WHEN I HEARD THAT CRY, I THOUGHT SOMETHING HAD HAPPENED.
NO ONE TOLD ME WE HAD GUESTS COMING.
WE'RE ALREADY SO BUSY AS IT IS...

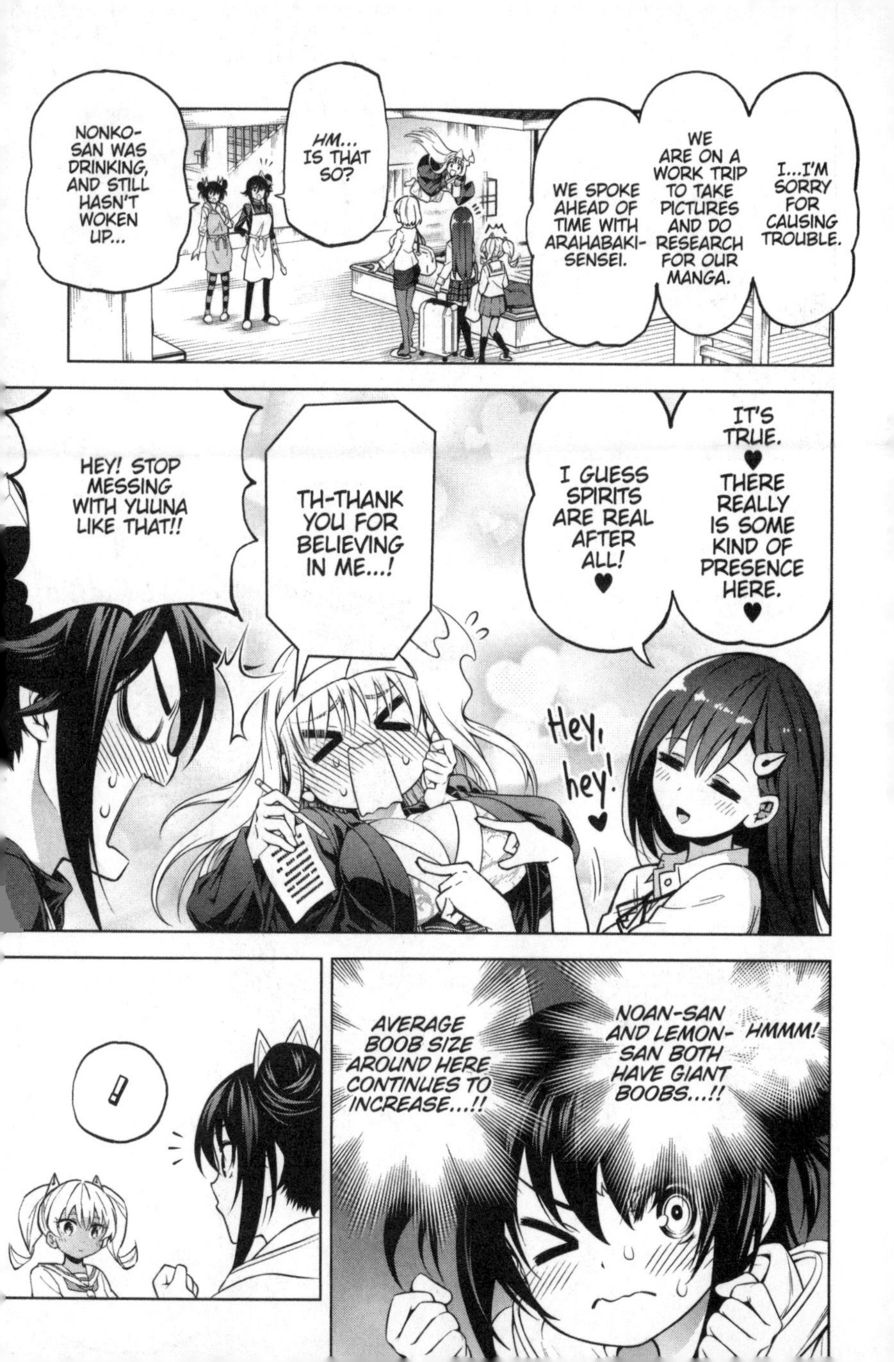
I...I'M SORRY FOR CAUSING TROUBLE.
WE ARE ON A WORK TRIP TO TAKE PICTURES AND DO RESEARCH FOR OUR MANGA.
WE SPOKE AHEAD OF TIME WITH ARAHABAKI-SENSEI.
HM... IS THAT SO?
NONKO-SAN WAS DRINKING, AND STILL HASN'T WOKEN UP...
IT'S TRUE. ♥ THERE REALLY IS SOME KIND OF PRESENCE HERE. ♥
I GUESS SPIRITS ARE REAL AFTER ALL! ♥
Hey, hey! ♥
TH-THANK YOU FOR BELIEVING IN ME...!
HEY! STOP MESSING WITH YUUNA LIKE THAT!!
HMMM!
NOAN-SAN AND LEMON-SAN BOTH HAVE GIANT BOOBS...!!
AVERAGE BOOB SIZE AROUND HERE CONTINUES TO INCREASE...!!
!

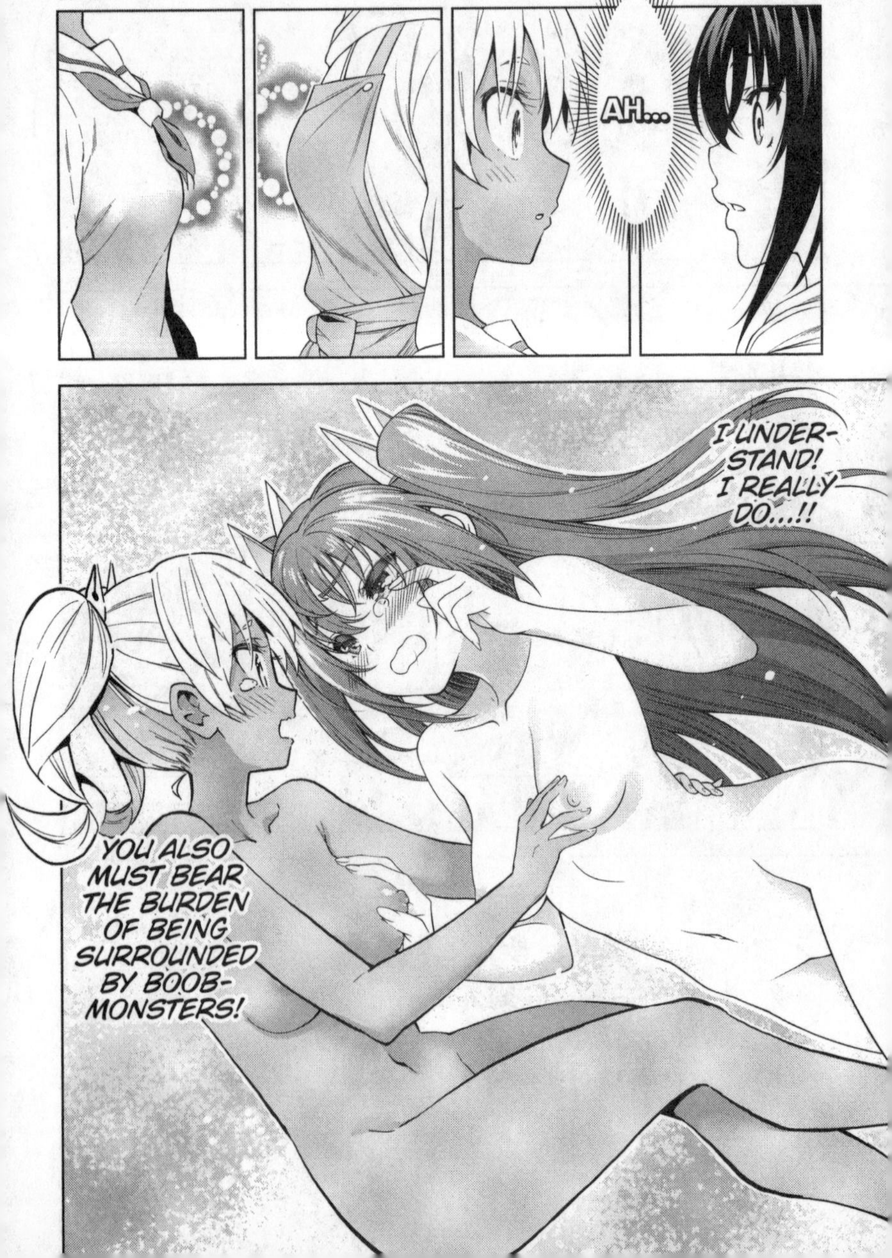
AH...
I UNDER-STAND! I REALLY DO...!!
YOU ALSO MUST BEAR THE BURDEN OF BEING SURROUNDED BY BOOB-MONSTERS!

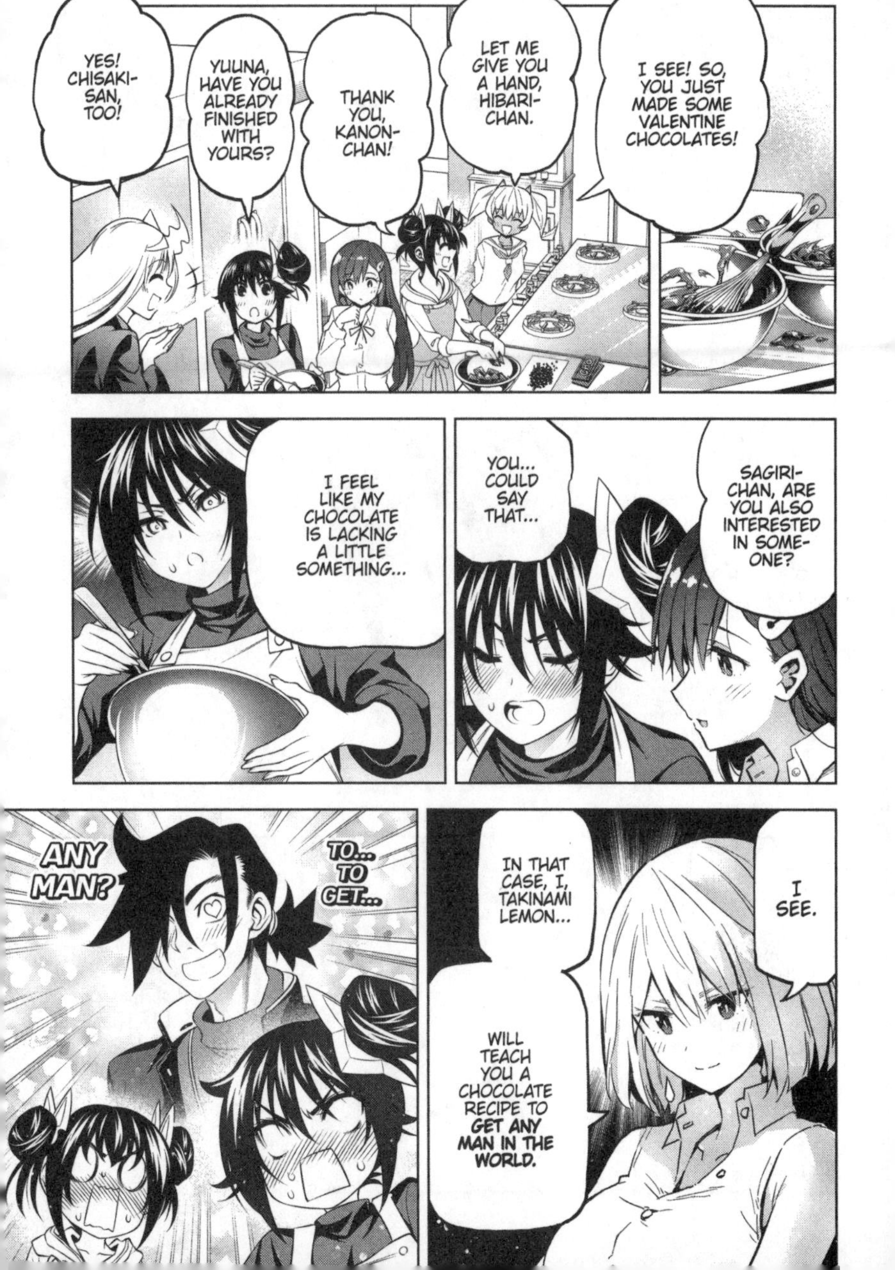
I SEE! SO, YOU JUST MADE SOME VALENTINE CHOCOLATES!
LET ME GIVE YOU A HAND, HIBARI-CHAN.
THANK YOU, KANON-CHAN!
YUUNA, HAVE YOU ALREADY FINISHED WITH YOURS?
YES! CHISAKI-SAN, TOO!
SAGIRI-CHAN, ARE YOU ALSO INTERESTED IN SOME-ONE?
YOU... COULD SAY THAT...
I FEEL LIKE MY CHOCOLATE IS LACKING A LITTLE SOMETHING...
I SEE.
IN THAT CASE, I, TAKINAMI LEMON...
WILL TEACH YOU A CHOCOLATE RECIPE TO GET ANY MAN IN THE WORLD.
TO... TO GET...
ANY MAN?

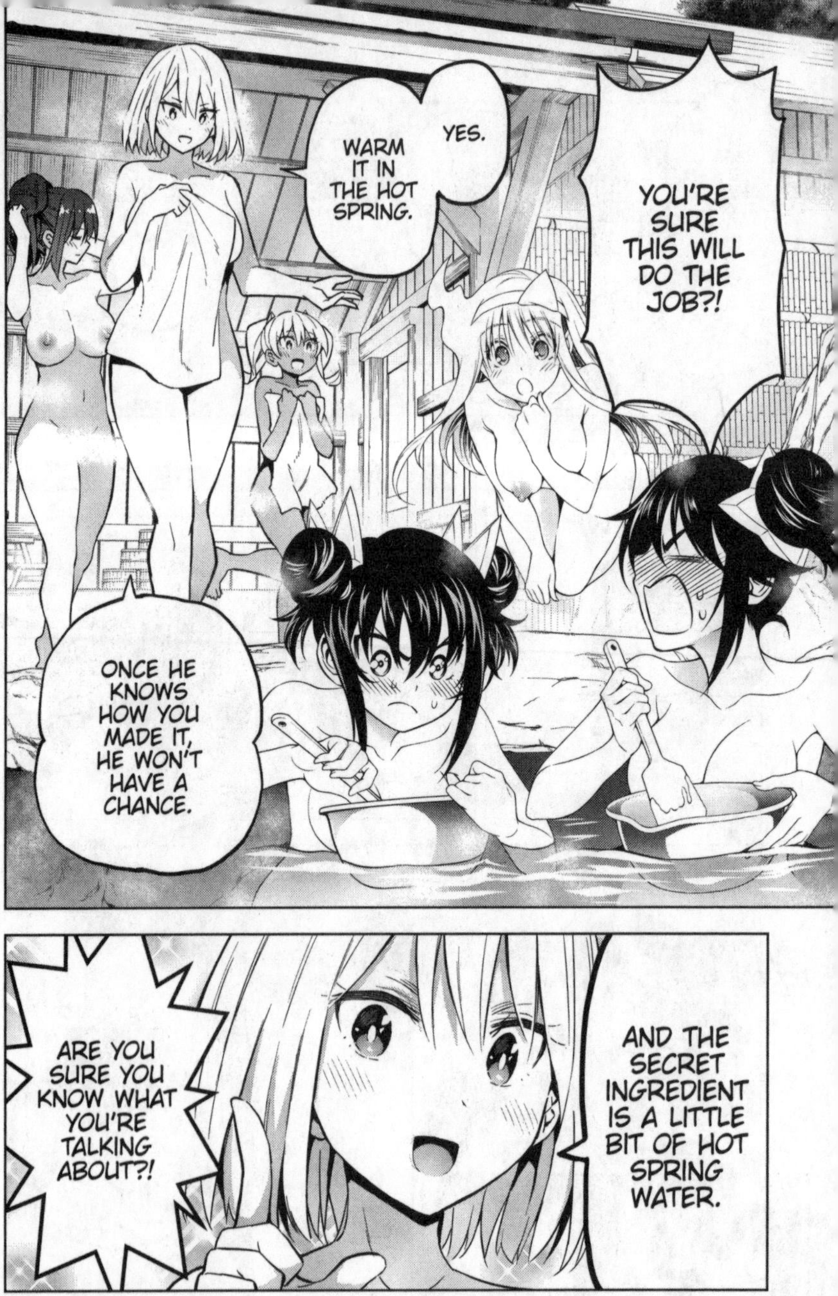
YOU'RE SURE THIS WILL DO THE JOB?!
YES.
WARM IT IN THE HOT SPRING.
ONCE HE KNOWS HOW YOU MADE IT, HE WON'T HAVE A CHANCE.
AND THE SECRET INGREDIENT IS A LITTLE BIT OF HOT SPRING WATER.
ARE YOU SURE YOU KNOW WHAT YOU'RE TALKING ABOUT?!

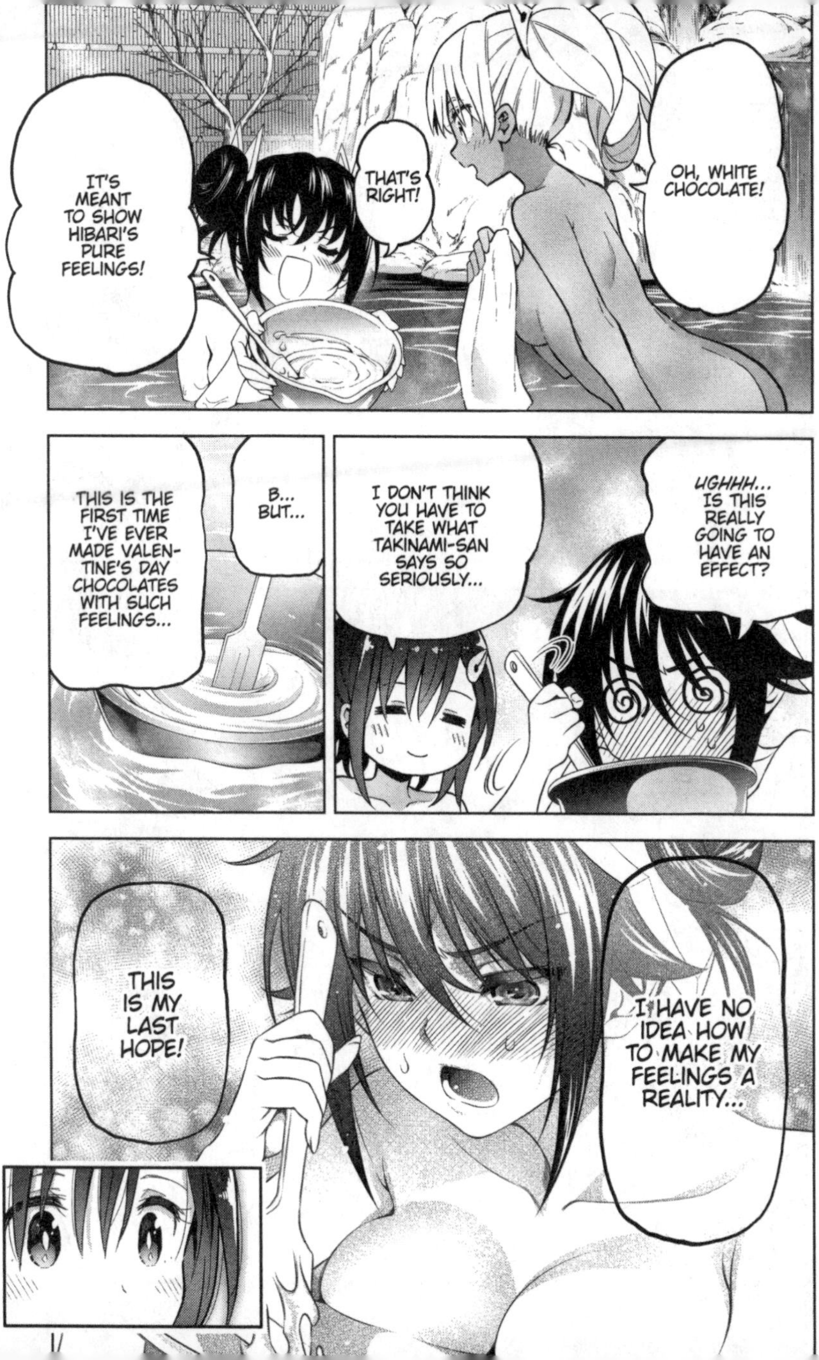
OH, WHITE CHOCOLATE!
THAT'S RIGHT!
IT'S MEANT TO SHOW HIBARI'S PURE FEELINGS!
UGHHH... IS THIS REALLY GOING TO HAVE AN EFFECT?
I DON'T THINK YOU HAVE TO TAKE WHAT TAKINAMI-SAN SAYS SO SERIOUSLY...
B... BUT...
THIS IS THE FIRST TIME I'VE EVER MADE VALEN-TINE'S DAY CHOCOLATES WITH SUCH FEELINGS...
I HAVE NO IDEA HOW TO MAKE MY FEELINGS A REALITY...
THIS IS MY LAST HOPE!

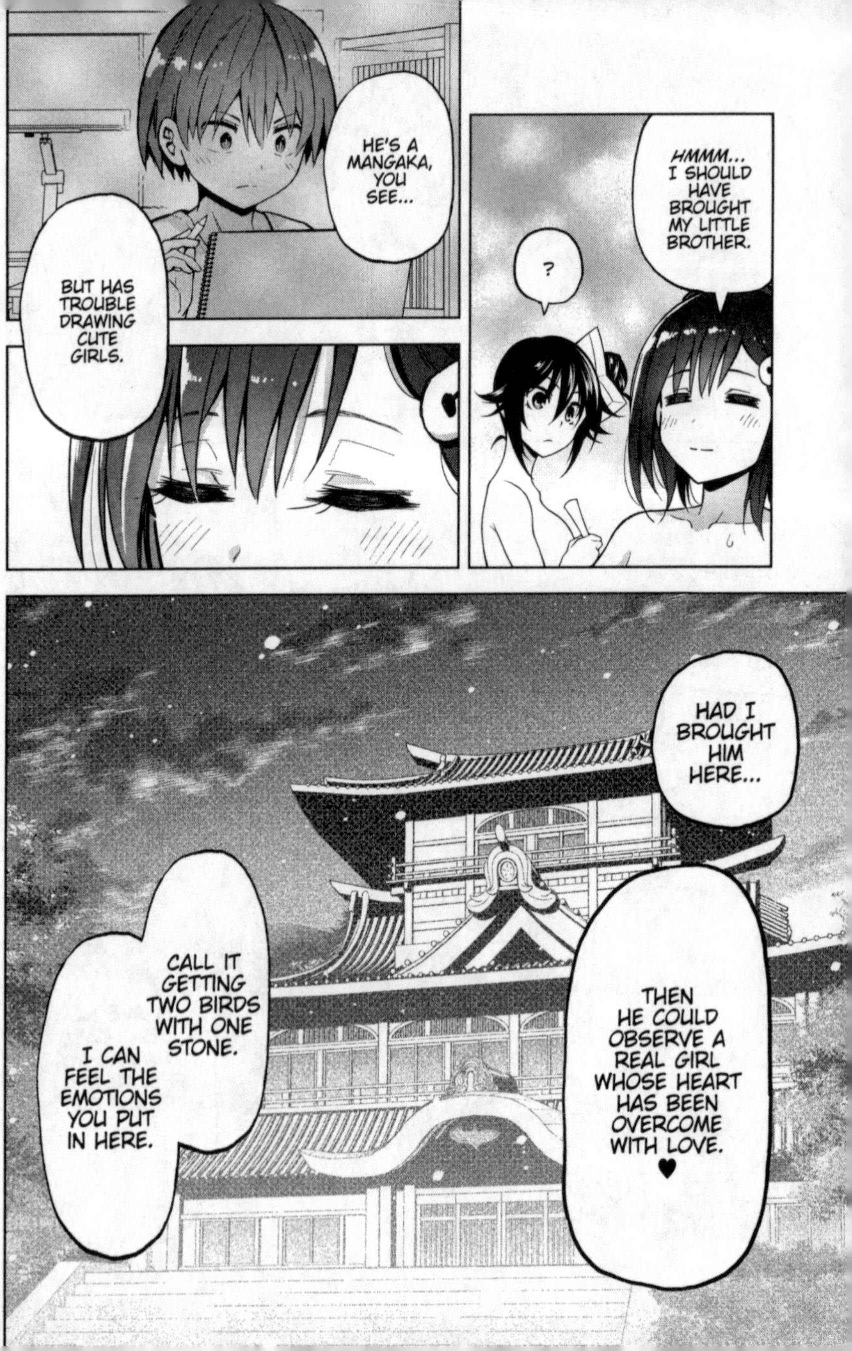
HMMM... I SHOULD HAVE BROUGHT MY LITTLE BROTHER.
?
HE'S A MANGAKA, YOU SEE...
BUT HAS TROUBLE DRAWING CUTE GIRLS.
HAD I BROUGHT HIM HERE...
THEN HE COULD OBSERVE A REAL GIRL WHOSE HEART HAS BEEN OVERCOME WITH LOVE. ♥
CALL IT GETTING TWO BIRDS WITH ONE STONE.
I CAN FEEL THE EMOTIONS YOU PUT IN HERE.

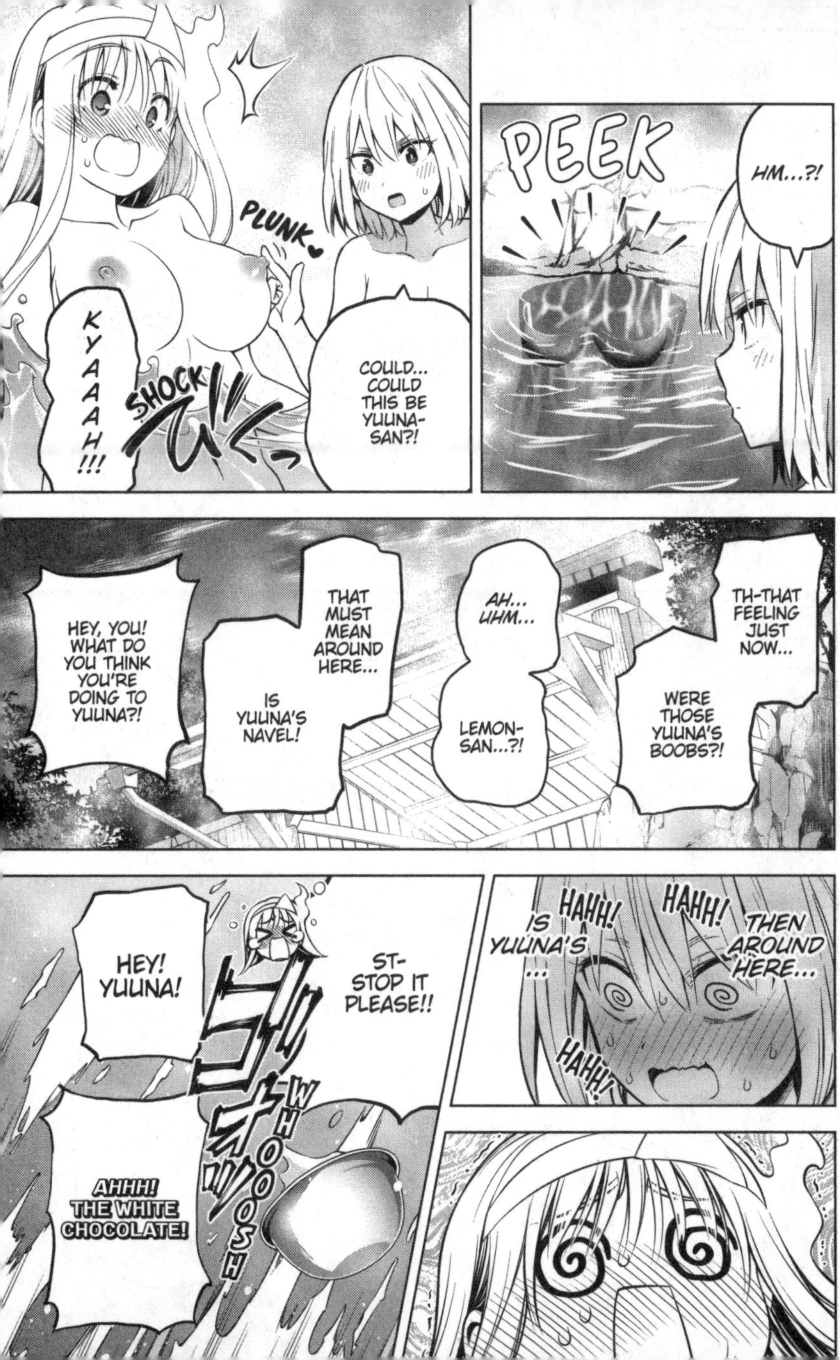
PEEK
HM...?!
COULD... COULD THIS BE YUUNA-SAN?!
PLUNK
KYAAAAH!!!
SHOCK
TH-THAT FEELING JUST NOW...
WERE THOSE YUUNA'S BOOBS?!
AH... UHM...
LEMON-SAN...?!
THAT MUST MEAN AROUND HERE...
IS YUUNA'S NAVEL!
HEY, YOU! WHAT DO YOU THINK YOU'RE DOING TO YUUNA?!
THEN AROUND HERE...
HAHH!
HAHH!
IS YUUNA'S ...
HAHH!
ST-STOP IT PLEASE!!
HEY! YUUNA!
WHOOOOSH
AHHH! THE WHITE CHOCOLATE!

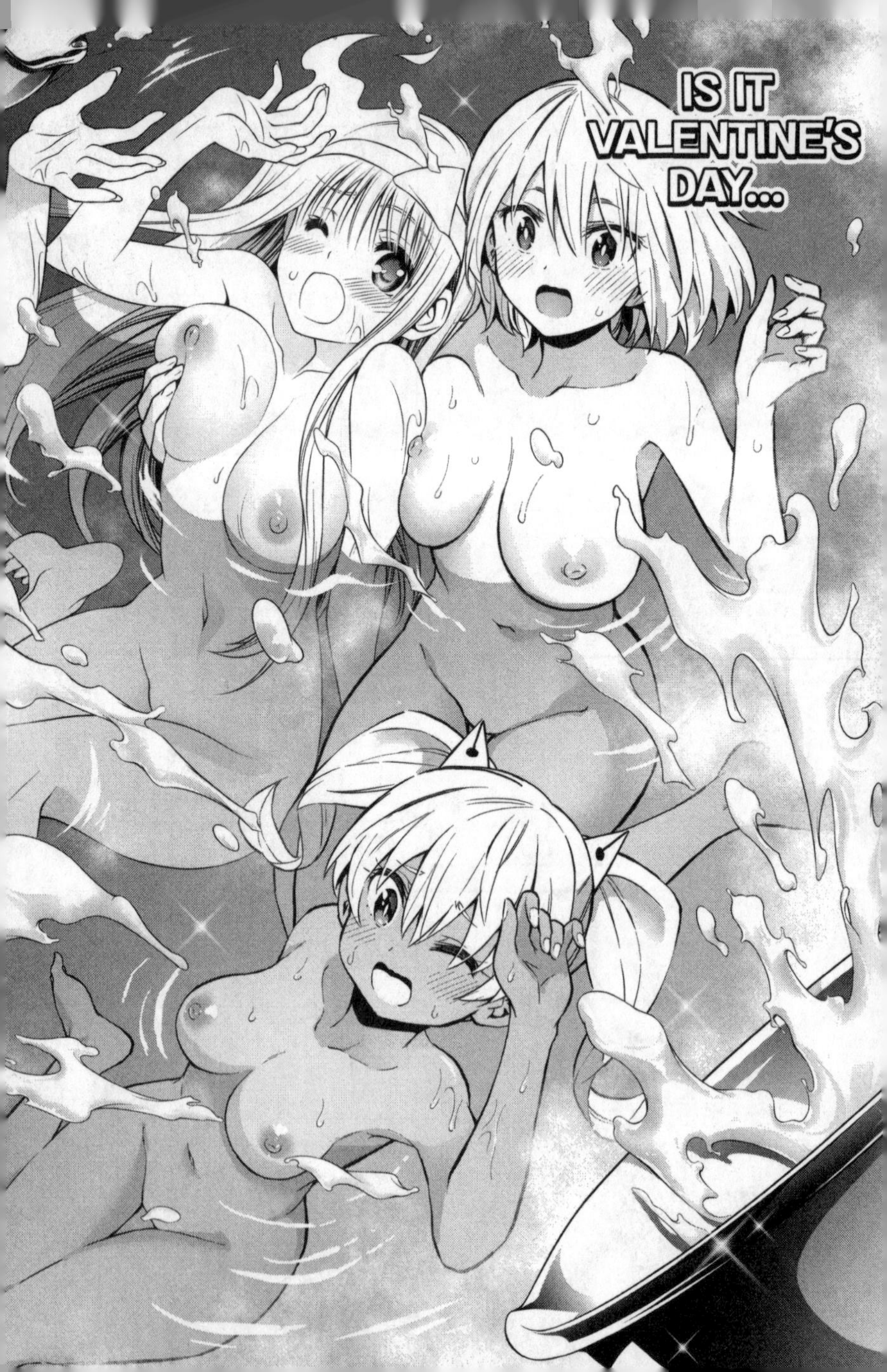
IS IT VALENTINE'S DAY...

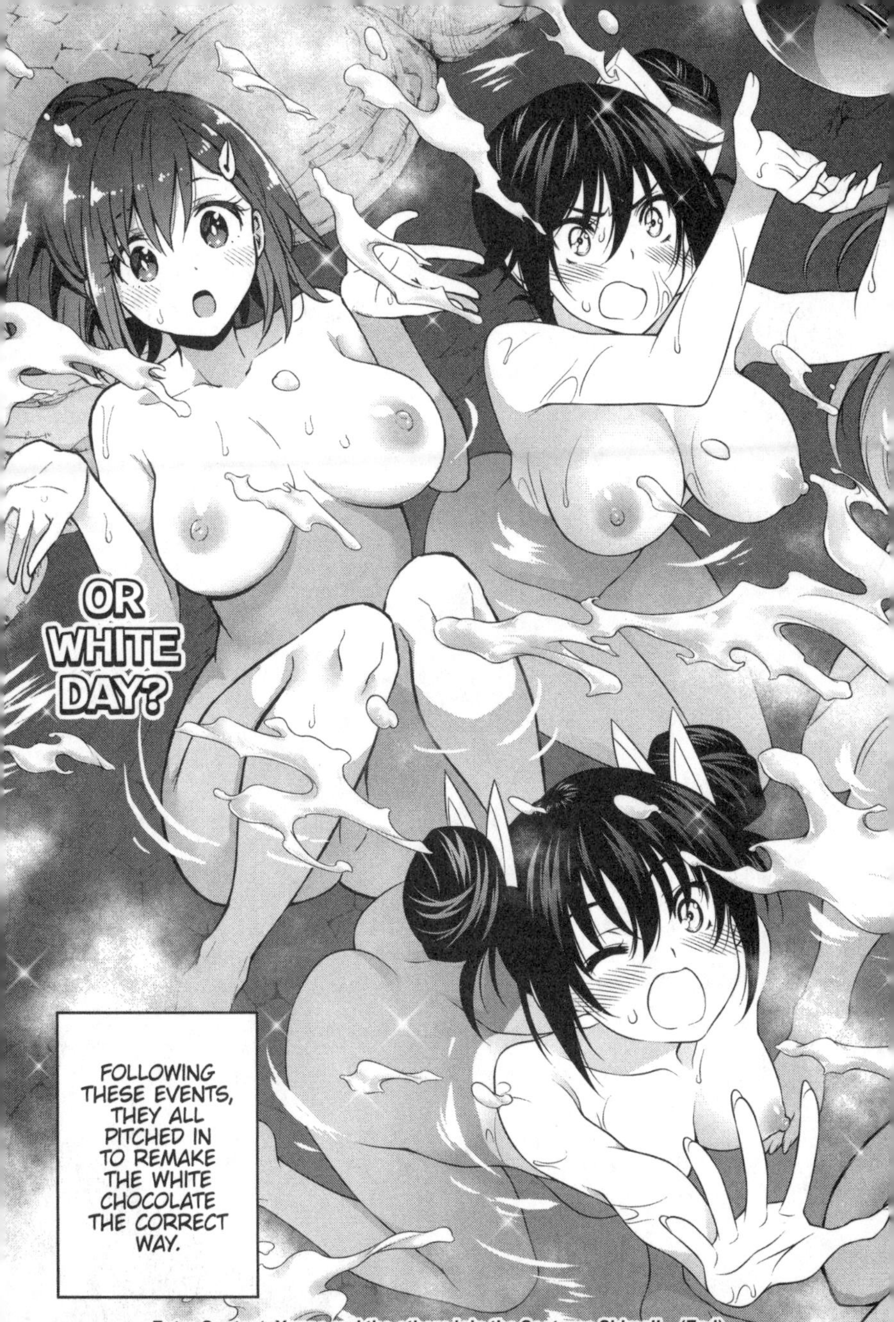
OR WHITE DAY?
FOLLOWING THESE EVENTS, THEY ALL PITCHED IN TO REMAKE THE WHITE CHOCOLATE THE CORRECT WAY.

Extra Content: Yuuna and the others join the Saotome Shimai! (End)

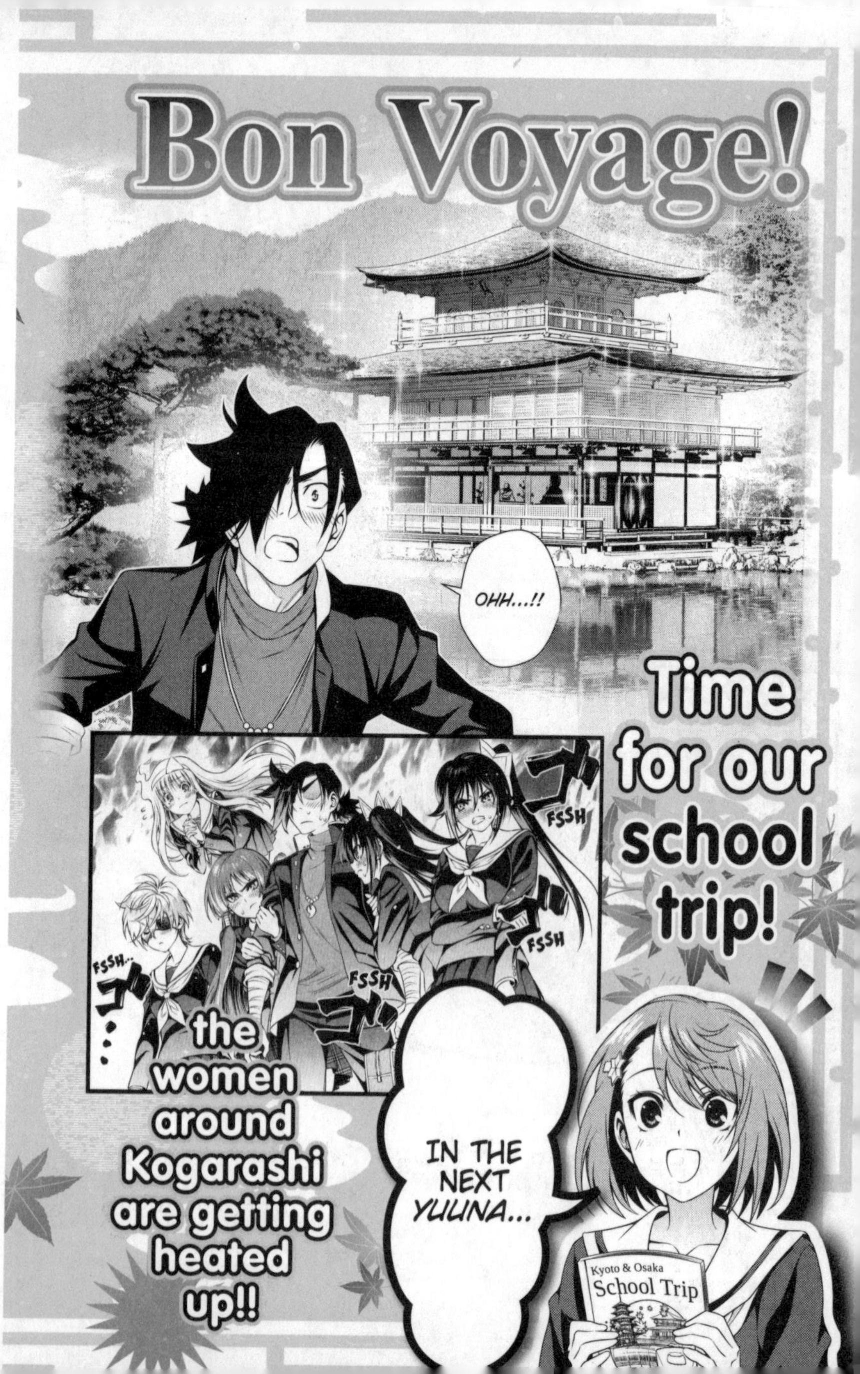
Bon Voyage!
OHH...!!
Time for our school trip!
FSSH
FSSH
FSSH...
FSSH
the women around Kogarashi are getting heated up!!
IN THE NEXT YUUNA...
Kyoto & Osaka
School Trip

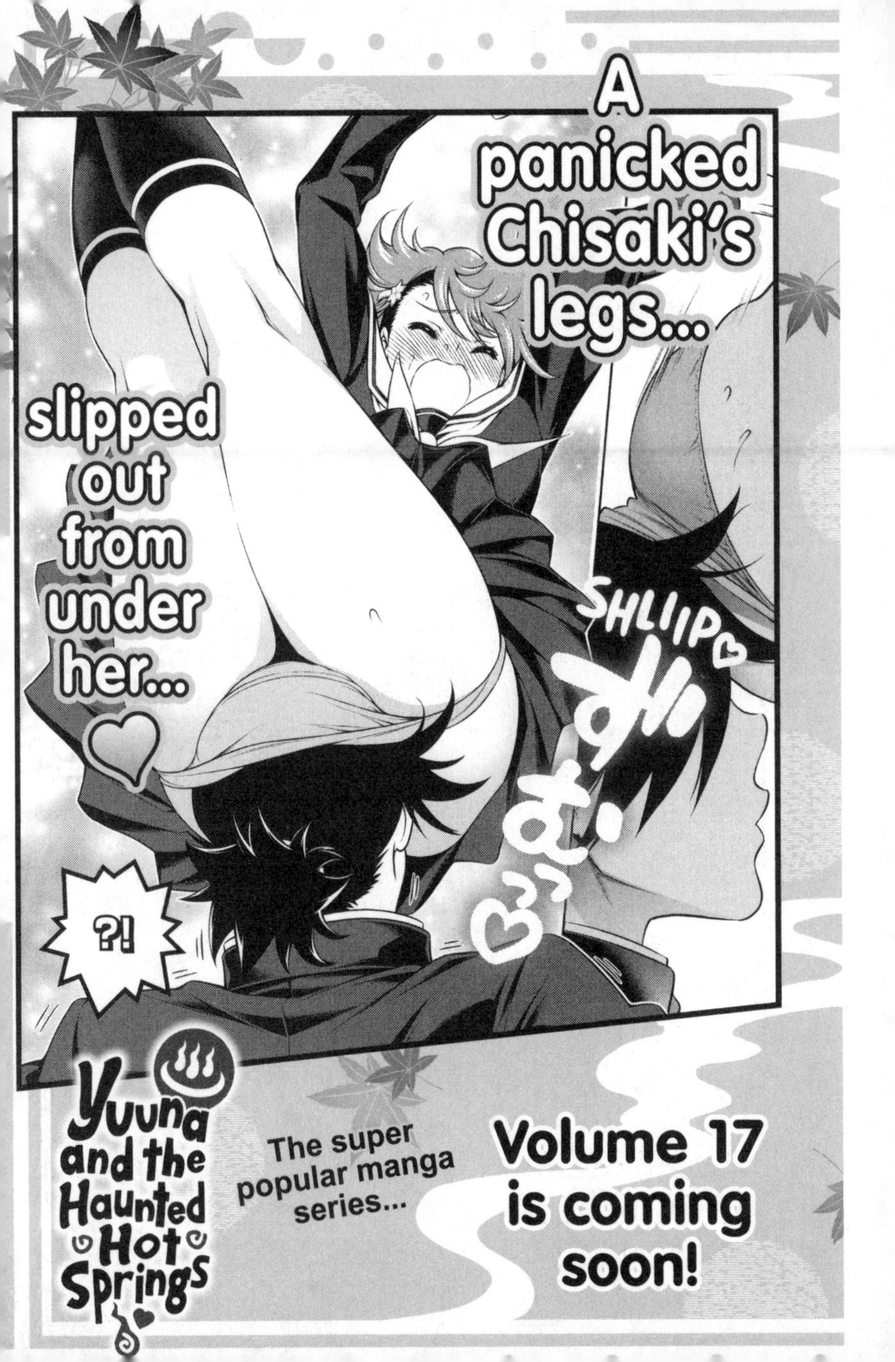
A panicked Chisaki's legs...
slipped out from under her... ♥
SHLIIP♥
?!
Yuuna and the Haunted Hot Springs
The super popular manga series...
Volume 17 is coming soon!